the simplicity connection

creating a more organized, simplified and sustainable life

c.b. davis

Trafford PUBLISHING®

*We at Trafford believe that it is the responsibility of us all, as both individuals and corporations,
to make choices that are environmentally and socially sound. You, in turn, are supporting this
responsible conduct each time you purchase a Trafford book, or make use of our publishing services.
To find out how you are helping, please visit www.trafford.com/responsiblepublishing.html*

*Our mission is to efficiently provide the world's finest, most comprehensive book publishing
service, enabling every author to experience success. To find out how to publish your book, your
way, and have it available worldwide, visit us online at www.trafford.com*

Trafford rev. 7/8/2009

 www.trafford.com

North America & international
toll-free: 1 888 232 4444 (USA & Canada)
phone: 250 383 6864 ♦ fax: 250 383 6804 ♦ email: info@trafford.com

The United Kingdom & Europe
phone: +44 (0)1865 487 395 ♦ local rate: 0845 230 9601
facsimile: +44 (0)1865 481 507 ♦ email: info.uk@trafford.com

table of contents

beginning

The market for self-improvement books may never be boring, but it is often littered with false hope. A better sex life? Lose weight in ten days by eating only Twinkies? Make more money than you've ever dreamed of from the comfort of your couch? These are promises left unfulfilled because they do not address the core of the problems they try to solve: *our society is destructively complex and dependent on consumerism.*

We are a country that brought its own symbol of freedom to the brink of extinction. In our "always on the cell phone," "$4 per gallon of gasoline," and "gimme more, gimme more" culture, there are, however, some rays of hope. Organic food and hybrid car sales continue to grow each year. The do-it-yourself revolution has become a hands-on way of life for gardeners, builders, and others who create. More people than ever before are saying *enough is enough*. We can simplify our lives on a local level and on a daily basis.

Fixing the problems of tomorrow (and yesterday) starts today. We have the ability to revitalize our health by saving our environment—cleaning the air and water, stabilizing the climate, refocusing our consumption with a plan for achieving sustainability. Finding out how to maintain our lives and relate to others are the first steps in making ourselves self-sufficient and peaceful.

But we still have a very long way to go.

What if, on the basis of one belief, we could start to rectify the larger problems of society? Solve global warming? Childhood obesity? The oil crisis? Chemical and environmentally induced sensitivities and diseases? Famine, drought, and poverty? What if one concept could teach us how to gain more time, more energy, more money, more happiness, and better health? Sounds too good to be true?

Simplicity is that cure-all, and *The Simplicity Connection* teaches us how to get back on a path of physical, emotional and mental well-being. This practical and comprehensive guide will help us rethink how we treat our bodies, our spirits, and our environment. It will show how even our smallest actions can lead to a simpler, better life.

What does clean air have to do with simplicity? What does driving your car to the mall have to do with rainforest destruction? What does your dinner choice have to do with the health of your neighbors? What does overpopulation have to do with social pathology? Everything. For starters, we must realize that *everything is connected*. When we understand this simple and basic truth, we can begin to solve the problems and focus on keeping our lives healthy.

The Simplicity Connection will also explain why we need simplicity in our lives and how we can overcome the perceived negatives of a simpler life:

✓ What will it take to fully realize how all our actions are interrelated and that every choice we make has an impact on our lives and on the planet itself?

✓ How can we begin to make ecologically informed choices in the thousands of decisions we need to make every day?

✓ How do we eliminate the complexities of life but maintain the comfort and convenience that our throwaway culture has given us?

✓ Can reducing scale and minimizing time demands fulfill the desires consumerism has created?

✓ What is the true answer to that age-old question, *what do we want from life?*

Simplicity is not necessarily about giving up your job, your home, or your possessions. On the contrary, in many instances, we need to stay where we are. What we need to do is to take a closer look at our lifestyles, our livelihoods, our activities, and see how we can make them simpler for ourselves and the planet. *The Simplicity Connection* will provide the information to show us how and where we can cut back, how we can change our actions.

The purpose of *The Simplicity Connection* is to present the problems, then provide solutions—"Okay," you say, "so what do you want me to do about it?" The answer? Think about what you did today. Almost anything you do can be reorganized, simplified, or made more ecologically sustainable. When we become more conscious of these connections, then we can learn to minimize their impact.

The Simplicity Connection is a comprehensive guide to creating a simpler life. It teaches us how to organize and simplify our time and finances so that we become free from the burden of not knowing what is enough and discover what we truly love to do. Too often, we focus only on materialistic personal goals—what kind of job we want, what kind of mate we're looking for, how many toys can we collect before we die. Our schedules are crammed full, our creditors keep calling, and our bodies are exhausted. What will it take for us to realize that we cannot find inner peace through trinkets and awards? It's deciding what is truly important in our lives that will help us find peace.

We live in—and, some say, worship—a culture that exhausts itself. Production to support our materialistic society depletes our environment. We need to regain control of ourselves and our habits. We need to see the connections between our selfish actions and their results, which affect us both physically and emotionally. Simplicity cannot be just about decluttering our lives. It must include minimizing our impact upon our surroundings.

Next we'll begin to apply sustainable solutions. *The Simplicity Connection* analyzes the problems associated with apathy and provides effective solutions for the individual, on the local level; small steps that can lead to community then global change. When we realize that everything is connected and every action has a greater consequence, we begin to see how changing the world can be accomplished through the daily actions of people like us. An ecological overview shows the environmental problems that mankind has created and gives solutions that can lead to recovery.

The path to simplicity should incorporate all aspects of our existence: body, mind, soul, and environment. We must question our modern so-called conveniences. We must learn about simpler and safer alternatives in regard to:

✓ What we consume:

Shopping: how we shop and why we can't stop.

Eating: becoming more conscious of what and how we eat.

✓ Transportation: changing the way we get there.

✓ Working: finding out what we truly love and doing it.

✓ Healing: strengthening the connection between mental and physical health and reducing our dependence on mainstream Western medicine.

✓ How we aesthetically enhance our lives:

Beautifying: improving our appearance without endangering our health.

Cleaning: seeing the dangers of common products and finding safer choices.

Housing and decorating: knowing how our physical environment directly affects our physical and mental health.

✓ Disposing: reducing waste and taking care of what we have created.

To live a simpler, saner life, we must consider not only the traditional issues of simplicity (minimalism, less consumption, less clutter) but also issues of sustainability, spirituality, creativity, environmentalism, frugality, organic living, conscious decision making, and common courtesy. *The Simplicity Connection* is about finding connections to simplicity in our daily lives and making simple changes. It can become a keystone to your life. As you read this book, you will find relationships you never expected and form a new plan for living. Balance the elements of sustainability and simplification and you will find the road to serenity. Welcome to *The Simplicity Connection*.

chapter 1

organizing

We don't need it, we don't want it, and we certainly don't use it. Then why do we still have it? The most troublesome byproduct of over-consumption is our collected clutter. Before we start tackling the greater problems of the world, we've got to get our own ducks in a row.

Step one: Organization. My childhood scrapbooks were organized in detailed chronological order, without any miscellaneous filler. When I was in college, I was mocked for my organizational skills because I color-coded my notes and labeled my drawers. As I moved out into the working world, those friends realized what I knew all along—that anal retentiveness can be pretty darn lucrative. Being organized saves not only time, but also money and energy. Knowing where to find things keeps the workplace running smoothly and keeps bosses and customers happy.

But organization is more than just nit-picky neatness. It includes efficiency, economy, scheduling, and keeping track of things, all which have become increasingly difficult to manage in our society of sensory overload. Although hundreds of products are available for sale to help keep us organized, we can easily get ourselves organized with little or no expenditure. This chapter will help you get and stay organized and put you on the path to a simpler lifestyle.

How far you take these organizational tools is entirely up to you. Maybe you just want to avoid late fees by remembering to pay all your bills on time each month. Maybe you want to transfer all those loose pieces of paper that clutter up your life into an electronic organizer. Maybe you just want to remember where you parked your car. ("Dude, where IS my car?") Whatever your reason, you will find that organization will allow you to spend more time doing things you want to do and spend less time worrying about or searching for missing information. When you get organized, you'll find that you have more time than you ever realized.

ORGANIZING FROM SCRATCH...

What is clutter?

If the first step to recovery is admitting you have a problem, the first step to getting organized is admitting that you have clutter. Before we begin, we should identify what clutter is:

- ✓ Too much stuff in too small a space
- ✓ Things we don't use
- ✓ Things that are messy and disorganized
- ✓ Things that are unfinished (and probably will never be finished)
- ✓ Things we don't like
- ✓ Things that confuse us and waste our time.

What clutter does to us:

- ✓ Costs us money.
- ✓ Makes us ashamed.
- ✓ Makes us feel guilty.
- ✓ Can become a source of conflict when Mr. Anal Retentive lives with Ms. Messy Kitchen.
- ✓ Is often a health and/or fire hazard.
- ✓ Makes us feel like we've lost control of our lives.
- ✓ Creates bad energy, makes us tired, keeps us stuck in the past.
- ✓ Creates confusion and a lack of focus.
- ✓ Makes us waste time looking for things.
- ✓ Creates more clutter. As we keep adding to one pile or building new piles, the piles take over entire rooms of our homes. Like the Blob, clutter is a contagious entity that seems to have a life of its own.

Clutter is also called "junk," but things only become junk when they aren't being used or are in the wrong place. Open a drawer and you may see a tube of lipstick, rubber bands, Chinese take-out menus, thirty-two ballpoint pens, a ticket stub from a Whitesnake concert, a leash for a dog you no longer own. Any one of these objects is fine if you actually use it on a regular basis and/or it's being kept in its proper place. Having a working flashlight doesn't do much good, though, when you can't find it. The first lesson in getting organized is to learn to store things where you can easily find them when you need them.

One of the hardest things to do is to look at your belongings and decide what is actually junk. Getting rid of old familiar junk can feel like giving up the family pet. You've carried some of these items (that ugly bookcase you've had since you were four years old) with you for years, lovingly transporting them across state lines, in one moving van and out the next. But now it's time to get ruthless. I have no pity for your *Charlie's Angels* lunchbox.

> *Test yourself*
>
> Take an inventory of all the gadgets in your world. How often do you use them? Have you ever bought something not realizing you already owned it or had something that would do the same job? This is a clear sign that it's time to clean house.
>
> How many of these "gotta have" items do you have that aren't being used—computers, aquariums, massaging foot baths, diet books, exercise doodads, stereo accessories, popcorn machines, bread makers, walkie talkies, guitars, food processors, CD players, board games with missing pieces, or parts of electronic equipment you no longer have. If it's been longer than a year since you've used these things, let them move on. What's the worst that could happen if you didn't have it anymore and needed it again?

Why we keep stuff:

- ✓ "Just in case"
- ✓ Because we think material purchases give us status among our peers
- ✓ For security
- ✓ Because we inherited it
- ✓ Because we believe that more is better
- ✓ We believe the "tightwad excuse": *I paid for it, I'll use it someday.*

We can now identify our clutter, but before going any further, we should analyze what originally held us back from staying organized. According to Julie Morgenstern, author of *Organizing from the Inside Out*, now is the time to ask yourself honestly, "Why can't I keep myself organized?" It's time to expose our excuses for not keeping ourselves organized.

Top Five Excuses For Having Clutter

1. "Don't know where to begin." Many people fear getting organized because we've got too much stuff and the task is just too big to pick any one thing to start with.
2. "Don't know how." Believe it or not, the fear of not knowing how to begin cleaning up keeps many people from starting to dig out.
3. "Too lazy." We just don't have the desire to go through all our stuff. While you may think removing clutter takes a lot of energy, the vitality gained once you're free of your junk makes up for the short-term effort.
4. "Too much like work." When we get home from a long day at the office, we'd

all much rather hit the couch than file bills. You're more likely to stick to an organization system if it's something you actually like doing and it doesn't feel so much like "work." Once we redefine how we see cleaning and caring for our homes, it becomes less of a chore.

5. "Not enough time." Procrastination, or some form of it, stops us from cleaning out, picking up, and putting away. But giving an initial investment to creating an organizational system can save hours of time, energy, and aggravation in the long run.

Where to Start Decluttering

If you're in need of a complete decluttering, tackle an easy room or a small task to ease into the project and get a feel for how long it will take you. Next, identify where your clutter lurks. When surveying a room, keep in mind these areas where clutter can hide:

✓ Drawers: kitchen, desk, bathroom
✓ Closets and lockers
✓ Shelves
✓ Under the bed, couch, dresser, or stairs
✓ Medicine cabinet
✓ Portable junk spaces: car, purse, wallet, address book
✓ Storage areas: attic, basement, garage, storage unit
✓ Refrigerator: outside and inside
✓ Bulletin boards
✓ Boxes: storage and jewelry
✓ Hidden spots: look under, behind, over
✓ Collections: Reevaluate why you collect things. Hobbies are great, but at what point does a hobby become an unnecessary excuse to bring more clutter into your life?
✓ Don't forget the junk room!

When to Declutter

Any time is a good time to declutter. If you begin to feel frustrated because you keep losing things or don't seem to have the energy to put things back where they belong, it's time to reevaluate the system you have in place and make some changes.

The ideal time to declutter is before a move. For a clean start, declutter as you pack instead of carrying clutter with you and unpacking it. You can save yourself the expense of trucking boxes of unwanted, unneeded stuff to your new home.

On the other hand

The amount of trash we create when moving is astronomical. Anyone who has ever strolled the streets of a college town in mid-May (or any urban alley) can attest to the wastefulness of our culture. We run out of time and energy and end up throwing perfectly useful things away.

Start decluttering in the morning and set aside a full day to complete the job. If this is your first time decluttering, you will need the time to get into the rhythm. Don't schedule anything all day and devote yourself to the task at hand. You'll be less stressed and less frustrated if you're not racing to finish because of dinner plans.

How to Start Decluttering

The first commandment of decluttering is *when in doubt, throw it out*. It's important to get rid of the things that no longer contribute to your life. *Throw out what you don't need or use*. This does not, of course, include things that have special sentimental meaning to you (like your Girl Scout sash).

Many organizational experts suggest throwing everything into the trash immediately. The purpose of this book is to teach you to act sustainably in all aspects of life, especially when disposing. If you're new to decluttering or in a rush, you may be tempted to just free throw everything into the garbage can. Instead, what you'll learn here is how to keep an emphasis on sustainable living and keep your trash pile as small as possible.

Outline your decluttering goals at the start of the day: Do you want a total overhaul or is there something in particular (a certain hobby, a room, an impossible drawer) that you want to focus on? This will help you plan ahead and get the tools you need. It may be just a box of garbage bags but my mother has to rent a dumpster when she does her biennial garage clean out.

Work as if you're on a schedule. If someone interrupts you, use the excuse, "I'm working under a deadline," and promise to call back when you have the time. Make sure you post a note conspicuously (near the phone, on your purse, by or keys) so that you don't forget.

> *Songs for your cleaning mix tape*
>
> One sure way to kick the job into high gear is to play positive music with an energetic tempo. The right music can make any task easier.
>
> "Wash That Man Right Outta My Hair" from *South Pacific*
>
> "Respect" – Aretha Franklin
>
> "Stronger" – Britney Spears
>
> "The Streetbeater" (aka the theme from *Sanford & Son*) – Quincy Jones
>
> "I Love Trash" – Oscar the Grouch
>
> "Moving Out" – Billy Joel
>
> "I'm Packing Up" – Elvis Costello
>
> "Enough is Enough" – Donna Summer and Barbra Streisand
>
> "The Final Countdown" – Europe
>
> "Yakity Yak" – The Coasters
>
> "Theme from *Chariots of Fire*" – Vangelis
>
> "Gonna Fly Now" (aka the theme from *Rocky*)
>
> "Ride of the Valkyries" – Wagner
>
> Plus any country western song with the theme of getting rid of excess baggage. My favorites include Roy Clark's "Thank God and Greyhound (You're Gone)," Dolly Parton's "Packin' it Up," and Tammy Wynette's "D-I-V-O-R-C-E."

Getting an objective buddy to help can make the day go faster, but be sure to offer to help them the following weekend. Maybe you can't see why you don't need four boxes of eight-track tapes, but a good friend sure can.

If you have trouble getting rid of things, start with baby steps. Set goals, like a number of how many things to get rid of each day. Pick ten items to start, then work your way up to more.

The most important trick to decluttering is *stay focused*. Oftentimes we'll come across things we haven't seen in years (a yearbook, old photos, souvenirs) and have an instant urge to reminisce. Resist that temptation! There'll be plenty of time later to pore through your summer camp scrapbook, but at 1:30 a.m., with the contents of your closets still in the middle of the floor, it's not the best time. I repeat: *do not put the prom dress on*.

THE FOUR PILES OF DECLUTTERING

While you declutter, you can practice getting organized by building the Four Piles of Decluttering.

- ✓ Pile 1—Garbage.
- ✓ Pile 2—Salvation.
- ✓ Pile 3—Maybe … maybe not.
- ✓ Pile 4—Has a purpose, needs a home.

If you've got a lot of stuff, use boxes. Your boxes will turn themselves into piles soon enough ... or possibly mountains. Remember to keep a pad of paper with a running to-do list on your person so you won't have to hunt for it when you need to make a note about something that needs to get done.

Pile 1. Garbage

This pile is explains itself. This is trash. This pile should only contain things that are unusable by any sane human being. But still, before you throw something out, think:
- ✓ Who else could use this?
- ✓ What else could this be used for?
- ✓ Can it be recycled?

❑ Sort through your *records* and *paperwork*. One of our biggest clutter problems is paperwork. Much of it we save only because of a fear we'll need it someday. The IRS says, "Generally, your records must be kept as long as they're important for any federal tax law" (IRS Publication No.552). If fear of throwing away old bills gets to you, at least separate them from your current expenses. Label them and store them in an out-of-the-way area. That way you'll still have proper documentation when your *Judge Judy* court appearance rolls around.

How long to keep paperwork

- ✓ Appointment books: 1 to 10 years (but this is mostly a personal choice)
- ✓ Auto payment book: until car is paid off
- ✓ Bank statements: 3 years, no more than 6 years back for tax purposes
- ✓ Car repair records: until car is sold
- ✓ Car title: until the car is sold
- ✓ Cash receipts for major purchases: until the item is sold or discarded
- ✓ Check registers: 3 years
- ✓ Canceled checks: for those of you who still dutifully write out "Pay to the Order of..." some banks will return cancelled checks to customers; others allow you to view them on-line. If you still feel the need to save checks, go for it. Six years is a recommended length of time.
- ✓ Credit card statements: 1 year, unless you need a statement as proof for a major purchase
- ✓ Health records: forever
- ✓ Loan papers: 3 years after final payment
- ✓ Manuals for appliances and electronics: until the product is sold or discarded

(cont'd)

✓ Medical bills: 3 years if needed to support tax returns
✓ Paycheck stubs: check annually against W2's, then discard
✓ Property lease or rental agreements: until you move and any claims are settled
✓ Traffic violations: 6 years
✓ Tax returns: 6 years. If it's a false return or no return filed, save forever.
✓ Utility bills: keep for as long as you need them. Usually utilities won't provide back copies of old bills, so if you need to save them for tax purposes, keep the current year. Otherwise, toss them.
✓ Warranties: until the warranty expires
✓ Vital records: permanently. This includes birth certificates, citizenship papers, adoption papers, wills, marriage / divorce / death certificates, passports, and titles and deeds to cars and property. Ideally, these items should be kept in a fire safe or a safe deposit box.

❑ *Mementos.* Minimize the souvenir, not the memory attached to it. Take photographs of yourself holding the item or keep only a small piece of it. Press a rose from a bouquet, take a small swatch of fabric from a dress. If necessary, save the shoelace from the pair of cleats that won you the state finals in soccer.

❑ Like rabbits, *photographs* have a habit of multiplying when they are left alone in a drawer. Decluttering them is relatively simple. Throw away all bad photos or photos that have no value to you. Give extra copies to the people who would appreciate them. Let go of negative energy by getting rid of photos that represent bad times of the past. (At least separate them from other photographs that still hold happy memories for you.) Save—but do not cut—only the negative strips of the photographs you'd want to replace or scan favorite pictures and keep the disk in a safe place. Sort all other pictures into albums or boxes.

Thinking outside the box: Scrapbooking

Scrapbooking combines photos, souvenirs, and memories with journaling, captions, and quotations. Not just a photo album, a scrapbook uses graphic design to expand the memory of an occasion with stories and backgrounds. There are classes and supplies offered to help the artistically challenged, but all you really need is a good quality book so that photographs are protected from chemical changes in paper. And don't forget the glitter. *Lots* of glitter.

❑ *Recipes.* Recipe boxes are clutter havens and rarely do we take the time to file correctly. The best way to organize your recipe collection is to use a three-ring binder and plastic sheet protectors. This way, you don't need to transfer the information, just slide the recipe card into the protector (you may need to tape smaller cards in place), and voilà—Julia Child, eat your heart out. You can create separators based on types of foods: desserts, pastas, appetizers, etc. While you're at it, also make a "takeout" section in the back and file all those paper menus that you can never seem to find when you really want them. You can also wipe plastic sheets clean when you forget to put the cover on the blender.

❑ *Newspapers and magazines.* Clip the article or information you want to save, then toss the rest of the paper. Keep a bibliographical file with the name of publication and the date so that if you ever need to locate the information again, you have a reference and know where to look it up easily at a library or on line.

❑ *Books.* I have only about four or five books in my personal collection. People know that if they give me a book, I will probably read it and then pass it on. If I want to read it again, chances are it can be found at the library. The same thing holds true for movies on videotape or DVD. Why does your personal library need to be bigger than your hometown's?

❑ *Your music collection.* Copy the few songs you like, then pass the CD or tape along.

Remember that 80 percent of what we file we never look at again. Ask yourself, do I really need this? Keep only what you absolutely need. Whittle the contents of every file drawer and box down to the essential information and toss the rest. Don't keep the envelope that something came in unless you have to prove the postmark date. Separate inactive files from active files you use on a daily basis. If possible store the old files in a box with the date when it can be destroyed written on the outside so that you don't have to waste time going through it again.

Stop & think

When going through paperwork that you're going to throw away, notice which pages are only printed on one side and save them for scrap paper. I print almost everything on scrap paper, knowing that if I ever need to forward it along to someone else, I can make a clean Xerox copy for them. Identity theft is a very real concern in this day and age, be sure to use a shredder for any piece of paper with your social security number or account numbers on it. The shredded strips later can be used as packing material or stuffing.

Things you can toss without a second thought:
- ✓ Maps older than five years
- ✓ Old calendars
- ✓ All but the current year's yellow pages. (Recycle old ones.)
- ✓ Old keys. Keep all extra keys on one ring, labeling them with a numeric code. (For safety's sake, keep the list separate.)
- ✓ Receipts from purchases that are not tax deductible and do not have any warranty.
- ✓ Anything expired, especially medication (both prescription and over-the-counter), milk, and meat. Note that, certain herbal supplements, vitamins, and spices also have expiration dates.

Expired medications

Many recommend flushing expired medications down the toilet so that they cannot be ingested accidentally, but medications are showing up in public drinking supplies because waste treatment plants are not designed to filter out these chemicals. Canada is experimenting with pharmacy return programs for proper disposal, but until the United States wises up, dispose of medications as you would any other hazardous waste. (Check www.earth911.org for recycling options.) You can also donate unopened and unexpired medications to health practitioners who are licensed redistribute them to developing countries that need them.

Some health and beauty aids also have expiration dates stamped on them. If not, use this rule of thumb: dispose of any makeup older than one year, sunscreen or toothpaste older than two, perfume one year after opened. Get in the habit of writing purchase dates on packaging in permanent marker.

The key to the garbage pile is to get it out of the house. *Immediately*. Subdivide as you go with recyclables, hazardous waste (very important if you're throwing away cleaners, expired medications, paint, or other chemicals) and a "truly trash" pile. If you cannot get rid of trash and recyclables right away, at least put them outside the house. You're going to need the room, and this way you won't be confronted with things you've already gotten rid of trying to sucker you into taking them back.

Pile 2: Salvation

I like to call this pile "salvation" because items here are being given another chance at use. If you're new to decluttering, your garbage pile will probably be the biggest (you might want to reconsider that dumpster…), but once you've become a seasoned simplifier, you'll be able to find salvation in almost anything.

Go through closets asking yourself, how often will I use my Rollerblades? Or that third blender? Or that fondue set? Make new piles based on what you have to donate—old books to the library, used clothes and furniture to the Goodwill, things you think friends might be able to use.

Make a "Personal Salvage" pile that includes unwearable clothing (missing buttons, stains, holes, etc.) that can be cut up for rags. Take off and save buttons or fasteners. This pile can also contain appliances or items that can be broken down for parts. Break these items down into their usable and workable pieces then discard the unusable pieces immediately.

On the other hand

Keep things in moderation. It's great to reuse grocery bags, but keeping a thousand plastic bags in your kitchen drawer is a sign of serious pack rat-itis.

Give yourself an extra week to work through the Salvation pile. If it hasn't been salvaged by the end of that week, then move it along. Stay disciplined. Use your running to-do list to write down what needs to be done for an item to receive a stay of execution.

I like to deal with decluttering clothing separately, usually at a time when I'm feeling like a supermodel. If you include clothes decluttering with everything else, you'll waste a lot of time trying things on. Instead, set aside a separate occasion when you can try everything on. This is another great opportunity to bring in that objective friend to tell you what works and what doesn't. Include shoes, belts, handbags, scarves, hats, and jewelry.

We can justify keeping any piece of clothing, whether it's "I'll diet back into it" or "this should come back in style in about ten years" or "when I was twenty, I spent a week's pay on this." Try not to let personal history come back and influence you. Any clothing you try on that causes you physical pain or any garment whose maintenance costs (alterations, dry cleaning, and upkeep) has more than exceeded its retail value should be relegated to the "pass-on" pile. Giving things away allows you to share their use and beauty with others who may need them more than you do.

Test yourself

Force yourself to wear something from the "haven't worn in a year pile" tomorrow. Nine times out of ten, you'll quickly realize why you haven't worn it and send it on its way.

Donate what can be passed along to the Salvation Army, Goodwill, or your church rummage sale. Every year natural disasters take the homes and possessions of thousands of Americans, to say nothing of people around the world who are suddenly without weather-appropriate clothing. Think about giving business attire to organizations that donate to the less fortunate who need interview and business clothing. This will help to lessen the blow of keeping something just because you paid "good money" for it. Many places offer a receipt for the merchandise you bring in that you can use as a tax deduction. Formal dresses can be donated through www.fairygodmothersinc.com to lower income youth for prom wear.

For what it's worth...

At most donation sites, it's up to you to fill out your receipt for the fair market value of the clothing you've donated. Use either 20 percent of the original retail value or these guidelines from the Salvation Army at www.satruck.com/donation_value_guide.

Some other donating tips:

- Give something you no longer need to a friend. But make sure the friend can actually put what you're giving them to good use. Nothing's sadder than seeing your stuff move to their junk pile.
- Try eBay (www.ebay.com), the online auction site, where your trash can find the person who actually thinks Thundercats action figures in their original packaging is treasure.
- Recycle old treasures at consignment shops or pawnshops. If there's still reasonable value in your stuff, you might try reselling it. Consignment shops usually buy women's clothing and either pay a percentage of the resale value in cash or provide merchandise credit. In case you're excavating in your closet back to the 1950s, vintage clothing stores also buy clothing.
- Free to a good home. When you don't have the time or energy to haul something around town or find someone who wants it, a simple "free for the taking" sign on an item on your front lawn or listed on craigslist.com is sure to get the item picked up in short order.
- Have a yard sale. You don't need a yard for a yard sale or a garage for a garage sale, but check your town laws before setting up your card table.

Successful yard sale tips

✓ There's strength in numbers. Consider throwing your sale with coworkers, neighbors, or friends.

✓ Location, location, location. The most successful yard sales are usually larger, well advertised, and in high traffic areas.

✓ Sell your sale. Those who shop the sales regularly know where to look for ads. Start with the free papers for the best advertising money can't buy. All you need on your sign are the words YARD SALE, your address (and an arrow pointing in the right direction), and the date and times (if you know you're not going to be able to get back to the sign in time to take it down after you're done). Some people put too much detail on their signs, listing what they have to sell. The more information you put on a sign, the smaller the important information gets. Stick to the basics.

✓ Have an extension cord with electricity at the ready. People are more willing to consider purchasing an appliance if they can see that it actually works. What about setting a loaf of bread by that toaster you're selling? An early morning round of toast can get folks in the mood to shop, and it will probably move that toaster before you get to the fight about who has to eat the end pieces. If you're selling clothing, provide a full-length mirror and a tape measure.

✓ Clean items for sale with a light solution of soap and water. Use rubbing alcohol and cotton swabs to clean out the grimy crevices.

✓ Save the sob story. You may think your sad tale will get you an extra $5 for the Barbie Dream House, but the folks came to shop, not to listen to your Poor Pitiful Pearl routine.

Of course, no one can tell you when to get rid of something. Sure, your landlord can threaten you with eviction and your significant other can walk out, but ultimately you have to make the decision to let the Atari 2600 and collection of ninety-eight games go.

Pile 3: Maybe … Maybe Not

This is the undecided, miscellaneous, "don't know what to do about it" pile. Save reviewing this pile until the end of your big cleaning day. That's when you're less discriminating about what you save because you're exhausted and more than ready to be done with it all. Some recommend sealing this pile up in a big box and marking it "Do not open until … [one year from this day]." If that year passes and you haven't missed or needed anything from the box, you can give it away.

Pile 4: Has a Purpose, Needs a Home

This pile should be everything you use often and need to keep but is currently located in an inconvenient place. Pick up any item. You should be able to easily defend why it is there without feeling guilty. While you're deciding what to keep, think about where things should go.

"Who's got my tap shoes?"

Keep a bag by your door for things you borrowed from friends or want to donate to them. Add to it, and when you're ready to visit that friend, just grab the bag and go.

KEEPING YOURSELF AND YOUR HOME CLUTTER-FREE

You've tackled the initial organization process and lived to tell the tale. Hopefully, your load is a little bit lighter and you're able to open closet doors without an avalanche of shoes and sweaters burying you. The hard part now is maintaining this same level of organization on a daily basis. If you develop a system that's easy to remember and maintain, keeping organized will be a piece o' cake. Without a system, you'll need discipline or maybe a personal drill sergeant.

Create an Enjoyable System

We all need a little discipline, but our organization systems don't need to feel like a tour of duty in the Marines. I personally went through some trial and error before I found the system that worked for me. I tried printing out a daily list, using a PDA, and writing down everything I needed to do, but none of these tricks got tasks done any quicker. It finally took just a packet of scrap paper cut in half and stapled together with a different page for each type of list (grocery, mail I was waiting for, projects, books and movies to remember, etc.) to kick my to-do list into gear. I also found that hand drawn boxes to check off were a great visual motivator. Try any of these tricks for keeping your proverbial ducks in a row:

❑ Use an in box and an out box. Find or create a system for moving things out of the in box and filing completed items. Try clearing the boxes out at least once a week. For items that stay in there forever, start new files: Pending Projects, On Hold, Follow Up. It may help you to treat your bills and personal paperwork as you would if you owned a business.

❑ Scrounge file folders and three-ring binders with dividers from your place of employment if they're throwing them away. These make great organizational tools. I don't recommend stealing office supplies; ask someone before taking. Defending your home organization system probably won't save your job.

❑ Learn to label. If you have a lot of stuff to keep, label boxes, cabinets, and drawers. Keeping a master list of where things are located will save hours of time spent searching. Make tab flags for books that you use often (this works great for phone books). Use Post-Its or make your own "stickies" from tape and paper.

❑ Try to avoid having a "miscellaneous" file. You'll be too tempted to throw anything in there and it soon becomes a wasteland of unfinished projects. Likewise, combine all those little scraps of paper into one main to-do list.

❑ Consider purchasing pre-designed books for certain tasks, such as keeping track of your financial, automotive, or medical records.

❑ Follow the "one goes in, one goes out" rule. One way to avoid creating another mountain of stuff is to follow this simple rule: for every item that you bring into the house, another item leaves. If someone gives you a sweater for Christmas, how about turning an old sweatshirt into rags? If your friend passes along several books she knows you'll like, how about trading some of your books with her?

❑ Break down enormous or complicated tasks. The things that remain longest on our to-do lists are usually there because we have difficulty getting them started. What's holding you back from completing them? Analyze what you need to do to complete a task and break it down into smaller steps. Instead of one large ominous job, you now have seven or eight smaller, more manageable tasks. The easier a task is to complete, the more likely you are to cross it off.

❑ Use a calendar to remind yourself of future events and errands (like getting an oil change in three months, rotating the tires on your car, flipping your mattress, checking your smoke alarm batteries, meeting due dates for bills, requesting a copy of your credit report once a year, changing water filters, and canceling services after limited-time free upgrades, to name a few).

❑ Schedule your chores and errands into your week. You'll feel less harried if you know that Monday is laundry day, Tuesday you clean the bathroom, and Wednesday you sort mail and pay bills. Maintaining this routine may seem difficult at first—and you may be tempted to skip a few days here and there—but in the long run, you'll free up more spontaneous time when you don't have to spend an entire weekend doing everything. Learn to schedule time to do things, especially if you're always late. Some people even go as far as to schedule their free time, writing in their day planners "read from 4 to 5 p.m., watch television from 8 to 10 p.m." If these tricks are what it takes to get organized, I say go for it, but remember—don't become a slave to your calendar.

❑ Store things near where you will use them and keep the things you use most often in the most convenient places. You're more likely to put the laundry detergent away if it's near the washing machine. Store things you use less frequently away from everyday traffic. There's no need to be tripping over the Christmas tree stand in May. Put like items together. If you can't find it where it's supposed to be, you will often assume you don't have it and go out and purchase another one.

❑ Keep all similar current information in one location. When you're ready to pay your bills, a small file box or basket lets you get down to business with stamps, calculator, and records easily at hand.

Do It Now!

Procrastination breeds clutter like Disney movies breed Dalmatians. Remember that it's a lot easier to clean dishes right after you've used them than it is to scrub off three-day-old mac and cheese. Stay current with these tips:

❑ Try to do everything as it comes up. Open your mail as you get it and, if you can, pay your bills immediately. Keep a checklist of all your monthly expenses (rent, car payment, insurance, student loans, gas, electric, phones) and check them off as you pay them. Be sure you check and write down every transaction in your checkbook. Late fees are punishment enough.

❑ Write ideas down as they come to you, but don't trust loose slips of paper or Post-Its. Use a small notebook and learn to keep all your notes in one place. Recopying information also helps to reinforce it.

❑ Learn how to prioritize your workload. Structure your lists so that you can see the importance of tasks and give them appropriate weight. You know instantly what needs to get finished first. You are better able to see if how you spend your time is meaningful and productive. Always tackle projects in order of pay-off and you'll discover more time almost immediately.

Tip for a to-do list

Be sure to add something easy (return videos), something fun (pick up a pie), something silly (paint fingernails green), and something routine (water plants) to your list. This way you'll always be able to cross something off. Psychologically, the visual of crossed off items makes us more likely to complete more tasks.

❑ Set goals for yourself. Keep them manageable and easy to accomplish at first. As you continue to succeed with them, up the ante. Keep your immediate goals posted in a highly visible place—on the refrigerator, the bathroom mirror, even a place relating to the goal—to remind you to keep focused on achieving them. To cut down on trash, I put a note over my trashcan, which I had to move every time I wanted to throw something away. A dieting goal could be attached to the refrigerator door handle, an exercise goal attached to the television remote control, a driving-less goal to the steering wheel of your car.

❑ Touch everything only once. Ever wonder how Mr. Rogers kept his clubhouse so neat? He didn't leave his clothes on the back of the couch, toss his shoes down by the door, and head to the kitchen for some Fig Newtons. He always took his jacket and shoes off at the closet and hung them up as he was changing into his sweater and Keds. Smart guy.

❑ Decide what to do with things as they come up. By opening your mail near the recycling bin, you can get rid of anything you don't need immediately. Place everything else where it belongs. Enter important events onto your calendar as you learn about them and transfer new addresses to your contact book. If you decide on a course of action as you sort, less information will get lost in the shuffle.

❑ Pay cash. As you'll learn in the next chapter, paying by credit card is essentially paying for something twice and leads you down the Yellow Brick Road to debt.

❑ Ask for help when you need it. Maybe the real reason you're not completing things is because you lack the right tools (or people) to help get the job done.

Be Conscious of Your Clutter-Creating Habits

As you get rid of unwanted items, think back on how they came into your life. Why have you kept this stuff so long? Be honest with yourself about why your life is so cluttered. Look deep at your habits and your fears to uncover what you're resisting by staying trapped underneath all your belongings, time commitments, and stress.

Clutter Habits

✓ Free samples: "Well, it's free, I can't turn that down."

✓ Gifts: "Someone took the trouble to buy me this, and I know they'd be upset if I just got rid of it."

✓ Fashion: "I've got to keep up with seasons and trends."

✓ Junk mail: "I'll just look through this later to see if there's anything interesting in here."

✓ Boredom purchases: "Why did I buy this, anyway?"

✓ Holiday clutter: "It wouldn't be right not to be festive!"

✓ Souvenirs from vacations: "How would we ever remember that trip and how much we paid for it without these quirky T-shirts and coffee mugs?"

Remind yourself with a notation on your calendar to audit your organization system every few months. Notice when piles start forming again, when you stop crossing things off your to-do list, or when a major life change has happened. Each event is a signal to check in on your organization system. Cleaning with the change of the seasons can be just what you need to break out of a rut.

Decluttering is the first step in simplifying your life. When we don't know where to find things, when we put things off, when our lives are so full of clutter, we rob ourselves of the full benefits of simplicity. As our possessions find appropriate homes, we free up time, money, and energy to devote to what we truly enjoy doing. Keeping organized will help us see what's been holding our lives back and pave a path for simplicity.

Do it today
Mark your calendar for three months from today. Are the organizing systems you put in place still working effectively? Get rid of thirty items you don't need, use, or want. Be ruthless.

ADDITIONAL RESOURCES
Aslett, Don. *Clutter's Last Stand.* Cincinnati, Ohio: Writer's Digest Books, 1984. Aslett wrote the book on decluttering. Actually, he wrote about forty of them. Trust me, he's the expert here.

Campbell, Jeff. *Clutter Control: Putting Your Home on a Diet.* New York: Dell Publishing, 1992. An efficiency expert gives solutions to cleaning and creating anti-clutter systems.

Morgenstern, Julie. *Organizing from the Inside Out.* New York: Henry Holt and Co., 1998. "The foolproof system for organizing your home, your office and your life." A primer for anyone who begins their organization from scratch.

Smallin, Donna. *Organizing Plain & Simple.* North Adams, MA: Storey Books, 2002. A ready reference guide with hundreds of solutions to your everyday clutter challenges. One of the best books connecting simplicity and organization.

Waddill, Kathy. *The Organizing Sourcebook: Nine Strategies for Simplifying Your Life.* Chicago: Contemporary Books, 2001. Waddill has created a blueprint for home and time organization using real-life examples, detailing how they were successful.

chapter 2

reconnecting

> Out of clutter, find simplicity.
> –Albert Einstein

Now that we've cleared out our clutter and gotten ourselves organized, it's time to reevaluate *how* we're living. The first question we can ask ourselves is, "How did it get to the point that I need to do a massive overhaul of my life just to find a pair of matching socks?" Do you often wonder why it feels like you don't have the time or money to do the things you really want to do? Or why you always feel so stressed?

Here's a hint. We've become a culture that's gone even beyond conspicuous consumption to a category that could be called "presumptuous consumption". We presume that everything will always be there for us. We take for granted things such as clean water, unlimited food supply and access to health care. Everything is easy and available. We've been conditioned to want it bigger, better, faster—every single minute of the day. We want more because we *can* want more. Freedom has taught us that it's our right as Americans to think we need it all.

It's time to examine the toll our lifestyle takes on our health and sanity and on the planet itself. Many of us are on a collision course with burnout. We're succumbing to the hazards of substance abuse and creating physical and mental health problems. *Simplicity offers an alternative to the out-of-control complexity of our lives.*

So what exactly is this simplicity I'm writing about? The definition of simplicity can be anything but simple but it is not about depriving ourselves of what we want. Simplicity is harmony and spirituality. It's frugality. It's oneness with the natural world. It's living sustainably. It's the connecting factor in all these concepts.

The simplicity movement is not new—we find it in the teachings of Jesus and it forms the basis for many faiths, such as the Quakers, Puritans, Amish, Shakers, and Mennonites. Simplicity also expresses itself through the philosophies of Lao Tsu and Aristotle.

However, the most notable name in the history of American simplicity is Henry David Thoreau, the 19th-century writer who moved to Walden Woods in search of a truer, simpler life. He took up residence in a one-room cabin for over two years to reflect on and write about a society that was already beginning to compromise itself with greed and disrespect for nature.

On the other hand: Thoreauvian misconceptions

Thoreau might have gone to live deliberately, but he wasn't the recluse many have considered him to be. He did not live in solitary confinement; he constantly had friends visiting, and he even had his mother do his laundry. He lived in view of a public road and was only two miles away from the center of the city of Concord, Massachusetts. His ten by fifteen foot cabin was practically palatial compared to the Unabomber's shack (at ten by twelve feet), but it's likely that cabin fever never set in because Thoreau was always outdoors.

Closer to our modern day, but hidden behind all the popular love of money in the early 1980s, simplicity experienced a resurgence with the publication of Duane Elgin's book, *Voluntary Simplicity*.[1] This book reacquainted people with Thoreau's ideas by offering an eighteen-part definition of simplicity that describes people who live simply as citizens who have a singleness of purpose, deliberateness, who are free of secondary complications and the distractions of vanity and ostentation, who live more consciously.[2] It was Elgin's work that put many on the road to a new way of living. But voluntary simplicity was, alas, no match for the luxuries and complexities of the Reagan era, and so the simplicity movement lapsed again.

As the nineties began, the twentieth anniversary of the first Earth Day brought recycling and concern for the environment back into our consciousness. Reaching middle age, baby boomers looked back fondly at the 1960s, when they imagined they'd lived an archetypal simple life. In April of 1991, the cover of *TIME* magazine read, "The Simple Life: Rejecting the Rat Race, Americans Get Back to Basics." The lead article[3] noted the beginning of a trend of Americans giving up the glamour and "godless consumerism" of the yuppie lifestyle of the eighties. The *TIME* writers painted a picture of the nineties as a time when we could all go back to churning our own butter and sitting by the fire listening to Pa read Thoreau.

The country seemed poised on the brink of a simplicity revolution: "We want to work less and spend more time with our families," we said. "We're ready to harvest our own crops." So what happened? When the Information Superhighway started accepting passengers, the economy got jumpstarted. Suddenly, all bets were off. ("Why should I sew my own clothes when J. Crew.com delivers them to my door?")

Today the majority of Americans still have a negative perception of simplicity. We claim to want change. We say we want to work less if we can, even if it means making less money. But at the same time, we all fall victim to the hypnosis of consumerism and advertising that permeates every waking hour of our lives. How do we minimize the complications but keep the comfort and convenience that our throwaway culture has given us? Can reducing time stress and scaling back still fulfill the desires that consumerism has created?

"Perhaps the biggest misconception about voluntary simplicity," Duane Elgin writes, "is that it's about frugal living and nothing more. The media portray it as a life of material sacrifice, which makes it easy to caricature and dismiss as irrelevant to mainstream Americans."[4] Living simply does not have to mean giving up indoor plumbing and moving to a cabin in rural Vermont. It doesn't have to mean sewing all your clothes by hand, giving up your car for a horse-drawn buggy, or tapping the trees on your front lawn for maple syrup.

There's a definite connection between minimalism and doing-it-yourself and those who choose to live simply, but these are not interchangeable lifestyles. Learning to live simply may initially feel like a sacrifice, but many people who try it feel that they're gaining a better sense of what is truly important in the world. Giving up unnecessary things in our lives often becomes easier than we expected.

Simplicity is also not just about reducing consumption. It's a *psychological transformation* that changes not only what we do, but also how we think and what we think about. It's a journey, a personal search for answers to the questions asked by the soul. It becomes a path of our own design, which we navigate using maps that often incorporate established paths.

We shouldn't fear the simple lifestyle. There is a deepening consciousness that accompanies it, one that allows us to focus more on our inner desires and less on trivial distractions. Living simply does not mean we have to drop out of society. On the contrary, in order to save our culture from eating itself alive, we need to direct the development of technology away from projects that waste time and money. Simplicity is not about curbing progress, but about not letting it get out of control. We need scientists, researchers, dreamers, and inventors to refocus their energy on finding simple, sustainable solutions to today's problems.

This book offers a variety of suggestions on how to keep every aspect of our lives at a level of simplicity that we are comfortable with. Ideas are presented to encourage us to develop a fresh perspective on how we can all change our lives to minimize our impact on the world and keep our minds, bodies, and the planet healthy. If we are unable to make large-scale changes to our lives (say, giving up our automobile), we can still take advantage of suggestions from the lists below as "baby steps" to start with. Doing small things is an alternative to just ignoring the problem until we can make the larger changes.

Guilt

One of the hardest parts of adopting simplicity is the inevitable guilt that accompanies always trying to "do the right thing." If we stray from what we believe is moral and good, we can feel that we're bad or wrong for doing so. Guilt is an emotion of our own creation. We may think others impose it upon us, but it's really our own choices and reactions that create guilt.

We feel guilty even when we have no reason to do so, and this emotion robs us of determination and efficiency. To avoid guilt, we must recognize the symptoms, identify the source, and decide to walk away from the struggle between low self-esteem and trying to please others. Let guilt go! It's an obstacle in our path to simplicity. Let's accept what the universe has provided and know that true simplicity implies no shame and no blame.

Ironically, there is no easy formula for simplicity. It's not *reading a book + giving up your car + cutting back your work hours = Simplistic Epiphany*! There are no right or wrong paths to simplicity. Fortunately, many of the paths have already been paved and choices are waiting. It's often called *voluntary simplicity* because, ultimately, only *you* can make the choices for your life.

INGREDIENTS THAT CHANGE OUR THINKING & RECONNECT OUR SOULS

Like a good stew, simplicity involves many ingredients to create a balanced flavor. Each batch is a creative expression of the chef, just like each person's path to simplicity is reflective of what their beliefs are. The ingredients of simplicity can help us choose how we want to make our own recipe.

1. Mindfulness
2. Return to nature
3. Spirit
4. Satiation
5. Balance
6. Who are we?
7. Slowing down
8. Solitude
9. Creativity

Let's consider each of these in turn.

1. MINDFULNESS: Living Deliberately

> I went to the woods because I wished to
> live deliberately, to front only the
> essential facts of life, and see if I could
> learn what it had to teach, and not when
> I came to die, to discover that I had not
> lived.
>
> –Henry David Thoreau,
> *Walden*

The most important concept related to voluntary simplicity is *being present in what is occurring*, having a continuous consciousness of your decisions. This is what Buddhists refer to as *mindfulness*. When we live deliberately, we take the time to see how our actions affect the world. A cup of coffee is no longer just a morning wake-up. It becomes the beans grown to make the coffee, the trees grown to make the paper cup, the chemicals cooked to make the plastic lid, the sugar cane harvested for the sweetener, and even the motivating factors that brought the gal behind the counter to sell us the cup of coffee.

Mindfulness can seem like a time-consuming burden at first, but the more simplified our lives get, the easier it becomes to make the choices that reflect our true beliefs. As mindfulness becomes second nature, we feel more passionate about our ideals. Best of all, we don't have to go to the woods as Thoreau did. We can easily learn to bring deliberate living into our daily lives.

By making our *state of mind* more important than what we're doing and making conscious choices about what we do, we can achieve a state of enlightenment. It's when we get caught up in searching so intently for the something "out there" that will complete us that we miss the miracles that occur in everyday life. What if it's not "out there" but actually within us?

Every routine task can be used as a focus for meditation. It is very simple to meditate: relax, focus your mind and begin contemplation. In his book *Wherever You Go, There You Are*, Jon Kabat-Zinn suggests using this meditation: "Trust that in this moment, 'this is it,' whatever and wherever 'this' is." Focus intently on the present, he writes, without "analyzing, discoursing, judging, condemning, or doubting" but "simply observing, embracing, opening, letting be, accepting."[5]

As Paul Roland likewise explains in his book, *How to Meditate,* our minds deceive us. Memory makes us think we can return to the past, and imagination makes us think we can anticipate the future.[6] We're easily distracted. We get bored. Nothing seems to be happening that is interesting enough to engage us. We think ahead to the promise of better times or back to memorable experiences of the past. Anything to keep our minds off the present moment. But why?

In reality, we truly exist only in the present. We have to accept that although we cannot control the world, *we can control our reactions to it*. Stay focused on here and now— the good in life. In boring times, it's good to remain mindful. In times of stress, it's good to remain mindful. In times of joy, it's good to remain mindful. In ordinary times, it's good to remain mindful. Just to be safe, *always remain mindful*. Practice Zen and the art of locking your keys in the car, Zen and the art of waiting for a table, Zen and the art of stupid boys who don't return your phone calls.

> Our true home is the present moment. To live in the present moment is a miracle. The miracle is not to walk on water. The miracle is to walk on the green Earth in the present moment, to appreciate the peace and beauty that are available now.
> –Thich Nhat Hanh[7]

Stop & think
Is there anything as beautiful as this moment?

Living in Reality

> You cannot find peace by avoiding life.
> –Michael Cunningham and David Hare, *The Hours* (spoken by Nicole Kidman as Virginia Woolf)

Simplicity is not just living for survival. It's living as if we truly want to live— making our own decisions, not being influenced by a mediated recommendation. Our culture has become completely mediated by television, radio, film, the Internet, books, magazines, advertising: all of these are beholden to the almighty dollar. "Madison Avenue" is now a cliché for the unseen man behind the curtain telling us what to buy to be cool.

Even people and materials that claim to lead us to simplicity can be controlled by advertising. (I'm looking at glossy magazines that advocate finding "simplicity" by way of purchasing $200 organizing systems.) We must learn not to instantly accept the word of the ubiquitous media as the answer to what our lives are lacking.

Our culture has taught us to live vicariously through televised images. This false reality may elicit emotional responses from us, but are televised experiences legitimate experiences? Are my choices my own? Or are they only my responses to how television, movies, popular culture want me to act? Am I merely watching someone else's life and not truly living my own life? Is watching a skydiver in a movie truly akin to the sensation of flying through the air? Simplicity encourages us to get up off the Barcalounger and out into the world.

Don't just sympathize with the impoverished and the ill. Live and shop among them and you will understand and respect them. Volunteering time to the less fortunate is just as important as donating money. Reject the altered realities that drugs and alcohol create. The emotions and perceptions they give us are not real. Escape mediated reality. The TV, stereo, and computer give us preconceived models and stereotypes; turn them off sometimes. Put the magazine down and experience life instead.

2. RETURN TO NATURE: Attending to Nature's Cycles

> Harmful side effects of consumerism and mass production become more apparent and start to impinge on our own lives. Many of us are becoming much more open to the bonuses of living in tune with nature rather than against it.
>
> –Rebecca Tanqueray, *Eco Chic*[8]

An incomplete picture of nature exists in our minds. We often fail to realize that nature is more than trees and wildlife. What nature really is, is the instinctual patterns that every living thing follows. The earth is a part of our extended body, involving all our senses. *Life is nature.*

People I call *Natural Simplists* are sympathetic to the plight of other creatures: From trouble in the rainforests, to rescuing a stray dog, to eating naturally and avoiding processed and refined foods and meat, simplists act in ways that express care and living in tune with nature's cycles. Environmentalism is not interchangeable with simplicity, but an intimate connection with nature is an integral part of both.

"The Great Outdoors"

We belong in nature, but we continue to close our homes off, feeling the need to separate ourselves from it. Our boxes should be climate controlled, keeping all the bugs and other pesky critters outside, but would it be too much to ask for a perfect view of the mountains? Madison Avenue tries to sell us nature by marketing SUVs as a way to have our own transportation into nature; in reality, their bulky design makes them dangerous to the great outdoors as they demand paved roads through the wilderness, lumber off-road and destroy habitat, and spew gas fumes into the air. We can sit in the safety of our living rooms and watch cable channels like *The Discovery Channel* and easily commune with nature.

In urban areas, nature tends to become "messy," so flowers are confined to manicured garden boxes, tree roots that break through the sidewalk are cut away, and vacant lots are quickly paved over and zoned for building. Nature invariably pisses us off and inconveniences us. The deer that steps in front of the car, mosquitoes that attack us at the company picnic, the rain on our wedding day—nature seldom gets our memos and rarely seems to follow our plan.

Our human response is to try to dominate nature. Our society sees nature as a dangerous force that needs to be civilized and subdued. We cut it down, burn it, kill it, destroy it, poison it, redirect it, pillage it, do anything we can to control it. Instead of letting nature exist on its own terms, we make it conform to our sense of beauty.

Biophilia is the psychological theory coined by the Pulitzer Prize-winning conservation biologist Edward O. Wilson, who defines the term as "the love of living things or the innate emotional affiliation of human beings to other living organisms."[9] There is an intrinsic need in all of us to relate to plants, animals, and the outdoors. The more we distance ourselves from nature, the less of an emotional connection we have with it.

Nature doesn't hurry. It doesn't waste anything. It has a way of fixing itself or adapting when left alone. Even after volcanic explosions, in time, growth will come from ash. (Unfortunately, with the totality of destruction we have inflicted on some parts of the earth, much will not be recovered in any amount of time that has meaning for us.) At its most basic level, nature will always come back, no matter what we mere humans do. There are many lessons we can learn just by observing how ecology manages and restores itself.

On the other hand

"Ecopsychology" is an alternative view of mental health that sees how people become physically and mentally ill because of the diseased state of nature. We need natural beauty just as much as we need sustenance and medication to remain healthy.[10]

Our inner struggles to find meaning in our lives inevitably lead us back to nature. Through simplicity, we find a deeper association to the planet. Before we cut down the old growth forest, pave the local wetlands, or burn another acre of rainforest, we must consider their connection to future generations. We must learn to respect and cherish our environment and the cycle of nature. We must fight to save and regenerate it, to preserve its resources. We must accept that plants and animals (not to mention other people) have as much a right to where and how they live as we do.

Test yourself

Thoreau advocated spending four hours a day outdoors. How long were you outside today?

Human Nature

Too often, we think of nature only as birds and trees and neglect to consider the human element of nature. People are part of the ecology, as much as redwood forests, Grizzly bears or Niagara Falls. We make our lives invariably more complex by trying to force nature to fit into our convenience. When we simplify our lives, we learn to respect the natural pattern of the human life cycle. Everything in nature has its own life cycle, and simplicity is acknowledging and respecting natural rhythms.

Currently, one couple in five has trouble conceiving. Now that we have created so many endocrine disrupters that lower sperm counts and cause sexual organs to malfunction or develop incorrectly, those who cannot have children try to manipulate nature with in vitro fertilization and fertility drugs. Moms and dads-to-be can induce labor or schedule C-sections to make birth more convenient. When conception is difficult, perhaps we should look closer at why it feels so necessary to have a baby in a world already overpopulated with so many unwanted children.

We enter the world in the most unnatural way possible: ripped screaming from our cozy home into a cold, sometimes drug induced, unnaturally lit, sterilized environment. Natural birth methods, like at-home birth with the help of a midwife or waterbirth, can lessen the trauma of the hospital experience (often save money, too).

Life is going great, you're looking forward to the big dance Friday night, and then— wham! You get the flu. Nature interrupts our lives by making us sick, but rarely do we see illness as anything more than bad luck. How often do we take our sickness as a sign to slow down and relax or look deeper at how our lives are affecting our physical health?

We will all experience loss in our lives, sometimes painful loss. By realizing that nature is cyclical and seeing loss as an unavoidable part of nature's process, we can learn to respect it, accept it, and move on. Grieving will not bring anything back, but it's a useful cathartic emotion that allows us to break away from the past and move into the future. Acceptance is an important quality in simplicity.

Even after a long illness when death is expected, death is often not treated as the amazing experience that it is. Families are kept away from loved ones, and though the patient may be ready to die, modern medicine is morally (and often legally) obligated to keep them alive. But many people are kept "alive" in a way I doubt any of us would choose. Hospice care provides an option for those who wish to finish their lives with dignity and some control. Terminal patients may also choose to remain at home, with medical attention coming to them if necessary. This often saves their loved ones the grief of turning off life support (not to mention exorbitant hospital costs).

Death is not neat and tidy. More often than not, it comes unexpectedly. It may be tragic. We feed our bodies unhealthy meals, breathe unclean air, and engage in lifestyles that stress us to the max. We must learn to see the connections between our complex lives and the physical toll that complexity may take. Some find comfort in the idea that when someone dies "it was their time," but others have learned to fear old age because of the impending sense of death it carries. We can choose to accept death as a passage and not focus on the pain and sadness it brings, but receive it with quiet reflection.

Modern American burials are controlled by an industry that, knowing people will pay for convenience, often price gouges the survivors because it can. Bodies have little chance of biodegradation when they are preserved with formaldehyde, sealed in a highly lacquered box then enclosed within concrete walls. But "green burials" are starting to change all that. These burials both respect the end of human life and the continuation of ecological life that exists around the burial plot. They advocate keeping the burial land as a natural habitat. When green burials are chosen, coffins must be made from biodegradable material and bodies cannot be embalmed. Some find that caring for a deceased loved one gives a sense of closure and intimacy that unnatural burials do not. (See www.finalpassages.org and www.memorialecosystems.com for more information.)

3. SPIRIT: Finding and Keeping in Tune

Because many beliefs of simplicity mirror those of organized religion (and as noted, the teachings of many spiritual leaders have formed the basis of the simplicity movement) it is not hard to see why many confuse simplicity with spirituality. But they are not transposable concepts.

Most us want to believe in something bigger than ourselves. We want to believe in a force that looks out for us, something we can rely on to know that ultimately everything will be okay. Our search for spirit leads us to our higher self, a place where compassion and quiet take charge. Our search for spirit can lead us to church, journaling, yoga, meditation, communion with nature, or unseen forces that guide us.

"Spirit" is often used interchangeably with religion and God. Generally, however, spirit is more than religion. It's not just religion that nourishes us. It's more a feeling of protection and guidance, being in tune with the world. It's the nonphysical, immaterial aspects of ourselves—the energy and essence that existed before and will exist after we cease to breathe—that bring us true simplicity.

On the other hand

Religion attempts to institutionalize spirit. When we connect simplicity to religion, this connection can frighten away many who would otherwise develop their spirituality. Some religions are anything but simple. Ten thousand seat churches? Jim and Tammy Faye? Muslim extremism? Like the separation of church and state, it's best to keep religion and simplicity connected, but not interchangeable.

Intuition

Feelings. Hunches. Inner urges. Daydreaming. Being "in the zone." The sixth sense. Call it what you like, each of these is an example of intuition and a window into our true selves. Our inner guidance can lead to the recesses of our mind where we can find hidden treasures of insight. Once we practice and get used to how intuition works, we can use it to get what we want. Notice what happens when you pay attention to what your mind tells you.

There are unexplained coincidences. Something you need appears exactly when you need it. You have a premonition of things to come. How wonderful it is when the universe provides. Are these unexplained moments truly just coincidences, or is the metaphysical world trying to manifest in your life? Coincidence sometimes feels dreamlike—but is it coincidence, or is it something deeper and more spiritual?

Be willing to accept what you attract into your life. Be honest with yourself and don't ignore signals that your intuition gives you. Notice which activities in your life give you more insight toward your true path. Does your morning commute allow you to have time for inspiration to strike? Do seemingly random thoughts enter your mind during your weekly yoga class? Why do you avoid that person who keeps calling you?

Tools for intuition

Look closely at these mystical or psychic paths, and you'll find their basis in the human mind. Ask the universe for a sign, and these tools can provide the medium for it to be revealed. Our interpretations of readings can lead to enlightenment.

✓ *Astrology*: The belief that the movement and locations of celestial bodies affect human beings.

✓ *Clairvoyance*: Psychic readers, fortunetellers, palmistry and Tarot readers use precognition (seeing future events) and retrocognition (ability to see the past) to make predictions.

✓ *Runes*: A Viking forecasting system. When we have a question, we draw a stone and interpret the symbol of the rune.

✓ *Dream interpretation*: Ask a clear question before going to bed, and when you first awaken in the morning try to remember your dreams. Don't get discouraged if you can't remember your dreams. Make up a dream if you want to. The basis for dreams and imagination is the same.

✓ *Visualization*: Imagine the situation in your head. How do you want it to turn out? Walking through the steps can reveal new ideas and foresight for potential problems.

✓ *I Ching*: The Chinese Book of Changes reveals that we already have the all the answers. Like other psychic sciences, it's just a tool to help us see what is in our subconscious. "Realize that all sickness, disease, failures, accidents are the embodiment of negative ideas or fears in your subconscious mind." –*The Secrets of the I Ching*[11]

✓ *Rebirthing*: A practice using hypnotherapy and breathing to recreate your own birth and thus revisit the initial events that led you to be who you are today.

✓ *Reincarnation*: Using a previous life to recall and learn from experiences held by the eternal being currently manifesting as you.

✓ *Magic 8-Ball*: My personal favorite. It can also be used to interpret answers to our questions.

I cannot tell you your definition of spirit. Spirit may be the most personal part of simplicity. While your definition may include religious faith, mine may be karma and the unseen hand that guides my intuition. But accepting a place of spirit in our lives will help us focus on a path to simplicity. However we come to define spirit, it accompanies a singleness of purpose and an emphasis on the less complex.

4. SATIATION: How Much Is Enough?

> Desire is the source of all suffering.
> –The Buddha

In our culture, the concept of "enough" is ceasing to have any real meaning. It seems that sufficiency is no longer an operative concept. How do we develop our sense of how much is enough? Since society won't define it for us, we can consider simplicity.

Simplicity can lead to a way of life based on knowing when to say, "That's enough." We can reevaluate our needs and buy less. When we do shop, we can learn to look for products that are durable, less complex, easy to repair, and nonpolluting in their manufacture and use. We can learn to recognize that advertising diverts our attention from the simple life and pushes us toward never-ending wanting where there is never enough.

Affluenza

"Affluenza" is a term created by the makers of a PBS documentary that explored the sociological effects of consumerism on our culture. It's the "painful, contagious, socially transmitted condition of overload, debt, anxiety, and waste resulting from the dogged pursuit of more."[12]

> To ask how little, not how much, can I get along with. To say—is it necessary?—when I am tempted to add one more accumulation to my life.
> –Anne Morrow Lindbergh

Greed

"Enough" manifests itself in jealousy and competition, arrogance and elitism. Greed does not have a satiation point because it does not fill the "need" it supposedly tries to fill. Wanting more leads to a never-ending class struggle. Because we want and are without, we learn to hate those who have. Americans hardly stop to enjoy the now. We are always focusing on the future and how can we do or get it faster, bigger, and better. Simplicity teaches us to accept what we have as plenty and not to covet those who feed the need to have more.

Needs vs. Wants

> Daddy! I want an Oompa Loompa! I
> want you to get me an Oompa-Loompa!
> I want an Oompa-Loompa right away!
> –Roald Dahl, *Charlie and
> the Chocolate Factory*
> (spoken by Veruca Salt)

Simplicity is about evaluating our own definitions of what we need and what we want. We need food. But can we survive without Kentucky Fried Chicken? Despite the finger-lickin' qualities of the Colonel's eleven secret herbs and spices, our existence will not be threatened if we never had another bucket.

Think about what else we convince ourselves we "need". True needs are shelter, food, and breathable air. But do you live in a house because of its ZIP code, eat out more than four times a week, and gas up your SUV twice a week with premium gasoline? How about living in a house you fit in, cooking at home with friends, and buying a bicycle? These are opportunities to explore the values of simplicity.

Possessions are fleeting. Events completely out of our control change our lives in an instant. A fire. A natural disaster. A traffic accident. A death. It often takes a life-changing event to make us see the difference between what we *think* we need but only want and what is truly important and necessary. With simplicity, we see the lines much more clearly.

Greed is more than just wanting more money and things. We also covet time and emotions. We feel that we need to "own" something (or someone), but then we hide it away to love it. Can we learn to appreciate things for what they are? Allow a flower to grow unpicked, a painting to hang where all can enjoy it, let the Oompa Loompas roam free?

> At some point in life the world's beauty
> becomes enough. You don't need to
> photograph, paint, or even remember it.
> It is enough. No record of it needs to be
> kept and you don't need someone to
> share it with or tell it to. When that
> happens—that letting go—you let go
> because you can.
> –Toni Morrison,
> *Tar Baby*

5. BALANCE: The Yin and the Yang

The national organization Simple Living America offers members, "balance in a complex world."[13] Without balance, voluntary simplicity becomes just another cult. Putting blinders on and shutting ourselves off from other ideas closes the door to tolerance and understanding. Keeping our minds open helps us to see both sides of a question and teaches us to weigh choices and explore other opinions.

When we apply the "balance process" to every aspect of our lives, we become more in tune with how our existence relates to the world. By changing the way we look at things, we will begin to see creative solutions to current problems and even begin to recognize potential problems before they occur.

> If you only read what you agree with,
> you'll never learn anything.
>
> –James D. Hodgson

The Balance Process

1. Listen with an open mind. Don't make any rash judgments.
2. Learn. Information allows you to make educated decisions.
3. Do you disagree? Why?
4. Is it rational idea?
5. Does it coincide with your beliefs?
6. See it from another's point of view. Why do they see it this way?
7. Accept the things that cannot change. Take the hand you're dealt and do the best you can.

The Balance Process in Action

Nonconformity vs. Go with the Flow

We want to be our own person—with a strong point of view. We should never just conform to someone else's ideas, we should always keep our own opinions. We should listen to many opinions, but always stay true to our own beliefs. We should listen to other people's arguments, but not force ourselves to see things another person's way just because their arguments may be overpowering.

Books should be tools for discussion, not everything will apply to everyone. Do not read and instantly subscribe to everything that is presented in a book (even this one). Take the information and put it through the balance process to see if it works for you. See if you can improve on some of the ideas. Ideas should foster discussions.

On the other hand: Be a river

When we decide to "go with the flow," we're flexible. Many people get upset about losing a job because they are trained to do only one thing. We resist new ideas because we often fear change. You will be less angry if you can see change as a challenge and an opportunity to grow in other areas of your life, to try new things.

Don't Take Life so Seriously vs. Playing Full Out

Stress is a direct result of putting too much importance on situations that in the grand scheme end up being insignificant. Everyone needs a little downtime—an opportunity to step back, put things into perspective, and find out it really is "only life after all." A sense of humor is crucial to getting out of this world alive.

On the other hand: 110 percent

Why do anything at less than 100 percent? The runner Steve Prefontaine refused to run any race unless he was running at full speed. He said, "To give anything less than your best is to sacrifice the Gift."[14] The path to simplicity does not have to mean sacrificing desires and goals. Evaluate what is truly important in your life and do your best at it.

Baby Steps vs. Getting the Job Done

Because our lifestyles rely on certain situations, habits, or addictions, many of the choices offered by simplicity can be lifestyle changes. Giving up our car-dependent life (and our car) may seem impossible because we are unable to visualize life with only public transportation or a bicycle. Some suggestions can lead to radical changes in how we live. This book tries to present several options so that we can baby-step our way into action.

To live more simply, the most important thing to do *is to get started* without worrying about immediately achieving every single goal at the same time. It will take a while to wean ourselves away from old habits. Picture training for a marathon. Go out and run twenty miles on your first day, and you're likely to hurt yourself to such a degree that you'll give up right then and there. But following a gradual training program and working up to reaching the 26.2 mile goal is less taxing on the system and greatly increases your chance for success. Staying simplified will get easier as you go along. You'll gain momentum as you gain physical and mental strength.

On the other hand: Just do it!

Sometimes you just need to rip the Band-Aid off. Elisabeth Kubler-Ross tells us, "When you live as if you'll live forever, it becomes too easy to postpone the things you know that you must do."[15] When we feel eternal, we assume that we'll always have the time to do what needs to be done. But life is finite and deathbed remorse is not something we often think about. What are you putting off to tomorrow that you could do today?

I Can Do Anything! vs. Knowing When to Ask for Help

The human mind is so powerful we can talk ourselves out of doing almost anything. Have you ever believed a superstition? Ever rationalized a fear so much that there was no way you were going to do something? The same logic can be applied to convincing yourself *into* doing pretty much anything. Refocus negative thoughts into positives ones by asking, "What *can't* I do?" Take the problem you have and ask, "Why can't I solve this?" until you can do it.

On the other hand: "Uncle!"

Knowing when to ask for help is crucial. You may empower yourself by learning how to fix your toilet, but keep the plumber's phone number handy just in case the bathroom ends up flooded. Watch the professionals closely while they're there and learn from them. Learn to see problems before they become catastrophic. Learn when to ask for help. Empowerment is important, but not at risk of personal health and safety.

By working to maintain balance (an even steady pace, taking a little from each side of the scale to even it out, seeing both sides of the problem), we can achieve tranquility, peace, and calmness. *It is the balance of organization, conservation, environmental practices, sustainability, and minimalism that will lead us to simplicity.*

6. WHO ARE WE? Simplicity and Personal Identity

Simplicity gives us a chance to discover our true selves by eliminating all but what is truly important. While we're heavily influenced by other people's opinions, we are still the creators of our own identities. We select from our experiences what we want to enhance in ourselves. Where did we come from? Where are we going? Why we are here? These are the questions that define who we are.

When we ask someone, "Who are you?" they usually respond by telling us what they do: "I'm a dentist," "I'm Bob's wife," "I'm an Olympic athlete." We also use events (weddings, retirement, deaths, 21st birthday) as temporary signposts that establish our identity. But if we associate ourselves only with something tangible or temporary, that sets us up for loss when it goes away. We don't need "things" or people to define ourselves.

When we lose something through death, tragedy, or natural disaster, we can succumb to painful emotions. Or we can say, "You may have taken [*fill in the blank*], but you haven't taken my true identity, the soul of who I truly am."

Identity through possessions says, "I am what I have." If we believe this, then we force ourselves to continually strive to have more, to own the most. We're constantly desiring the unattainable. Our lack of "stuff" (a shiny new Mercedes, a beach house in Malibu, Brad Pitt as our husband) becomes the key to our incompleteness and leaves us feeling like we have no true identity. We come to believe that we're not worthy. Our identity is not found in another person or in having "stuff". The only person who can make us truly happy is ourselves.

Test yourself

Our society loves labels. Without labels attached to our identity, we feel, well … like nothing. We all need something important to do, to be. But these labels keep us trapped. If you feel the need to label yourself, pick something that defines you that no one can take away from you (and it can't be self-deprecating). Here are a few of my favorite labels: Viking, Warrior, Defender, Goddess, Angel, Eccentric, Random, Extraordinary, Wonderful, Light-traveler, Sensitive, Radiant, Rare, Fascinating, Wild, Amazing, Nonconformist, Free Spirit, Miraculous.

Body Image: Who We *Aren't*

Too fat, too thin, too short, too tall—it's the body image lament. How to satisfy the voice within that says, "Your body's not good enough"? Reconciling personal image issues allows us to focus our attention on more productive experiences. Reallocate time spent worrying about eating the French fries instead of the salad to taking an afternoon nap. Accept your shape, color, or size for what it is, a unique work of art.

Scary stats

✓ Approximately 50 percent of the female population is on a diet at any given time.
✓ Over one person's lifetime, at least 50,000 individuals will die as a direct result of eating disorders.
✓ Most fashion models are thinner than 98 percent of American women.
✓ 80 percent of ten-year-olds are afraid of being fat.
✓ In America, $40 billion is spent on dieting and diet related products each year.

The final answer, I know, is always inside. But the outside can give a clue, can help one to find the inside answer. One is free, like the hermit crab, to change one's shell.

–Anne Morrow Lindbergh, *Gift from the Sea*

Imperfection: Choosing the Charlie Brown Tree

We all remember the drawing, the tiny single branch with the two pieces of plywood as a stand, each needle threatening to drop off with the slightest breeze. The final punctuation—a single shiny ornament that when tied on causes the tree to bend over, almost in two. It's Charlie Brown's Christmas tree.

What was really so bad about it? Why does it make us laugh with ridicule or cry with pity or cheer its courage? Because Charlie Brown's tree doesn't fit the typical image of what a Christmas tree should be. It isn't majestic, it isn't healthy, and it's incapable of holding all of Martha Stewart's one hundred and fifty handmade angels, ribbons, stars, glass balls, gingerbread men, candy canes, strings of light, popcorn garlands, and chains of organically grown cranberries.

But that modest little tree teaches us a very important lesson. What if it were okay to celebrate Christmas with a tree like that (or even no tree all)? What if tradition allowed imperfection? What if "imperfection" ceased to have meaning?

The Japanese concept of *wabi sabi* tells us that there is a beauty in flaws. If we let go of our pursuit of needing to be perfect, we can just enjoy the way things present themselves. I always try to pick out a Charlie Brown tree. I've adopted pets that have wandered into our yard, unwanted by their original owners. The bumper of my car had been held on by a yellow bungee cord for more than five years. And why bother fixing that scar on my forehead? It's seen me through life and is part of my identity.

Don't wait for "perfection" to arrive before doing what you want. It's not coming. Don't wait for someone else to say it's okay. If we expect an ideal, we're always disappointed in the results. Waiting will rob you of much time and many chances to live.

Learn to see potential in the imperfect and just let something be, as if it had no potential. To accept the idea that everything happens for a reason means waiting for these reasons to present themselves, but not to force a reason from anything. So go ahead and put a big daisy patch on your worn out favorite pair of jeans. Put a frame around that strange stain on the wall. And hang your Christmas ornament on the ficus tree, the cactus, or the floor lamp.

Recipe for imperfection

Amish quilters add a mismatched patch onto each quilt as a reminder that only Spirit can create perfection. Zen Buddhists place a flaw in each ceremonial teacup, lest the potter think he is perfect. Especially in our overly hectic lives, we should learn to accept imperfection.

✓ Success is not defined by perfection.
✓ There is no need for pedigree.
✓ Accept with gratitude what is there.
✓ Don't feel the need to "count" everything and validate your existence at all times.
✓ Know that no one is perfect or indestructible.
✓ Understand that mistakes are normal. Accept them and move on with your life.

---

7. SLOWING DOWN: You Move Too Fast

> If you can spend a perfectly useless afternoon in a perfectly useless manner, you have learned how to live.
> —Lin Yutang

I know what you're thinking. "I don't have time to make my life simple. I've got too much work to do." But why do we feel the need to rush? It was John Lennon who said, "Life is what happens while you're busy making other plans." Believe it or not, we have no time because we move too fast. We don't have enough time to do the things we truly want to do, so we speed through our lives embracing time-saving devices, trying to salvage some of those lost minutes.

We have a million timesaving devices that are supposed to free up our time, but just where is all this time we've gained? The gadgets that are designed to save time only end up accelerating it and conditioning us to want everything faster and faster. They also eliminate any *downtime* we may find when we would normally be waiting. Like nature, life on "American time" abhors a vacuum. While it may look like we have more time, the time we "create" is instantly filled up with more things to do.

> ### Time savers?
>
> Microwave cooking, instant macaroni and cheese, TV dinners
>
> Vitamin supplements (quick hits of nutrients that replace eating)
>
> Fast food drive-thru lanes (note the abbreviated, time-saving spelling of "through"; even going into the restaurant has become faster)
>
> One-hour dry cleaners, half-hour photo, 15-minute workouts
>
> Cell phones and PDAs
>
> Auto-deposit, auto-pay, and Automated Teller Machines
>
> Automatic tollbooths, self-checkout lanes
>
> FedEx, UPS, and Express Mail at the US Postal Service
>
> On-line shopping
>
> Multitasking
>
> Combination items like the spork, the skort, and brunch.
>
> Abbreviated speech and communication: Eliminating grammar, spelling and punctuation and even whole sentences in e-mail with the use of "emoticons."

Time equals money and busy people are productive people. Right? The concept of "wasting time" makes us feel guilty because time has become too valuable to "waste" on leisure activities. The Protestant work ethic taught us that "idle hands are the devil's tools" and that every minute we're not working is losing us money.

We feel more successful when we're able to accomplish more in a day. We think people who are too busy to talk to us must be very important. Some of us go on vacation and take every gadget we own with us so we can keep in touch with the life we left behind. Is this newly "found" time, really time well spent?

The nine-to-seven workday has given us twenty-four-hour grocery and convenience stores. The Internet never closes, which means we can shop whenever we want to. But "always open" has also has created a culture of employees and shoppers who operate through the night and weekends.

With so many products on the market, we also experience "brand clutter." We think we'll make the wrong choice if we decide too quickly. With only an antenna on our TV, we're lucky to get ten channels. But, God bless America, now we have 500 cable, satellite, or digital television channels to choose from. But I ask you—when do we have time to watch a whole TV show, anyway?

It's hard to know what we want because we want everything and try to squeeze everything in. We want to be able to afford more stuff, so we are forced to work more hours to pay for it all.

Sadly, for many people it takes a catastrophic experience to make them stop and reevaluate how they view their time and spend it. It's why some cancer survivors actually claim to be thankful for their illness and say that they wouldn't trade their experience because it taught them to cherish every moment and spend their time wisely. For some, it's being exposed to other cultures that make them reexamine their lives. Take time now to briefly analyze the quality of what you're doing with your time.

> Speed is irrelevant if you're traveling in
> the wrong direction.
> –Gandhi

Going through life at top speed gives us an addictive adrenaline rush. But anxiety affects our health. Could our physical symptoms (heart attacks, ulcers, tension headaches, insomnia) be a result of all this rushing? In his book Timelock, Ralph Keyes describes "time sickness." The American need to the beat the clock manifests as stress, elevated heart rate, and high blood pressure.[16]

We believe the whole day must be filled with projects and that everything must be done immediately because time is running out. We become conditioned to life at such a hectic pace that when we're stopped, we become angry at having to wait. Sitting at a stoplight, we honk when the car in front of us doesn't move the instant the light changes.

On the other hand

Sometimes we don't fear not having enough time but having *too* much. We're unemployed, we've got a boring Sunday afternoon ahead of us, we're waiting for our tax appointment. As the sailors in the 1955 movie *Mister Roberts* learned, sometimes trying to survive during times of boredom can be as mentally draining as being on the front lines. Learn to balance your free time and relax when it's available. Use slow times to be economical with your actions and conserve your strength. Allow your body to recover and get ready for the next time you might need that extra boost of energy.

How do you want to spend your time? Commuting? Working late? Waiting in line? Or would you rather have a nice dinner with friends? Take a class and study something you've always wanted to learn? What do you want to do with your life? When we think beyond what we expect of ourselves, we can realize that simplicity can help us reevaluate time.

Chronological time is measured in seconds, minutes, and hours. Qualitative time is measured by how our souls grow. Qualitative time is the feeling of "losing track of time" we get when we're totally engrossed in something we truly love. Athletes call it being "in the zone" or "in the flow." This trance-like altered state of mind is often where we're most successful and most happy. It's true timelessness, a flowing condition where our physical and spiritual states become one and we are fully in tune with what we're doing.

Tips for Gaining Back Some Time

❏ If you don't want to do something that doesn't have to be done, *say no*. Know that very little absolutely has to be done. When confronted with a request you're not sure you want to agree to, a good answer is, "Can I let you know once I've checked my schedule?" But if you're unable to fulfill an obligation (whether you have a legitimate excuse or have changed your mind), let the person know as soon as possible.

❏ Cut out things that you do just for the sake of doing them. What would happen if you didn't watch TV for an evening? How many magazines and books do you read because you think you need to read them?

Test yourself

Clocks are everywhere—on the VCR, in the car, on our wrists, stoves, and cell phones. The mere act of turning on the television or radio tells you the time by what's on. A clock that audibly ticks away seconds can give us a stressed feeling, like we're under the gun. How does having so many clocks affect your sense of time?

Try not to look at the time for an entire day. Cover every clock in your house, put away your watch, let the VCR blink at 12:00 all day. Allow your body to accept its natural rhythms, eat when you're hungry, sleep when you're tired, and see how your perception of time changes. Are you more rushed or less rushed?

❏ Relax and learn to be still. Take time for yourself. This may feel counterproductive to achieving a goal, but studies show that taking small breaks during long projects helps us finish faster with fewer mistakes.

❏ Use technology as a supplement to life, not in place of it. The Internet limits our field of view by instantly directing us to what we want—clicking on prompts, we don't stumble across things as we would in the open world. Use computers to communicate but not as a substitute for actually seeing people. Use computers for research, not instead of actually visiting a national park or a museum. Technology can be used for good without succumbing to the pointless distractions of *moderndrunkardmagazine.com*.

❏ Say what's on your mind. Communicate simply by being honest and to the point. Many troubles could be avoided if we told the truth at the onset. Sugar-coating what we say often causes more problems than we think it may solve.

❏ Change gears every once in a while by varying your routines to keep them from getting stale. Push yourself to do the things you've always wanted to do. Keep a wish list, do things on it, and cross stuff off. Jump out of that plane. Ask that special someone out. Remember, we're all just food for worms, so—seize the day.

❑ There should be pleasure in the process. Don't work so hard that you miss the enjoyment that comes from simply performing a task. If we learn to enjoy routine tasks, we'll find ourselves feeling less like they're time-consuming chores.

When things aren't happening as fast as we would like, ask yourself, "What more do I have to learn? What lesson is here? What is this waiting trying to teach me?" There are no "lose" situations. You can learn not to repeat mistakes. Every experience has worth and can be a chance to learn. Realize that every tragedy has a meaning and a lesson.

Simple living won't create more than twenty-four hours in the day, but it can help us to see what is truly important and reevaluate how we spend our time. When we lead simpler lives, we can learn to work more efficiently, redistribute tasks to maximize our time, and be more selective in what we choose to do.

8. SOLITUDE : Alone or Loneliness

That pesky World Wide Web may bring us closer to a pen pal in Cameroon, but how come we still don't know our neighbor's first name? We can turn our car into an office on wheels by plugging in the fax machine, phone, television, satellite radio, DVD player, and other gadgets. But these so-called conveniences shield us from and distract our attention from the real concerns of life. They isolate us from other people and keep us alone.

Solitude is underappreciated. We've become afraid of being alone. Even when we're physically alone, we're so afraid of loneliness that we fill our time with distractions. We form surrogate relationships with our television, radio, and computer. We need to change the perception of what "being alone" is.

Sometimes we fear being single forever. We're afraid we'll die alone with no one to care for us in our time of sickness. What could be worse than never finding our ideal mate? Stop and think. Maybe it's really okay to be single. It may not be easy when the world is lining up by twos around us, but discovering our own identity makes it simpler to find a compatible partner with similar desires (if that's what we truly want). It's easier to finish the puzzle when we know exactly what piece we're missing.

Another fear of being alone is that we'll fall prey to some kind of emotional sickness, psychological disorders with symptoms of anxiety, alienation, and isolation. Pathological aloneness includes fear of people, addictive disorders (like workaholism, over/under eating, and excessive computer use), obsessive-compulsive disorders, and codependency. It is being able to balance our time alone with time spent with others that will help us stay emotionally healthy.

Anne Morrow Lindbergh thought that it was not physical solitude that kept us distanced from others, but spiritual isolation. With a spiritual understanding that we find through simplicity, we can discover who we truly are and what we truly want. Then we'll enjoy the time we spend by ourselves that much more.

Rewards of Being Alone

> In solitude we give passionate attention to our lives, to our memories, to the details around us.
>
> –Virginia Woolf

Solitude is characterized by deliberate contemplation and it is distinct from other types of aloneness: loneliness, isolation, privacy, alienation, withdrawal, and even silence.[17] We can make a conscious choice to be solitary *and* happy.

Examine the negative feelings you have about being alone, and then look at the many benefits to being on your own. Solitude can be an important time when we can travel into our hidden thoughts for reflection, for learning about passion, for asking what our heart truly desires. If we practice being alone, we can learn not to fear it and it will help us end cycles of codependency. Private moments can become welcome diversions from the hustle and bustle of everyday life.

As Patricia Webb Levering wrote in *Disciplines for Discipleship*, solitude replenishes us. "We find ourselves better able to be for others after we have had some time apart to be internally refreshed. Solitude of the heart creates an inner spaciousness, unhurriedness, and reflectiveness that leave room to be open to another person."[18]

What to do when you're "at a loss"

When something awful happens, or if you're just feeling lonely, you can feel sorry for yourself or you can...

- ❏ Treat yourself to a movie.
- ❏ Write.
- ❏ Bust out of the humdrum of everyday life by trying something new and different.
- ❏ Exercise, even if it's only a twenty-minute walk to the store to buy a pint of Ben & Jerry's.
- ❏ Meditate.
- ❏ Open your address book and call the first person you find that you haven't talked to in at least a year.

❑ Open your wish list and reread your secret stash of personal desires and goals you want to accomplish.

❑ Open your "smile file," an inspiration box or book with things that make you smile when you need it. What makes you happy? Start building this file today so you'll have it when you need it. Include inspiring pieces and quotes; lists of favorite movies, letters, or cards; funny books; photographs and images that invoke favorite memories; mementos or souvenirs.

❑ Accomplish the most long-lived task on your to-do list.

❑ Go on an adventure.

❑ Visit a coffee house. It seems everyone is always comfortable being alone there.

Thinking outside the box: Peace Pilgrim

On January 1, 1953, a woman calling herself only "Peace Pilgrim" began a monumental journey by following the Rose Bowl Parade in Pasadena, California. When the parade ended, Peace kept on walking, alone, for well over thirty-five years. On her journey, she carried only a map, a comb, a ballpoint pen, a folding toothbrush, and a few copies of her message: "This is the way of peace: overcome evil with good, and falsehood with truth, and hatred with love." After walking 25,000 miles, she stopped counting the miles, but kept on walking.

She said, "When you find peace within yourself, you become the kind of person who can live at peace with others. Inner peace is not found by staying on the surface of life, or by attempting to escape from life through any means. Inner peace is found by facing life squarely, solving its problems and delving as far beneath its surface as possible to discover its verities and realities."[19]

Peace and Quiet

How can we listen to our hearts and dreams when there's so much noise? Our lives are filled with hype, jolts, and shock. We channel scan and surf the Net for brief "hits" of information. Everyone competes to get our attention. Instead of allowing this sensory overload to drag us under, we should focus on learning to be still. If you want to grow and cultivate a simplified life, you need some quiet time by yourself.

Being still can be difficult, especially when we're so caffeinated and overstimulated by visual and audio cues. But stillness and time alone are necessary to the regeneration of the soul. Times of peace and quiet give us a chance to stop and collect our thoughts. Spend a day without mediated distractions (television, radio, the Internet) to help create a clean mental environment for yourself. Walk without concern of time, distance or heart rate. When we allow our minds and bodies to stop running at warp speed, we begin to realize not only what is truly important, but also what is missing. This realization will focus our concentration on quiet introspection and open a path to simplicity.

Noise

In 1996, the World Health Organization declared noise to be a significant health problem. It doesn't have to be loud to be damaging to the human body and spirit. Even relatively quiet noise can cause changes in sleep patterns, blood pressure, and digestion. We turn the radio up in the car to tune out the sound of our loud muffler. We put headphones on at work to drown out our co-workers' elevated voices. In the early 1900s, the brass bell on a fire truck was enough to clear traffic, but today's sirens need to be decibels louder than jet engines or firecrackers to compete with every-day city noise.[20]

---

9. CREATIVITY: Finding Your Own Solutions

One of the best byproducts of living simply is finding your creativity. Instead of immediately taking the easy way out, *we can learn to find our own solutions*. We can begin to think, "How could I do this differently? How can I do this hands-on?"

A certain amount of desperation often breeds creativity out of necessity. (This is "involuntary simplicity.") Think of the "starving artist," the tortured, down on his luck soul who paints over canvases because he cannot afford to buy new ones, the singer who sings in a subway station, and the ballerina who welds by day and strips by night to afford ballet school. Sheer survival is often the motivation that fans this flame of creativity. Think of times in your own life when money was tight. What did you do to carry on?

The trick to successful voluntary simplicity is to move beyond living desperately but to keep a mentality of living creatively. Seeing your situation as desperate makes you a victim, and creative people are not victims. Many of us live simply out of necessity when we are young and just out of school, where simplicity arises because we're poor. Unfortunately, the frugality and environmental benefits that accompany this involuntary simplicity are often abandoned as our income increases.

Fostering Creativity

Like our muscles, our creativity needs to be exercised to remain strong. The following tips will help you practice using your creativity so it will be there for you when you really need it. Don't fear becoming a "kooky artist type." Anyone can be trained to be creative. Yes, even you.

❑ Test it. The best way to increase creativity is to put it through the paces. Each time we experience something new, a creativity seed is planted and we become more receptive to inspiration.

- ❑ Write near water: the ocean, a stream, or a fountain, if that's all you've got. Too many positive ions generated by electrical appliances and pollution can cause headaches, fatigue, and depression. Water releases negative ions, which make us more creative and energetic.

- ❑ Listen to classical music, which is stimulating to intellectual and creative development. Steven Halpern, author of *Sound Health*, says, "carefully created and selected music can aid relaxation, concentration, creativity, meditation, muscle response, digestion, mood, healing, and positive mental states."[21] Don Campbell's book *The Mozart Effect* also cites studies that have also shown classical music's positive effect on making plants grow, promoting the development of premature infants, and helping people cope with pain.[22]

- ❑ Get a new perspective on your life. Try using your non-dominant hand for writing, using your computer mouse, or doing anything else that you usually automatically use your dominant hand for. Look at the world upside down for a while. Lie on the floor, get up on a chair, survey from a different angle. Experiment with new ways to learn. If you are typically a person who learns better visually, try learning aurally or by touch.

- ❑ If you're not used to solitude, seek it out. If you're always surrounded by people, try spending some time alone. You may find a change in company brings creativity and a new outlook.

- ❑ Relax and visualize peace. Eliminate from your life the people, places, and situations that drain your creative potential. Let go of stressful things that don't support your creativity.

- ❑ Hang out with a child for an afternoon or be a kid again for a day. Listen to a three-year-old tell you a story. Get out the crayons, finger paints, or play dough and see what you can create.

At some time in our childhood, someone probably told us (whether overtly or through actions we witnessed) that our ideas and dreams were "not okay." So we put them aside, studied math and science and reading, went on to college, got a job, and started a family. Somewhere along the line, we gave up our "weird" ideas and dreams and even began to see them ourselves as silly and childish.

Try to think back to your childhood. What did you like most? What fascinated you? Can you remember what you wanted to be when you grew up? What made you change your mind? Regardless of how immature those old ideas seem now, think about what made you happy back then. What could you be doing now if someone had nurtured your silly ideas and dreams and told you they were okay? What qualities of these memories remain in your current life? Which ones could you integrate into your daily routine?

Creative Simplicity Tests

> It is good to be tested. We grow and learn through passing tests. I look upon all my tests as good experiences.
> –Peace Pilgrim

We are all born creative, but as we get older society tells us to conform to an image of what is expected of us. We get lazy because we think it's no longer necessary to be creative. It may not always seem like it, but our lives are easy and convenient. We no longer need to do physical labor to accomplish most tasks. What were once challenges now have shortcuts.

A shortcut solution is available to almost every problem and everything is available for a price. Can't find an answer? Google it. Bored? There are twenty-five movies playing down the street. Hungry? A drive-thru awaits. But challenges are important because they help us realize how strong we can be. And no matter how creative we think we are, there's always room for more creativity. Follow these tips to increase your creativity:

- ❏ Don't allow yourself to buy something to solve a problem. Try to find another solution without spending any money. What could you do instead of buying a formal dress or having a night out on the town? What would you make for dinner using only items you have on hand?
- ❏ Bring along a pen and a single sheet of paper when you know you'll have to wait for a long time (I find a trip to the post office ideal for this exercise). The first rule is to not focus on the wait being an inconvenience in your life. Use the time to daydream or people-watch. You'll be amazed how many creative thoughts come up during your wait. The next great American novel could be started while you're in the line at the DMV. I've found the smaller the paper, the more ideas I can think of … and it's always the time when I haven't got a pen that the brightest inspiration strikes.
- ❏ Spend a day with no distractions. Shut the television off. Unplug the phone. Hide your car keys.
- ❏ Play MacGyver. How would you "get out" if you were trapped with only what's in the top drawer of your desk?

MacGyver, The Coolest Creative

Angus MacGyver, played by Richard Dean Anderson from 1985 to 1992 on ABC's nonviolent action-adventure series, is by far the coolest creative of modern pop culture. A "MacGyverism" now means any trick that uses normal items to create something extraordinary. Some of my favorites are:

✓ A police siren created by whistling through a piece of aluminum foil and an ordinary comb.

✓ A thumbprint impression lifted with pool chalk and candle wax.

✓ It's a bird, it's a plane, no, it's MacGyver in a homemade hot air balloon made with a shed, a tent, and gas cylinders.

❑ Are you already creative at something? Try something completely different for a change. Pick one item from this list and go off and try it right now: sing, dance, draw, plant a garden, make a collage, write a story, cook, act a scene, write a poem, paint, sculpt, sew, play a musical instrument, blaze a new trail. Play a game, but make up your own rules. If you're struggling with a fear of your own creativity, start with a prepackaged "kit" (think: paint by numbers).

GETTING STARTED

Okay, let's recap. If we act now, getting simplified will give us:

✓ A greater awareness of our natural environment and a focus on sustainability

✓ Time to live life on our own terms and at our own speed

✓ A greater sense of purpose, a life with meaning, value, and fulfillment

✓ A more concrete identity, a better idea of who we really are

✓ Less clutter and consumption because we've learned to cut back and see what we don't really need

✓ A better understanding of money and how it can help us achieve our goals

✓ Greater control over our mental and physical health

✓ More choices and more freedom.

We can live simply in the country or in the city, and our future depends on both suburbanites and city dwellers embracing the practices of simple living. We need people to believe in simplicity and can extol its virtues to the masses. That's why even though I roll my eyes at every celebrity who visits a talk show and goes on about their new hybrid car, I know that this promotes the cause more than a thousand newsletters printed on tree-free paper.

If at first you don't succeed, try again. And don't get discouraged. When you try to live simply, and if you're serious about making your life simpler, there is often more than one alternative. Just because you were unable to give up your car after trying for several weeks, you should not take it as a failure.

Remember, *guilt is not allowed.*

Thinking outside the box: The simplicity circle

Cecile Andrews brought the Scandinavian concept of study circles to the topic of simplicity in her book *The Circle of Simplicity*. She devised a ten-week program where groups of six to ten people meet regularly to discuss reading assignments on the nature of simplicity. Because people find it difficult to start "getting simplified" and maintain their simplification, these circles create support groups that offer both encouragement and new ideas. Groups are leaderless and each week rotate facilitators (the person who is in charge of watching the clock and keeping other members on topic). The book provides the meeting structure, but the format encourages spontaneous discussions.

Know that *simplicity is not about deprivation.* It should be a voluntary and enjoyable process. Simplicity is balancing how we want to spend our lives with what is necessary to survive. The path to simplicity is a personal decision, however, and the suggestions in this book may not be compatible with your lifestyle. Only you will know what's right for you.

Simplicity should be about low maintenance. If you are practicing something and the energy you put into it is not rewarding you mentally, spiritually, or physically, then maybe it's time to reevaluate and change paths. When simplicity lowers your stress level, you'll notice your time, energy, money, and health being saved.

The Simplicity Connection will lead us through all parts of our lives on the quest for simplicity. Together we will develop physical, emotional, spiritual, and mental capabilities. I hope your desire to never stop learning will lead to a goal of inner peace and fulfillment, to authentic living.

Simplicity takes practice and discipline. It takes conscious focus. On the path to simplicity we find many personal freedoms: freedom of spirit, freedom of action, freedom from worry. When we find a simpler life, we find an escape from work we don't enjoy. Living simply may not be the solution to all of our problems, nor is it a cure all for the ills of society, but it will allow us to be better prepared to make decisions that are healthier for our sanity, our society, and for the planet as a whole.

Reconnecting to the basic elements of simplicity may seem daunting at first, especially if you are implementing some of the benefits for the first time. Take it slowly and know that every little step you take brings you closer to building the foundation of a simplified life. Remember mindfulness, a connection to nature and spirit, finding the point of "enough" and balance, knowing your true self, taking life at a slower pace, learning to use alone time to your advantage and exercising your creativity.

Do it today

Conserving energy is not just about turning off lights. It's also being economical in everything we do. Not overreacting. Expending less physical energy. Thinking smaller. Schedule some time this week to just relax.

ADDITIONAL RESOURCES
SIMPLICITY

Andrews, Cecile. *The Circle of Simplicity.* New York: HarperCollins, 1997. A guide for starting a simplicity circle. (www.simplicitycircles.com)

Ban Breathnach, Sarah. *Simple Abundance: A Daybook of Comfort and Joy.* New York: Warner Books, 1995.

_____. *Something More: Excavating Your Authentic Self.* New York: Warner Books, 1998. Two books with daily meditations on simplicity.

Burch, Mark. *Stepping Lightly.* Gabriola Island, British Columbia: New Society Publishers, 2000.

Elgin, Duane. *Voluntary Simplicity.* New York: Fawcett Books, 1998. "Toward a way of life that is outwardly simple, inwardly rich." The book that made him the father of the modern simplicity movement. (www.awakeningearth.org)

Longacre, Doris Janzen. *Living More with Less.* Scottsdale, PA: Herald Press, 1980. Despite its copyright date, very little of this book had to be updated when it was re-released. Both the topics and Longacre's style of writing are timeless. See also *The More-With-Less Cookbook* for more than just eating tips and recipes.

Luhrs, Janet. *The Simple Living Guide.* New York: Broadway Books, 1997. A comprehensive guide to the simple life.

Pierce, Linda Breen. *Choosing Simplicity*. Carmel, CA: Gallagher Press, 2000. A study of people who are living simply coupled with lessons learned. A good book for anyone who has trouble believing that they couldn't possibly get simplified any time in this century.

St. James, Elaine. *The Simplicity Reader*. New York: Hyperion, 1998. Three books in one: *Simplify Your Life, Inner Simplicity*, and *Living the Simple Life*. A very comprehensive guide to simple living.

CREATIVITY

Cameron, Julia. *The Artist's Way*. New York: G.P. Putnam's Sons, 1992. An eleven-week program to help tap your hidden well of creativity.

SARK. *Creative Companion*. Berkeley, CA: Celestial Arts, 1991.
_____. *Transformation Soup*. New York: Simon & Schuster, 2000. SARK's writing helps unlock the creativity of the child within and her "Further Reading" lists play like the greatest mix-tape ever.

Sher, Barbara. *Wishcraft: How to Get What You Really Want*. New York: Ballantine Books, 1979. Discover what you want. Turn your fears into strengths and your dreams into reality.

ORGANIZATIONS

Countrylife.net is an on-line simplicity village and a resource for learning about the practical arts of simple, self-sufficient living with discussion boards and articles by experts on topics like baking, gardening, and homesteading.

For those seeking "Balance in a Complex World," look no further than Simple Living America (www.getsatisfied.org) which has partnered with the PBS series *Simple Living with Wanda Urbanska*, to create the only national, nonprofit organization working to build a strong voice for voluntary simplicity.

The Simple Living Network (www.simpleliving.net) provides resources and community services for help in living more simply. They publish a free online newsletter that highlights the latest happenings in the simplicity movement and list simplicity groups by geographical location.

chapter 3

budgeting

The more money we've got, they say, the more problems we see. We are so consumed by our struggle with and our pursuit of the almighty dollar that money scares us and makes us angry. It's both how we perceive monetary worth and our inability to manage our finances that cause this anguish. And regardless of how much bacon we each bring home, most of us feel we could use a better pan to fry it in (if not a cast iron skillet from Williams-Sonoma). But if, the best things in life are free, why do we struggle to accumulate more money and more stuff?

As you probably know (hopefully not the hard way), get-rich-quick schemes are not the answers to money troubles. If it sounds too good to be true, it almost always is. There's no easy way to get rich quick, but here is the foolproof way to actually become wealthy. The first step is to change your perception of "rich"; the second step is to scale back and live within your means.

We've heard of those who use the interest from their savings as their sole source of income. We're sure there's no way we could ever get there ourselves, and even if we tried, how much fun could we possibly have getting there? We think, "Go back to your own planet, pod people!" but also, "Hmmm, I kind of wish I could do that..."

The Simplicity Connection is for realists. We're going to help you see the reality of how money affects us and what we all can do to change how we spend it. I know we all want to save money. I also know that you want to keep on living while you're at it. *Simplicity is about being conscious in our decision-making.* It's also taking care of both our needs and wants.

MONEY REEVALUATION

> The idea of more, of ever increasing wealth, has become the center of our identity and our security, and we are caught up by it as the addict is by his drugs.
>
> –Paul L. Wachtel, *The Poverty of Affluence*[23]

For many of us, our self-worth equals our monetary worth. People see their net worth as a reflection of their social status and keep trying to keep up with the proverbial Joneses. We want more to support our lifestyles and feel like failures when we don't have enough. To merely survive in the capitalist society, we assume we need even more. It's not only how we judge ourselves, but also how we judge others and how they judge us. Because those who have money are both envied and despised, we keep our finances secret; knowing how much someone else makes changes our impression of that person.

Instead, we can use simplicity to help us personally come to terms with wealth.

> In a society in which the dream of success has been drained of any meaning beyond itself, men have nothing against which to measure their achievements except the achievements of others.
>
> –Christopher Lasch, *The Culture of Narcissism*

Scary stats

✓   90 percent of all crimes are committed because of money.
✓   89 percent of all divorces are related to money problems.
✓   1.3 billion people on the planet live on $1 a day or less.

"Rich" is a relative concept. Jane survives comfortably on her earnings of $20,000 a year, while John makes $60,000 and considers himself destitute. Ask Jane how much money it would take to make her well off, and she thinks $60,000 would be more than enough. Ask John the same question, and he sets the bar much higher—maybe $600,000 would do it for him. Why is it the more money we make, the more money we seem to need? Ben Franklin noted that money doesn't bring happiness. "Instead of filling a vacuum," he wrote, "it makes one."

How did we become such slaves to money? If money were no object, we like to say, all our problems would be gone. But if money is *everything,* then why are there depression support groups for lottery winners and so many professional athletes and celebrities with drug problems?

Financially, the simplest thing we can do is to reevaluate our perception of what being rich actually is. Take a few minutes now and analyze how and why you've become so singularly focused on the almighty dollar. Is it family pressure that causes you to strive for more? Is it the media—specifically, advertising—that has focused your attention on wanting more? (We'll learn more about the pitfalls of advertising in the *Shopping* chapter.) Or is it something else that drives you to chase money?

We often confuse our emotional yearnings with material wants, thinking that an object we can buy will fulfill our soul's desires or that peace of mind comes from how much money is in our checking account. Worse yet, we don't make this decision for ourselves, but instead accept someone else's lifestyle as our yardstick. We can change all that. We can learn to find our sense of identity through our spiritual pursuits rather than through material goods.

What are you truly striving for? What do you think will happen once you finally achieve it? In a poem called *The Station*, Robert Hastings writes about how we're all passengers on a train. We're excited about our final destination. We think that when we finally arrive, we know our dreams will be realized and our lives will be complete. But we must understand that *there is no station*.[24] "The true joy of life is the trip. The station is only a dream. It constantly outdistances us." Hastings encourages us to let go of regret of the past and fear of the future and focus instead on living for the moment.

> I am not quite sure what the advantage is in having a few more dollars to spend if the air is too dirty to breathe, the water too polluted to drink, the commuters are losing out in the struggle to get in and out of the city, the streets are filthy and the schools so bad that the young perhaps wisely stay away, and the hoodlums roll citizens for some of the dollars they saved in the tax cut.
>
> –Economist   John Kenneth Galbraith[25]

Decide what your monetary priorities are. Do you really want or need it all? How would you act if there were no one you had to impress? Maybe you would even enjoy making $7.00 an hour if you weren't dependent on your job for income. Instead, let prosperity equal your contribution to the world. When we stop equating amount of income with self-worth we change our perception of wealth.

> ### *Voluntary Poverty*
> In our society, "poverty" is a dirty word. It conjures up desperation and sadness. Deciding to live in *Voluntary Poverty* is a conscious decision to need and have less money. It's a path to create satisfaction in your life by getting rid things you don't need or use.

SCALING BACK TO LIVE WITHIN YOUR MEANS

Now that you've begun to rethink how money affects your life, are you ready to simplify your spending? Good, let's continue with simple tips on how to make your wallet happier...

1. Budgeting
2. Focusing on simplicity
3. Paying cash
4. Stopping shopping
5. Buying for durability
6. Waking up
7. Doing it yourself
8. Using your taxes
9. Doing it now

1. BUDGETING: Every Penny Counts

Balancing your budget or your checkbook often seems like trying to find the missing sock in the dryer. But the money has to go somewhere and it's important to remember that *every penny counts*. Start by writing down *every penny* you spend for a month and what you spent it on. Train yourself to get receipts for everything when you pay cash. Writing it all down (separate from your check register) starts a discipline that makes you more conscious of how much you spend. Write down the fifty cents you put in a parking meter. The $5 you put in the office lottery pool. The $1 you put in the stripper's G-string at the bachelor party. *Every single penny.* When the month is up, gather your receipts and start dividing into piles by categories of expenses. Here's a sample worksheet.

The Every Penny Counts Budget Worksheet

TRANSPORTATION

Fuel, insurance, maintenance, tolls & parking, service, oil changes, non-car transportation costs such as bus and train fares

FOOD

Groceries, meals dining out, "treats" (non-essential food items), alcohol

HEALTH

Medical and dental insurance, doctor's visits, medicines (both prescription and over the counter), vision coverage

CLOTHING

Including: work-related and uniforms, laundry, dry cleaning

ENTERTAINMENT

Cable TV, nights out, movies & video rentals, theater tickets, CDs, magazines, video games

WORK/EDUCATION

Computer software, job-related or industry magazines, books. Separate these expenditures into two categories: things you'll be reimbursed for and others you won't. Include things you buy that will further your knowledge about things you would like to do with your life. Keep receipts for this category and ask your tax person whether or not anything is deductible.

BILLS

Rent or mortgage, insurance, student loans

FEES

Credit card interest, bank fees, professional dues

UTILITIES

Phones (landline, mobile, and long distance service), Internet connection, natural gas, electricity, garbage pick-up, water

OTHER PURCHASES

- ✓ Health and beauty aids (cosmetics and toiletries)
- ✓ Postage
- ✓ Travel
- ✓ Household expenses (such as cleaning products, decorating supplies, and light bulbs)
- ✓ Pets
- ✓ Investing

FOR OTHERS

Charitable giving, gifts

SCREW-UPS

Expenditures that could have been avoided with a little common sense and attention to detail: library fines, parking tickets, late fees on rentals, emergency purchases when something is forgotten.

BAD HABITS

Smoking, drinking, anything you know you do too much of that isn't good for you.

MISCELLANEOUS

Avoid putting things in this category. It's a wasteland where you lose money because it isn't itemized.

Do not include credit card payments in this list. Instead, *itemize each line in your credit card bill*, including each charge in the appropriate category. Don't forget to add the interest to the FEES category, an obvious wasted expenditure. You'll see this at the end of the year when you can see that you've paid hundreds of dollars in interest.

If you buy things in separate categories from the same store, break the amounts on the cash register tape out. If I buy shampoo and a six-pack of beer at the grocery store, I account for the shampoo under health and beauty aids and the beer under alcohol. Now that supermarkets have become the all-purpose one-stop shopping experience, many things we buy at the grocery store aren't food. If you want to be even more diligent, note the taxable items you buy and attach the tax to these purchases.

In order to see how much money we can comfortably live on, we must also budget our income. Record your salary from all sources of employment, keeping a separate line for each job. Create a category for gifts, reimbursements, and earned income from investments. Also list any miscellaneous income and keep documentation for tax time.

There are computer programs that will do the math for you and keep everything organized, but I don't recommend going out and purchasing one (remember, we're trying to save money here) unless you're still having trouble keeping organized. I've created a simple spreadsheet and I do my calculations by hand (which keeps my math bone strong). Take your total incoming and subtract your total outgoing. This is your profit for the month. Well ... it is if it's a positive number.

People who only look at their bills when they're making a budget forget small miscellaneous purchases paid for with cash, then wonder where the rest of their money went. The beauty of the *Every Penny Counts Budget* is that we can see where every penny in between goes.

Let's see how this works: Let's say my friend Julie heads down to Starbucks every workday. Let's take a look at Julie's COFFEE line item. (She's got it tucked nicely away under FOOD. I'd suggest moving it to BAD HABITS, but I know better.) At five times a week, $1.60 a pop, times fifty weeks a year equals $400! "But," she protests, "I love my ridiculously overpriced little hyper beans! I need my coffee!" Okay, we'll deal with addictions later. For the moment, let's look at alternatives to the daily coffee ritual. What if you made the coffee yourself? What if you cut down to three times a week? These two steps are a good start.

Continue to create new categories to fit your lifestyle. For example, I love my diet soda. I wanted to know exactly how much money I was wasting on this nasty habit I really didn't want in the first place. So I created a SODA category and was able to see the hundreds of dollars I was drinking away just to get the caffeine rush.

After your first month with your budget, restructure categories to help you figure out where your own sucking hole is. When the "miscellaneous" category amount keeps getting larger, you'll start to wonder what you've been spending all that money on. When I noticed this happening I looked at my receipts and realized it was time to reevaluate and break out a HOUSEHOLD category to account for items I consider necessary to maintaining my residence: a new refrigerator, cleaning supplies, fabric to make curtains. Separating the miscellaneous column into necessary versus nonessential expenses revealed a new area I needed to be conscious about.

We rarely alter our spending habits unless there's a drastic change in our income, but looking at a detailed budget of our finances can be a conscious reminder and a visual index of how our money is being wasted. Does it feel like you ate $500 worth of food? Was the $150 you spent on movies worth it? Did you need $300 worth of additional clothes? Do you really want to spend $200 a month on gasoline? Then don't. What would you rather have used that money for? Seeing concrete numbers helps us better realize what our priorities are and what we really want them to be. It also pinpoints the expenditures that we can cut back on.

On the other hand: Penny wise and pound-foolish

Don't overlook savings on large items because you're too focused on your coffee habit. Use your energy to research value on large purchases before wasting hours clipping soup coupons.

---

2. FOCUSING ON SIMPLICITY: Simplify, simplify, simplify

As chapter 2 taught us, simplifying doesn't just make our lives easier, it can actually end up saving us money, too. When we start simplifying our personal belongings, for example, we begin to reevaluate our place within the larger world. This extends to our environment, how we interact with one another, and our personal economy. The true costs of goods and services should reflect their social, environmental, and financial impacts for their entire lifecycle, from creation to disposal.

There are two types of expenditure in our budgets: those that are *unavoidable*, and those that are *unnecessary*. Look again at your budget and pinpoint your unnecessary expenditures. Analyze each line item to decide whether that expenditure helps or hinders you on your path to simplicity. Maybe you discover that you can be happy driving a fourteen-year-old car. Maybe it doesn't matter so much where you live. Get out that red pen and start slashing.

Remember the ingredients of reconnecting to simplicity from chapter 2? Let's see how they apply to our finances.

❏ *Mindfulness.* As our lives become more deliberate and simplified, we are better able to see where else we can cut back. When we are conscious of how we spend our money and what we spend it on, we learn to pause before making purchases. *Is this purchase really necessary?*

❑ *Return to nature.* How does money affect nature? We can connect our spending habits to the larger world by realizing that certain purchases are more harmful to the environment and humanity than others. A trip to the local big-box store for a cheap new pair of sneakers may seem harmless, but supporting a business that disrespects local wildlife habitats and buying a product manufactured with sweatshop labor ultimately costs much more than you pay at the register.

❑ *Spirit.* A simplified spiritual life shows that money doesn't buy happiness. We also realize the more we simplify our personal spending habits, the more money we have available to help others with.

❑ *Satiation.* Even the bills that are unavoidable can be reevaluated when we change our perception of how much we can comfortably live on. Shopping second-hand can make you impervious to advertising, reexamining where you live can drastically reduce rent, and saying "no more" to trivial purchases are a few ways to show that *enough is enough.*

❑ *Balance* is increasingly important in the capitalist society we live in. With a culture that urges us to spend, using the balance process helps us make decisions that favor both the health of the planet and our personal desires.

❑ *Who you are & Imperfection.* We are not what we own. We are not what we covet. "Perfection" cannot even be purchased.

❑ *Slowing down.* When our pace is slower, we can become more mindful, more aware of what is enough. We pay greater attention to what we truly desire. Remember, even the richest man cannot buy more than twenty-four hours per day. Will buying that time saving device really gain you more time or will it only make you more hurried?

❑ *Solitude.* Yes, it's true that being alone usually means we're not spending any money. When we develop our personal identity through solitude, we are better armed to decide what we need and do not need.

❑ With *Creativity*, we can more easily see opportunities where we don't really need spend money. A substitute for an expensive evening out at the theater? Volunteering your time as an usher. A new dress to wear for the occasion? A second-hand gown bought for a third of the price. A nice treat after the show? A seat at the counter at your favorite greasy spoon to split an ice cream sundae with a good friend.

When simplicity reveals what is truly important in our lives, we realize the true nature of our desires. Then it becomes easier to reallocate our money. We must understand the connection between our complicated spending habits and the complications in our lives. Spending more will not make us happier and more productive in the end. Throughout the book, we'll find hundreds of ways to scale back and refocus our attention.

3. PAYING CASH: And Pay As You Go

The best way to live within your means is to *pay cash*. Shopping becomes much easier and less tempting when you have to actually fork over the dough at the time of transaction. When we bring only enough money to buy what we need, the deal is officially done once the register closes and change has been handed over. With credit, we can conceivably pay for an item many times before it's paid off.

Scary stats: Credit horror

✓ 6: The number of credit card offers mailed to the average American household in one year, regardless of their credit history.

✓ $4,617: Average balance per open credit card in 2004.

✓ $1,164: Average household interest payments in 2004.

✓ $43 billion: Amount the credit industry made off late payments, over-limit spending and balance transfer fees in 2004.[26]

Try these tips for keeping up with your money.

❑ Pay off your credit cards and maintain clear credit balances. Only use a credit card for convenience when you're able to pay off the entire balance at the end of the month.

❑ If you're having credit card problems, get rid of all but one credit card, and keep that one for emergency use only. If you're serious about wiping out your credit card debt, start paying cash or using a debit card for everything you buy. Consolidate all your credit cards into one with the lowest interest you can get. There's always a credit card company offering a low introductory rate for balance transfers.

❑ Know that paying only the minimum balance on your bill is not going to make it go away. When you pay less than the balance of a credit card bill, you're living in the past. By using a card with a balance, you're adding more to a pile of debt and the interest continues to accumulate. If you have money saved elsewhere, consider using some of it to pay off large bills. Five thousand dollars in a money market account could earn you $300 a year, but $5,000 on a credit card can end up costing you almost $1,000 a year.

❑ Never pay an annual fee. There's no need to pay a bank for the privilege of using their card when you can get them for free.

> ### On the other hand: What about those store credit cards?
>
> They offer you a discount right then and there for signing up for one. "Today? Right now? All I have to do is give you my Social Security number?" The offer seems too good to be true, the reward benefits are enticing. But ask yourself: *do I really need another card?* Many sign up for the instant discount, then cancel the card right away. Beware though; all this goes on your credit report. Some of these cards are actually good deals, but only accept the new card if you can do three things:
>
> 1. If you're able to pay off all your bills when you get them and never carry a balance.
> 2. If it's a store you frequently patronize because they offer good value, high-quality merchandise and fair and ethical treatment of their employees.
> 3. If you intend to use the card for purchases you would already be making. Companies know that customers who sign up for their cards spend on average hundreds of dollars more in their stores than those who shop without a handy card. Getting their card will get you on their mailing list, so expect lots more junk mail.

- ❑ Never use a credit card for cash advances. You'll be charged interest as soon as you take the money out.
- ❑ Choose carefully when signing up for a credit card that supports a cause you believe in. Just because they're donating a portion of your interest to charity, doesn't mean that their interest rate is any better. It may, in fact, be higher to offset the amount you've donated. You're better off making your own tax-deductible donation at the end of the year.
- ❑ Double check credit card statements for double billing, charges you don't understand, and incorrect amounts before automatically paying them.

4. STOPPING SHOPPING: Find Better Ways to Amuse Yourself

When you can't avoid it, get what you need for less or buy it used. Sooner or later, we're going to run out of toilet paper and have to leave the house, but we'll be leaving with the exact amount of money we need and we're going to be armed with some tricks of the trade.

- ❑ Forget the coupons. Those ladies on TV talk shows who say they spend $13 a week on groceries to feed a family of seven, spend way too much time clipping coupons and mailing in rebates. We, however, have better things to do than flipping through a thousand coupons a week to weed out the expired ones. Coupons can be great if they're for something you really need and use. Otherwise, don't waste your time.
- ❑ Find the sales. We're afraid to buy something because we know it will go on sale the instant we walk out of the store. Many stores offer price adjustments (giving the

difference between regular and sale price if the item does go on sale within a set period from the time of purchase), price matching (agreeing to charge the same price as a competitor advertises), and honoring previous sale prices. The trick is often just asking if they have any of these policies. Since retail is so highly competitive, they will often do almost anything to get our sale, even if it means shaving a few bucks off. But then again, *it's only a bargain if it's something we'll actually use.*

❏ Try bartering. Who says we have to pay money for everything? What do you have to trade? What if you want piano lessons? Maybe the teacher will trade your lesson for several hours of yard work each week. How about a gym membership? Maybe the owner will trade you several hours of working out for working behind the check-in desk. These trades are usually not based on how much the object costs, but how much it's worth to both parties involved. A gym membership may cost the owner nothing, while thirty-two hours of desk shifts may cost him $600. Try advertising on bulletin boards at the grocery store, Laundromats, health clubs, and community centers. If you can get a good dependable group interested, try a "Free, Trade or Barter" box or list serve. For larger trades, the IRS requires that you report the fair market value of what you traded.

❏ Substitute what you already have for what you think you want. Before heading to the mall, use your finely tuned creative sensibilities to think of alternatives.

❏ Keep in mind the perks of buying used: no or minimal fuel used in shipping, a product saved from the landfill, no new resources consumed in production, and usually a used item is less expensive. Look for more alternative ideas in the *Shopping* chapter.

On the other hand

Frugality is a part of simplicity, but many think saving money is the same thing as being simplified or environmentally conscious. Neither is interchangeable with the other.

The line between frugality and simplicity gets more visible when we see people stuffing their pockets with sugar packets and napkins at restaurants. I have a problem with those who call themselves simplified but advocate unethical practices in the name of pinching pennies. Entering places you haven't paid to be, paying less than reasonable value for something, swapping price tags, buying something and returning it without parts, and taking more than your share is not being a frugal. It's stealing, plain and simple.

Sustainability should be our first consideration, saving money, second. Sure, you can buy almost anything at the "for-a-buck" store, but under what conditions (and in what decade) were those products made? What is the environmental impact of the byproducts of manufacturing? How much do the clerks who work there earn and do they have health benefits? In the long run, the sociological cost of that purchase may far outweigh the dollar you spent. The connection between cheapskate or frugal living and thinking green is using less. If it's not environmentally responsible, the point of saving money should be irrelevant.

5. BUYING FOR DURABILITY: Making It Last

Take care of what you have and use it until it wears out. Research new purchases for durability, value, and multiple uses. Be aware that there are some people who subscribe to a conspiracy theory that products are designed for planned obsolescence (or "death dating") and manufactured so the item (or certain parts of it) will wear out after a certain time to ensure future sales. Other products, they say, are designed to wear out to coincide with our "getting tired of them." In a country that considers "durability" lasting about three years, we should learn to be suspicious of products without warranties. Put more consideration into products you'll use on a daily basis and consider an initial higher cost for better quality and greater savings in the long run.

❑   Look at purchasing quality products that can last lifetimes. Buy beautiful things to be cherished and preserved. L.L. Bean products may be slightly more expensive than other brands but the company stands behind their 'guaranteed for life' policy.

❑   Try to select items that will require less maintenance.

Stop & think

Mass customization is the building of products on demand, such as when computers and cars are made to order. This process can be adapted to fit books, appliances, DVDs, and music. On-demand is more efficient than overstocking warehouse stores with enough copies for everyone who might wander in.

❑   Take some preventive measures. If we know something will wear out in a certain spot in a certain way, we can reinforce it before we need to replace it. Even if you didn't go to Yale, sew those suede patches onto the elbows of your jacket. Purchase replacement parts, instead of buying a whole new item. Applaud that guy who rescues a junked out version of his car solely for the parts.

❑   Alter items that you already have. If you can't bear to part with clothing you don't wear, for example, have the clothes professionally altered so that you'll be able to wear them comfortably and happily.

Creative clothing

With a little creativity and elbow grease, you can avoid a trip to the mall and probably salvage any piece of clothing.

- ✓ Dye or bleach it.
- ✓ Add accents: lace trim, ribbon, beads, sequins, silk flowers, ruffle, fur trim, bows, iron-on decals, patches, or replacement buttons.
- ✓ Wear it as is. A friend adapted the phrase "arrogantly shabby" (which actually refers to an architectural style of the Carolinas) to refer to any piece of clothing worn to flaunt its imperfections. There are plenty of Ubiquitous Mall Stores that sell clothing that is purposely "distressed"; be in fashion for free!
- ✓ Make your own pattern by tracing the shape of an existing piece of clothing onto a piece of craft paper.
- ✓ Transform it. Make a skirt into a scarf, pants into shorts, a dress into a skirt. Take the sleeves off a shirt or shorten a skirt.
- ✓ Pull a Scarlett O'Hara or Maria von Trapp. Pull down your drapes and sew them into clothing. Old clothes, sheets, and tablecloths can also yield fabric for a new item. There are even some who unravel old sweaters and use the yarn to knit something else.
- ✓ Get thee to the nearest garment district. For creative ideas, an afternoon spent walking through fabric and notion stores is good for more ideas than a year's worth of *Martha Stewart Living*.
- ✓ Pick up a good guide for making simple alterations and fixing common clothing injuries.

---

6. WAKING UP: Become Conscious of How You Spend Your Money

It's time to become conscious of everything you spend money on. As Francis Bacon said, "Knowledge is power," which means ignorance is a waste of money. What do you know about the bills you pay? Do you just automatically write checks every month? Do you understand your phone service? Can you explain your car insurance? What's covered by your health insurance? Not following directions makes everyone's lives more difficult. Keep your head up, your ears and your eyes open. E.F. Schumacher said, "The gift of material goods makes people dependent, but the gift of knowledge makes them free—provided it's the right kind of knowledge of course."[27]

- ❑ Call ahead to find out if the store has what you need and if they're going to be there when you need it.
- ❑ Read directions carefully.
- ❑ Deal only with ethical companies and know the law. The Better Business Bureau is

accessible on line with a searchable database of companies at www.bbb.org.

❑ Research major purchases through *Consumer Reports*, which does not accept advertising and provides unbiased ratings.

❑ Be observant ... and patient. Rushing to get to an appointment usually gets me a parking ticket for failing to read the sign that says Tuesdays are street cleaning days.

❑ Always question. And if your questions aren't answered to your satisfaction, go somewhere else.

❑ Get it in writing (or take notes), especially if someone tells you something and you're afraid they may renege in the future.

❑ Avoid becoming emotional when you negotiate or argue. Like it or not, some companies will overcharge because they don't like your attitude. It may not be fair and it may not be legal, but it happens.

❑ Let your fingers do the walking on the Web or the phone. Any company worth its salt has a customer service department.

❑ Find out if anyone you pay regularly (rent, utilities, etc.) provides discounts if you pay several months in advance. Sometimes you might get a free month of service in exchange for their receiving an investable fee early.

❑ Take it back if it doesn't work to your satisfaction. Always ask to speak to the manager. Don't get angry. Just explain that you're a good customer.

❑ Summarize warranties and expiration dates in plain English on the receipt. "Car part is under warranty for 30,000 miles (when my car odometer reaches 67,402 miles) or two years (until 1/13/10), which ever comes first." This will help avoid confusion and help you take full advantage of the warranty. Use a calendar to mark dates. "September 15th: Must cancel subscription to *New Couch Weekly* or pay for full year."

7. DOING IT YOURSELF: Saving Money by Learning Self-Reliance

If we can handle simple problems (for example, basic plumbing, carpentry, and gardening), we can easily eliminate some of the middlemen we have to pay. We can learn self-reliance and reduce our dependence on others. Learning new skills and finding out how things work allow us to take pride in our abilities. We also gain the confidence to tackle other projects.

❑ Rent how-to videos and books from libraries or hardware stores to help you get started on a project.

❑ Call for tips. Many appliance manufacturers will give repair advice over the phone. Before calling Mr. Fixit, call the company and explain your symptoms. A fifty-cent washer always beats a $90 labor charge. See more about 'Doing it Yourself' in the *Housing and Decorating* chapter.

❑   Consider creating hand-made inexpensive gifts. See page 76 for suggestions.

❑   Cook. There are alternatives to the fast food "ultra bargain meal," which is just empty calories and makes you feel sluggish by mid-afternoon, anyway. Bake from scratch and bring lunch to work. How's this for simple math? The cost of a daily muffin is $2.00 at the corner chi-chi coffee place. Baking your own muffins—a week's supply at a time or more—from a pre-packaged mix brings it to about thirty cents each, and the price goes down the more you make. When you cook, you avoid fast food places and create a "garbage-less lunch." Use reusable containers (instead of plastic sandwich baggies), silverware, and cloth napkins.

8. USING YOUR TAXES: Taking Full Advantage of What They Pay For

I'm not advocating trapping your cat in a tree just to check out the latest recruits in your town's fire department, but few of us are even aware of what our taxes are used for, such as schools, parks, libraries, police, community events, community centers, and senior and youth services. Take advantage of all of these services. One should only be allowed to complain about taxes if they actively fight for or against them and vote.

❑   Head for a national park. See the National Park Service (www.nps.gov). Your federal taxes pay for maintaining national parks, which provide inexpensive activities set against the backdrop of nature and history.

❑   Check out Matthew Lesko's book, *Gobs and Gobs of Free Stuff*, which lists government resources to help you find what you want … for free.

❑   Trek on down to the public library. Why buy the cow, when you can get *The Da Vinci Code* for free? There are some books that we should all own (Roget's Thesaurus, the *Worst Case Scenario Handbook*, and *Growing Up Brady, I Was a Teenage Greg*, come to mind), but for all the rest, chances are that some library, somewhere, has a copy of it. Using interlibrary loan, libraries are able to lend books throughout communities and counties, and the Internet has made it ridiculously easy to search the entire library system and place the item you want on hold. Many systems will even ship to your local branch and contact you when your book has arrived. If that fails, interlibrary loan allows you to locate the book at any library in the country and have it sent to your branch for a nominal fee. But wait—there's more. For the average of $20 a year each American pays in taxes to support libraries, you can also rent videos, audio CDs, even works of art. These community-minded organizations often offer free or low-cost meeting spaces and Internet access and computer use.

❑   Contact elected officials with your concerns and questions. Whether you voted for them or not, your taxes do pay their salary. Contact the president at (202) 456-1111 or president@whitehouse.gov. Contact your senator or congressional representative at (202) 224-3121 or www.house.gov/writerep. They have operators standing by to take your comments about whatever's on your mind.

> If you're not outraged at your government, then you haven't been paying attention.
>
> –Mickey Michels

Wake up for change

Mahatma Gandhi said, "Almost anything you do will seem insignificant, but it is very important that you do it." Everyone has the power to affect change, even little ol' you. We may feel like we're only one person, and that one person has no power at all, but we can make small changes that eventually affect the world. Use these tips to help open your eyes to your community and keep an eye on your tax dollars at work.

✓ Question authority.

✓ Monitor legislation. Keep an eye on the powers that be.

✓ Make contact. Write, call, e-mail, and visit lawmakers, manufacturers, and retailers. Write letters to the editor of local papers.

✓ Boycott. Believe it or not, boycotts work. The Boycott Action News (www.boycotts.org), published by Green America (formerly Co-Op America), supports the use of boycotts as a powerful economic strategy that consumers can use to enact social change. The site lists, but does not necessarily endorse, active boycotts.

✓ Recognize propaganda, which uses fear to try to scare us into believing its message. Don't believe it, even if it's propaganda that forwards your own beliefs.

✓ Get on the Web. Create a Web site, start a blog, join a message board. Check out www.thepetitionsite.com, where you can create and post your own petition.

✓ Support and campaign for environmental candidates. When "my government" doesn't represent *my* ideals, I know it's time to take a stand. We need to care enough to fight to put people we truly believe in, in power and not get discouraged when we feel our votes don't count, especially when all we see is the rich and powerful winning.

✓ Don't stop thinking just because you've gotten a "satisfactory answer." Continue to develop critical thinking. As the Opposing Viewpoints series of books published by Greenhaven Press states, "Those who do not know their opponent's arguments do not completely understand their own."[28] Get both sides of the story and read beyond the headlines.

✓ Educate others. It's said if you teach a man to fish, he'll eat for a lifetime. Teach a woman to lobby Congress, she'll fight forever.

9. DOING IT NOW: Stop Procrastinating

Not procrastinating is the key to keeping organized, and you often get the added benefit of saving money, too. When we put bills off, it only increases our chances of missing deadlines or having them fall through the cracks. Learn to prioritize tasks and solve financial problems as they arise. Monitor your credit card usage and don't miss a payment.

If you've fallen far into debt and the creditors have started mailing notices, calling, or sitting in your driveway, it's best to face the music. In the long run, you'll be better off by taking responsibility sooner rather than later. That overdue bill or debt won't go away and will only get worse if you don't acknowledge it. The first step in recovery is admitting you need help. You may think you're bad off now, but having to declare bankruptcy is a curse that will follow for many years.

Springboard

Try the nonprofit Consumer Credit Counseling Services from Consumer Credit Management at 1-800-WISEPLAN or www.credit.org for help getting back on track.

In addition to addressing our financial woes right away, we should also start saving immediately. That's *not* once you have the credit card or the student loan paid off. It's today. Right now. Especially if you currently have no savings at all. Do not let your debt stop you from starting to save. Even if it's only $5 a month, it's a beginning.

For many of us, the object of our working lives is to make enough money so that we're financially able to stop working and still be able to afford to do the things we love. But retirement is a distant goal, something we don't have to consider right now. Right? *Wrong.* It's like the story of the eighty-year-old man entering college. The seventeen-year-old asks him, "Don't you realize you'll be eighty-four by the time you have your degree?" The eighty-year-old answers, "Yes, but I'll be eighty-four anyway." When we're eighty-four, chances are Social Security will be dried up. The $5 a week we could have been saving in a Roth IRA could be financing our trips to Atlantic City.

Many of us enjoy our work, especially when it's something we're truly passionate about, but there's freedom involved with financial solvency. If we have enough to live on, we can be more secure in our choices. We'll be able to work because we want to, not because we have to, and we're more apt to use the money we have for things we truly want to do. "If I had enough money to pay my bills, I'd quit my job and work part time on my novel and part time volunteering at the children's library." "I'd use my savings to pay off my mortgage. Then I'd work for less money on film projects that my friends from college are putting together." "I would just play video games all day." Do any of these sound like a good idea? Double check your budget and see if you're ready for your life of luxury.

It's imperative that we understand where our money is and what it's doing. Patience is important in investing, but so is research. Now that we've got all this new-found time on our hands, that won't be a problem for us. Get to know your money by reading up on investing. Find out what works for you. Be on the lookout for free financial seminars and always ask questions.

Who's getting rich off your money?

Unlike major banks, credit unions are nonprofit, cooperatively owned organizations. By switching, we can save interest on loans because there's no corporation making money off our interest. Often, we can even see where our money goes. Large banks invest worldwide, but credit unions keep their money local and support our neighbors. They were created to promote thrift among their members and they're regulated and insured just like banks. Many have certain criteria you must meet to join, but they're often open to relatives of people who meet their criteria.

Investing

Here's the basic, bare-bones introduction to getting your portfolio in order. Rule number one: *diversify*. As in, *don't put all your eggs in one basket*. The trick to investing is to put money where it will make the most money for you. Find the investment with a maximum return, minimum time, and minimum risk, and you've found the golden ticket. Meeting with a financial advisor can help you find out which plan is best for your needs.

According to *Girls Just Want to Have Funds* (boys, don't be shy; you can read this one, too), diversify your savings by spreading your money over at least four different types of funds or investments.[29]

❏ Keep your *In the Now Fund* in an easily accessible a checking account for day-to-day expenses.

❏ Prepare for the unexpected by keeping a *Rainy Day Fund* to cover job loss, medical distress, or other emergencies. Some experts recommend keeping up to six months of your regular income in this account in order to cover rent, utilities, and other bills if you get laid off or laid up. Use a savings account or money market mutual fund. These accounts have a higher rate of interest than checking, but are still easily accessible.

❏ Set up a *Short Term Goal Fund* for down payments, vacations, holiday plans, etc. Give a savings account a tangible goal. Name it. Instead of saving for "a vacation," try saving "to go skiing in Aspen over December break." You'll notice this focus will help achieve your goal quicker. Try money market mutual funds, certificates of deposit, or bonds, which have higher interest rates but are less accessible.

❏ Also establish your *Long Term Goal Fund* for buying a house, starting a business, saving for retirement. Put long-term savings in an account that is difficult to access and have money directly deposited into it from your paycheck. Try mutual funds or individual stocks, which may be volatile over the short term; in the long run, they'll provide a higher return.

Thinking outside the box: Ethical investing leading to social change

Socially Responsible Investing (SRI, also known as Sustainable and Responsible Investing) lets you be true to your values while you build your investment portfolio. Many SRIs provide competitive returns, but more importantly they look beyond the bottom line and research the ethical practices of the companies they support.

You can pick the types of companies you want in your fund. Want to stay away from "sin stocks" like liquor, gambling, and tobacco? How about companies that operate sweatshops or treat women and minority workers poorly? How do you feel about military weapons, nuclear power, animal testing, and fair trade? You don't like 'em? They're outta there.

SRI also supports community investing that channels money to communities in need of economic development. To find SRI, look outside the larger investment companies and try Calvert, Parnassus, Domini, Pax World, and Social Funds.com. To research these companies, check out Paul Hawken's www.responsibleinvesting.org.

GIVING BACK

I know what you're thinking. "Charity? *I'm* charity! Have you seen my student loan bills?" Okay. So maybe we're not quite ready to tithe 10 percent of our income, but sooner or later, after organizing, simplifying, and getting out of debt, I guarantee you'll be faced with an excess of income that someone will promptly ask you to hand over, whether it's a homeless person on a street corner, a kid selling candy in front of the post office, or your coworker raising pledges for their walk-a-, bike-a-, dance-a-, jog-a-, or hoochie-coo-athon. Do I sound jaded? Good. And so should you.

There are thousands of charitable organizations out there, and it's easy to pick the wrong one. "Wrong" is meant subjectively. The "wrong charity" is the one that uses our money in any fashion that we don't agree with. Before we make a donation, therefore, we should always have a little background so we can make an informed decision.

Several years ago, for example, I raised a good sum of money to participate in an event. I felt so proud of myself. I was making a difference. I was doing something proactive for the people in my life who were suffering. Midway through the event, however, I figured out that the money I'd raised was going to early detection, not research. And only a portion of the money raised was being returned to the charity, at that, the remainder was used for production expenses such as safety, signage and recruitment. It was my own fault that it took me that long to figure that out. The company had clearly presented the information, but I'd chosen to ignore it. I'd interpreted it the way I wanted to.

As it turned out, I am very glad I participated in this event, anyway. I continued to have a long-standing relationship with them, but the experience taught me to be more aware of to whom or what I donate.

Five Steps to an Informed Donation: Picking A Charity Wisely
1. Ask for a Record of Impact. A reputable organization will gladly provide literature about the event or cause and state how much has been returned to charity in the past.

The information card

Charities soliciting for donations in Los Angeles County are required to provide an "Information Card" that accompanies all requests. To make your own, call the charity and ask these questions.

✓ Activity: What is the letter you received for? Is there an end date? ("Appeal for donations until 12/31/08.")

✓ Purpose: What is the activity for? ("Net proceeds to support local meal program to people living below the poverty line.")

✓ Expenses: How much money is spent on administrative costs, including printing, postage, salaries, direct mail, and miscellaneous expenses?

✓ Previous Activity: How much money has been raised and returned to the charity in the past by this organization? ("2007 appeal raised $1,342,401 from gross receipts of $1,631,942 at an expense of $289,541 or 17.7 percent of gross receipts.")

✓ Chair: Contact information for the person(s) in charge of the organization.

If you are still unsure of the legitimacy of the organization, ask for a 501(c)(3) document, which gives the federal nonprofit tax identification number. If someone connected to the charity seems suspicious about this, be wary. If they don't have this number, they may be a for-profit company that could be making money from donations.

You can also research charities at the Better Business Bureau Wise Giving Alliance (www.give.org), Philanthropic Research Inc.'s searchable web site for charitable organizations (www.guidestar.org), or www.charitynavigator.org.

2. Ask the person raising the money about their connection to the event. Try not to be swayed by sentimentality. Though we may feel compassion for a friend whose brother died of cancer, if the charity they're supporting doesn't agree with our beliefs, we should consider alternatives. Never give just because of pressure or out of guilt.

3. If you have to refuse, be polite and as honest as you can be. "I'm sorry I can't support a cause that does vaccine research on animals." Stay true to *your* conscience.

4. Money is not the only thing we have to donate. As we simplify our lives, we'll have more time to devote to charitable pursuits. If you can't donate money but feel the cause is worthy enough, consider donating time or skills.

5. If all else fails and you still want to support a friend but can't in good conscience support their cause, be honest. Consider giving them something that shows you support their decision to make a difference. Examples include sneakers or a gift certificate to a sporting goods store for someone participating in an athletic event. Food supplies to someone who is raising money by throwing a party. Donating time to a child's school instead of buying candy from the kid at your door. With any luck, your concern will help them raise their own awareness for the charity.

IDEAS FOR SIMPLE MONEY-SAVING GIFTS

What is the value of a gift? As the MasterCard commercials show, most items have set monetary values, but the emotions that accompany them are priceless. Think of the things in your life that have meant the most to you. They're probably times spent with family, a wedding or a birth. A gift can remind us of feelings, but memories reside in our souls. Before giving, ask yourself, *am I giving just to cross a name off my list?*

It can be very difficult to get people—especially children—to understand our not wanting to give or receive gifts. It's also hard not to seem ungrateful when we tell someone we don't want a gift. Be prepared for some resistance when telling people you're not doing gifts this year. You may feel insulted or ridiculed.

There are two major types of gifts: services/experiences and goods/products. As we learn to simplify our lives, consider giving a service or an experience (movie tickets, sky diving lessons, a massage) over a product (Big Mouth singing bass, meat-of-the-month club, or slipper socks). Give a gift that won't add more clutter to the recipient's life. Think about gift certificates for goods and services they need, such as their veterinarian, the post office, or their gym.

Take a look at the gift line on your budget worksheet. If it's December, we may wonder how the amount of the GNP of Trinidad ended up right here. There are endless choices for giving gifts that cost little or even nothing and still show how much we care.

Anyone can grab a pair of mittens from The Gap and charge them, but it's a special gift when they're hand-knitted in their favorite sports team's colors.

New Neighbor or a New House

❑ For the tea drinker, a teacup and saucer set filled with assorted teabags. Buy loose teas (which can cost only pennies per cup) and separate them into tins to make assortments for several friends. Include a tea strainer or infuser.

❑ Got a green thumb? Look on line for resources for proper techniques for propagating one of your houseplants. If you can't grow things to give away, give small flowerpots filled with packets of seeds and soil. For cat lovers, how about a packet of catnip seeds?

❑ Give gifts in a jar: candy, cookies, pasta, coffee or cocoa mix, or potpourri in a jar. Tied with ribbons, they look good enough on their own and don't need to be gift-wrapped.

❑ Create a fruit basket or a wine and cheese basket. The pre-made baskets sold in stores invariably seem to be twice as expensive as the total amount of the ingredients in the basket. A better way is to select the items yourself. This is also a good way to avoid that one item that ends up repulsing the recipient. But then again ... maybe they're the one that likes the cheese log.

Birthdays and Holidays

❑ Try a holiday free from "store bought presents". Instead, make things for each other and rediscover the simplicity, traditions, and true spirit of holidays.

The regift

The New England tradition of the Yankee Swap (sometimes called White Elephant) is a creative solution to ridding your home of previously given unwanted gifts, giving regifting a comic twist. The object of the game is to find something in your home that is truly the ugliest, most useless, most impractical gift you've ever received. The trick is to make sure the giver of this gift isn't within your Yankee Swap circle, (unless of course it was given at a previous Yankee Swap, in which case etiquette states that it's not a social faux pas to regift). Wrap your gift, gather your friends, and, one by one, everyone picks a present from the pile. Swapping gifts is encouraged, especially if something actually can be put to good use.

Some classic Yankee Swaps I've been to have included: ceramic cat made by donor in junior high school, pair of brown plaid platform shoes circa 1979, and a plastic fish-shaped handbag. White Elephants differ in that gifters are given a limit (usually no more than $10) to actually purchase a gift that is tackier than a drug store box of wine.

❑ What's your secret skill? Are you an artist? Can you build with wood? Do you make a mean batch of chili? Think of all the things you do for yourself, and you're sure to find at least one gift you can make.

❑ Give the gift of your time or a coupon for a service you can provide. Do you know someone who seems to be burning the candle at both ends? Offer to help with errands or babysitting. Offer to help cater a party for a friend. Once you learn to change your own oil, you'll have gifts to last a lifetime.

❑ Think twice about jewelry. For one 18-carat gold ring, Oxfam estimates that 20 *tons* of mine waste is created.[30] Instead, a more sustainable option for gold can be found at www.greenkarat.com for recycled and ecologically responsible jewelry.

❑ Reveal your social responsibility. Give gifts that show what you believe in. Make a donation to a charity in a friend's name or ask that in lieu of a gift for yourself, they donate to a charity of your choosing. Seek out organizations like the following:
   - ✓ WindBuilders (www.nativeenergy.com) help to build wind farms.
   - ✓ Organic Farming Research Foundation (www.ofrf.org) sponsors research and educates the public and lawmakers on organic farming issues.
   - ✓ Heifer International (www.heifer.org) sends animals to hungry families around the world as a way for them to become self-reliant and create a sustainable culture. Not just cows, but goats, pigs, chickens, ducks, bees, trees, rabbits, sheep, llamas, buffalo, or a knitting basket can be ordered as a donation.

❑ Keep it nearby. If you want your donation to remain in your community, check your local Better Business Bureau for a list of local charities.

❑ Make or buy a calendar and write special dates on it. Include simple reminders to make your friends smile. Don't forget: June 11th: *Ferris Bueller's Day Off* and July 12th: *Richard Simmons's birthday*.

❑ Has someone always complimented you on a recipe of yours? Give them a copy, plus some of the ingredients. This works especially well with cookie recipes. Measure out the ingredients, make sure to note which ones you've included. (Do not, however, include the eggs.)

❑ Buy inexpensive picture frames or scrounge for nifty ones at flea markets to use when you create a collage of things you've done together through the years. Arrange quotes, photos, pressed flowers, souvenirs, then frame the collage.

❑ Create a spa in a basket: candles, bath oils, a natural sponge, a CD of relaxing music, and a rubber ducky. Make your own bath salts from the recipe on page 268.

❑ Make a movie night in: a basket with a DVD, popcorn, beverage of choice, and some candy treats that didn't cost $4.50 a box.

> ### *Wrap it up*
> Almost any paper can be used to wrap a present. Think of new and interesting ways to cover your packages, like plain brown paper with a homemade stencil, a fabric remnant, a fancy department store bag cut down to size, old maps, wallpaper samples, or an old book with a hole cut out of the middle to hide the present inside. Reuse tissue or wrapping paper by ironing it to remove wrinkles. Wrapping gift boxes allows them to be reused many times.

Cards

The greeting card industry has us by the heartstrings. They know that we have no idea what to say to a loved one when their pet has died. We don't know how to simply say, "I love you." "How can I express my love to you, my valentine? Roses are red, violets are ... *Line, please!*" We run to the card store every time a national holiday rolls around because it's convenient and easy (and, invariably, because we've forgotten Grandma's birthday yet again). By arming ourselves with a box of plain note cards and envelopes from a stationary store, we can create our own line of all-purpose cards.

- ❏ Go through a pile of not so flattering photographs. Glue them to the front of the card. Write captions. Hilarity ensues.
- ❏ Keep a collection of favorite quotations. Earmark which ones remind you of friends and which ones may offer consolation if tragedy strikes.
- ❏ To make an envelope, place a card or letter diagonally in the middle of a square piece of paper and fold the corners inward. Seal it with tape or a sticker.
- ❏ Consider sending holiday cards sold by charitable organizations instead of the glossy ones from the stationary store.

I find that the "just because" gifts are the ones I most remember. Why does there have to be an official holiday before I can give someone a gift? How about taking something to a friend who is ill or sad ... or just because?

> At the deepest level, there is no giver, no gift, and no recipient ... only the universe rearranging itself.
> –Jon Kabat-Zinn, *Wherever You Go, There You Are*

As we simplify our finances, we can see the direct connections to simplifying how we shop, how we choose to work, and how we reconnect to our personal and professional aspirations. There is a ripple effect that accompanies conscious spending and scaling back: when we think smaller, we use fewer resources, and minimize the impact on the planet. We can focus on what's truly important: eliminating the worry about paying bills, pursuing our own goals, giving to others, and most of all, relaxing.

Do it today
Pull out your latest list of goals. Are you giving them enough financial and emotional support? What can you do this week to focus more on helping them come true?

ADDITIONAL RESOURCES

De Graaf, John, et al. *Affluenza.* San Francisco: Berrett-Koehler Publishers, 2001. Companion book to the PBS series that coined the word "affluenza."

Dominguez, Joseph R. and Vicki Robin. *Your Money or Your Life: Transforming Your Relationship With Money and Achieving Financial Independence.* New York: Penguin Books, 1999. When you've abandoned all hope about ever being able to save any money or simplify your spending, Joe and Vicki's book is there for you. YMOYL and its companion web site (Financial Integrity, www.financialintegrity.org) provide practical approaches for managing finances and reevaluations of our love affair with the almighty dollar.

Goodman, Susannah Blake. *Girls Just Want to Have Funds: How to Spruce Up Your Financial Life and Invest Like a Pro.* New York: Hyperion, 2000.

Hunt, Mary. *The Best of Cheapskate Monthly: Simple Tips for Living Lean in the 90's.* New York: St. Martin's Press, 1993.

Lesko, Matthew. *Gobs and Gobs of Free Stuff.* Kensington, MD: Information USA, 1998.

McKibben, Bill. *Hundred Dollar Holiday: The Case for a More Joyful Christmas.* New York: Simon & Schuster, 1998.

Kobliner, Beth. *Get a Financial Life: Personal Finance in Your 20's and 30's.* New York: Simon & Schuster, 2000.

chapter 4

balancing the ecological connection

One of the most important effects of simple living is how it can minimize our impact on the planet. Scientists can postulate many things, but the truth is that no one knows for sure what long-term effects our actions will have upon the earth. Does this scare the human race into conscious conservation and sustainability? Hardly. Thanks to the pervasive influence of affluenza, we keep pushing concern for the environment to the back of our minds to make room for the latest Britney Spears tabloid story.

We must begin to make the connection between our every-day activities and their effect on ecology as a whole. Why is the ski season shorter? Why are so many beaches closed? Why are so many of my friends having trouble starting a family? What does one event have to do with another? What is the connection between how I live and the health and well-being of those around me? When will we realize that ecological problems are more than nature being sick?

We can agree with Thomas Jefferson when he stated that while the earth belongs to the living, *we are not its owners.* We are merely house sitting for a while. But we have taken this duty about as seriously as the typical 80's movie teenager takes house-sitting when his parents leave him alone for the weekend. We act with little consideration of the consequences. When will we realize it's already Sunday night and it's past time to start cleaning?

The full range of the world's ecological problems is too long to list here, but effects on human health become increasingly more visible. For starters, consider cancer, endocrine disruption, multiple chemical sensitivities, and other environmental illnesses. None of these are one-cause conditions. Each arises from a mixture of several substances that build up over time in our bodies. This makes tracing the genesis of the condition back to a single toxin nearly impossible.

The ecological issues we face today are in danger of turning into major health and food supply crises. These problems are snowballs rolling down an endless hill, getting larger and larger and more difficult to control. How do we protect ourselves against these effects of unknown combinations?

Our health will depend more on how we are able to remedy ecological problems than on how successful we are at discovering cures. Education will lead us to understand hazards and hopefully change our attitudes about the destruction of our environment. The first step in balancing how we want to live and how we *need* to live to protect the planet is to focus on the five most important crises of our environment:

1. Air
2. Water
3. Energy
4. Chemicals
5. Deforestation.

1. AIR: Climate Change & Pollution

> Man, it's hot. It's like Africa hot. Tarzan couldn't take this kind of hot.
>
> —Neil Simon's, Biloxi Blues

We can just throw away that old *Farmer's Almanac*, because it ain't gonna make a difference. Why is it so darn hot? Nine of the planet's ten warmest years on record, have been since 1995.[31] Since 1979, 20 percent of the polar ice cap at the North Pole has melted.[32] And higher temperatures don't just make it hotter, they contribute to creating extreme weather events like hurricanes and tornadoes. There's more catastrophic weather on the horizon: shifts in seasons with longer, hotter summers and colder winters; drier droughts and deserts, extreme global thermal contrasts; and bigger, wetter, more intense winds that will cause more frequent storms that result in higher sea levels and tidal surges.

This change in weather events is part of a concept that Thomas Homer Dixon describes in his book *The Ingenuity Gap* as the "revenge effects" of nature fighting back.[33] Our insistence on progress and industrialization makes us cut down the trees that provide shade and cooling. Cutting down trees destroys habitats, which causes animal and plant species to become extinct or forces them to adapt to what we've created. We're rewriting the environmental rules, but when will we realize that if we mess with Mother Nature, sooner or later She'll mess back with us?

The start of any discussion about climate change should begin with the big three: the *ozone layer*, the *greenhouse effect*, and *global warming*. These are important terms, but what exactly do they mean?

The ozone layer is a thin layer of gas located between twelve and thirty miles above the earth's surface that shields us from the effects of the sun's most hazardous radiation. When everything goes the way it should, the ozone layer provides a protective screen that filters out shorter wavelengths of ultraviolet A and B radiation before they are able to reach ground.

In 1985, however, we began to hear about a noticeable hole in this protective cover. We would later learn that this hole was created by our use of CFCs, hydrofluorocarbons, and methyl bromide. The radiation that slipped into our atmosphere through the hole began to cause damage to living cells that led to increased cases of skin cancer, lowered immunity, "snow blindness" (a condition where the cornea is burned), and crop damage. UV radiation also can destroy microscopic sea creatures called krill, leading to an effect that ripples clear up the food chain to us. Fortunately with legislation we have reversed some of the damage, but we still have a long way to go.

Scary stuff

Ozone produced at ground level, commonly known as smog, contributes in its own way to the greenhouse effect. Learn more about ground ozone in the *Transporting* chapter, page 178.

The *greenhouse effect* is normally a beneficial and natural process that regulates the climate of the planet. Greenhouse gases (mainly carbon dioxide [CO_2], carbon monoxide, and methane) maintain temperatures by absorbing sunlight and radiation. They prevent the earth's heat from radiating out into space. This is a necessary process, and without it temperatures would drop so low that oceans would freeze and life as we know it would not be possible. It's only when an excess of greenhouse gases becomes trapped within the earth's stratosphere that a crisis occurs.

A rough estimate is that half of the negative effects of the greenhouse effect occur when burning fossil fuels release carbon dioxide, which comes mainly from wood (primarily the burning of forests), coal, oil (from automobiles and airplanes), and natural gas. The most important issue is the altitude at which these gases are released—the higher the altitude, the fewer molecules to help break them down. Those released into the air at least five and a half miles above sea level (as airplane exhaust), will stay in the atmosphere one hundred times longer than if released at ground level.[34]

Another quarter of the greenhouse effect is attributable to methane, which is largely released from landfills when organic waste (such as manure) breaks down. Methane is also released as gas from the stomachs of cows and by termites eating wood.

The final quarter is a result of chlorofluorocarbons (CFCs), a double whammy, which both speed up the greenhouse effect and deplete the ozone layer. At low levels in the atmosphere, CFCs are pretty much inert. At higher levels, stronger UV rays break down CFCs, releasing chlorine atoms that destroy ozone. CFCs were invented in the 1930s and were once used commonly in aerosol propellants. One pound of CFC can destroy 70,000 pounds of atmospheric ozone, and a molecule of CFC is about 10,000 times more destructive than a molecule of CO_2.[35] CFCs were banned from aerosols in 1978, but loopholes in the law allow hundreds of products to continue using CFCs. Currently, sixty million pounds of CFCs, used in refrigerating units and air conditioners, are still on the market.

On the other hand

Styrofoam was also composed of CFCs, but what we refer to now as "Styrofoam" is in fact polystyrene, which contains no CFCs.

Although *global warming* is not solely the result of human activities, we are still the leading culprits as we burn fossil fuels to power our cars, heat our homes and run our factories. You think it's hot now? Scientists predict that if we continue our careless consumption of fossil fuels, global temperatures will rise between 2°F and 9°F by the next century. It may not sound like much, but this is a faster change than any that has occurred within the last ten thousand years.

"Okay," you say, "so it's just gonna be a little warmer, right? I can deal with two degrees." Guess again. As the climate changes, the earth's temperature rises, which means that more solar radiation gets through the ozone layer, which causes the polar ice caps and glaciers to melt. When the ice caps melt, sea levels rise. When sea levels rise, coastal areas begin to erode. When coastal areas erode, the habitat for species that live there is destroyed.

But wait—there's more … trapped heat within the earth's atmosphere creates more intense storms, which causes flooding, which eventually results in exploding populations of disease-carrying insects and rodents within thirty-five miles of a coastline—where one third of the planet's population lives. We're talking Biblical stuff now.

As all these things are occurring, species are forced to adapt. As the ice caps melt, phytoplankton (the basis of the food chain) is destroyed by excess solar radiation. It's all part of a chain effect that only seems to get worse.

Hope for the Future

While these atmospheric crises may seem dire, we possess the tools and knowledge—simple every-day actions we can all take to help balance the effects of these dangers to our climate.

❑ Reduce meat consumption and we'll help reduce the number of cattle raised and, subsequently, lessen the production of manure and decrease the production of methane.

- ❏ Reduce dependency on coal and petroleum energy. Burning oil, gas, and coal are the main causes of climate change.
- ❏ Use less electricity by increasing energy efficiency and insist on the use of renewable energy sources. (See page 98.)
- ❏ Lobby to increase fuel efficiency standards for cars, SUVs, and pickup trucks.
- ❏ Fight against deforestation. Trees help balance CO_2 levels.
- ❏ Learn to slow down when it gets hot. The minute the mercury gets over 80 °F, we lock ourselves indoors or in the car and crank the AC full blast. Ironically, these same air conditioners raise the planet's surface temperature, which makes it even hotter. Try taking it easy on hot days and if you don't have to drive, don't.
- ❏ Limit sun exposure and avoid it as much as possible between ten a.m. and three p.m., when solar rays are strongest. Don't rely too much on sunscreen, which gives a false sense of protection (and possibly contributes to at least some of the increase in skin cancer cases). When using sunscreen, make sure it blocks both UVA and UVB radiation. Sunblocks containing titanium dioxide or zinc oxide are the safest and most effective. Develop a light, natural tan slowly through repeated short exposure to the sun in early mornings or late afternoons.
- ❏ Wear sunglasses with 100 percent UVA and UVB protection, not only in summer months but also especially in winter months where snow can magnify the sun's effects and cause cornea damage.
- ❏ Eat foods high in beta-carotene (carrots, broccoli), vitamin C (citrus, peppers), vitamin E (almonds, sweet potatoes), and selenium (Brazil nuts, tuna, turkey). Research shows that these may provide some protection for skin from UV radiation.
- ❏ Buy organic strawberries and tomatoes. Methyl bromide, the leading ozone depleter still being produced, is most often used as a pesticide on these crops.
- ❏ Recycle halon fire extinguishers, which contain compounds that are more destructive to the ozone layer than CFCs. See www.halon.org for information.
- ❏ Have all air conditioners (including car units) regularly checked for leaks. If your system is leaking, do not use it until it's fixed.
- ❏ Recycle refrigerants properly when replacing an air conditioner or refrigerator.
- ❏ Reduce car trips. If we all eliminated one ten-mile car trip a week, we could each save over 500 pounds of CO_2 from being released each year.
- ❏ Cut down on usage of synthetic materials and chemicals. If no one buys them, they won't have to be manufactured.
- ❏ Plant smog resistant trees and shrubs to help clean the air. Male gingko trees (the females produce a smelly fruit) are very resistant to infection and pollution. If you have the space, plant grass instead of trees (grassland or fields are more efficient at removing carbon from the air than trees).

Climate neutral

"Climate neutral" is a concept where companies take responsibility for the pollution their product creates, whether through manufacture, use, or disposal. Companies offer to help offset this pollution by performing other acts, such as planting trees to compensate for CO_2 emissions, supporting wind farms or donating energy efficient lighting to local schools.

Air Pollution

Each year the average adult breathes in (and out) seven million liters of air (give or take a few million), which is seven to fourteen liters of air every minute. When we exercise, we can take in up to fifty liters per minute. The more air we breathe, the more pollution we take in. Suddenly, it's not just asthmatics, children, and the elderly who need to be concerned about the dangers of air pollution. In many large cities, the air is not fit for anyone to breathe.

Scary stats

Eighteen million Americans now suffer from asthma.[36] In children under age five, asthma cases have increased 160 percent since the mid 1980s.[37]

Health officials are beginning to realize just how dangerous poor air quality can be, and it doesn't need to be visible to be damaging. In her book, *When Smoke Ran Like Water*, Devra Davis writes, "Pollution never shows up on death certificates," but there's a correlation between higher death rates on higher pollution days.[38] Although when someone dies the listed cause of death is a heart attack, could pollution have caused the symptoms that led to the ultimate damage?

When it comes to something as necessary as air, why are we not more worried? Where air pollution is concerned, *acid rain, volatile organic compounds,* and *radon* are especially critical. Remember, if we simplify our actions that affect the ecology, we'll help create a healthier planet.

Acid rain is a result of sulfur and nitrogen oxides (released by cars and factory exhaust) coming into contact with water and morphing into sulfuric and nitric acids, both of which are harsh, toxic chemicals. When any type of precipitation falls, the toxic mixture returns to earth, spreading it over a larger area.

Acid rain can peel paint off buildings, destroy plants, and kill fish and aquatic wildlife by raising the acidity of lakes and streams. It can damage our (and other mammals') health by creating respiratory problems. Think of acid rain as the messenger that brings chemicals right to our door.

Volatile organic compounds (VOCs) are substances that readily become volatile at room temperature, which makes them easy to inhale. A VOC is any carbon-based chemical that creates unstable particles that are released into the atmosphere in a process called out- or off-gassing. VOCs can be both indoor and outdoor pollutants and can come from synthetic and natural substances.

Some chemical VOCs we're likely to come into contact with every day are xylene, toluene, benzene, styrene, formaldehyde, chloroform, and trichloroethylene. Adhesives, carpeting, cleaning products, fabrics, floor coverings, paints, paper towels, photocopiers, upholstery, and wall coverings can also contain VOCs. Inexpensive appliances are usually made with low quality plastics. When the product heats up, the materials off-gas. Chemical substances that may have been banned in the U.S. still reach us by way of products and parts made in other countries.

VOCs contribute to respiratory problems, allergies, environmental illness, and multiple chemical sensitivities. Long-term exposure can result in neurological effects, a weakened immune system, and possibly cancer. Some even cause birth defects or mutations.

Indoor Air Pollution

Ah, home sweet home. After a long hard day at the office breathing copier fumes, the long ride home breathing bus and car exhaust, and walking anywhere breathing any other kind of air pollution, when we walk through our own door we might think we're home free. But indoor air pollution can be just as damaging to our lungs as outdoor pollution. Because we spend so much time inside and seal our homes to make heating and cooling more efficient, we've trapped stale polluted air inside with us.

Stop & think

What exactly is in the air inside your home, office, or car? Indoor air pollution can come from formaldehyde, synthetic fibers, adhesives, inks, paper goods; particle board, furniture; paints, varnishes, off-gassing from paints; appliances and other plastics; molds and pesticides; vapors from cooking (heated metal, natural gas, food odors); fumes from household cleaning products; fragranced cosmetics; radon and asbestos; and tobacco smoke. Some of these air contaminants are released immediately, whereas others are released slowly over time.

Hope for the Future

❑ Know this warning: a product labeled zero-VOC says nothing about its general toxicity. Certain chemicals, such as propylene glycol, are vegetable based and nontoxic, yet they are still classified VOCs.

❑ The EPA regulates VOCs because they contribute to smog, but legislation for indoor air quality is virtually nonexistent.

❑ Use the nonelectric version of an appliance. As small appliances run, their mechanisms heat cheap plastic and off-gas. Instead try a hot water bottle for a heating pad, air dry your hair instead of using a hair dryer, pick a wind-up alarm clock instead of an electric one.

Radon is a naturally occurring radioactive gas that breaks down into solid, radioactive particles. When inhaled, these particles become lodged in the lungs and radiate into our tissues. Because radon cannot be seen, tasted, or smelled, the link between symptoms and radon is not always immediately recognized. But the longer our exposure or the higher the level of radon in our homes, the greater the risk to us and our families. Radon is considered to be the second leading cause of lung cancer in the U.S.

Radon naturally occurs in certain rocks, groundwater, and soil. Food grown in radioactive soil will pick up some of the radon as it grows. Radon can also enter homes through holes or cracks in basement or foundation floors or walls. It can also enter when released from well water when we bathe or wash our clothes.

Hope for the Future

❑ When television sweeps periods (February, May, and November) roll around, there always seems to be at least one news story about radon. ("Coming in the six o'clock hour! The silent killer that lives in your basement...") Don't overreact to overhyped news teasers. The EPA estimates that about 6 percent of American homes have elevated levels of radon. Who should be concerned? Those with well water and basements should probably think about testing.

❑ Ventilate. Outdoors, radon poses little threat because it's diluted by air. It's only when radon is trapped in a structure that it can accumulate and reach dangerous levels.

❑ Test your home. Testing is simple and inexpensive. Request a brochure from the EPA and National Safety Council by calling (800) SOS-RADON. If the radon levels in your home are low, take corrective steps as soon as possible. Find where the radon is coming from and either plug up its entry point or redirect the air back out of the house. Close off areas of high concentrations. If you discover elevated radon levels, see www.nsc.org/issues/radon/fixit.htm for removal solutions.

Indoor Air Quality Tips

❑ Change or clean the filter for your cooling or heating unit regularly. If you don't, it will continue to circulate not only VOCs but also rodent feces, dust mites, bacteria, and mold.

❑ Purchase high efficiency particulate absolute (HEPA) air filters that are able to remove VOCs, odors, and over 95 percent of particulates from the air.

❑ Air out your house, especially during the winter. Open the windows in your bedroom at least once a week for a few hours let stale air out. Keeping the air circulating ensures that rooms don't get too wet or too dry, which prevents the growth of molds.

❑ Remove as many petroleum-based products from your house as possible: fabric softeners, air fresheners, detergents, paints, perfumed cosmetics, marking pens, and synthetic cleaning products.

❑ Set new products that have a noticeable odor outside and let them "breathe" before you bring them indoors.

❑ Keep rooms well ventilated when using any flame, including candles and fireplaces. All flames consume air, and carbon monoxide poisoning is a threat if the air doesn't circulate. Gas appliances produce large amounts of carbon monoxide, carbon dioxide, nitric oxide, and nitrogen dioxide, as well as smaller amounts of formaldehyde and sulfur dioxide. When the flame burns consistently orange instead of blue, call the gas company for a tune-up.

❑ Choose candles wisely. Petroleum-based and lead-wick candles contribute significantly to dangerous levels of indoor air pollution. Buy (or make) candles made from beeswax, soy or vegetable oils, lead-free wicks, and pure essential-oil fragrances.

❑ Deep clean your carpets. Get rid of dust, dust mites, and other noxious thingies so you won't be inhaling them with every step you take.

❑ Pick up some houseplants. While opinions vary about the ability of plants to remove large amounts of chemicals from the air, there's significant evidence to show that given a static amount, certain plants will absorb chemicals. According to Plants for Clean Air Council and NASA, plants cannot metabolize chemicals as fast as they are produced but the bacteria in the roots will consume formaldehyde and use it for food.[39] Fifteen to twenty plants should be enough for an average sized home. Repot every two years to rejuvenate roots.

Plants that make good air filters

According to the book: *How to Grow Fresh Air* by Dr. B.C. Wolverton,[40] the top ten houseplants that act as air filters for removing formaldehyde, benzene and trichloroethylene and regulating indoor humidity are:

1. Areca palm
2. Lady palm
3. Bamboo palm
4. Rubber plant
5. Dracaena palms

6. English ivy
7. Dwarf date palm
8. Ficus
9. Peace lily
10. Boston fern (best at removing formaldehyde from air)

For carbon monoxide, use a philodendron (but caution: philodendron is toxic to cats). For formaldehyde, use chrysanthemums, gerbera daisies, snake plant, spider plant, corn plant, and golden pothos.

---

2. WATER: Pollution & Conservation

> The future of civilization depends on water. I beg you to understand this.
> –Jacques Cousteau

Potable water is the key to life. But we take clean water for granted and we're unaware of how each drop is connected to the world at large. The water we drink once ran in a stream through the Himalayas, flowed through polar ice caps, and even drained into the Pacific Ocean via a sewage pipe. How truly "pure" is the water that flows from our tap?

The government says our water is safe to drink, but life in the private sector shows a different cup of agua. How safe or pure it is when we turn the tap and water comes out with a rusty color, smells of chlorine, or stains the porcelain green? How could drinking this water possibly be good for us?

Bottled water seems to be a good immediate solution. If the government won't protect us, we'll buy our own water. But bottled water is sometimes little more than just tap water from someone else's tap with minerals added to change the taste. Regulation of bottled water is currently no stricter than regulation of municipal water. A study by the Natural Resources Defense Council found that one third of 103 brands of bottled water studied contained contaminants including arsenic and *E. coli*.[41]

Soda water?

The water bottled and sold by Coke (*Dasani*) and Pepsi (*Aquafina*) are no more than mineral packets sold to local distributors allowing them to bottle their tap water and sell it for upwards of $2 a bottle.

Municipal water treatment is not foolproof, and the government is not responsible for the water supply beyond the point of entry into our home. This means our residence can be the cause of the problem. Many municipal water treatment facilities were only designed to disinfect and clean the water supply by killing disease-causing bacteria, but they neglect other hazards, such as heavy metals, volatile chemicals, and medications.

On the other hand

We may build up a tolerance to the impurities in our water, but our guests will have an adverse reaction to it. (Think about that trip to Mexico or the mouth sores you got when you drank the water at your cousin's place upstate.) Tolerance, however, does not mean safety. Many hazardous chemicals found in water can accumulate in fat cells over time.

Water pipes may contribute pollutants to our drinking water through the leaching of cadmium, copper, iron, lead, and zinc. Lead can come from pipes or solder, and corrosive water can react with the pipes or fittings. You can reduce the amount of lead in your water by running cold water for a minute or two before using it for drinking or cooking. Polyvinyl chloride (PVC) pipes also contaminate water by leaching petrochemicals.

Fluoride, which is added to some municipal water supplies, is actually a toxic substance recycled as a byproduct of metal refining. If you notice mottling or white staining on your teeth, you are probably getting too much fluoride; it adds up from the potential fluoridation of the public water supply, the amount contained in toothpaste and mouthwashes, juices and other beverages, and the amount naturally contained in foods.

Chlorine, also added to water supplies as a disinfectant, creates trihalomethanes (THMs), tiny dangerous particles formed when chlorine reacts with natural organic matter in the water (dead leaves, humus, silt, or mud). The worst exposure to THMs is from shower steam, where we breathe in chemical particulates, but it's also easily absorbed through the skin. To reduce your exposure to THMs, install a shower filter.

Traces of medications and caffeine are also found in public water supplies. Over 50 percent of all drugs pass right through our systems, and we re-ingest some of these chemicals through our drinking water. Trace amounts of estrogen (from birth control pills and hormone replacement drugs), antibiotics, pain relievers, perfumes, codeine, antacids, cholesterol medications, sunscreens, hormones from animal feedlots, antidepressants, and chemotherapy agents have all been found in tested water.

Keeping the Water Clean

Any chemical washed into a storm drain, flushed down a toilet, or applied to the environment inside or outside the home will ultimately end up in someone's local water and then in the food chain itself. Sewage treatment plants dump 5.9 trillion gallons of wastewater into coastal waters every year.[42] Traces of household and garden chemicals can interfere with the reproductive cycles of a variety of fish and other organisms. Cars leak all sorts of goo onto our roadways. One rainstorm, and this mixture of toxic fluids (possibly lead, mercury, gasoline, and arsenic) are washed into municipal water supplies. (See the *Transporting* chapter, page 179 for more information.)

One way to make our drinking water safer is to lighten the burden on water treatment plants by keeping the water going out of our homes as clean as possible. Here are some tips:

❑ Do not put grease, fats, and oils down the drain, sink, garbage disposal, or toilet. Freeze animal fats in a can and then deposit the can in the trash. These slippery substances can clog our sewer pipes and restrict the flow of wastewater away from our homes. Blockages force wastewater up onto streets, where it drains into the storm drain system.

❑ Scoop the poop. Picking up after the dog doesn't just keep the neighbors happy. It keeps sewers happy, as well.

❑ Never flush tampon applicators. In communities that still dump to the oceans, the plastic pieces break apart and may be ingested by marine animals. Pieces can also clog mechanisms at water treatment plants.

❑ *Avoid using toxic substances.* If you have to use one, dispose of it properly. See page 296, for tips.

❑ Pack it in, pack it out. Bring it to the lake or ocean, but take it home when you leave.

Scary stats: Travel waste at sea (Baby, please don't take me on a sea cruise!)

It is actually legal for cruise ships to dispose of human waste and ground up food beyond three miles from shore. They are allowed to dump "gray water" (used water that doesn't contain human wastes) anywhere. According to the EPA, a typical week-long cruise carrying upwards of 3,000 passengers and crew and will generate eight tons of garbage, one million gallons of gray water, 25,000 gallons of oil-contaminated water, and 200,000 gallons of sewage.[43]

Help clean your drinking water at home. Request data sheets from your water provider to get an idea what you're up against.

❏ Testing your own water will help determine if the contamination is coming from within you home (pipes, point of entry, faucet). Tests can be expensive (up to several hundred dollars), but we shouldn't be ignorant with something as vital as water.

❏ Use filters to help remove some chemicals from drinking water. Be sure that the filter you use takes out the chemical you are concerned about. Keep track of when to change the filter.

Water Conservation

Humanity's use of water quadrupled between 1940 and 1990. Half of that increase can be attributed to population growth, but the other half is the effect of an increase of per capita consumption. Americans love water: we want our sports teams to play on lush lawns, our yards to be green and healthy, our cars always freshly washed, our swimming pools filled and cleaned. Even our toilets need to be flushed with potable water! Every day, we each use between eighty and one hundred gallons of water, while the average European uses about half as much.

While it may look like there's plenty of water, the 320 million cubic miles of water on earth are all there will ever be. Almost 98 percent of the water on earth is actually seawater. Another 2 percent is trapped in polar ice caps and glaciers or stored underground. This water is inaccessible, leaving well under one percent available as fresh water. This amount needs to support all the humans, animals and plant life on earth, but two billion people do not have access to sanitized drinking water and three million people die every year from water-related diseases. Ninety percent of the Third World's wastewater is discharged into local rivers and streams. Eighty percent of disease in poorer countries is spread by drinking unsafe water.

American Water Usage

Thermoelectric Power - 48%	Aquaculture - less than 1%
Irrigation - 34%	Livestock - less than 1%
Public Supply - 11%*	Mining - less than 1%
Industrial - 5%	Domestic use - less than 1%[44]

   * The 11% for "public use" is misleading because the water in that slice includes domestic use, industrial use, and even more thermoelectric power.

As we can see from these stats, our domestic water use is almost insignificant compared to water being used for thermoelectric power, which extracts, uses, and then releases back (at a considerably greater temperature) 195,000 million gallons of water per day. After that big chunk of the pie is removed from the chart, the next biggest slice goes to irrigation and industry. For example, it takes 105,000 gallons of water to make one car. Computer manufacture uses massive quantities of fresh de-ionized water and produces billions of gallons of wastewater. Oil extraction requires water to be pumped into wells to increase pressure in the reservoir and enhance production, but the water cannot be reused because it contains high levels of minerals and pollutants.[45]

Saving Water: Every Drop Helps

That tiny sliver of total domestic water consumption is still 3.5 billion gallons consumed every day. We could drastically lower this number if we each just used 10 gallons less a day and by making some simple lifestyle changes.

Domestic water use[46]	
Toilets - 40%	Laundry - 8%
Bathing - 25%	Dishwashing - 5%
Drinking & Cooking - 20%	Gardening & Car - 2%

Try the following tips to cut back on your water usage.

❑ Reuse gray water. The rinse water from showers and baths, dishwashing, washing machines, and sinks doesn't contain sewage, even though it's not suitable for drinking. It can be used, however, to water non-edible plants and to flush toilets. Before using gray water outdoors, check local health regulations to make sure it's legal. Never use soaps that contain phosphates.

❑ Fashion a flush bucket. Place a five-gallon bucket to catch shower or bath water and use that water to flush the toilet. For those living in snowy areas, five buckets of melted snow a day can both reduce your indoor water usage and help spring arrive sooner outdoors.

❑ Collect the water that runs while you're waiting for it to heat up and use it for watering plants or cooking. Use water you boiled vegetables or pasta in to water plants. The nutrients will help the plants thrive.

❑ Gather rainwater. Keep your collector securely covered if is outdoors. Some communities (particularly on the east coast) have laws against standing water that can lead to mosquito infestations.

❑ Turn the water off when you're not using it. This seems like a no-brainer, but turning the faucet off while shaving, brushing teeth, or washing can save ten to twenty gallons a day.

❑ Let the dishwasher do its job. Don't prewash. Most dishwashers have strong enough water pressure and hot enough water to get your dishes clean.

❑ Run only full loads in the dishwasher or washing machine or set water levels to accommodate smaller loads.

❑ Fix leaks sooner rather than later. A leaking toilet or faucet can waste up to fifteen gallons of water per day. To check for toilet leaks, add drops of food coloring to the tank. If color appears in the bowl, there's a leak.

❑ Put a displacement device in your toilet tank to save water. Sink a small plastic soda bottle or a glass jar with a tight lid and filled with sand or rocks in the tank. As long as it sinks, the object will raise the water level, requiring the toilet to use less water when flushed.

❑ Switch to low-flow. By law, all toilets sold after 1994 are low-flow and use between one and two gallons of water per flush. Older models can consume as much as seven gallons.

❑ Let it mellow if it's yellow. Here's one that may get some strange looks. If it's just urine, don't flush so often. (This one works best if you live alone and aren't expecting company.)

❑ Consider a dual-flush toilet that has two flushing options, one for solids, which uses more water (about 1.6 gallons), and one for liquids, which uses half as much (only .8 gallons).

❑ Install showerhead aerators and low-flow taps. Restrictors control the amount of water flowing through the faucet or showerhead, while aerators actually expand the stream of water, giving a more satisfying flow.

❑ Go military. For a military shower: get in, get wet, shut off the water, lather up and then turn the water back on to rinse.

❑ Water lawn and outdoor plants in the early morning or after sun has gone down to reduce evaporation. Use a hose with a spray nozzle to cut the water supply as you move around the yard. Soaker hoses provide drip irrigation that is the most efficient way for lawns and soil to retain water.

❑ Try xeriscaping. Design your yard to reduce the need to irrigate lawn and plants. Plant native flora to make the most of climate and rainfall and ground covers that are more tolerant to drought. Find other methods of making the soil hold more water. Mulch and shade netting also reduce the amount of water that evaporates. Learn to water plants when they need it, not automatically whether they need it or not.

❑ Have a salad instead of a burger. According to the U.S. Geological Survey, it takes 2,607 gallons of water to produce a single serving of steak, 408 gallons for a serving of chicken, and only six gallons for a salad.

On the road again

> It just proves a point. Once a traveler leaves his home, he loses almost 100 percent of his ability to control his environment.
>
> –Agent Dale Cooper, reporting from the Great Northern Hotel in *Twin Peaks*

A vacation is a break from our usual routine, a reward for working so hard all year. On vacation, we stop counting calories, pennies, and drops of water down the drain. But how we get there and what we do once we're there can create enormous waste and pollution. A vacation from home doesn't have to be a vacation from our values.

While staying in a nice hotel is akin to living like a queen for a day, think of the amount of water needed for cleaning bathrooms, washing linens, and preparing food for hundreds of rooms every day, not to mention maintaining landscaping and fountains. Many hotels now allow guests the option of having sheets changed every other day. Keeping your hotel room clean minimizes expended energy and lowers electricity and water use. There are however, many alternatives to the usual corporate hotels or motels:

✓ American Youth Hostels. No one will ever accuse a youth hostel of being a four star accommodation, but that's not the point. What began as a safe haven for American students traveling abroad is today a place where anyone is welcome to stay the night. (www.hiusa.org (202) 783-2294)

✓ Sanctuaries. Looking for a break from the Motel 6? Jack and Marcia Kelly have written *Sanctuaries: A Guidebook to Lodging in Monasteries, Abbeys and Retreats*, which lists places they have visited, with advice on what to expect when you get there and what is required. While the majority are religious centers (of varying denominations), all are centered on hospitality: they open their doors to travelers seeking retreat or a peaceful refuge. (Try that at HoJo's.) Donations are encouraged.

✓ Find information on free or low cost recreation ideas and camping locations through the searchable National Park Service web site (www.recreation.gov).

✓ Visit www.greenmap.org for a collection of hundreds of worldwide city maps that feature locations of their city's sustainable businesses and services.

✓ See www.ecotravel.com and www.ecotourism.org for more ideas on living lightly while on the road.

✓ While traveling isn't often the most ecologically sound of activities, www.terrapass.com and www.myclimate.org sell carbon offsets for automobile and air travel to help even out the amount of pollution created by these means of travel.

3. ENERGY: Conservation Saves More Than Money

We want it cheap and we want it easy. Most of all, we want it the instant we flip the switch. As blackouts threaten and energy rates soar, the government tries to sell us on the need for new power plants to combat the crisis. Oil, coal, and nuclear power only seem cheaper because long-term ecological and medical costs are not factored in. We have already picked the "low hanging fruit"—the easy-to-get, nonrenewable energy sources. Now it takes more and more energy and resources to recover each additional barrel of oil or lode of coal.

Although nuclear energy has been a frightening concept since its inception, in reality it has kept our country powered for well over fifty years. Nuclear power stations produce virtually no carbon dioxide emissions and cost one third to one sixth the cost of fossil fuel energies.

At what cost does this immediate savings come? A typical reactor will generate 20 to 30 tons of high-level nuclear waste every year. There's no known way to safely dispose of this waste, which can remain dangerously radioactive for a quarter of a million years.

Other environmental consequences of nuclear power include the daily discharge of billions of gallons of thermal pollution (hot water), which adversely affects marine ecosystems near power plants. The temperature of this wastewater can be up to twenty-five degrees hotter than the water into which it flows.

With nuclear energy, we're supporting a system that's tenuous at best while sustainable sources go underfunded. If we take nuclear power out of the U.S. fiscal budget equation, over $4 billion could be reallocated each year rather than spent on the restoration and management of sites contaminated by nuclear materials.

Three quarters of the world's energy consumption comes from nonrenewable sources. Fortunately, alternatives are not only being researched, but implemented. Renewable energy sources such as solar, wind, and water power are being sold to consumers at rates comparable to those set for nonrenewable energies, and homes can be set up to run off a combination of several types of electricity. If we put the same amount of time and money into developing these renewable technologies that we put into creating a smaller cell phone, imagine what we could accomplish.

Test yourself

Although 50 million people in northeastern U.S. and Canada lost power for approximately twenty-four hours during the blackout of August, 2003, over two billion people in the world live every day without electricity from transmission lines. Spend a day without electricity. Unplug everything, even your refrigerator (if possible). How prepared are you to live without electricity if you needed to?

Hope for the Future: Renewable Forms of Energy

✓ Solar energy is clean, safe, and quiet. Best of all, it's a "free" and completely renewable source of energy. In one minute, the sun provides enough energy to fulfill the world's energy needs for an entire year. Power can be produced in as little as 5 percent full sunlight. Currently, more than 100,000 homes in the U.S. (largely in rural locations) depend on solar as their primary source of power. Solar is also used for roadside emergency phones, animal warning-trigger signs, and temporary construction signs, where the cost and trouble of setting up utility power outweighs the expense of photovoltaic panels. Homes that combine solar power with electricity often can receive credit from their energy company if they generate more solar power than they need.

President Sunshine

Back in June 1979, President Jimmy Carter installed solar panels on the roof of the White House to provide hot water for the West Wing. As soon as Ronald Reagan took office, they were removed.

✓ As the Dutch have known for centuries, wind power is a simple concept. Wind turns blades around a rotor connected to a shaft, which drives a generator. The stronger the wind, the more energy it yields. Because stronger winds are found at higher altitudes, some wind turbines can be as tall as two hundred feet. Because cold air is denser than hot air, wind turbines are able to generate about 5 percent more power at any given wind speed in the winter than in the summer. Between 1994 and 1998, the wind industry grew by 40 percent and currently powers millions of homes. Many farmers have moved away from the unpredictability of crops and livestock and switched to "raising wind" because there's more money to be earned. In some locations, wind farms have as many as 5,000 turbines harvesting free energy.

✓ Hydropower usually means a dam and a reservoir used to retain water from a river. When the stored water is released, it passes through the dam, rotating turbines that spin generators to produce electricity. Hydropower is currently the largest and least expensive source of renewable electricity produced in the U.S. There has been some concern about hydroelectric power, however, because large-scale dams are built to hold water, which changes how the water flows and where it flows to. Dams can thus alter natural habitats of wildlife, including fish migration, which affects water quality. Large-scale dams can also put stress on continental plates and subsequently raise the probability of earthquakes. Less obtrusive "run of the river" hydropower doesn't require large dams but diverts water into a canal or pipe to spin turbines.

A Few Others Sources of Renewable Power

✓ Tidal power harnesses the energy created during the twice-daily change in sea level.

✓ Co-generation directs energy created as a byproduct of one industry (e.g., excess steam from manufacturing) for use somewhere else.

✓ Geothermal energy captures energy from contained water heated in underground reservoirs.

✓ Biomass energy burns waste wood products (plants and trees) to create biodiesel fuels (including ethanol) to produce steam that spins a turbine.

✓ Methane to energy is a promising method of power generation that harnesses the destructive greenhouse gas from landfills or livestock manure and uses it to generate electricity.

Energy deregulation

Are you willing to pay slightly more for sustainable choices? Several states have begun deregulating energy so that different companies can compete for our business. This allows us to not only choose which company we want to provide our power, but also what type of electricity we want. Many use this as an opportunity to seek out alternatives to nonrenewable energy sources, specifically green power (also called "green-e" or "clean power"). Costs for green power are slightly higher but the small premium you pay goes to support cleaner technologies.

Tips for Saving Energy

The cheapest and safest way to free ourselves from dependence on nonrenewable fossil fuels is to use less energy. For heating and cooling, follow these simple tips:

❑ Prevent drafts by weather-stripping doors and windows and insulating walls and windows. Hold a lit candle near a window frame to check for leaks. Remember to keep air circulating, however; a completely sealed home increases your exposure to VOCs.

❑ Weatherproof electrical outlets by keeping them covered.

❑ Put a sweater on. As Jimmy Carter urged the country in the late 1970s, bundle up instead of turning up the thermostat. Wearing a hat indoors will also help you keep warm.

❑ Wrap your water heater in an insulation blanket (sold at hardware stores) and try turning it down to 120 °F. If you'll be away from home for more than two weeks, turn the heater off.

❑ Keep cooler in the summer by drawing the shades on sunniest side of house to block sunlight and heat during the day. Open windows in the evening to let in cooler night air. Conversely, keep the shades open in winter during the day for added solar heat.

❑ If your gas-powered heating unit has a pilot light, call the gas company to have it shut off during the summer months.

❑ Keep your air conditioning unit (if you must have one) clean and in good working order.

❑ Plant trees and shrubs around the perimeter of your house to provide shade, which cools the house in summer months.

❑ Light colored exterior walls will reflect heat away from the house.

❑ Consider a solar greenhouse that can offer all the benefits of heating a room with almost none of the heating costs. Be sure to have a way to cut the room off from the rest of the house when it gets dark and cools down later in the day.

Stop & think

What if we could find a way to harness all the energy we create at the gym when we're running on treadmills and peddling stationary bikes to power electrical appliances?

Kitchen

Our kitchens are home to some of the biggest energy wasters in our homes. We can greatly decrease our energy load by purchasing more efficient appliances and using these tips to reduce usage.

❑ Move the fridge away from stove and also keep it a few inches away from the wall, so it doesn't overheat and run more often. Keep the condenser coils on the back dust-free by vacuuming them at least once a year.

❑ Switch to bottom drawer freezers, which are more energy efficient than side-by-side models.

❑ Think about trading in your old fridge for a newer, more energy-efficient model. Only purchase appliances with the Energy Star label: they adhere to strict energy efficiency guidelines.

❑ Consider buying a smaller refrigerator. If you live alone, is there really any reason to buy a full-sized unit? Using a smaller unit will help condition you to buy fresher food more often.

❑ Fill freezers and fridges with filled water jugs, sugar and flour containers, or bottles of alcohol. A full fridge runs more effectively and loses less cold air when the door is opened.

❑ Make sure the door gasket seals tightly. Place a dollar bill between the door and the unit. Close the door and try to remove the bill. If it pulls free easily, you may need to replace the gasket. Test several places along the door.

❑ Set the fridge between 37 °F and 40 °F and the freezer to zero degrees, which should be plenty cold enough.

❑ Allow hot foods and liquids to cool off before covering and placing them in the refrigerator. The moisture released by uncovered warmed containers increases energy use.

❑ Cover the pot when you boil water. The water will get hotter faster.

❑ Unplug appliances when they're not in use. Many electronics, including televisions, continue to use electricity even when they're turned off.

❑ Avoid running appliances during peak hours, between 5 and 9 a.m. and 4 and 7 p.m., especially during summer months.

❑ Save energy by only washing full loads in the dishwasher and washing machine.

❑ Wash your clothes in cold water.

❑ Let your dishes air-dry. A dishwasher uses more energy to dry dishes than to wash them. If the dishwasher doesn't have an automatic air-dry switch, turn the unit off after the final rinse and prop the door open to let moisture escape. Ventilate the kitchen to dissipate dishwashing detergent fumes.

Lighting

Twenty-five percent of electricity consumed in the U.S. is used for lighting. Half of that is being wasted every day.

❑ Turn off the lights. It's a mantra Mom and Dad have repeated since before we were tall enough to reach the light switch. There's a good reason for it.

❑ Maximize the daylight. Open the shades on a sunny day to let the sunshine in. Go outside and read during the day.

❑ Use task-oriented lighting. Instead of lighting an entire room, set up lamps to focus on what you're doing where you're sitting.

❑ Switch to compact fluorescent bulbs that use a quarter the energy of incandescent bulbs and last ten to thirteen times longer. Call your utility company to see what kind of incentive they offer to entice customers to replace incandescents with compact fluorescents. Select models that use full spectrum light that mimics sunlight.

❑ Don't forget … candlelight is very sexy.

As if there weren't enough to worry about with the health and safety of our energy choices, how electricity affects our bodies is becoming a major concern. *Electromagnetic fields* (EMFs) are generated by the sun, moon, and planets. Our bodies naturally adapt to the earth's EMF (7.83 Hertz), but when electricity became common in our homes, humans suddenly became exposed to an almost constant current of 60 Hz. EMF now refers to the low-frequency fields derived from use of electric power.

On the other hand

EMF is not the same as the radio frequency (RF) waves (at 3 MHz to 300 GHz) produced by such sources as radar, microwave ovens, cell phones, and radio and television broadcasting, which can also be controversial. Some believe these RF waves can lead to an increased risk of brain tumors and suppressed immune function, but no long-term studies have been done.

Anything that carries an electrical current has an EMF that produces invisible rays; anything with a transponder will have higher levels. This includes all electronics (television sets, VCRs, cable boxes, stereos, computer monitors and terminals) and appliances (alarm clocks, dishwashers, hair dryers [literally a ray gun pointed at our heads], microwave ovens, and electric blankets). Airplanes keep us captive in a vessel with readings up to 30 mG (milligauss) and sensor activated security gates at retail stores can have readings over 100 mG. The walls in our homes are filled with electrical wires and a source of high EMFs is found in "askew" buildings, as a result of faulty grounding and wiring. EMFs are also emitted from high-tension power lines that criss-cross above our heads, electrical line transformers, and electrical power stations.

Scientists feel that exposure to EMFs at a level of less than 3 mG is safe, but extremely high levels of EMFs are possible human carcinogens, notably a leukemia risk for children. It's beginning to be discovered that EMFs also interfere with the body's own electrical-magnetic field (our aura), creating tenseness and irritability. Positive ion environments cause tiredness, foggy-headedness, depression, and a disruption to our immune systems. Could our desire for everything electric and the accompanying EMFs have anything to do with why we feel the need to rush all the time?

Hope for the Future

❑ Live unplugged. When there's a choice, use a non-electric appliance: can opener, mixer, blanket, hair dryer, or leaf blower. Switch to solar or battery powered appliances. Remember that manual powered is also usually quieter than the electric version.

❏ A tip for those with VCRs and DVRs, as long as your cable or antenna is routed through the VCR, the television does not need to be plugged in to be able to record programming. Unplug the television for all times when you aren't watching it, to save electricity and eliminate electromagnetic fields. (It will also allow you to fast forward through all those commercials too.)

❏ Avoid using electric products, such as an electric blanket or a heating pad, that come in direct contact with your body for extended periods of time. Pregnant women should never use these products.

❏ Don't stand so close to me. Move away from the source of EMF and unplug it when you're finished. Put the alarm clock and the humidifier further away from your head when you sleep and stand back from the microwave when cooking.

❏ Use an EMF blocking screen for computer monitors, available from office supply stores. (This is not necessary for laptops or flat screen LCD displays.)

❏ Buy or rent a gaussmeter, a device that measures the amount of EMFs emanating from electrical appliances. Though scientists have deemed levels of less than 3 mG safe,[47] common appliances commonly emit much higher levels. Tube televisions and computer monitors give readings of 30 mG directly in front, but readings are well over 100 mG in back where the tubes are. Dishwashers can emit over 100 mG when running, 50 mG when off. The microwave oven is too high to register a reading when on, but levels drop to 50 mG at two feet, then 1 mG at six feet.

❏ Get a negative ion generator. Ionizers emit negative ions to counteract positive ions given off by electrical appliances, static from synthetic clothes, smoking, and polluted, dry, dusty air. Models are now reasonably priced and available for the home, office, car, or even to wear on your person. There are also combination units that feature other air purifying options.

4. CHEMICALS: Toxic Compounds in Our Environment

Our air, water, and environment are filled with a variety of toxic elements—some are naturally occurring, but many were not even in existence before World War II. It's these chemicals and heavy metals that are to blame for many of the health and ecological problems we face today.

The most frightening collision between health and ecology could be the staggering rise in hormone disruption. Hormones tell the body what to do and when to do it. *Hormone disrupters* (also called endocrine disrupters) are chemicals that can mimic human or animal hormones, the messengers created by glands to control their many functions.

Chemical disrupters enter the body in minute amounts via contaminated water and food. Once they're in the bloodstream, hormone disrupters behave like imposter hormones and deliver false messages to our cells. These imposters cause things to happen when they shouldn't; at the same time, things that should be happening, don't. Where hormone disrupters are concerned, the amount of chemical is not always really "important," and sometimes a higher dose will produce less of an effect.

Xenoestrogens are chemicals that mimic estrogen—a group of fifty-one synthetic chemicals that include not only polychlorinated biphenyls, dioxin, and DDT, but also organic heavy metals, such as mercury, lead, cadmium, and arsenic. These xenoestrogens are found in plastics (PVC and Polystyrene), canned goods (metal cans lined with plastic to prevent a metallic taste from leaching into food), detergent breakdown, and in meat and poultry (from hormones fed to animals).

The people most at risk for harm caused by hormone disrupters are those who work in the production of chemicals or live in neighborhoods surrounding incinerators or hazardous waste landfills and firefighters who brave toxic fires. But no one is safe. Death is slow, invisible, and indirect. Although chemicals can trigger hormonal cancers, such as prostate and breast, it is, sadly, our obsession with cancer that can blind us to these other dangers of hormone disrupters, which can also:

  ✓ Affect our hormonal systems by blocking receptors and alter hormone receptor levels.
  ✓ Cause premature puberty. Grammar school-aged girls develop breasts, boys grow mustaches.
  ✓ Lower sperm counts.
  ✓ Increase the number of males who have higher estrogen levels.
  ✓ Cause underdeveloped and deformed sex organs and hermaphroditic qualities.
  ✓ Cause sterility.
  ✓ Mimic the effects of natural hormones.
  ✓ React directly and indirectly with natural hormones.
  ✓ Alter natural patterns of synthesis of hormones.
  ✓ Cause developmental damage such as learning disabilities and attention deficits (ADHD).

Let's focus on just four persistent bioaccumulative toxins that happen to be four of the most dangerous substances on earth. Two are manmade: dioxin and polychlorinated biphenyls (PCBs). Two are organic: mercury and lead.

Dioxin is frequently referred to as the most toxic chemical known. The FDA has considered no amount safe, and in fact, an amount of dioxin the size of a fist is toxic enough to kill every person on earth.

Dioxin is not a single substance but actually seventy-five chlorine-containing chemical compounds that are not created intentionally, but as a byproduct of chlorine-based industries, such as pesticide manufacturing and using chlorine to bleach paper. Dioxin can leach from bleached papers: from coffee filters into coffee, from tea bags into tea, from diapers and tampons, from milk cartons into milk, and from paper trays into microwaved food. It is also found in some deodorants and antibacterial soaps.

A minimal amount of dioxin is created by naturally by volcanoes and forest fires, but burning of fossil fuels and incinerating trash that contains plastic and paper also releases dioxin. Toxicity is also a result of activities such as preserving wood, refining oil, and smelting metals. Agent Orange, a defoliant widely used by the U.S. armed forces during the Vietnam War, exported dioxin to the far reaches of the globe.

Dioxin is a bioaccumulative toxin. That means it is passed up the food chain and stored in the fat cells of every organism that ingests it. It's both lipophilic (fat loving) and hydrophobic (water hating) and it doesn't readily break down. Dioxin has been detected in almost every person tested and in every location on earth, including members of Inuit tribes who live thousands of miles from anything we would call civilization and have probably never seen antibacterial soap or a coffee filter. But wait—dioxin is not just a hormone disrupter. It's also a known carcinogen that affects immunity and causes liver damage, weight loss, and skin disfiguration.

Hope for the Future
- ❑ Call manufacturers and ask if they use chlorine to bleach their products. Purchase products that have not been bleached with chlorine.
- ❑ Use cleaning products that do not contain chlorine. Hydrogen peroxide is a safer alternative.
- ❑ Call for a worldwide ban on chemicals known to disrupt hormonal systems.
- ❑ While the EPA may not be perfect, it is still our government environmental watchdog. Our taxes support EPA research and programs. Use the following phone numbers to get in touch with the EPA:
    - ✓ Indoor Air Quality Information Clearinghouse (800) 438-4318
    - ✓ Safe Drinking Water Hotline (800) 426-4791

The EPA's Food Quality Protection Act and Safe Drinking Water Act requires the EPA to "develop measures designed to test chemicals for endocrine effects." The EPA also maintains the Toxics Release Inventory, an online database (www.epa.gov/tri) that anyone can access for information about chemicals flowing into the air, water and land in any community. See also www.epa.gov for listings of local EPA offices.

Thank you, President Nixon

Presidential Aide John Ehrlichman explained that Nixon only created the Environmental Protection Agency because he assumed Ed Muskie, who lobbied for clean air and water, would be his main opponent in the presidential race of 1972. Nixon saw the 20 million Earth Day participants as a group of voters he didn't want to take a chance on.[48] Despite this public show of support for the environment, however, Nixon still kept the air-conditioning turned up in the Oval Office so that he could have a fire going year round.

Our next toxic bad ass: *Polychlorinated Biphenyls* (PCBs) were introduced in 1929 and soon became a family of 209 chemicals. By the time they were banned in 1976, 3.4 billion pounds had been produced.[49] PCBs were mainly used for industrial purposes: plasticizers, fire-retardants, insulating electrical transformers, and in the production of lubricants, hydraulic fluids, cutting oils, and liquid seals. Some were used for household products: to make wood and plastic nonflammable, to preserve rubber. They were added to paints, varnishes, inks, and pesticides. From 1957 to 1971, manufacturers put PCBs in carbonless carbon paper. Like dioxin, PCBs disrupt hormone systems, cause reproductive problems, and have been found to cause cancer in laboratory animals.

PCBs are truly "the thing that would not die." They are nonflammable, very stable, and don't test as toxic. These persistent "hand-me-down poisons" can be absorbed through the skin and drawn into fat. They are not excreted, and when an animal is eaten by another or when a body decomposes, PCB molecules remain attached to cells and travel with the cells wherever they go next. Levels remain high at the top of the food chain (in humans) because PCBs do not dissolve readily in water and resist the bacteria that break down most chemicals.

Hope for the Future

- [ ] The ban on PCB production was a start, but it's easy to see that because they don't break down they will continue to be a problem well into the future.
- [ ] Be careful if you work in an older industrial building. Seek professional help in disposing of transformers and old files that may contain carbon paper.
- [ ] Avoid eating contaminated fish. See the *Eating* chapter, page 166, for tips on finding healthier seafood.
- [ ] Start taxing "bad" things. Taxes are levied, which places a burden on the taxpayers, to clean up water supplies and public lands after polluting companies are often absolved from total responsibility. We can counter this trend with tax breaks for companies that work for sustainability. Much like a luxury tax, higher taxes can be

placed on products and services that cause environmental or health degradation. Cigarettes and gasoline are already taxed, but companies that pollute the environment and deplete resources should pay for the cost of cleaning up their messes.

Mercury is a persistent heavy metal and potent neurotoxin that accumulates in water and in the tissues of humans, fish, and animals and causes nerve, memory, and motor problems. It takes only one gram of mercury to contaminate all the fish in a twenty-acre lake. According to the Agency for Toxic Substances and Disease Registry, "exposure to excessive levels of elemental (metallic), inorganic or organic mercury can permanently damage the brain and kidneys of people of all ages and interfere with fetal development."[50] Insomnia, loss of appetite, fatigue, changes in behavior, muscle tremors, blindness, weakness, and weight loss are additional symptoms of repeated exposure to mercury.

Mercury was declared a hazardous pollutant by the EPA in 1971 and is slowly being phased out of many commercial uses. Nevertheless, every year, 4.3 tons of mercury is used to make thermometers sold to consumers and hospitals. But this is only one percent of the total mercury used in the U.S. The greatest amount of mercury is currently used for industrial switches. It's also used in many industrial processes and included in such products as fluorescent lights, home and appliance thermostats, weed killers, fungicides (a 1990 ban on fungicides reduced mercury in latex paint), computer components, laser and copier toner, and in the manufacture of some glassware and jewelry, notably the processing of gold and silver. Mercury is also released when coal is burned by electric utilities.

Despite all the dangers of mercury, the American Dental Association (ADA) still denies that there is any risk from using dental amalgam (a mixture of metals dissolved with mercury). The association only admits that an adverse reaction to dental mercury use is confined to "a very small number of people" who are allergic to amalgam fillings.[51]

Hope for the Future
❑ Look for alternatives to products such as pesticides, wood preservatives, flu shots, and contact lens solutions that contain mercury derived ingredients with the aliases: thimerosal, methylmercury, phenylmercuric acetate or nitrate, pentachlorophenol, methiolate, mersalys, mertiolate, mercumatilin, mercuramide, mercurophylline, mercaptomerin, merethoxylline, merbromin, mercurius, formalin, and chlorhexidine.

❑ Look for the car companies, including Volvo, who have phased out mercury use. Most have not. Cars manufactured before 2003 most likely contain mercury switches.

❑ Switch to digital thermometers and dispose of mercury thermometers as hazardous waste. California has banned the sale and manufacture of mercury fever thermometers in an effort to lower the amount of disposed mercury.

❑ Ask for non-mercury fillings when having dental work done. Older fillings can be replaced if you feel they are affecting your health.

❑ Properly recycle compact fluorescent light bulbs (which contain mercury) as hazardous waste.

Lead, which has been used for millennia, is a basic element that is malleable, resists corrosion, and cannot be destroyed. Lead remains in the environment or is absorbed through skin and lungs. Once in the body, it will accumulate in the bones or brain over time. Baby teeth have been used to determine how much lead children were formerly exposed to. Children with higher exposures to lead are more likely to suffer from behavioral abnormalities such as hyperactivity, attention deficit disorder, to engage in violent and delinquent behavior, and to have impaired mental development and lower intelligence.

Long-term lead exposure can lead to kidney cancer, nerve damage, paralysis, and reproductive system impairment and miscarriages. Brain damage can be severe and permanent. It's coupled with hallucinations, tremors, insanity, and death. Lesser symptoms include headaches, abdominal pain, weight loss, muscle weakness, lethargy, leg cramps, numbness, photosensitivity, anemia, and depression.

Lead-based paint was banned in the U.S. in 1978, but millions of tons of lead paint probably remain on the walls of homes built before this date. The soil and water around homes that contain or once contained lead paint can also be contaminated. Some lead paint was used on antique dishware, some lead inks were used on bread bags.

We are also exposed to lead from tobacco smoke (and smokers ingest 25 percent more smoke than nonsmokers). Lead is also used in car batteries, X-ray and radiation shielding, computer components, some craft and art supplies, leaded crystal, and certain hair dyes. Lead chromate is used as a pigment in plastics, and lead oxide is used as a catalyst in the polymerization of PET, a common plastic.

Lead was added to gasoline in 1922 to raise the compression and power of the internal combustion engine. By the mid-1970s, 90 percent of gasoline contained lead. During the sixty years that leaded gasoline was used in U.S., thirty million tons of lead was released from exhaust pipes, leaching into the ground or evaporating into the air. It's estimated that five million tons of lead remains in the soil near busy roadways.[52]

Follow these tips to reduce your chances of lead poisoning:

- Run water through faucets for at least a minute if it has been sitting in the pipes overnight or longer. (Don't forget to reuse that water for flushing.)
- Test water and soil with inexpensive kits found in hardware stores. They are not always 100 percent accurate but can give a ballpark estimate of lead contamination.
- Get a simple blood test, which can tell if your body has high levels of lead.
- Lobby for a global ban on leaded gasoline. In 1986, when the U.S. banned leaded gasoline, lead levels in blood fell by 80 percent almost immediately.[53] Focus on the following countries, which have no set plan to ban lead: Nigeria, Saudi Arabia, Venezuela, South Africa, Indonesia, Iraq, Libya, Algeria, Iran, Kuwait, Turkey, United Arab Emirates, Syria, Israel, and Malaysia.
- Check your china. Antique dishware could be coated in paints or glazes that contain lead. To check your pattern, the Environmental Defense Fund has compiled a list of china patterns with low-levels of lead that can be found online at www.environmentaldefense.org/documents/994_LeadChina4.htm.
- Keep an eye on the Golden State. In 1986, California passed Proposition 65, The Safe Drinking Water and Toxic Enforcement Act (commonly known as the Green Labeling Law). If a product or facility contains more than a set limit of a chemical known to cause cancer (including lead), birth defects, or reproductive harm, it must be labeled. This shifts the burden of proof from the user of the product to its manufacturer. There remains some debate that the standard levels for some chemicals are too low and some federal legislature supercedes local laws. There are currently over 550 chemicals on a list that's updated once a year.

Thinking outside the box: Leading the way in destruction and restoration

Being the sixth largest economy in the world and representing 15 percent of the U.S. marketplace, California is a trendsetter for the rest of the country, if not the world. Problems arise in California, usually more quickly, including running out of resources first. Laws established in California have caused companies to reevaluate and reformulate products to meet the state's requirements and sell the new versions to the entire country, rather than deal with different models of the same product. California was first to impose automobile emission standards, the first to have an air pollution control agency, and the first to test car engines on a regular basis.

Plastics

> Mr. McGuire: I just want to say one
> word to you ... just one word."
> Benjamin: Yes sir.
> Mr. McGuire: Are you listening?
> Benjamin: Yes sir, I am
> Mr. McGuire: Plastics.
> –Buck Henry /
> Calder Willingham,
> *The Graduate* (1967)

When we think of the "oil crisis," most of us think no further than how close to $4 a gallon we have to pay for gasoline at the pump. We sit and express our hatred for atrocities in the Middle East, but we rarely connect the oil crisis to petroleum's hundreds of additional uses. Ten percent of crude oil goes to manufacture "ordinary consumer goods" such as medications like aspirin.

Petroleum-based products	
Videotape	Polyester fabrics
Pesticides	Carpets
Floor wax	Rubber boots
Crayons	Paint
Shoe polish	Ink
Golf balls	Contact lenses
Vitamins	Cosmetics, including perfume, shaving cream, deodorant, nail polish, toothpaste

There's no doubt that plastics have saved millions of lives and made our existence easier and more convenient. They are used for practically everything and have easily replaced many safer materials (specifically glass). Plastic has been good to us: bulletproof vests, medical supplies, and lightweight containers for food products that reduce weight and size of packaging and lower transportation costs.

Plastics have revolutionized our world. But will they also destroy it? Problems can exist at every phase of a plastic product's life: with the chemicals and nonrenewable petroleum used in manufacturing, in off-gassing fumes after production, in its poor ability to biodegrade in landfills, in the release of toxins if plastic is incinerated.

Of the two types of plastics, 80 percent are thermoplastics, or soft bendable plastics.

Thermoplastics tend to cause vapors when heated (like in a microwave) and give off volatile organic chemicals that pollute our air. Thermoplastics include PVC, PP, polyethylene, acrylics, nylon, polystyrene (the new "Styrofoam"), polycarbonate, polyvinyl butyl, and cellulose. These plastics can be melted down to be recycled, but not completely.

PVC

Polyvinyl chloride (PVC) is the soft plastic being blamed for the abundance of phthalates (softeners that make the rigid, flexible) in our environment. PVC is used to make pipes for plumbing, shower curtains, wall coverings, siding, windows, doors, furniture, and plastic bottles. It's also found in certain cosmetics, such as nail enamels, and often used as a plasticizer to make food wrapping, which can leach into products from packaging. PVC is often used to make infant and pet soft chew toys.

When PVC is burned, it creates dioxin. Off-gassing fumes from new products can cause environmental illness and symptoms of multiple chemical sensitivity (see *Healing*, page 224). Prolonged exposure has caused tumors in rats.

With the growing awareness of the dangers of PVCs, many companies (and European countries) are phasing out their use in construction. Avoid products with the "3" recycling symbol and choose a non-plastic alternative instead.

The second type of plastics is thermosets (rigid plastics), which, once hardened, cannot be softened. Since thermosets cannot be vaporized, even at extremely high temperatures, they are generally regarded as safer than thermoplastics. The two exceptions are urea-formaldehyde resins and polyurethane foam, which off-gas and contribute to upper respiratory problems and allergic reactions. Other thermosets include phenolics (Bakelite, of which the handles of pots and pans are made), polyesters, and silicones.

Plastics are thus problematic from creation to disposal. The worldwide process of making 70,000 manmade chemicals from nonrenewable fossil fuels contributes greatly to air pollution. When companies use cheaper materials to create cheaper products, this often causes the product to lose function quicker; we are forced to dispose of them and buy new ones. We justify purchasing products in plastic packaging with the theory that they can be recycled, but plastics are seldom recycled and, unfortunately, won't biodegrade within any reasonable span of time. When plastics are buried, they can last for hundreds of years.

Eventually, somewhere in the distant future, that plastic bottle will break down into plastic chunks. Though the plastic may get smaller, it will always continue to exist. If pieces of plastic end up in streams or the ocean, they can harm marine life. Fish commonly get stuck in six pack yokes and turtles and sea birds mistake small chunks of Styrofoam for food, which when ingested makes them float.

The incineration of plastics can emit toxic chemicals like hydrochloric acid and the toxic metals that were added to give color or rigidity to the plastic. Thousands of Americans are killed each year as a result of inhalation of toxic smoke created by burning plastics in fires in homes and commercial buildings.

Hope for the Future

I love my yoga mat, my running shoes, and the hard plastic bumper on my car. Plastics are an indispensable part of our society, and, yes, they've made our lives simpler. Eliminating all plastic from our lives is virtually impossible; it's something even the most hard-core environmentalist would have difficulty implementing. But we can learn to pick our plastics wisely and not abuse them for our convenience. Follow these tips for reasonable use of plastics:

❑ Lower your exposure. The only way to fully protect ourselves from the dangers of toxins is to not be exposed to them. When shopping, always ask, *Could I find this product in a non-plastic version?* and *Where will that plastic product go when I'm not using it anymore?*

❑ Try to reuse and recycle if the plastic version is the only option.

❑ Purchase appliances that use minimal amounts of plastic.

❑ Look for alternatives to petrochemical plastics by seeking out plastics made by ingenious companies that use plant products such as glucose from corn (a fiber called Ingeo) or algae to create a foam fiber.

5. DEFORESTATION: It's Time We Start Seeing the Forest for the Trees

Each year of its life, a single tree can absorb fifteen to twenty-five pounds of carbon dioxide while at the same time releasing oxygen. It can remove 1.5 pounds of dust, soot, and smoke from the air and remove nitrogen and phosphorus compounds from groundwater. Tree roots in forested areas control flooding by maintaining soil structure and increase water evaporation by drinking water up from the soil. Branches and leaves tame winds with a drag effect. Trees create cooler air by making shade and increasing humidity.

To counteract the climate problems we face, we must fight deforestation, which is more than just rainforest destruction or removal of old growth forests. *Sprawl* also leads to deforestation. The main cause of pollution in the twentieth century has been industrialization, and with industrialization comes the need to cover as much free space as possible. Factories and automobiles contribute to pollution we can see, smell, and taste, but every year, more trees are taken down to make way for another big box store, super highway, or suburban subdivision. Seven thousand acres of land are lost to sprawl every year, totaling well over 50,000 square miles since 1970.[54]

How much for a book of stamps?!?

Do you wonder why first class postal rates have risen by almost thirty cents in last thirty years? An ex-postmaster general explains that the increase goes to supplement the cost of fuel needed to transport mail through rain, snow, sleet, and hail to the widening suburban fringe.

We want everything we could possibly ever need to fall within convenient distance. A handy "shopping sphere" that surrounds us. One edge is our home, another, our work, another, our gym, grocery store, and shopping center. As these places move further away from one another, the sphere gets larger and we become more dependent on our cars. Crime and urban development have pushed many people out to the suburbs in search of safety and quiet. We commute back to the city for work, spending more time, money and gas on traveling. With monopolistic practices of the big box stores that force smaller competitors out of business, we are forced to drive even further to get to our one-stop shopping.

Many of us don't think about sprawl until it hits us where we live. We love the convenience of that one-stop shopping. (Cat litter, prescription medication and snow tires, all at rock bottom prices—all in one handy location!) But move that wholesale club store into our personal sphere, and suddenly our claws are out. No one wants sprawl in their own backyard.

Sprawl gives a false sense of economic recovery. When the discount mass merchandiser swoops into your town with its big box, they try to give the illusion of an economic upswing. Consumers are lured by the convenience of one-stop shopping rather than stopping at several at local merchants. Big box retailers promise new jobs but neglect to acknowledge jobs that will be lost when they drive local businesses to close.

Sprawl creates a myriad of ecological problems. When it rains, rainfall runs off the sprawling pavement into sewers that drain back to rivers, lakes, or the ocean, where it becomes salt water. Asphalt suffocates the soil, preventing air from connecting with organisms that live in the earth. Quarrying takes millions of tons of stone to create the raw materials used for the buildings and roads of our urban paradise.

Aesthetically speaking, sprawl eliminates the creativity in architectural design. A plan (or formula) for a shopping district often duplicates previous designs for brand standard and ease in construction. Once you're within the confines of a shopping mall fortress, you can't tell whether you're in Boise or Boston. Stores in chains or franchises are cookie-cutter replicas of all the others because individual expression is not part of "brand standard." Rarely can a small local business afford the overhead in a new mall, so they are usually relegated to an impermanent kiosk amid foot traffic where potential customers stopping to browse run the risk of being run over by shoppers on their way to another Ubiquitous Mall Store.

As we clear the land to build more malls and boxes, we lose natural habitats, open space, unique natural areas, and historic commercial centers. Developers cleverly name these malls "Village," "Commons," or "Square" to evoke the olden days and help compensate for the lack of remaining outdoor historic public spaces.

On the other hand: What vitalizes cities?

✓ Community
✓ Safety
✓ Sense of pride and belonging
✓ Respect for heritage
✓ Bringing back local government to make local decisions
✓ Bringing back conversation between residents

To get out of the mall, follow these tips:

❑ Chat with friends and neighbors about shopping at local, possibly historic, businesses to keep money in your community.
❑ Encourage local organizations and businesses to buy locally.
❑ Talk with local business owners and find out what their challenges are and how you can help them.
❑ Organize against sprawl and advocate for new legislation. Keep an eye on your Chamber of Commerce.

Thinking outside the box: Sprawl-Busters

"Your quality of life is worth more than a cheap pair of underwear."[55]

There may be over 6,000 Wal-Marts worldwide, but Al Norman is still ready to fight against the one coming to your town. He doesn't even need a Wal-Mart to get him riled up. He'll take on a Home Depot, a Target, or any other big box developer, any day of the week. Maybe it's because he's from New England, where he's seen quite a few casualties to the Wal-Mart takeover. (Anyone remember Ames, Caldor, Zayres, or Bradlees?) Any unwanted development, he's the guy to call. For tips on how to start your own grass roots campaign against the big boxes, see www.sprawl-busters.com and Al's book *Slam Dunking Wal-Mart*.

Another eco-victim of our need for progress has been *old growth forests*. This is an ecosystem that's never been cut and provides a habitat for trees of different ages. The importance of old-growth forests is, however, more than just saving endangered species like the spotted owl or marbled murrelet. Like the rainforest, the old-growth forest creates a unique ecosystem that may not exist anywhere else on the planet.

Like every forest, old-growth root systems maintain the shape of the soil, creating a web that prevents flooding and soil erosion. Tree roots also help absorb pollutants before they enter water and run off into lakes and rivers. But over 78 percent of the earth's original old-growth forests have already been logged. Many foresters are trying to practice "sustainable yield" by not cutting more than can be regrown, but while replacement forests do provide some benefits, they are often planted in industrial-sized evenly spaced rows, which reduces their ability to most effectively sustain a biologically diverse ecosystem.

The *rainforests* are "nature's green lungs" and the earth's oldest living ecosystems. Despite their longevity and all that's been written about the attempt to protect them, rainforests are still being destroyed at a staggering rate. As vegetation is cut or burned, vast reserves of carbon are released into the atmosphere as carbon dioxide, the second largest contributor to the greenhouse effect. According to the National Academy of Science, at least fifty million acres a year are destroyed by indigenous people who cut down trees so that they can plant crops, by ranchers who cut sections to provide grazing areas for their cattle (which become our steaks and Big Macs), by oil and mining companies who cut to locate nonrenewable reserves, and by logging companies for building materials and paper products.[56]

But when left intact, the reason these forests work so efficiently is because they are self-contained ecosystems. Plants store nutrients in their roots rather than in the soil, so removing trees removes critical nourishment for the forest. High temperatures also help naturally decompose matter within six weeks, quickly recycling it for use by new organisms.

Rainforests are both compact and diverse—they may contain more species, but fewer individuals of each, making each critter particularly vulnerable to extinction. The destruction of an entire population creates a ripple effect for other, dependent species. It doesn't take the loss of very many individuals to devastate an entire population or to scatter it so thinly that individuals can no longer find each other to reproduce.

Though they may be thousands of miles away from where we live, rainforests are nonetheless part of our daily lives. Foods such as bananas, chocolate, coffee, cola, tomatoes, and sugar and spices such as vanilla, ginger, cinnamon, cloves, black, cayenne, chili pepper, allspice, and cardamom all grow in the rainforest. Commonly used woods from rainforests include teak, balsa, mahogany, sandalwood, and rosewood. One quarter of the medicines available today owe their existence to rainforest plants. The National Cancer Institute states that 70 percent of plants useful in cancer treatment are found only in the rainforest. We get fibers such as bamboo, kenaf, kapok, and rattan from rainforests.[57] Careful and sustainable harvesting can protect the rainforest and still yield products our culture wants.

Although they cover only 2 percent of the earth's surface (6 percent of its land mass), rainforests house over half of the world's plant and animal species. According to the Rainforest Action Network, a typical four square mile patch of rainforest contains as many as 1,500 species of flowering plants, 750 species of trees, 125 mammal species, 400 species of birds, 100 species of reptiles, 60 species of amphibians, and 150 different species of butterflies.[58]

Other Examples of Deforestation
- ✓ *Mangroves* are coastal forests whose webs of tree roots act like sponges, soaking up excess rain and snow that would otherwise cause flooding and erosion. These web roots also strain nutrients and filter out contaminants before the water reaches lakes and rivers. Protecting mangroves preserves a sheltered natural habitat for indigenous plant, animal, fish, bird, and reptile species.
- ✓ Inland *wetlands* like the Florida Everglades are also an important part of the world's ecosystem. Half of the world's wetlands have been lost over the last century, mostly as a result of developers that rank the bottom line as more important than the species that inhabit these areas.
- ✓ *Coral reefs* are the ocean's rainforests. They contain microscopic plants that provide fish and ocean mammals with food and give them their vibrant colors. The greenhouse effect has raised ocean temperatures, resulting in coral bleaching, which damages or kills entire reef systems. More than just a source of income for tourism and fishing industries, coral systems protect coastal areas from extreme weather events. They are also being studied to find ingredients for new medications.

Hope for the Future

The first step in preventing deforestation is to learn about forests and think about the world beyond our backyards. Knowledge of how ecosystems work makes us more conscious of the decisions we make that affect them. Although a coral reef may be thousands of miles away in one direction, a rainforest thousands of miles away in another, and the old growth forest three states over, their survival still has a daily effect on all of us. To help protect the forests, follow these tips:

- ❑ Minimize paper and wood consumption. If possible, use tree-free paper alternatives like kenaf and hemp, where not a single tree is cut down for production.
- ❑ Reduce (and recycle) aluminum, which requires mining bauxite from rainforests.

Aluminum

Aluminum is used for more than just cans and foil. It's an ingredient in personal care products such as antiperspirants, toothpaste, and antacids. It's used as an anti-caking or bleaching agent in everyday foods such as salt, processed cheese, pickles, bleached flour, and baking powder. In large quantities, aluminum can be toxic; it attacks the kidneys and brain. Autopsies of the brain cells of some, but not all, Alzheimer's patients have found increased concentrations of aluminum.[59]

- ❑ Reduce beef consumption. Beef used for fast food hamburgers or processed beef products is not typically labeled with country of origin. It's likely to come from cattle raised on land that used to be a rainforest.
- ❑ Hold corporations accountable for socially and environmentally destructive business practices. Write, call, or e-mail corporations about important issues. Boycott their products.
- ❑ Invest in and support rainforest communities, organizations, and grassroots efforts. The Rainforest Action Network's "Protect-an-Acre Program" supports the rights of rainforest communities, protecting both their livelihood and their environment.
- ❑ Choose products bearing the Forest Stewardship Counsel (www.FSCUS.org) or Smart Wood label, which are certified to be harvested sustainably from managed forests with strict environmental, social and economic standards.
- ❑ Shop for shrimp and shellfish that are sustainably raised and harvested. Shrimp and shellfish farming destroy mangrove forests and it takes about 2 pounds of wild fish to grow one pound of farmed shrimp.[60]
- ❑ Ask questions. We can avoid illegal trade that leads to endangered species and extinction by asking storeowners if the plants and animals they sell were taken from the wild.
- ❑ Learn to respect the earth and understand nature. Don't just think about just your immediate family, think about other cultures and other species. Think about the future and how the next generation will have to live. The more of the planet and the environment we destroy, the less choice our descendants will have in how they exist. Search for your own profound connection.

The connection between the air, water, energy, chemicals and deforestation cannot be ignored: harm one, the others will suffer as well. Balancing our effect on the environment is critical. We can keep the style of life we are accustomed to and save the planet, but only with major renovations to how we create and consume products.

Do it today

Step up your conservation efforts by being mindful of your ecological impact. Keep your water and electricity use to a bare minimum today.

ADDITIONAL RESOURCES

SOLUTION-ORIENTED READING

Barlow, Maude and Tony Clarke. *Blue Gold: The Fight to Stop the Corporate Theft of the World's Water.* New York: The New Press, 2002.

Colborn, Theo, et al. *Our Stolen Future: Are We Threatening Our Fertility, Intelligence, and Survival? A Scientific Detective Story.* New York: Dutton Books, 1996.

Davis, Devra. *When Smoke Ran Like Water: Tales of Environmental Deception and the Battle Against Pollution.* New York: Basic Books, 2002.

Fagin, Dan, et al. *Toxic Deception.* Secaucus, NJ: Birch Lane Press, 1996.

Hayes, Denis. *The Official Earth Day Guide to Planet Repair.* Washington D.C.: Island Press, 2000. Offers solutions to help save the planet. Written by the chairman and CEO of Earth Day.

Hill, Julia Butterfly. *The Legacy of Luna.* San Francisco: HarperCollins, 2000. A young woman shows the power of determination by spending two years in a redwood tree to save it from logging company.

Lughole, Jeffrey, PhD, and Kelly Turner. *You Can Prevent Global Warming (and Save Money!): 51 Easy Ways.* Kansas City, MO: Andrews McMeel Publishing, 2003.

Marks, William E. *The Holy Order of Water: Healing Earth's Waters and Ourselves.* Great Barrington, MA: Bell Pond Books, 2001.

McKibben, Bill. *The End of Nature.* New York: Doubleday, 1989.
_____. *Hope, Human and Wild: True Stories of Living Lightly on the Earth.* Boston: Little, Brown and Co., 1995.
_____. *Deep Economy: The Wealth of Communities and The Durable Future.* New York: Times Books, 2007.

Schildgen, Bob. *Hey Mr. Green: Sierra Magazine's Answer Guy Tackles Your Toughest Green Living Questions.* San Francisco: Sierra Club Books, 2008.

Schumacher, E.F. *Small is Beautiful: Economics as if People Mattered (25 Years Later … with Commentaries).* Point Roberts, WA: Hartley & Marks. Originally published in 1973.

Stauber, John C. and John Sheldon. *Toxic Sludge is Good For You!* Monroe, ME: Common Courage Press, 1995.
_____. *Trust Us, We're Experts!* New York: Jeremy P. Tarcher, 2001. The public relations viewpoint on environmental issues.

Williams, Joy. *Ill Nature.* New York, Lyons Press, 2001. "Rants and reflections on humanity and other animals."

The Earth Day Network (www.earthday.net) web site contains links to many other related sites.

The Green Guide (www.thegreenguide.com), once the newsletter of the now defunct Mothers and Others for a Livable Planet, the Guide is now back and filled with product information and advice.

The Environmental Health Sciences publishes *Environmental Health News,* a website about public health and environmental justice. (www.environmentalhealthnews.org)

The Union of Concerned Scientists (www.ucsusa.org) is more than 100,000 scientists and ecologically concerned citizens working together to create a better world.

ENERGY
The State of California (www.consumerenergycenter.org) energy conservation homepage.

Evangelista, Anita. *How to Live Without Electricity and Like It.* Port Townsend, WA: Loompanics Unlimited, 1995. Advice on alternatives to electric heating, cooling, cooking, and lighting. Everyday solutions for those who don't have the patience to deal with maintaining solar panels on their roofs.

DEFORESTATION
The Rainforest Action Network (www.ran.org) organizes and educates to bring the plight of the rainforests and the human rights of those living in and around them to public attention.

Duany, Andres, et al. *Suburban Nation: The Rise of Sprawl and the Decline of the American Dream.* New York: North Point Press, 2000. The authors, owners of a community design firm, explore how sprawl has negatively impacted our communities.

KEEPING A GREEN EYE ON THE GOVERNMENT
The League of Conservation Voters (www.lcv.org) is a national, nonpartisan organization that works to elect environmental candidates into office. Their web site offers a scorecard listing the voting records of Members of Congress on environmental issues and a weekly e-mail update of upcoming votes.

Public Citizen (www.citizen.org), consumer advocate Ralph Nader's citizen watchdog group, has worked since 1971 for government accountability. Their motto: "Protecting Health, Safety and Democracy."

MoveOn.org (www.moveon.org) Don't think your voice matters? Think again. MoveOn is bringing the little guy back to politics. MoveOn tells you who to call, when to call, and even gives you the phone number (they'd probably even dial the phone for you if you asked). Members help by proposing and prioritizing issues and even create their own political action committee.

GETTING INVOLVED
Blaustein, Arthur. *Make a Difference: Your Guide to Volunteering and Community Service.* Berkeley: Heydey Books, 2002. A sourcebook listing over 140 worthy organizations in need of volunteers.

McMillon, Bill. *Volunteer Vacations*. Chicago: Chicago Review Press, 1999. A guidebook featuring hundreds of national and international listings for anyone considering using their time off to assist others. Whether it's working on a railroad in New Mexico, trail building in Alaska, or community development in Belize, adventures usually come with free room and board. Updated regularly, this guide also contains testimonials from former volunteers.

The Center for the New American Dream (www.newdream.org) offers practical tips and resources for making positive changes toward a more fulfilling and sustainable way of life.

The Earthwatch Institute (www.earthwatch.org) creates volunteer programs around the globe focusing on scientific research projects. No previous experience is necessary (except scuba certification for diving projects), but volunteers bring talents such as photography, carpentry, computer skills, teaching, language ability, cooking, or surveying. They'll match your qualifications to a team or train you in the field. The only requirements are flexibility and a sense of humor.

VolunteerMatch is an online agency that can help anyone find their ideal volunteer opportunity (www.volunteermatch.org).

chapter 5

shopping

> The things you own end up owning you.
>
> –Jim Uhls, *Fight Club*
> (spoken by Tyler Durden)

More than anything else, it's our consumption habits that define us as Americans. What is behind the psychology of why we always want to buy something *right now*? Advertisers try to create a need where there really isn't one by convincing us that shopping will to fix everything that's "broken" or "missing" in our lives. We've learned to believe that without purchase of their product or service, we'll feel deficient.

We use shopping in an attempt to move ourselves away from who we truly are. Shopping depersonalizes us. Is the "need" to buy a response to a mediated request? A quest for a status symbol? An extension of power? Next time you go shopping for non-essentials, ask yourself, "Why am I shopping?"

Scary stats

✓ 59 million people in the U.S. are addicted to spending.

✓ 53 percent of all grocery purchases are spur of the moment.

✓ There are more shopping malls than high schools in the U.S.

Shopping gives us a rush. It's the art of the deal and the thrill of acquisition. There's a high from purchasing and ownership. We feel successful when can make a profit by exchange or find a bargain or think we were able to get the better of a company.

Previous purchases soon become stale and boring. We need something new and exciting to entertain us, so we head off in search of new stimuli. There's never a dull moment at the mall. Consumerism provides a continuous stream of products; there's always something new and exciting out there. Companies are always trying to outdo each other with something bigger, better, shinier, and faster. Suddenly, our Diane von Furstenburg wrap dress is several minutes out of style. Off to the mall in search of what the plastic, headless, size zero mannequins are wearing this season. Manufacturers create artificial obsolescence so that they can change styles often and sell more goods.

Shopping becomes the path to the Holy Grail: Coolness. We search and search for that item that will make us stand out and be respected at the same time. We fall victim to false prophets because what Fonzie had is just not available in stores.

We also indulge in sport shopping, a weakness advertisers are happy to exploit. Full-page newspaper ads announce an amazing two-day sale at the local department store, and we immediately get on the phone with friends to arrange an excursion. In the mall—our modern jungle—bargain hunting becomes a true survival skill. If we can manage to sort through the eight pounds of advertisements we receive in the mail each week to find the one store with the lowest price, we deserve that toaster at 25 percent below market value.

Consumption gives us a feeling of accomplishment. Like Mom, who told us to eat our peas or else we wouldn't get dessert, consuming rewards us. According to Erich Fromm, author of *To Have or To Be*, consumption is also a form of ownership. The more one consumes, the more one has, and—as defined by our society—the more we have, the better we are.

The draws of consumerism offer temporary relief from our everyday problems. But it's just that: temporary. The emotions that make us want to spend money? Loneliness. Boredom. Depression. Feeling unloved. Wanting more out of life. We shop to reward ourselves or to bribe others. But shopping as therapy is merely the Band-Aid we put on deeper problems.

Stop & think: Shopping as patriotism? The consumerism of war.

During World War II, propaganda that said, "waste during war is sabotage" covered the country. "Use it up, make it do, or do with out" was born. Citizens were required to ration items from sugar to scrap metal in order to save raw materials for the war effort. Money was invested in war bonds instead of consumer goods. People felt they were an active part of the war as they altered their lives to support America.

Soon after the war ended, everyone was rewarded for their hard work. Within five years, the baby boom had exploded and the suburbs were born. Television—and TV ads—became common, the country prospered and it seemed as if everyone was rich and happy.

This is quite a contrast to our present-day wars, where we're now strongly encouraged (begged) by the government to keep our money circulating when the economy slumps. (Could you imagine our society rationing sugar or gas?) Our most recent wars have occurred when unemployment and underemployment were high. Why should it take a war to produce jobs and spark the economy?

(cont'd)

What is the best way to financially ride out a war? I think it is to live as we should always live: organically, sustainably, with passion and compassion, and most importantly, *simply*. It's easy to feel small and helpless when we're not in the trenches, but don't fall victim to thinking your trip to the mall is going to create an economic stimulus. Americans as a whole are resilient and creative and will survive by any means necessary.

When simplicity takes root in our lives, we discover how much shopping for convenience we really do. How often do we just grab something off the shelf and throw it in the cart instead of even thinking about what we already possess that could do the job? We should realize that purchases do not generate self-esteem. We should remember that the people with the most stuff often don't think very highly of themselves. The costs of these items of instant gratification are longer-term suffering from our accepting of someone else's ideals and losing touch with our own identity.

ADVERTISING

Advertising is a powerful force that permeates everything. Each year, well over $100 billion is spent on advertising in America. This translates to over $500 per target reader or listener, which manifests as the more than 1,500 ad messages we're exposed to every day. Two thirds of newspaper content is advertising. Half the mail we receive wants to sell us something. Outdoor advertising—including billboards, ads painted on the sides of buildings, on the insides (and now even shrink wrapped on the outsides) of buses, on hubcaps, on kiosks, and even as flip book-type moving pictures that we can see as subway cars move through tunnels—is now a $5 billion industry.

On the other hand

Largely due to Lady Bird Johnson's Highway Beautification Act of 1965, four states have banned offsite outdoor billboards: Maine, Vermont, Alaska, and Hawai'i.

Everywhere we look, in almost every corner of free air space, someone is trying to sell us something. Recently, Swiss companies have even taken the bull by the horn (so to speak) and started painting advertisements on the sides of cows. In the 1990s there was discussion that Pepsi would start projecting their logo onto the moon. What happens when this becomes a reality? Will we be subjected to a different ad each night or will it change every thirty seconds? Will ads change with the phases of the moon? And exactly who owns the advertising rights to the moon?

According to ACNielsen, the average American watches more than four hours of television every day, which works out to fifty-two full days a year. That's almost two solid months. Television commercials have become shorter and faster, packing more information into fifteen-second blocks and squeezing in more breaks per hour. VCRs and digital recording systems like TiVo help us fight back, however, and will force companies and broadcasters to rethink how they market products and create programming.

It's the advertised products that are successful. Without advertising, no one knows your name. Advertising tells us if we buy this car we'll be cooler, this shampoo, and our hair will look bouncier. We're given the secret key to the American dream ... if only we drink this soda. The reality is that these products are just things. We may think we aren't being affected by ads, but advertising is so powerful, so all present, that now it's like a wise voice in our ear and we believe what we hear. Advertising is ingrained into our every thought and action.

Corporate sponsorship has been a common presence since the creation of mass media in the early twentieth century. Companies would sponsor a program and use the actors to promote their products during the broadcast. These days, sponsorship has moved on to sports stadiums and athletic teams. In Southern California, the Disney sponsored hockey team, the Anaheim Mighty Ducks, plays in the Arrowhead (a brand of bottled water) Pond.

Stop & think

How soon before corporations start sponsoring bridges and tunnels? Highway cleanup already allows companies to promote themselves when they sign up for trash removal, but when budget crises arise, will cities and towns begin selling off their freeways? When will we be taking the AOL Cross Country Information Super Highway to exit 31 Flavors to Baskin Robbins®? Or taking an auto tour of the Delaware Water Gap™?

Corporate sponsorship also influences news coverage, which leads to biased reporting when companies threaten to pull advertising from stations that broadcast programs and stories that reflect negatively on their interests. Companies send out press releases and video newsreels to stations that air this commercial footage as real news.

We often watch television as a way to escape a stress in our lives. That's when we're most vulnerable to advertising, which doesn't just sell a product, but creates wants where none originally existed and promotes consumerism as a way of life. When it tells us, "Do this, now!" we believe that we can satisfy our needs by buying something. Buying thus becomes an addiction.

Advertising has also taught us how to complicate even the simplest of activities. There are now specialized stores filled with merchandise on any topic we can think of.

Running, a sport that used to involve only a pair of sneakers, now requires shorts, keep-us-cool singlets, heart rate monitors, energy bars and electrolyte replacement drinks, reflectors, sports gels, running radios, cold weather gear, warm weather gear, rain gear, and six different types of shoes (with special insoles) for optimum training.

The advertising industry is well aware of the reasons we shop. Advertisers know more about us than we know about ourselves. Every time we swipe a bar coded card at the supermarket or drugstore, a marketing company collects a little more data on us. The threat that Aldous Huxley dreamed up in *Brave New World* is here: we have become a series of numbers, with all of our hopes and desires coded into a series of lines.

Most advertising is focused on what we lack and what can make us "cool." When we're in high school, it's fairly easy to tell "what's cool." What's cool is what the popular kids are wearing or using. What's cool doesn't get us ridiculed. What's cool gains us the respect of our peers (and probably the scorn of anyone over age twenty). In *The Culture of Narcissism*, Christopher Lasch writes that "we allow experts to define our needs for us and then wonder why those needs never seem to be satisfied."[61]

Peer pressure marketing was fully realized in 1992, the first year since 1975 in which the number of teenagers in America increased. Suddenly the focus of advertising shifted to a younger generation. Capitalism now thrives on the manipulation of children. Lost in the shuffle of fear that kids will get addicted to smoking or drugs, the possibility that they will get addicted to shopping can be equally dangerous. A lifetime of poor spending habits can begin at an early age.

> Having too many THINGS, Americans spend their hours and money on the couch searching for a soul. A strange species we are. We can stand anything God and Nature throw at us save only plenty. If I wanted to destroy a nation, I would give it too much and I would have it on its knees, miserable, greedy and sick.[62]
>
> –John Steinbeck, in a letter written in 1959 to Adlai Stevenson, complaining about the "cynical immorality" of the U.S.

If Steinbeck could only see us now.

So how do we maintain our organized and simplified lives in the face of a system with so much money and power behind it? How do we fight back against this inundation of mediated influences?

MEDIA LITERACY

To retaliate against the almighty power of the advertising dollar first we must fully realize the magnitude of what we are up against. Media literacy is a study of the way information is presented and a way to dissect advertised images. We should always be aware that sometimes the way things are presented is not necessarily the way they truly are. Nothing is 100 percent objective. Media are first and foremost tools for business and entertainment.

When money changes hands, it nearly always influences how stories are reported in the news. Who funds the information we're receiving? Most of the time, it's not obvious. Large corporations own smaller companies, and it's not always easy to see relationships. If we're media literate, we watch with a cynical open mind. We have to assume that there's an ulterior motive for everything.

Due to government deregulation in the 1980s, a handful of mega-corporations now own media conglomerates that control television and radio stations; film production, distribution, and theater companies; amusement parks and video game companies; magazines, newspapers, book publishing companies, and record labels; and Internet web sites. It's this monopolistic control that influences what we see, hear, and buy. Without a second thought, we can skim an article in *Entertainment Weekly* magazine on what the cast of *Friends* are doing now, watch a New Line Cinema movie trailer on our Netscape web browser, sign onto America Online (connected by Road Runner DSL), and look up information about the soundtrack on Electra record label web site—all without ever leaving the umbrella of *one corporation*. (It's possible, of course, that some of these companies will have changed hands again after this book is printed…)

One small beam of hope is that media literacy is now being taught in schools that are finally struggling out of contracts with Channel One, an in-classroom video program that was mostly advertising. Media literacy teaches children to become more aware of how advertising affects them. It helps them analyze messages so they can see for themselves how they're being manipulated. When we learn that the messages we're exposed to are an altered reality, we're better able to make educated decisions and resist the temptations that a big advertising budget offers.

Fighting Back Against the Tricks of the Trade

❑ Hold the media accountable for PICAN. As part of the Communication Act of 1934, broadcasters must operate "in the Public's Interest, Convenience and Necessity" (PICAN). Because of this law, television broadcasters have a strict obligation to serve the public. The mass media won't tell us about simplicity and rarely will it tell us about frugality or spirituality. Unless we're up at 6 a.m. on a Sunday for "Urban Focus" or "Church Chat," few of us are exposed to PICAN in action.

Stop & think

There's no glamour and there's little budget. There's no doubt about it, much of public broadcasting can be pretty dry. Sitting through a broadcast of a school committee meeting leaves many in a comatose state. Where's a concerned citizen supposed to go for entertaining public information television? What interests you? What are your ideals and how could you turn them into a half hour public access program? Contact local broadcasters and see if you can get yourself some airtime to have your voice heard.

❑ Be aware of advertising watchwords. How many of these terms have we been victims of: "on sale," "new and improved," "once in a lifetime," "in style," "for a limited time only," "not sold in stores," "space age material," "doctor recommended," "special edition," "laboratory tested," "largest selection available," "but wait—there's more," "buy two and save," "professional grade"? These phrases are carefully selected to elicit a "buy now!" response from consumers.

❑ Stick to your guns. Advertising undermines our commitment to brand loyalty by making us want to try new products. There's always something better just about to be released. But if a brand or product works for you and always has, why switch?

❑ Remember that imperfect is okay. Advertising sells perfection. Appearance is given higher consideration than performance. We're conditioned to believe that if something has a blemish, it's of lesser quality. Notice the model with the flawless skin, the house with the perfectly manicured yard. Advertisers use airbrushing, lighting, camera angles, and add food coloring to make pictures of products look their most appealing. (White glue is used in photographs of bowls of cereal to look like milk.) But when we get it home, it looks nothing like it looked on TV and, worse yet, sometimes actually makes us look worse. Take the produce section in your grocery store. It's a work of art. Rows upon rows of apples, oranges, pears, peaches, plums. Without a bruise or a speck of mold, they're uniformly colored and sized and displayed in geometric patterns. No bad apples spoil this bunch. We've been taught to expect a higher standard. We scrutinize our produce—sure those bruised apples may be okay for someone, but not us. The olfactory nerves and the taste buds cannot often overcome the visual cues.

- ❏ Stop watching. Or listening. Or reading. If you can't quit cold turkey, try limiting your media intake of television, movies, magazines, newspapers, and the Internet. When we cut back on these influences, we learn to think for ourselves. Go on an "information diet" by cutting back to topics that truly interest you. This "diet" will help foster creativity, and research shows that the amount of television we watch is proportional to the amount of money we spend.
- ❏ Affirm that your happiness cannot be bought.
- ❏ Avoid wearing clothing with logos on them. Do you really want to be a walking billboard?

Social Conscience

As we learn more about moving our lives toward simplicity, we have more choices to weigh when choosing a product. In the good old days, we shopped for convenience, aesthetics, and price. All we wanted of the product was for it to perform as advertised. Now there are new questions to ask and a lot more pitfalls to be aware of. Can this product be recycled? Were ethical ideals considered in its manufacture and sale? How is it packaged? Were animals and humans treated fairly in its production? Is it nontoxic? Does the company practice sustainability?

Remember that cup of coffee from chapter 2? It's still not just the trees that were cut to make the paper for the cup, the chemicals that were heated to make the plastic for the lid, the beans that were harvested by migrant workers, the hormone-free milk from the cow fed on organic grain, the twelve trucks, and the 500 gallons of fuel needed to transport all the pieces to where we stand right now. Every facet and every action has an ecological ripple connected to the larger world.

Each time we go shopping, we have an infinite number of choices. Consider shopping as voting. This choice is support of their business plans. When we buy something, we're casting a vote and letting the store know what kind of product we want to buy. Our act of buying signals the manufacturer to make another. "Crunch all you want, we'll make more," the Doritos commercial yelled. If we buy it, they will make more.

There are hundreds of different reasons why we buy something, but it's virtually impossible to separate ourselves from the economic and political community. We want the best deal for our money, but not at the expense of our personal values and beliefs, especially relating to the environment. To ensure that our votes are cast for people who share our beliefs, we need to be conscious shoppers. This is the closest we can come to ethical consumerism and still be good Americans supporting our capitalist society.

Unconscious consumers often unknowingly support sweatshops, drugs, apartheid, rainforest destruction, and tobacco companies.

Thinking outside the box: Working Assets
"Saving the world, one call at a time."

A media conglomerate that puts social responsibility above the bottom line? Since 1985, Working Assets has generated over $50 million in donations to nonprofits working for peace, equality, human rights, education, and a cleaner environment. When we sign up for services we need and already use, such as long distance, cell phone service (under the name Credo Mobile), Internet access, or a credit card (at rates and terms of service comparable to other companies), Working Assets donates a portion of our monthly charges to non-profit organizations, which are causes customers help select. Founded on the belief that building a business and a better world aren't mutually exclusive, Working Assets isn't shy about standing up for what they believe in. (See www.workingassets.com.)

The Lesser of Two Evils

So which company is worse? The one that tests its products on animals but has an innovative and sustainable packaging system or the one that publicly proclaims it's cruelty-free and "pro" indigenous cultures but packages in heavy glass bottles and ships from thousands of miles away? Do we buy the locally grown apples at a cheaper price to support local farmers or the organic apples trucked in from South America? Is the shampoo made with propylene glycol, but otherwise 95 percent organic ingredients at $7 a bottle, really that much better than the 99 cent supermarket version we've been using since we were five?

Every time we shop, we're faced with these decisions and many more. A trip to the grocery store can make us crazy as we collapse in the frozen food section trying to pick a carton of ice cream. Choice equals freedom, but deciding can be exhausting. Sometimes living simply becomes a study in finding the lesser of two evils.

How difficult is it to find a company that is completely "clean"? Living in a capitalist society, it's rare to find one that is prolific enough to be widely available, socially conscious and sustainable enough to win the support of even the most hard-core environmentalist, effective enough to be better than other brands, and economically priced for the cheapskate consumer. How products are made, what is included, how workers are treated and what the effects of ingredients are, are often simply unknown.

Many companies are concerned about the environment, but when they try to publicize their concern, their other business practices are attacked, often by environmentalists who hold these companies and organizations to a higher standard. These companies are scrutinized with the same fine-tooth comb used in the Watergate hearings. Because they present an image of social responsibility, when one branch is attached to a scandal, the whole tree can come crashing down. We want them to be faultless. We get mad when we discover they're not.

What's the solution? Unless we're truly committed to our convictions, it's not easy to choose the lesser of two evils. Each decision we make helps us create our identity of personal values. Considering our choices helps us make better decisions in the long run. For the time being, we may have to accept the "less bad." And remember, sometimes the better choice between the lesser of two evils can be neither.

Stop & think

How can we expect businesses to change regarding environmental sustainability if we denounce those who have an environmental commitment? Companies often remain quiet about their eco-improvements, rather than call attention to other practices. Small, socially aware companies like Tom's of Maine, Ben & Jerry's and Stonyfield Farms have become part of huge multinational corporations that produce other products that cannot be considered sustainable. Nike, often under attack for their labor practices in the Third World and for contributing to the consumptive culture of our country, also explores means for tanning leather without questionable toxins, recycles rubber into athletic tracks and playing fields and is one of the world's largest buyers of organic cotton.

Cut those who are giving the effort some slack. Use your value system to guide yourself through the maze of products. Complain about what you dislike and praise what sets your little ecological heart aflutter.

Questions to think about when deciding between the lesser of two evils:
- Do I really need it?
- Could I buy it second hand? Rent it? Borrow it? Share the cost with someone? Could purchasing a used version be just as good or better?
- Could I create it myself?
- Do I already own something that could serve the same purpose?
- Do I understand how what I'm buying works?
- Is the product built to last? Could its faults be hidden? Would I be able to repair it if it broke?
- Do the materials used to create it use resources that are rare, limited, or nonrenewable?

❑ Does manufacturing this product contribute to the greenhouse effect, acid rain, or destruction of the ozone layer? How does manufacture affect local wildlife habitats? What kind of air, water, noise, ground, or visual pollution is created?

❑ How was the product transported to the retail outlet?

❑ How is the product packaged?

❑ What is the afterlife of the product? How will it be disposed of? Will it easily biodegrade or can it be recycled?

❑ Will the "life cycle cost" of the product outweigh the initial lowest price? Think about the additional costs hidden within the item we're purchasing: money spent on electricity required to run it, maintenance costs involved in repairing it should it break down, and costs to dispose of the item properly once we've finished with it.

Buying Locally

In the 1970s, scientist and philosopher Rene Dubos coined the phrase, "Think globally, act locally." This advice is another way to keep our values in check when we head out to the market.

While the big box stores offer lower prices, greater variety, and more convenient locations, they've all but obliterated the "mom and pop shop" that can't compete with a giant corporation. These moms and pops are our neighbors. When we support smaller local businesses, we keep money in our community. Service is usually hands-on and knowledgeable and mom and pop are more willing to help us one on one. We need to remember that we're paying to have the big boxes stay open every hour of the day, every night of the week. We're paying for a parking lot the size of Rhode Island.

SUSTAINABILITY

Sustainability is thinking about tomorrow by acting today. Between the years 1960 and 2000, the population of earth doubled; at current rate of growth, it will double again to twelve billion by the year 2040. The U.S. population is only 4.5 percent of this number, but we use 30 percent of world's materials.[63] As populations continue to grow, we need to be even more conscious of how we impact the earth and each other.

Sustainability is harvesting or using resources so that they are not depleted or permanently damaged. Sustainability is about shopping for durability and remembering that every product we buy has a past, a present, and a future. Deciding whether something is environmentally sound requires looking at its entire life span. To live lightly upon the earth, we must reevaluate our daily activities and purchases.

Clothing Without a Conscience

We've all heard of Third World laborers being paid pennies a day to mass produce the clothing we sift through in the bargain bin at the Super Save. Human rights are the main issue of sweatshop practices. You think your job sucks? Sweatshop workers are often subjected to dangerous working conditions and physical and verbal abuse while they're working for wages far below a reasonable standard of living. Everyone should have the right to earn a living wage in a safe and decent working environment, and those who profit from exploitation should be held accountable.

Clicking for your conscience: The National Green Pages

While sweatshops may never be extinct, there are now many companies committed to eliminating the exploitation that occurs in the garment industry. The National Green Pages (published by Green America) is an online database that screens and refers only companies that are committed to environmental and social responsibility. With over 150 categories of businesses, including clothing, toys and pet care, stop by their site before you shop. See www.coopamerica.org/pubs/greenpages.

Fabrics

Better dressing through chemistry was unleashed upon the world in 1950 when DuPont bought the patent for polyester. Mostly derived from petroleum, synthetic fibers are not sustainable. Synthetics will sometimes off-gas bothersome chemical odors, and clothing dyes can contain toxic chemicals that can leach onto and into our skin, especially when we sweat.

When we buy a T-shirt, we almost never consider eventual disposal problems. These fabrics may be strong, colorfast, and resistant to corrosion and chemical attack, but thanks to these qualities, they cannot be recycled. With the exception of acetate and rayon, they biodegrade very slowly. Some fabrics will release toxic fumes when burned in incinerators.

Buy clothing that is wash and wear. Avoid "Dry Clean Only" fabrics, which can use formaldehyde-based resins for anti-wrinkle or anti-stain finishes, doubling or tripling the amount of toxins we're exposed to. Low levels of formaldehyde can continue to be released throughout the life of the garment.

Companies will often use different shops to manufacture garments, even within the exact same style and color. While the tag may tell us the country where the shop is located, it won't tell us where the fabric originated, which may be a country that still uses pesticides that have been outlawed in the U.S. (like DDT). Learn to read product labels when shopping for clothing and to recognize fabrics that are more ecologically conscious.

On the other hand

Note that not all synthetic fabrics are bad. Rayon is made from sustainable plant based fibers. EcoSpun and PCR Synchilla fleeces are both made from recycled plastic soda bottles.

Natural Fibers

It's best to seek out natural fibers, if only for their disposal purposes. But be warned: there are processes that can make these natural fibers just as hazardous as synthetics.

✓ *Silk* is produced from an ancient and complicated process wherein silkworms produce continuous unbroken strands of silk fibers that are carefully drawn out and woven into fabric. Silk is extremely strong and absorbs moisture without feeling damp. It's insulating (considered by many to be the warmest when used to make long underwear), breathable, naturally heat resistant, and it will only burn when flame comes in contact with it. Silk is used to make delicate shirts, undergarments, and other lightweight clothing. The only caution is that it's sometimes treated with formaldehyde to prevent water spotting.

✓ *Linen* comes from the stem of the flax (or linseed) plant, which is grown worldwide. The fibers are stiffer than cotton but have a smooth texture that makes them well suited for tailored or delicate clothing and for household items such as tablecloths. Linen feels cool and comfortable in hot weather because it absorbs moisture and dries quickly. Though it wrinkles very easily, the fabric is strong and durable and resists deterioration in sunlight. Good quality linen is expensive because it's imported; pure linen fabrics are very rare now. Currently, most "linen" is actually a linen-cotton blend.

✓ *Ramie* is made from the shrubby ramie plant (also called China grass) grown in Asia, Brazil, and the U.S. It's durable, flexible, and lustrous, and it doesn't shrink. It's used to make napkins, tablecloths, and towels. Ramie is usually blended with cotton and other fibers and has a texture similar to linen.

✓ *Hemp* comes from the stems of *Cannabis sativa*, which creates a strong coarse fiber used for cord, rope, matting, paper, and cloth. The use of hemp dates back many thousands of years because it has always been very durable and resists rotting in water. It's stronger than weeds and pests, so herbicides and pesticides are not needed where it's grown. It's very absorbent, so it dyes well. It's similar in feel and appearance to cotton, but it isn't used as often as it could be because of the illegality of planting it. Though it contains very low levels of cannabinoids (THC), properly grown hemp has virtually no intoxicating effects when used.

> ### Not just for Cheech and Chong any more
> Today in the U.S., hemp (meaning the roots, stalk, and stems of the cannabis plant) is legal to possess. Marijuana flowers, buds, and leaves are illegal and come with stiff fines and possible jail terms for possession. Seeds are legal to possess and eat, but only if they are sterilized so they won't grow to maturity. Since it's not possible to grow the hemp plant without being in possession of marijuana, the U.S. doesn't produce any industrial hemp products and must import them. It is possible to grow hemp legally, but this involves filing an application with the Drug Enforcement Administration, which rarely grants permission.
>
> Unlike many crops, hemp can be grown in most locations and climates with only moderate water and fertilizer requirements. It resists UVB light that can damage other crops. It puts down deep roots, which prevents soil erosion, and can be grown in the same location for many years in a row without any noticeable soil depletion. Its growth cycle is only 120 days, making it an efficient and economical crop for farmers to grow.
>
> Hemp has thousands of uses: rope or twine, paper, textiles, building materials, paint, detergent, varnish, oil, ink, cosmetic products, and fuel. Medically, marijuana can be used to ease symptoms associated with multiple sclerosis, cancer, AIDS, glaucoma, depression, epilepsy, migraines, asthma, and severe pain. Patients have found it to be extremely effective in fighting nausea. Hemp seed is also highly nutritious source of protein and essential fatty oils with almost no saturated fat. As a dietary supplement, these oils can reduce the risk of heart disease.

✓ *Cotton* is derived from the fuzzy puffs that surround the seeds of a cotton plant. It's easy to mill, is soft and absorbent, and dyes well. While Egyptian cotton is considered the best quality, the finest U.S. cottons are Pima and Sea Island cotton from Caribbean and Gulf areas. The higher the thread-count the better. While cotton is important for its part in making T-shirts, towels and medical supplies, one third of U.S. cotton is used to make denim.

Be aware, however, that cotton is the most chemically intensive crop grown in the U.S., using upwards of thirty-five million tons of pesticides and fertilization each year. The plant is very delicate, requiring pre-emergence herbicides to protect it from weeds, herbicides to protect the seed before it germinates, and the application of insecticides when the crop finally grows. A defoliant is dropped when it's time to harvest the cotton, causing leaves to drop off the plant making puffs easier to pick. By the time it becomes fabric, one yard of cotton cloth has required one third of a pound of toxic chemicals to control insect and weed problems. Once cotton becomes fabric, it's often treated with ammonia, formaldehyde (to prevent wrinkles), other chemicals, and heavy metal color dyes, all of which can be absorbed through the skin, especially when we perspire.

Consider cotton alternatives:

- ❏ Shop for "certified organic cotton" products, which are subjected to the same organic guidelines as food crops. Because organics constitute less than 1 percent of the cotton planted in the U.S., it can be more difficult to find and more expensive than other fabrics.
- ❏ Pick "unbleached cotton," which is cotton in its natural beige color.
- ❏ Select clothing made from "green cotton," which is treated with chemicals during the growing process, but the fabric is unbleached, undyed, and not treated with formaldehyde.
- ❏ Look for growers who are experimenting with growing colored cotton by breeding the plants to produce color puffs.

✓ *Rayon* is manmade fiber, made from natural ingredients. Made from reworked cellulose, the material that makes up the cell walls of plants, it has a cotton-like texture that is easily blended with other fabrics. It wrinkles easily, however, because it has a lightweight silken texture, so watch for chemical treatment for wrinkle prevention.

✓ *Wool* comes from the fleece of sheep, angora rabbits and goats, yaks, camels, llamas, alpacas, and vicuñas. It's loved for its softness and cushioning, warmth in winter, coolness in summer, water resistance on the outside but absorbency when wet, and for being naturally flame retardant. A few of the sustainable qualities of wool are that it can be recycled, is easily biodegradable, and that very few chemicals are used in manufacture. Fibers are light-colored and easy to dye.

Types of wool

✓ *Organic wool* is when the animal is raised chemical-free. Organic farming prohibits the use of prophylactic antibiotics and chemicals to control insects.

✓ *Untreated wool* has not been bleached, dyed, or undergone mothproofing treatments.

✓ *Virgin wool* means the wool in the garment or product has not been recycled from other products. *Shoddy wool* has been reused from another garment.

✓ Use caution when selecting merino wool (which is often from sheep kept in huge confinement sheds) and vicuña wool (some vicuñas are killed when being fleeced because they won't hold still).

SHOPPING ALTERNATIVES

By changing where we shop, we can change the effect advertising has on us. It's been said before, but it bears repeating: *buy only if you need something.* Instead of succumbing to presumptuous consumption, we can become conscious consumers. If you need to shop, follow these suggestions:

❑ Avoid department stores. The "latest styles" come with the largest price tags. What are we actually paying for when we buy retail? Store overhead (including excessive lighting and cooling bills), advertising, and possibly unfair labor practices.

Foot fetish: A brief history in shoe UNsimplicity

"The secret of life is one thing ...
comfortable footwear."

– Cliff Claven, *Cheers*

Sure, that $450 for a pair of Jimmy Choos could clothe and shoe a Third World child for life, but, oh, they look so swell upon our feet. Did Carrie Bradshaw really need enough pairs to correspond to a down payment on a house? Someone should have reminded her that no matter how many shoes we have, we can still wear only one pair at a time. Declutter your shoe rack and teach yourself to shop for functionality and durability.

✓ Imelda Marcos, quite possibly the world's greatest shoe fetishist, claimed she owned (only) 1,060 pairs of shoes at the height of her reign. Meanwhile 200,000 of her fellow countrymen and women worked making shoes at below living wages.

✓ Though many companies have switched from killing animals for leather (and the toxic chemicals used to tan it) to synthetic materials, it lessens the quality of goods, causing them to break down quicker and release the particulates into our environment.

✓ Even though we usually toss our old shoes in the trash when we're done with them, there are plenty of recycling options available: Run the Planet offers a list of organizations that recycle used athletic shoes including Nike which takes the "rubber" and turns them into Nike Grind, a mixture for athletic courts, tracks or playgrounds (www.runtheplanet.com/shoes/selection/recycle.asp). Cobblers might be a dying breed, but check your local listings, they can give your favorite cowboy boots or sassy sandals another few years of wear.

❑ Hop on over to the flea market. Used products have already paid most of their ecological debt to society.

❏ Shop in antique malls or junk stores. On the surface, these may seem to be two different kinds of shops, but, deep down, they're pretty much the same, even if they do cater to clientele at opposite ends of the economic spectrum. Going antiquing has turned into a yuppie cliché and caused prices to be inflated, while junk stores recognize their wares for what they are: junk.

❏ Check out church bazaars. A good cause often prompts many to finally clean out their closets. Fabulous bargains can be found amid the hand-knitted teapot cozies.

❏ Go to garage and yard sales to find a second hand item that you don't need in mint condition or just want to test out.

❏ Dive into the dumpster or cruise the curb on trash day. Not for the faint of heart, dumpster diving is an elite sport all its own.

❏ Patronize consignment shops. Consignment shops resell good quality and stylish clothing with small amounts of wear and tear. Shop owners take items and attempt to sell them within a preset time frame. If the garment is sold, the shop owner pays the consigner usually between 40 and 60 percent of the selling price. If the garment isn't sold, it's up to the consigner to reclaim it.

❏ Visit vintage clothing stores. Vintage has character and history—dresses from the 1950s, bowling shirts, handkerchiefs from the World War II era. Just because some of the clothing is antique, doesn't mean it's on its last legs. Handmade clothes were often made to higher standards. Be sure to thoroughly clean everything bought at a vintage shop, chances are, the original owner didn't clean it before dropping it off, and who knows how long it has been sitting among the polyester leisure suits.

❏ Head to a thrift store. The old stand-bys, the Salvation Army (www.salvationarmyusa.org) and Goodwill (www.goodwill.org), are the best bets. When you treasure hunt here, the funds often go to charity and used goods are kept out of the waste stream.

What to bring on a thrifting excursion

✓ Moist towelettes. Hands get grimy quickly, and who knows where the nearest source of running water is.

✓ Sack lunch and lots of water. Maximize time (by bringing sustenance) and funds (by bringing it from home).

✓ A hat and sun block. Outdoor markets are usually held in the sunny months.

✓ Comfortable clothes and shoes. Dress down. Wearing a Chanel suit will probably not help you in the bargaining process.

✓ Get friendly with someone who owns a truck and let them know the days you're thrifting so they won't be caught off guard when you call and ask them to pick you and your new steamer trunk up.   *(cont'd)*

✓ Bring a tape measure and carry a notebook that contains the dimensions of the rooms in your house. No use buying that piano for $5 if you won't be able to get it through the front door.

✓ Know your body measurements, too. Many thrift shops and flea markets don't have dressing rooms and sometimes sizes aren't given, either because the garment is handmade, it's a vintage piece, or labels have been cut out.

✓ Play it safe and don't leave home without it—cash, that is. Some retailers accept credit cards, but the majority deal on a cash-only basis.

✓ Bring a keen eye. The return policies of these outlets are slim to none, so check the item thoroughly and be sure you really want it before you buy it.

❑ Try shopping at a dry cleaner. Many places sell clothing that has been abandoned after a certain period of time to try to recoup the loss of the cleaning bill.

❑ For services, look for beauty academies, dental schools, medical colleges, or massage schools. An instructor should supervise your service and prices can be substantially lower.

❑ Try public auctions of government seizures and abandoned property. If you don't mind capitalizing on someone else's misery, the U.S. Treasury auctions off real estate, jewelry, cars, boats, electronics, carpeting, and even planes to the eager public. (See www.treasury.gov/auctions.)

Where to look

Try the phone book under Clothing: "Secondhand" or "Vintage." "Used goods." "Charitable organizations," "Consignment," "Resale," and "Women's apparel, used." Look in college towns or areas that cater to bohemian types. Newspapers list yard sales and flea markets in the classified section.

SHOPPING DEFENSE

Okay, so you think you're ready to face the mall again? Relax. I'm going to send you out with a few more tricks up your sleeve so you can come home happy with your wallet still full of cash.

❑ Shop without a cart. Retailers have related Parkinson's Law to shopping. Parkinson's original "work expands to fill the time available for its completion" becomes "stuff will fill the space it has been allotted." That's why retailers have increased the size of their shopping carts. Research has confirmed it: the bigger the cart, the more money people will spend to fill it. (Stay tuned for "Parkinson's Law of Traffic" and "Parkinson's Law of Garbage" later in the book.)

❏ Don't shop when you're hungry. Try to wait until you get home before breaking open the box of cookies or at least wait till you're through the checkout line.

❏ Shop only the perimeter of the grocery store. This is where fresh foods are located: deli, seafood, bakery, and produce. Wandering down the aisles is like walking down the Bourbon Street of processed foods. This same concept is applied in other retail outlets. They place what you need the most (for example, pharmacies in drug stores) in back corners so that you'll have to walk through the whole store to get there, hoping something else will catch your eye on the way.

Thinking outside the box:

Who is Paco Underhill and why does he know what retailers don't?

He knows where we're going when we enter a store. He's watched us shop and he knows what we want. He knows that the "butt-brush effect" (the fact that we don't like being unexpectedly jostled while shopping) will influence whether or not we buy something. His work is more authentic than those kids at the mall who say, "Wanna take a survey?" His research won't disturb our dinner.

Underhill is a *retail anthropologist* who goes beyond examining register receipts. He ponders the sociology and psychology of shopping. He's the man with the clipboard hiding behind the potted plant, and his worldwide behavioral research company, Envirosell, has spent millions of hours watching retail shoppers in person and on video tape to find out what exactly makes us tick.

Underhill wants to teach retailers how to be nicer to us so we'll buy more and with more pleasure. He's also the guy fighting for our right to test the product before we buy it. He tells us not how retail spaces manipulate us so much as how they fail and succeed at stimulating us. His book, *Why We Buy: The Science of Shopping*, is not a must-read only for the retail manager; it should also be at the top of the reading list for the conscious consumer.

❏ Avoid buying things at eye level and on end caps (the shelves at the end of an aisle). This is where marketers place heavily promoted products. And they only want us to see them so they'll end up in our carts.

❏ Do you wonder why we have to crouch and crawl on the floor to get our favorite organic cookies off the very bottom shelf at the grocery store? "Slotting" is the factor that gets certain products the prime real estate in stores. New manufacturers have to pay thousands of dollars just to get on the shelf, and they get no guarantee how long they'll be there.

❏ Shop with a list and stick to it. The time we spend in a store is proportionate to the amount we buy. With a list in hand, we know what we need and can cut our shopping time in half. Go directly to fresh peas. Do not pass frozen corndogs.

❏ Designate one day a week to do all shopping and errands. We can cut down on travel by planning all our trips and calling ahead. We'll be able to get in, get what we need, and get out. Most stores will hold the item you're looking for, and if you developed a relationship with the places you shop, they'll take care of you. Sitting on the phone on hold for five minutes always beats a twenty-mile round trip when they don't have what you need.

❏ With larger purchases, write out the pros and cons of buying it and do your research in *Consumer Reports* (www.consumerreports.org).

❏ Only use coupons on items you buy regularly. Two dollars off dog food doesn't do much good if you don't have a dog.

❏ Just because it's on sale, doesn't mean it's a bargain. "Look at these pants! Two dollars!" Forget the fact that they're green plaid and four sizes too big. "I have to buy this dress. It's $15 down from $495!" Just because we can buy something, doesn't mean we should.

Test yourself
Find out how many days you can go without spending money.

❏ Sleep on it. Give yourself a day before purchasing anything you want. I try a one hour per dollar ratio: if an item is $40, then I'll force myself to wait at least forty hours before purchasing to see how I still feel about it.

❏ Leave the tags and labels on for a week without touching the item. Usually after a week, the "have to have it" impulse has passed. Then you can return it.

❏ Leave your money at home when browsing at the mall. Better yet, avoid the mall altogether.

❏ For the seriously addicted spender: tape a note around your credit card as a conscious reminder to yourself. When all else fails, freeze your lack of assets by placing the credit card in a plastic container filled with water in the freezer.

❏ Stop buying your way out of problems. If you had no money at all, what would you do instead? Try to find creative solutions or alternatives to shopping.

❏ Go generic. Because they don't advertise (or the advertising is built into advertising the store), store brands cost considerably less than national brands. Look for generic drugs, cleaning products, food items, and health and beauty aids. Store brands are sometimes made at the same location as the national brands.

❑ Watch expiration dates. Check dates on perishable foods like dairy, eggs, and breads, but also makeup and over-the-counter medications. Fresh organic food is highly perishable because it doesn't contain preservatives. When buying a loaf of organic bread, I always freeze half of it because I know I won't eat it all before it starts to mold. You can also freeze mushrooms, popcorn, coffee, vegetables, nuts, sugar, and flour (keeps out clumps and bugs). Shop the back of the rack or shelf in the grocery store. They tend to move the oldest items to the front to get them to be the next sold.

❑ Maximize your time and you can save money. Time truly does equal money. Shop at off-peak hours. Call stores and ask what time of day they are slowest. You can get in and out or get undivided attention if you need it.

❑ Know the difference between advertising and opinion. According to the First Amendment, people can say or write anything they want about a product as long as it isn't an advertisement. In advertising, if the claim is false, it's illegal. If it's only misleading, it's up to the consumers to figure it out for themselves. People who have a vested interest in whether or not we buy their product make advertising claims.

❑ Retailers fear that when products are made to last, businesses will eventually run out of customers. That's why some companies create "planned obsolescence," making products of lower quality so they'll fail and we'll have to buy another one. Shop for quality, durability, and warranty.

❑ How much do we really need? Products shown in advertisements use more than necessary. Have you ever tried to brush your teeth with the amount of toothpaste shown on TV commercials? We also don't need a cleanser for every room of the house or every appliance. Bathroom cleansers are marketed with one especially designed for the tub, another for the toilet, still another for the sink. Kitchen cleaners are available for the counter, the stove, the appliances, and eating surfaces. (Instead see *Cleaning*, page 282, for the ten simple nontoxic cleanser ingredients.)

❑ Consider unit price. For those of us with a math deficiency, one of the few good things about big box grocery stores is the unit price listed on every shelf. It lists how much per unit (pound, ounce, quart, etc.) the item costs so we can easily compare different brands for value. By looking at the shelf strip, we can see that the bottle of shampoo at 20 cents an ounce is clearly a better value than one at $1.19 an ounce.

❑ Think about the ecological impact of the packaging you're purchasing. Avoid over-packaging by buying loose produce and reusing produce bags. Packaged produce that will last only a few days is often sold in plastic and foam that can last for centuries.

❑ Watch the weight. We've all fallen for the air puffed bag of potato chips only to find a bunch of measly crumbs at the bottom of the bag when we get them home. Sometimes manufacturers will even change the amount of the contents without changing the size of the packaging. Tricky, but true.

❑ Remember color tricks: Does the color of the package match the food inside? Green is often used on lettuce bags and orange for packaging carrots to make them look "fresher." Grocery stores also use pink lighting to make meat look redder.

❑ Buy concentrated foods, such as juices and detergents. Add your own water and save weight and space for transport.

❑ Buy refills for products such as razor blades or cleaners.

❑ Buy flexible packages: pouches, "bricks," or cereal in bags.

❑ Buy in bulk. There are two types of bulk shopping: The first is large quantities from the big box stores like B.J.'s, Costco, and Smart and Final. Like using coupons, only buy large quantities of something you already buy. And make sure that you've taste tested it before buying a quantity large enough to feed the local junior high school. Break it down into meal-sized portions before freezing it. Buying in bulk saves us from going back to the store more often. It also saves packaging.

The second type of "bulk" is pack-it-yourself. Many organic food stores have extensive bulk sections with everything from flour, sugar, coffee, spices, nuts, granola, and rice, where we can buy as much as we'll use. Buy spices in smaller quantities because they will lose freshness and potency over time.

On the other hand: Impulse buying

We've been in line for ages (probably about two minutes, but it seems like a year and a half when the three-year-old behind us is singing the Wiggles theme song at top volume). We look for anything to divert our attention from the supermarket lothario in front of us trying to get our attention. What's this? J.Lo is planning a mission to Mars? Batteries, I could use some 9-volt batteries … and M&M's makes a fat-free peanut butter caramel version? The impulse buy has struck again.

It doesn't matter what is placed at the checkout area. Marketers know they have our undivided attention. We're a captive audience. To make the most of this time waiting, take a book when you go shopping or keep yourself focused on the purchases you have in your cart and use this time to read ingredient lists or fabric labels.

COMMON COURTESY

The credo of the service industry has always been, "The customer is always right." But somehow this information leaked out to the public and we've learned to work this golden rule to our own advantage with little regard to the effect it has on unsuspecting sales clerks. Take a step back and think about the person behind the name tag.

The View From Behind the Cash Register: Service Industry Pet Peeves

- ❏ Try to see yourself from the perspective of the service industry (restaurant, retail, etc.) employee. If you've ever worked in retail, you may find yourself going into other stores and unconsciously straightening their shelves or rehanging the clothes. Once we've been in their shoes, we're a lot more conscious of how we shop. Treat servers and clerks as you would want to be treated.
- ❏ Relax. Patience is a virtue. You were the new guy on the job once.
- ❏ Put it back where you found it, or at least in a restocking location. Just because you always wanted to feel like a runway model during fashion week, that doesn't mean you should throw piles of clothing on the fitting room floor.
- ❏ If you think there's any chance you might bring your purchase back, save your receipt. Learn the store's return policy (some even print it on the back of your receipt). Many stores bend the rules slightly, but they have policies for a reason.
- ❏ Don't take advantage of "No-Hassle Return" policies. Cigarette smoke and food odors, pet hair, makeup or deodorant stains on clothing, lost or destroyed packaging, and buying a product for the purpose of stealing parts can become loss of merchandise for the company. This creates more waste. Rule of thumb: keep it in the condition you would want to buy it in.
- ❏ Unload groceries onto the conveyer belt in the order of heaviest first to speed up the bagging process.
- ❏ Don't take out your frustrations on a cashier when the corporation is to blame. Yelling at a sales clerk who makes $8 an hour may make you feel better in the moment, but chances are they didn't set the policy you're rebelling against.
- ❏ Be discreet if you have a problem. We all want justice for our suffering, but you catch more flies with honey than vinegar.
- ❏ Ask for help. Most of the time, sales people are more than happy to help us get what we want, especially if it means they don't have to refold that entire table of sweaters we're about to ransack.
- ❏ Don't open packages without permission. Ask an associate for help. Would you want to buy a mangled package? We may say we wouldn't mind, but we still reach for the pristine package.

❑ Have realistic expectations. Just because we're paying for something, doesn't mean that we're the Queen of Sheba.

Remember tipping is a gratuity, not a must, but in most places, wait staff are paid as little as $2.13 per hour before tips, and then they have to share those tips with busboys, aides, and other employees. Of course there are bad apples in the service industry and employees should have a certain measure of accountability for their company. There's rudeness, ineptitude, and ignorance in any business, but when you find it, that's when you go to the top. Be sure to praise as well as condemn.

Simplifying our shopping habits can be the transformation to simplicity. There are visible connections to our budget, how we dispose, and how we organize our lives. If nothing else when shopping, stop and think about these 4 quick questions:

✓ How did product come to be at this place?
✓ Why are you buying? (And if it's a "want", what will it bring to your life?)
✓ How will it eventually be disposed?
✓ What is an alternative to this purchase?

Sometimes "because I like it" or "because I want to" is an okay answer. But notice when you're using that as a cop out to avoid thinking about the future of the product. With these four simple questions, we can transform our shopping habits. And every little bit helps.

Do it today

Continue to avoid trivial conveniences, throwaway products, and anything created for one time use.

ADDITIONAL RESOURCES

MEDIA LITERACY

Klein, Naomi. *No Logo: No Space, No Choice, No Jobs.* New York: Picador USA, 1999. Commentary on the proliferation of branding in our mediated culture.

Schecter, Danny *The More You Watch, the Less You Know: News Wars/(Sub)Merged Hopes/Media Adventures.* New York: Seven Stories Press, 1997. Whybrow, Dr. Peter C. *American Mania: When More Is Not Enough.* New York: W.W. Norton & Company, 2005.

Lasn, Kalle. *Culture Jam.* New York: HarperCollins, 2000. Adbusters (www.adbusters.org) are artists, activists, writers, pranksters, students, educators, and entrepreneurs who want to fight the power behind the information age with a dose of its own medicine. They sponsor Buy Nothing Day and TV Turnoff Week and provide exhibitions for subversive work through ads, videos, and posters.

SHOPPING WITH A CONSCIENCE

Begley, Jr., Ed. *Living like Ed: A Guide to the Eco-Friendly Life.* New York: Clarkson Potter, 2008. A companion piece to Begley's HGTV television series (*Living with Ed*), he makes eco-living accessible to everyone.

Bongiorni, Sara. *A Year Without "Made In China": One Family's True Life Adventure In The Global Economy.* Hoboken, NJ: John Wiley & Sons, 2007. A mother of two sets out on a yearlong mission to avoid purchasing all products with the 'Made in China' label.

Pearce, Fred. *Confessions of an Eco-Sinner: Tracking Down The Sources of My Stuff.* Boston: Beacon Press, 2008. Pearce takes off on a world tour to discover the ecological impact of creating items such as his wedding ring, his cup of coffee and his computer.

Timmerman, Kelsey. *Where Am I Wearing?: A Global Tour To The Countries, Factories, And People That Make Our Clothes.* Hoboken, NJ: John Wiley & Sons, 2009. Timmerman traveled to China, Bangladesh, and Honduras to uncover how his favorite items of clothing were made.

CHEAPSKATE SOLUTIONS

Craftster (www.craftster.org) is a great online community where crafty hipsters share clever ideas.

Dacyczyn, Amy. *The Complete Tightwad Gazette.* New York: Villard Books, 1998. Promoting thrift as a viable alternative lifestyle. What began as a newsletter published from 1990 to 1996 has turned Amy Dacyczyn into the guru of frugality. After she making the talk show rounds, subscription numbers skyrocketed, and this mother of 6 was able to retire. This is all three of her books of newsletters compiled, with a few new articles thrown in for good measure. She tackles such topics for tightwads as travel, Halloween costumes from scrounged materials, inexpensive gifts, tricks to help us move, saving on groceries, avoiding credit card debt, and lots of quick and cheap recipes.

Knapp, Jennifer. *Cheap Frills: Fabulous Facelifts for Your Clothes.* San Francisco: Chronicle Books, 2001. Creative ideas for salvaging women's clothing.

Yankee Magazine's Living Well on a Shoestring. Yankee Publishing, Inc., 2000.

HOT ON THE TRAIL OF ALTERNATIVE SHOPPING

Hoff, Al. *Thrift Score.* New York: HarperCollins, 1997. Hoff has turned her online 'zine ThriftSCORE into a manual on how to conquer thrift stores. Where to shop, how to score, what to do with it once we've got it home, and rational reasons behind it all.

Zubrod, Sheila and David Stern. *Flea.* New York: HarperPerennial, 1997. "The definitive guide to hunting, gathering, and flaunting superior vintage wares." They list the major flea markets in the U.S. and offer strategies on hunting.

For cleaning products, household goods, and gardening supplies, specializing in companies that care:

- ✓ www.abundantearth.com Providing products, services, and information to promote an ecologically sustainable culture.
- ✓ www.ecomall.com Search engine that will search hundreds of sites that offer green products.
- ✓ www.enviroyellowpages.com The environmental industry's worldwide directory. 350,000 listings.
- ✓ www.gaiam.com Gaiam was formerly Real Goods and several other smaller sites that focus on sustainability.
- ✓ www.greenculture.com "Products for an enlightened planet." Includes a network of several sites that feature furniture, natural fiber clothing, gardening and composting supplies, solar products, lighting options, pest control, and pet care.
- ✓ www.worldwise.com Pet, home, and garden products. Environmental news, stories, links, and a bi-monthly newsletter from Debra Lynn Dadd.

chapter 6

eating

> Don't put that in your mouth.
> –Mom

At age five, we paid little attention to what we put in our mouths: mud pies, paste, crayons, cat food. But would you be surprised to learn that even after we've grown up, we still don't pay much attention to what we're eating? We wonder why our health is poor, our moods erratic, our energy levels low, and our skin and hair weak. Maybe we should take a closer look at our diets.

We don't think about what we buy in the grocery store. We don't try to read and understand labels. We trust the decisions made by government agencies that regulate food. Just because something has been deemed "safe," however, doesn't mean that it's the best choice to put into our bodies. Knowing exactly what some legally "safe" products contain might change our minds about ingesting them.

WHAT WE'RE EATING THAT WE SHOULDN'T BE

Complex lives lead to complex food. We may think fast food and the prepackaged meal are simple choices but the overall cost is ecologically and medically far greater than the few bucks out of pocket. Being able to identify preservatives, additives, and genetically engineered ingredients and knowing what their effects are, are the first steps to improving our eating habits and keeping healthy.

Scary stat

Ninety percent of food dollars are spent on processed food.

Preservatives

Without preservatives, a traditional grocery store would be a very empty place. While it may be impossible to go completely preservative-free in our diets, learning the dangers of chemical additives can help us decide which are not necessary.

Nitrates and *nitrites* are used in products to preserve color and prevent the growth of bacteria. They are often listed as sodium nitrate or nitrite on the ingredient lists of pork products, poultry, fish, cheese, and processed meats like hot dogs, bacon, sausage, and lunchmeats. Alone, nitrates and nitrites are benign, but when combined with amines (chemicals that naturally occur in the stomach), they can create nitrosamines, which are potent carcinogens. To help flush the body of nitrates and nitrites, it's recommended that we take a 1000-milligram (mg) dose of vitamin C when we eat these foods. (Get that extra large glass of OJ with your Grand Slam breakfast.)

BHA (butylated hydroxyanisole) is used as an antioxidant to extend the shelf life of products by preventing oils from becoming rancid and preserving food odor, color, and flavor. *BHT* (butylated hydroxytoluene) is similar to BHA, but possibly more toxic. BHA and BHT are found in foods containing fats and oils—butter and processed foods such as snack foods, potato chips, cereals, crackers, meats, baked goods, chewing gum, enriched rice, and beer. Both are also used in pet foods, animal feed, food packaging, cosmetics, and rubber products.

BHA and BHT are controversial because there are many points of view regarding their safety. Some studies have implicated the compounds in enlarging livers and kidneys, causing behavioral changes, and changing enzymes that make the bodies of test animals more susceptible to cancer and reproductive disruption.[64] But other studies have shown BHA and BHT to be beneficial in treating symptoms of herpes and AIDS. If food is manufactured in order to be consumed during a normal time frame (a week or two at most), BHA and BHT are unnecessary additives.

Food irradiation is another method of preserving foods. During the 1950s, the Atomic Energy Commission developed food irradiation as a way to recycle radioactive waste from nuclear weapons. Exposing food to high-level radiation (the equivalent of ten million medical x-rays) kills insects, mold, and bacteria (such as salmonella, *E. coli*, and campylobacter). This process—which proponents want to rename "cold pasteurization"—also inhibits sprouting and slows rotting. The U.S. has approved the irradiation of beef, poultry, pork, spices, dehydrated herbs, teas, strawberries, white potatoes, wheat, and wheat flour. Currently, food that has been irradiated doesn't have to be labeled as such.

Irradiation also kills the good bacteria that create the warning bad smell in contaminated meat; the contaminants can be feces, urine, vomit, and pus. The effects on our health of consuming irradiated products are unknown, but research has shown some reproductive and genetic damage in lab animals. Irradiating also causes chemical changes in the food, reducing the level of essential nutrients and vitamins such as thiamine, which plays a vital role in normal nervous system function. Some people have noticed a slight alteration in taste of irradiated products. Avoid irradiated food by looking for the irradiated product symbol (a flower in a circle). Know also that certified organic food cannot be irradiated.

Waxed fruit is not the old-fashioned table decoration but edible produce coated with waxes made from petrochemicals, such as polyethylene. This process increases shelf life by sealing in moisture, but it can also seal in surface pesticides and fungicides. Apples, watermelons, tomatoes, oranges, tangerines, peppers, pineapples, cucumbers, and squash are a few items that are commonly waxed.

Produce waxes are generally considered safe because they pass through the body undigested, but they have no nutritional value and you're still ingesting a petroleum product. The law requires stores to note the presence of waxes on produce, including the organic waxes made from plant and insect extracts that are approved for use on organic produce. Always wash your produce thoroughly, but know that rinsing in plain water won't remove wax or pesticides. Hot water and soap or produce washes will remove most of the wax coating. Pesticides are trickier. Many will have already leached through the skin and settled in the fruit before you take your first bite.

Additives

The world of processed food would be nothing without additives. Dyes and bleaches brighten or alter food colors. Flavors and sweeteners change the taste of food. Thickeners, humectants, and anti-caking agents modify the texture of food. Often, these additives outnumber natural ingredients.

Food dyes are used only to promote aesthetics and have no nutritional value. They are listed with Food, Drug and Cosmetic use (FD&C) code names. The term "color" also denotes an additive. Juices, gum, cosmetics, and candy are a few products that contain chemical colors. Specialty kids' foods are made in bright unnatural colors to make them more appealing to younger taste buds. (Raspberries are *not* blue, lemons are *not* pink.) Read ingredient labels for coloring additives and choose only foods that do not contain colors or dyes. Since many artificial dyes are made with coal tars, it's best to avoid all colors if possible. (For more on dyes and coloring in cosmetics, see *Beautifying*, page 259.)

Artificial sweeteners are found with the chemical names *aspartame, saccharin*, and *sucralose*. The cost of these artificial sweeteners is roughly one tenth that of sugar and though they may save teeth and calories, they still raise concerns for people who want to eat healthily.

Aspartame (brand names *Nutrasweet* and *Equal*) was considered revolutionary when it was introduced in 1981 and it easily replaced saccharin (*Sweet and Low*) when reports began implicating it in cases of cancer in laboratory rats. But life isn't always so sweet. Aspartame can change the levels of chemicals in the brain and negatively affect people with underlying Parkinson's disease and insomnia. To a lesser extent, it can cause headaches, vision problems, depression and mood swings. The Food and Drug Administration says aspartame accounts for over 75 percent of the reported adverse reactions to food additives.[65]

Sucralose (*Splenda*) is a newer sugar alternative. Despite its safety rating and claims that it passes through the body unabsorbed, it's still created by chlorinating sucrose.

It's often difficult to notice how much artificial sweetener we swallow on a daily basis. It's used in diet soft drinks, toothpaste, vitamins, cold preparations, breath mints, candy, chewing gums, yogurt, snacks, and juices. Instead of white sugar, which has almost no nutritional value and is treated with multiple pesticides and chemical bleaches, if you need a little sweetness choose unrefined sugars. For natural simpler sweeteners try the following:

- ✓ Honey, which has traces of vitamin C, thiamin, riboflavin, niacin, calcium, iron, phosphorus, and copper. It's also the only sweetener not refined by chemicals.
- ✓ Molasses. Of the three types (unsulfured, sulfured, and blackstrap), unsulfured molasses is the finest quality with the best flavor, but blackstrap molasses contains more calcium, potassium, and iron than most foods. Per tablespoon, molasses has the lowest amount of calories of the natural sugars.
- ✓ Organic, "formaldehyde free," pure maple syrup. Brands tapped in Canada do not use formaldehyde pellets inserted in trees to increase sap production.
- ✓ Brown rice syrup, natural unbleached sugar cane ("Sugar in the Raw"), or vegetable glycerin can be substituted in recipes for white sugar.

Pop goes the dentist bill

How has colored sugar water become so influential in our society? More American than apple pie, the image of the soft drink is young, sexy, and refreshing. We're easily hooked when we're kids; this is not helped by the trend of 5,000 schools with soda vending machine contracts.

The average North American consumes fifty-three teaspoons of sugar a day. For those who drink sugared sodas, a twelve-ounce can averages seventeen teaspoons. Americans drink fifty-six gallons of soda a year or approximately 600 cans per person. These soft drinks also rob the body of calcium and magnesium and create a dependence on caffeine.

How about a glass of water instead?

- ✓ Lack of water is the number one trigger of daytime fatigue. Dehydration gives us difficulty with short-term memory, with basic math, and with focusing on a computer screen or printed page.
- ✓ Even slight dehydration will slow your metabolism down as much as three percent.
- ✓ In a University of Washington study, a glass of water shut down midnight hunger pangs for almost all of the subjects tested.
- ✓ Drinking five glasses of water daily decreases your risk of colon cancer by 45 percent, breast cancer by 79 percent, and bladder cancer by 50 percent.[66]

Monosodium Glutamate (MSG), adopted for use in late 1940s as a flavor enhancer in Asian cooking, is now common in all kinds of American processed foods. The flavor of MSG is difficult to describe and it lacks any nutritional value. What it does do is enhance the tastes of certain foods and make us feel dehydrated, encouraging us to eat and drink more. Rarely is MSG listed on ingredient lists, but keep your eyes open for these aliases: hydrolyzed vegetable protein (HVP), hydrolyzed plant or vegetable protein (HPP), textured protein, sodium caseinate, calcium caseinate, autolyzed yeast, hydrolyzed oat flour, yeast extract, yeast nutrient, malt extract, barley malt, Chinese seasoning, Kombu extract, and PL-50.

"Chinese restaurant syndrome" is actually a chemical sensitivity that is triggered after ingesting MSG. Symptoms include headaches, nausea, abdominal cramps, visual disturbances, diarrhea, fatigue, and weakness. To avoid consuming MSG, patronize restaurants that stand behind their "No-MSG" policy. Read processed food labels for MSG aliases.

Genetically Engineered Foods: Better Eating Through Chemistry?

Genetic engineering (GE) involves modifying the genetic code of an organism (plant, animal, micro-organism, or human). Using gene guns, scientists transfer foreign DNA from one or more organisms (often from an entirely different species of plant or animal) into a host, creating a new, genetically engineered species.

The concept of genetic engineering isn't complex, but the technology is anything but simple. When food is genetically modified, the transferred genes can alter the original genes in unknown ways. An altered genetic code can cause the plant to produce fewer nutrients and change the compounds it produces. Companies patent altered genes and the resulting seeds and products—also known as Genetically Modified Organisms (GMO), transgenic plants, "designer" foods, or Franken-foods—to protect their investment.

Because one of the most common genetically engineered foods is the soybean, as much as 60 percent of all prepared food in a typical American supermarket contains genetically engineered ingredients. Monsanto, the leading GE manufacturer, has created both a genetically engineered product (*Round Up Ready Soybeans*) and a companion herbicide (*Round Up*). *Round Up* is so powerful that it kills any plant that gets in its way ... with the exception of Monsanto's *Round Up Ready Soybeans*. Ingredients made from soybeans include soy oil (the top edible oil used in the U.S.), lecithin, soy meal, protein, bread, mayonnaise, ice cream, cookies, dog food, nutritional supplements, and bakery goods. Avoiding these products is not enough if you want to steer clear of GE soy, however, because most soybean meal is used as livestock feed.

Some GE corn is engineered to contain *Bacillus thuringiensis*, a natural pesticide that causes every part of the corn plant to produce a toxin that repels pests. Corn is found in soft drinks, breakfast cereals, fruit drinks, chips, and other snack foods. Other crops that have become victims in the GE revolution are tomatoes (except the Roma tomato), potatoes, cotton, canola, and papaya (currently the only GE fruit).

Genetically engineered dairy products are created from cows injected with Recombinant Bovine Growth Hormone (rBGH, also called recombinant bovine somatotropin or rBST). rBGH replicates a natural hormone, tricking cows into producing more milk. It can, in fact, increase milk production by up to 25 percent, but it usually yields only around 10 to 15 percent more for a country that already produces more milk than it uses. Unlike some other GE foods, there is no test for milk that can distinguish between cows treated with rBGH and not those not treated.

Science has created soybeans that resist herbicides, corn that kills insects, and rice that provides more vitamins. Each sounds like a good idea, right? What's the catch? If GE foods are so safe, why have they been banned in Europe and Japan?

An initial concern is health problems like allergic reactions. When we splice genes from something we are allergic to (like Brazil nuts) into something we aren't allergic to (like soy beans), the resulting plant can become allergenic. We can have an allergic reaction to the food made from that genetically engineered plant. Plants that are engineered to contain antibiotics can cause humans to build up a tolerance to the drugs that treat pneumonia and other bacterial infections.

---

rBGH

The use of rBGH has led to an increase in udder infections and levels of pus in cow milk. Milk containing rBGH also contains more bacteria, fat, and antibiotics (the result of farmers trying to treat infections). Research has shown that drinking rBGH milk can create an elevated level of IGF-1 (insulin growth-like factor) in humans, which has promoted breast and gastrointestinal cancers.[67]

With genetic engineering, there is the possibility that some tomatoes may contain fish genes. Without proper labeling regulation, there is no choice for consumers, specifically those with special diets, those who don't eat meat for ethical reasons, and those with religious restrictions.

But when a farmer decides not to use GE seeds, his crops may *still* be contaminated with what can be considered biopollution. His neighbors can render his decision obsolete as winds carry pollen from farms that use GE seeds to farms with non-GE plants, cross-pollinating the crops and genetically engineering the non-GE farmer's crops in spite of his efforts to grow pure plants.

Some GE seed companies make farmers sign agreements that they won't save or distribute GE seeds. Farmers who break the agreement are punished with fines, and sometimes the seed companies send their high priced legal teams after small farmers. Genetic technology can thus be tempting to struggling farmers. While farm subsidies pay farmers not to plant, higher, more consistent yields make the farmer more successful.

The Terminator

"Terminator seeds" is a technology that causes the plant to become sterile after only one growing season, genetically shutting off the plant's ability to germinate a second time. This ensures that farmers won't save and distribute seeds and forces them to buy more seeds next year.

Currently the U.S. government does not require stringent testing or labeling of GE foods. In fact, U.S. agencies treat genetically engineered foods no differently than other foods. They are often rushed into stores without chemical and nutritional analyses.

But Mother Nature always fights back. Despite their annoyance to humans, weeds and other pests are part of the web of life. When pushed to the wall, nature will find a way to perpetuate itself. Bugs mutate and adapt to pesticides. Weeds evolve into super-weeds that resist herbicides. Bacteria and viruses transform themselves and cause diseases that outwit antibiotics. It may sound like a cheesy science fiction novel, but when engineered plants let their new genes loose in the environment, it's possible that "super-species" might be created with the ability to conquer all obstacles to their domination of the planet. Including us.

Genetically engineered food is about the quest for the one type of seed that grows faster, yields more, and is harvested more easily. As in any modern industry, once these goals are achieved, the GE food is mass-produced with the hopes of identical results and sales to reflect its success. But the lack of diversity thus created can require more pesticides because insects and diseases have also adapted to the crops. Farming with chemicals contaminates the soil and decreases the number of birds, animals, insects, and spiders around farms.

Variety is not just the spice of life. It's essential to existence. With biodiversity, there is strength in nature. It's monoculture that leads to weakness. Biodiversity is a web of individual species woven together with interlocking tasks. Remove any of these threads, and the whole cloth becomes less stable. No part of an ecosystem is insignificant. A system that has more species is better able to handle stress and evolve into a stronger, more diverse system.

In Ireland between 1845 and 1850, 1.5 million people died of starvation or disease caused by the hunger and poverty of the potato famine. Because all of the potatoes in Ireland were genetically identical, they all rotted, which either killed the people who ate them or led to the starvation of the people who didn't eat them. The livelihood of the Irish people was thus destroyed. Had there been more diversity in the potato crop, perhaps one of the varieties could have survived, people might not have starved and their society might not have been decimated.

It might be easy to dismiss the Irish potato famine as the ignorance of an earlier generation, but currently in the U.S., 90 percent of all eggs (white eggs) are produced by one breed of chicken, the White Leghorn.[68] What happens if a disease or pest cripples this breed? An all too real crisis faces the only breed of edible banana (the Cavendish), as pests and disease threaten the genetically non-diverse crop with extinction.

Who is to blame for lack of diversity? It's not just the seed companies owned by large multinational corporations. It's not just farmers who want higher yields and consistent harvests that stand up to mechanical gathering. It's also us, the consumers who insist on cheap food.

Biodiversity tips

✓ Set up a bird feeder to invite local species back to your neighborhood. Fill sparingly during summer months so that birds do not become dependent on you for food.

✓ Toads, bats, and rabbits ... what other species are native to your area? Research habitat and encourage diversity of local critters in your backyard.

✓ Buy exotic local produce in order to encourage diverse production in your community.

Genetically engineering food is clearly akin to playing God. What makes us think that we have the right to manipulate nature? When stem cell research and human cloning are in the news, citizens revolt. Ironically, this is the same methodology used to genetically modify crops and animals. We have not explored the potential hazards that could come with this technology. Worse, we are not moving cautiously into the future, but rushing in with only the thought of success. The absence of experimentation and regulation is like flying without a parachute.

The truth is that genetically engineered products have not proven to be any more nutritious than nonengineered food. They haven't even reduced the use of pesticides. At the current time, it's extremely difficult to eat a non-GE diet. Livestock eat feed containing GE ingredients. Soy and corn derivatives are used in thousands of products. Pollination drift is widespread. With so much of supermarket food containing at least one GE ingredient, the odds are high that we consume genetically engineered products every day.

Since GE food is thus already integrated into our diet, the only way to be sure we're eating GE-free in the U.S. is to become more conscious of how and what we eat. We can grow our own food. We can eat and drink completely organic and patronize brands that have decided to go GE free, such as Wild Oats and Whole Foods store brands. Or we could just all move to Europe, where they have made genetic engineering illegal and taboo and where companies have had to remove all GE ingredients from their products.

Learn to lobby for accurate labels. Pro-GE companies fight against companies that label themselves GE-free. Without labeling, we are denied the right to choose—we just don't know which item of supermarket food includes us in the giant genetic experiment.

Cookware and containers

If it weren't bad enough to have to worry about what's in our food, now there's concern about what we put food *into*. When space age technology plastics and coatings come in direct contact with food, the transfer of chemicals can endanger our hormonal systems.

- ✓ Teflon contains perfluorochemicals (PFCs), a fluorine-based plastic that is used to create the nonstick cookware coating. The EPA is concerned about an increase in birth defects and reproductive problems as a result of flakes of Teflon that chip off and end up in food.[69] PFCs are also used in the lining of microwave popcorn bags. One of the reasons PFCs work so well as a coating is that they virtually never break down in the environment.
- ✓ Restaurants often use aluminum pans because they heat up faster. Aluminum is suspected of being connected with Alzheimer's disease.
- ✓ Stainless steel is generally safe, but if it is scratched, chromium and nickel can leach into food.
- ✓ Try to choose glass over plastic storage containers, but if plastic is the only option, choose containers with Δ1 PET or Δ2 HDPE recycling codes. These plastics are frequently recycled and not been found to leach toxins into food. Regrettably, most plastic is intended for single use and those who reuse it can encounter problems. Washing containers in hot water may cause the plastic to break down quicker and leach chemicals into whatever is put in the container next. Instead of reusing plastic water bottles, use the heavier plastic or aluminum bottles made for camping.
- ✓ The softer the plastic, the more chances it can melt into our food. Avoid using plastic utensils, especially for stovetop cooking.
- ✓ Never use plastic containers in the microwave, even the "microwave safe" containers and those that come with microwaveable foods.
- ✓ Avoid plastic wrap or transfer food as soon as possible to unbleached wax paper, aluminum foil, or a safe container.

Hope for the Future: What We Should Be Eating

Avoiding what's bad for us can help keep us healthy, but it takes modifications of our diet to naturally boost our immunity and protect us against toxins. (Look for more tips of boosting immunity with food in the *Healing* chapter, page 230.) Here are some tips for simpler and healthier eating:

- ❑ Eat closer to nature by avoiding processed foods and sticking to simple ingredients. Eat as much raw food as possible. Lightly steam vegetables and fruits to preserve their full benefits. Vary and rotate your diet. Eat lower on the food chain and limit your intake of meats and cheeses.

- ❑ Assist and repair your immune system with produce that is dark, ripe, fresh, and raw and that offers a full spectrum of vitamins.

- ❑ Look for rice and flour that are unbleached and unrefined. The refining process of turning brown grains into white ones robs the grains of most of their fiber, protein, vitamins, and minerals. Enriching doesn't begin to put back what was lost. Try whole-wheat grain products, not only breads, but also cereals, pastas, and flours.

- ❑ Just because something is labeled "fat free," "low fat," "caffeine-free" or "no sugar," doesn't necessarily mean it's good for us. Sometimes the process required to make it fat free can do more harm than good. "Low fat" means no more than three grams fat per serving and that does not mean the product contains fewer calories.

- ❑ Be cautious: "natural flavoring" may not necessarily be any healthier than artificial flavor. Many flavorings can be derived from both natural and synthetic methods.

- ❑ Watch out for products labeled "fresh." This is not a universally defined term and government regulation is subjective. A chicken labeled "fresh" can be frozen at twenty-six degrees for several weeks, "fresh" fish may be several weeks old, and meat can be called "fresh" up to six weeks after slaughter. Some produce (apples, potatoes and squash) can be washed in an acid solution and called "fresh" for up to a year. Many of the "fresh" vegetables we find at the chain grocery stores were harvested six weeks ago and trucked in from another state or country.

Going Organic

In order to trust that we're eating safely, going organic is the only way to go. Organic is a legally defined term: any food product carrying that word must be approved by a government agency. There are clear rules for what constitutes organic and what does not. Giving a legal definition to the word helps to create a standard of excellence. For more details and the current legal specifications for "organic" products, check out www.ams.usda.gov/nop.

Although there is no conclusive scientific proof that organic food is better for us, it often contains less water and has a higher nutrient content because rather than taking in pesticides from the soil, organic crops take in more nutrients and protein.

Organic produce is grown in a natural, environmentally safe manner without the use of synthetic chemical pesticides, herbicides, or fertilizers. Vegetables and fruits are grown with natural farming methods and are free of genetically modified ingredients and irradiation.

Organic meat is reared "free range," that is, without use of hormones to speed maturity or stimulate production of milk or eggs. Sick animals must be treated with homeopathic remedies rather than antibiotics.

Products labeled "100 percent organic" must contain only organic ingredients. Products labeled "organic" must be composed of 95 percent organically produced ingredients. The remaining five percent of ingredients are severely restricted to items approved by the USDA. Processed products labeled "Made with organic ingredients" must contain at least 70 to 94 percent organic ingredients. Products with less than 70 percent organic ingredients may identify specific ingredients that are organically produced on the ingredient list but may not use the term "organic" on the front of the packaging.

Organic certification agencies are agents of the USDA and have to be satisfied that the manufacturer is meeting standards for production. Know that not all organic produce is certified, however, even though it may meet standards, because certification is an expensive and time consuming process that many small local farmers cannot afford. Supporting those who farm organically encourages certification.

Good chocolate

Africa's Ivory Coast supplies 43 percent of the world's cocoa, but employs child labor in a region that still uses leaded gasoline, which pollutes the air, water, and soil where the crops are produced. To avoid these unhealthy practices, we can buy products made with organic cocoa beans (nothing organic is grown on the Ivory Coast). The leading organic brands of chocolate are also certified fair trade products that support better conditions for workers. Also look for the words "shade-grown," meaning the cacao was grown in its natural habitat (the shade of taller trees), which restores the natural habitat of wildlife. Cocoa is grown in direct sun only for higher yields.

Traditional farming methods used by organic farmers include integrated pest management (IPM) that lets natural predators—insects (such as ladybugs), butterflies, hoverflies, spiders, toads, birds, and bats—defend crops against harmful creatures.

By changing the locations of where crops are planted each year, organic farmers prevent a buildup of pests, regenerate the soil, and replenish nutrients. Each crop has its own diseases and pests. Cover crops are planted during the off-season to help keep the soil regenerated. Farmers also plant green manures. These include alfalfa, red clover, and fava beans, which hold nitrogen in their roots and enrich the soil. Soil that is rich in nutrients keeps pests and diseases at bay.

Organic farmers plant sacrificial plants around the crop for the insects and birds to feed off of instead. Companion plants also help protect the crop. Onion family plants (garlic, chives) are planted near roses to repel aphids, basil helps tomatoes resist insects and disease, and mint fends off mice and rats. Weeding and picking off pests and dead leaves is often done by hand.

Instead of chemical fertilizers, organic farmers use natural alternatives like organic compost, worm castings, seaweed, organic manure, and rock potash. Sewage sludge cannot be used.

Organic farmers may use pesticides only as a last resort, and even at that point only natural, biodegradable products: copper salts, sulfur, rotenone pyrethrum (a plant extract that harms fish and some beneficial insects as well as the pests), boric acid, and a soft soap that controls aphids. Diatomaceous earth (the shells of critters that lived long ago) is a natural pesticide that slices into the exoskeletons of insects such as ants, aphids, and slugs. Organic farmers should be able to tell when spraying a pesticide is necessary and when the plant is just dying from old age.

On the other hand

"Organic" doesn't always mean the product is free of chemical pesticides and fertilizers. While farmers are prohibited from directly applying pesticides to crops, chemicals are so pervasive in the modern world that they have entered water and air supplies where they can't be controlled.

In organic farming, animals raised for meat are allowed to live "free range." They follow their natural patterns of behavior in their natural habitat, remain with their mothers longer after birth, develop natural immunities to diseases, and lead a more dignified life and death. They are fed natural diets, as opposed to the "cannibal cow" diet of ground up dead, dying, or diseased animals found in many commercial feeds. (Cows don't actually need feed to make protein, they're fine with grass.) Their feed cannot contain GE grains. Farmers agree to abstain from cruel factory farm tactics such as debeaking chickens and docking piglets' tails.

Thinking outside the box: Newman's Own Organics

There are hundreds of organic food companies. What makes Paul Newman's company different? "Shameless exploitation in pursuit of the common good," says its founder, the blue-eyed movie star. The original Newman's Own, established by Paul Newman and A.E. Hotchner, has helped return over $250 million to charity since 1982. In 1993, Nell Newman, Paul's daughter and a self-professed "gourmet environmentalist," merged her passion for organics and her dad's altruistic tendencies to create Newman's Own Organics, which has since become a separate company. What started with a batch of organic pretzels now includes a full line of organic cookies, chocolate, popcorn, fair trade coffee, and pet food.

One of the few negative aspects of organic farming is the higher retail cost of the veggies and other products. As we support this industry, we help it mature and allow prices to stabilize. Initial higher costs do not factor in the savings of ecological resources. In organic garden and farm plots, soil is saved and remains nutrient rich and water absorbent. Runoff water is not polluted by chemical pesticides and fertilizers. The health of farm workers is respected, traditional seed varieties are kept alive, and more people are employed. Organic farms average about 50 percent less energy use, 97 percent less pesticides and about half as much fertilizer as larger factory farms.[70]

There are many favorable arguments for going organic. These include not only the chance of our improved health, but also supporting an industry whose foremost goal is farming responsibly and sustainably and reducing toxic chemical use.

Above all

If it's not possible to eat a full organic diet, consider focusing on the following products. According to the Environmental Working Group, these products are often imported from countries that allow chemicals that the U.S. has banned.[71]

Apples	Nectarines
Bell peppers (Red and green)	Peaches*
Celery	Pears
Cherries	Potatoes
Grapes (Chilean)	Spinach
Lettuce	Strawberries

* (Often have the highest rates of illegally applied pesticides)

Organic produce may not always win the pretty produce beauty contest, but in order to achieve the rows of uniformly-shaped, richer-shaded apples, waxes and pesticides may have been applied to make them last longer. Fruits and vegetables may have been pumped full of chemicals to enable them to grow in poor soil and survive thousands of miles of transport. Learn to overlook superficial flaws in organic produce. If you're still not convinced, try a blind taste test.

The little stickers found on produce do more than help the grocery checker ring your apples up at the register. The PLU (or Price Look Up) codes can help us determine how and where the product was raised. Organic produce carries a five-digit PLU code beginning with a 9, while genetically engineered or modified produce carries a five-digit number beginning with an 8.

Organic flowers

Flowers supplied to florists and supermarkets are often imported from other countries where pesticide regulations are far more lenient than they are in the U.S. To find organic flower growers near you, go to www.localharvest.org/organic-flowers.jsp. To order organic bouquets, try www.organicbouquet.com.

TO MEAT OR NOT TO MEAT: THE CASE FOR VEGETARIANISM

Once upon a time, vegetarians were considered skinny and pasty-complexioned oddballs who only ate bean sprouts, brown rice, and tofu. Today, over twelve million Americans are practicing vegetarians. At the same time, worldwide, meat consumption is at an all-time high. If the facts were known about meat production, many carnivores would probably reconsider their meat-loving ways. While vegetarianism is not for everyone, the case against meat is a strong one. And even if you can't go full on veggie, this might help you decrease the number of times you eat meat each week.

Raising animals for food consumes massive quantities of natural resources and generates a tremendous amount of pollution. Let's take a half-pound of hamburger. Raising the animal from which we get the meat for that one burger requires 3,500 pounds of water; it's estimated that we'd save more water by not eating a pound of California beef than we would by not showering for an entire year. The fossil fuels used to produce one hamburger could be used to drive a small car twenty miles.

Meat production destroys habitats, which leads to the extinction of a variety of species. In tropical beef production, one hamburger requires over 100 square feet of rain forest destruction. A large portion of U.S. land, about 860 million acres, is devoted to grazing land for meat producing animals, which could be better apportioned. Raising cattle on a ten-acre farm feeds only two people. When corn is grown on those ten acres, ten people are fed. When wheat is grown, twenty-four people are fed. When soybeans are grown, sixty people are fed.[72]

That same hamburger also creates twelve pounds of livestock manure and other pollutants. In fact, farmed animals produce more greenhouse gases through their tailpipes than all the cars and trucks in the world combined.

Three companies produce sixty percent of all hogs in America, and each of these animals creates two to four times as much waste as a human being. There are no sewage treatment plants for hog farms. The manure is stored in lagoons that emit at least 130 different gases, including ammonia. In 1995, a record spill occurred in North Carolina when a dike surrounding a hog waste lagoon collapsed. According to the EPA, over 20 million gallons of excrement and urine were dumped. (Other sources set the figure higher, at 35 million gallons.) Virtually all aquatic life was killed, an estimated 10 to 14 million fish, and 364,000 acres of coastal shell fishing beds had to be closed.[73] This was not an isolated incident. Damaging spills have also occurred in Virginia, Maryland, Iowa, Minnesota, and Missouri.

It's the cultures that base their diets on meat that suffer from more "diseases of affluence"—heart disease, stroke, and hormonal cancers. A diet of less meat and more plants tends to be lower in overall fat and cholesterol, lower in calories, and higher in dietary fiber. The vitamins, minerals, and antioxidants found in a plant-based diet can also help fight cancer by attacking free radicals. A high-plant diet also elevates the amount of sex hormone-binding globulin (SHBG) in blood. This hormone stabilizes menstrual cycles, reduces incidences of hormone-based cancers, and may affect our moods and behaviors.

Thinking outside the box: Innately vegetarian

Dr. Peter J. D'Adamo, author of *Eat Right 4 Your Type*, has studied the connection between our blood type, our diet, and our good health. Based on a theory pioneered by his father, D'Adamo developed lists of foods that are compatible with the four main blood types, including one that recommends vegetarianism. Our inability to lose weight, our predisposition toward certain diseases, and even so-called allergic reactions may be a result of eating the wrong foods for our blood type.[74] (See also www.dadamo.com.)

Each year thousands of people are admitted to hospital emergency rooms with complaints of food poisoning. It's estimated that there may be upwards of 80 million less severe cases that are assumed to be something else. It should make us wonder—"What's in the beef?" When we realize the majority of food diseases originate from animal products, another check goes in the vegetarianism column.

Staphylococcal bacteria, present in humans in the nose and throat as well as in skin infections, cause diarrhea, cramps, and vomiting. The bacteria enter our food by way of contact with infected people, who may sneeze on or handle meats, cheeses, egg products, and poultry. Staph bacteria are killed by heating or freezing, but they tend to multiply in food that has been frozen, then heated, then refrozen.

Salmonella is the most common bacterial food-borne illness with over 2,300 types. It multiplies by dividing in poultry, raw meat, fish, eggs, unpasteurized milk, even in vegetables, and causes upset stomach, cramps, diarrhea, headaches, and (in severe cases) death. Bacteria are killed by irradiation, bleach, and cooking.

There are hundreds of types of *E. coli* bacteria, but *E. coli 0157:H7* is a rare strain that produces large quantities of a potent toxin that destroys our intestinal lining. When meat is contaminated during unsanitary slaughter conditions, the E. coli survive and multiply at refrigerator and freezer temperatures. They can be killed by cooking and using bleach on cooking surfaces. Symptoms of infection are severe diarrhea and abdominal cramps.

Listeria are found in soil and water and transmitted through manure used as fertilizer. Animals can carry these bacteria without appearing ill and contaminate dairy products and meats. Listeria infection can take up to six weeks to show flu-like symptoms (fever, fatigue, nausea) and can lead to septicemia or meningitis if not properly diagnosed and treated. Cooking foods thoroughly kills the bacteria.

Bovine Spongiform Encephalopathy (BSE), or mad cow disease, is the Big Scary of the meat world, the one that turned Oprah off hamburgers and drops the price of fast food stock any time it's mentioned in the news. BSE is a degenerative brain disorder of cattle caused by feeding cows a cannibal diet of animal feed containing "rendered byproduct" (also called "ruminant protein"), which can include ground-up sick beef, lamb, and pork meal. Normally herbivores, cows fed a carnivorous diet grow faster and meatier. Human consumption of infected meat can lead to brain damage and death. Testing can be done before slaughter, but cooking and freezing won't kill the cause of the disease.

On the other hand: Food disparagement laws

A group of Texas cattlemen sued Oprah Winfrey in 1996 over a specific comment she made on TV about never eating a hamburger again after learning about mad cow disease. (They didn't win the suit.) Thirteen states have laws to protect farm groups and food companies from media reports that might cause consumers to avoid their products.

To steer clear of food-borne diseases on meat, poultry, and eggs:

- ❏ Never cut vegetables with the same knife used to cut meat.
- ❏ Never thaw any meat on the counter. Keep it in the refrigerator.
- ❏ Rinse preparation surfaces, hands, and utensils in boiling water immediately after use. Wipe with a light disinfectant solution. (See *Cleaning* chapter for some all-natural, non-chlorine bleach alternatives.)
- ❏ Use clean dishtowels every time you prepare meat products.
- ❏ Cook food thoroughly. Cover leftovers and put them away as soon as they have cooled.
- ❏ When in doubt, throw it out. Is food poisoning really worth taking a chance on that old ham sandwich?

No discussion of vegetarianism is complete without an analysis of animal rights. While some choose not to eat meat for dietary reasons, others make the choice solely for ethical reasons.

> A rat is a dog is a boy.
>
> –Ingrid Newkirk, PETA

This infamous quote implies that all living beings are created equal. But should animals have the same rights as humans? Do animals have souls? Should a cow be equal to, say, Katie Couric? If not, and if only some animals have rights, where is the line of demarcation between those with rights and those without? What makes a dog more important than a mountain goat? What about reptiles and microscopic organisms? The fact that this argument will probably never end makes vegetarianism a very personal decision.

We've all heard stories of brutality toward animals and the farm factory practices that turn livestock into fast and easy food. While the number of American farms has decreased, the overall size of farms has increased. Factory farms (sometimes called Concentrated Animal Feeding Operations) are structured to produce maximum returns with as many animals as possible.

Livestock are not covered under the animal welfare act and are often considered only property or machines. Factory farm animals have become so overly crossbred that they are among the stupidest animals on earth. They are kept in very close quarters. When one gets sick, the entire pen (sometimes upwards of 10,000 animals or birds) must be treated with antibiotics as a prophylactic measure, whether or not other animals show signs of disease.

Stupid poultry

✓ Chicken embryos have been successfully grown with four legs instead of two.

✓ Chickens are hyper-stimulated with artificial light to get them to lay eggs sooner.

✓ Turkeys, which lack the instinct to feed themselves, often have to be taught to eat and drink by placing a chicken in their pen.

Is it the same hormones fed to poultry that are causing young women to reach puberty earlier, older women to reach menopause earlier, and even creating fewer male babies?

Cuts of meat used for food are not the only products made from rendered parts of animals: Gelatin is created from boiled hooves and horns and used in marshmallows, gelatin desserts, and vitamin capsules. Tallow or fat from livestock is used in candles, margarine, lubricants, waxes, lipstick, soaps, film, and cosmetics. Collagen, extracted from bones, hides, and hooves, is found in moisturizers and lotions. Pet foods can contain road kill, byproducts of the food and beverage industry, parts of livestock, and even euthanized dogs and cats from shelters.

The average meat-eating American consumes about twice the amount of protein the human body needs, and it's a misconception that those who don't eat meat don't get enough protein. The vegetarian diet can be completely balanced and provide all the vitamins and nutrition of a meat diet. Besides, vegetarian foods have been designed to mimic flavors and consistencies of meat products, making the line between telling the difference between real and faux meat less obvious.

Types of vegetarians

✓ *Lacto-ovo vegetarians* don't eat meat, poultry, fish or seafood, but they do consume milk, milk products, and eggs.

✓ *Lacto-vegetarians* are similar, but don't eat eggs.

✓ *Piscitarians* or *pescetarians* do eat fish, but don't eat meat or poultry.

✓ *Vegans* avoid all animal foods and products, including eggs, dairy, and even honey.

✓ *Fruitarians* are similar to vegans, but avoid processed and even cooked foods. They eat raw fruit, grains, and nuts.

✓ The *macrobiotic diet* is a modified vegetarian version of the traditional Japanese diet that means eating more whole grains, beans, and fresh vegetables. It's also a philosophy of living in balance with nature, eating only those foods that grow regionally and in season, and foods that balance the forces of yin and yang within your body. Many turn to macrobiotics for recovery during heart disease, cancer, and diabetes.

SEAFOOD

Fish may be the most efficient source of beneficial essential fatty acids, but the demand for higher yields has created a "catch as much as you can" mentality in the fishing industry, leading to over-fishing and killing more than necessary. Sixty percent of the fish that the Food and Agriculture Organization of the United Nations traces are categorized as "fully exploited, overexploited, or depleted."[75] Fish are now being located by sonar or spotter aircraft, which is the equivalent of shooting fish in the proverbial barrel.

Over-fishing has not only depleted fish stocks but also subsequently impacted other sea life that relies on these disappearing species. The demand for fish doesn't equal the amount of fish being wasted as a result of bycatch. Each year, 60 billion pounds of fish, sharks, and seabirds die when they are caught accidentally as a result of industrial fishing techniques. Shrimp fishing is the most destructive; for each pound of shrimp caught, between four and ten pounds of dead or dying marine life are returned back to the ocean.[76]

> If cod and haddock and other species cannot survive because man kills them, something more adaptable will take their place. Nature, the ultimate pragmatist, doggedly searches for something that works. But as the cockroach demonstrates, what works best in nature does not always appeal to us.
>
> –Mark Kurlansky, *Cod: A Biography of the Fish That Changed the World*[77]

Fish hatcheries (where fish are hatched, then released into the wild) limit diversity in much the same way as producing the same variety of white eggs does. When these fish are released, they can crossbreed with wild fish, raising the possibility of passing on the new genes to offspring. This dilutes the gene pool of genetic characteristics that allow wilder fish to better adapt to predators and natural conditions.

Farm fish are raised in metal or mesh net cages located along the ocean coasts of the U.S., Canada, Norway, Scotland, and Chile. Rather than relieving pressure on ocean fish stocks, farmed salmon actually increases it. Pens can contain hundreds of thousands of fish that grow to full size in half the time, but approximately three tons of wild fish are needed to raise one ton of farmed salmon.[78]

These fish farms are chemically intensive and damage the ecological balance. They are breeding grounds for parasites that require treatment with pesticides and antibiotics. Wastes from these fish farms pollute ocean beds. Decomposition of dead fish leads to a shortage of vital oxygen in nearby waters. Farmed fish occasionally escape and negatively impact wild populations by introducing diseases and parasites. The diet of fishmeal fed to farmed salmon produces a pale gray or yellowish flesh, so chemicals are used to recreate the bright coral color of wild salmon meat.

Industrial and civilian pollution of waterways contaminates fish and shellfish in our rivers and lakes. These contaminated fish store toxins like mercury and PCB in their fat. Unfortunately, despite all the benefits of eating seafood, environmental concerns have made it necessary to be cautious when selecting that lobster from the tank at the A&P, pointing to the catch of the day on the menu of our favorite land-locked restaurant, or even dropping a line off our own dock.

Hope for the Future

As good as eating fish is for us, trying to remember which fish to eat can be terribly confusing. Is cod over-fished? Is this salmon farm-raised? Is Atlantic halibut likely to contain mercury? To eat safely as well as tastily, remember these tips:

- ❑ Pick deep cold saltwater fishes (haddock, cod, salmon, tuna, snapper, and flounder), which are recommended because they are considered to be the least contaminated by pollutants.
- ❑ Avoid coastal and freshwater fish, especially if you are unaware of the water quality of the area the fish came from. Safer options are fish from high mountain lakes and streams.
- ❑ Select smaller, leaner, and younger fish. These are preferable because the fish has had less time to accumulate toxins. Fish low in fat content are bass, rainbow trout, and white perch.
- ❑ Be warned of fish more prone to mercury contamination: tuna, king mackerel, Atlantic halibut, pike, sea bass, shark, and swordfish.
- ❑ Look for Alaskan salmon, which are guaranteed to be wild because salmon farms have been outlawed in Alaska.

THE HOW, WHERE, AND WHY OF FOOD SHOPPING

The more complex we make our food processes, the less control we have over what we eat. In the 21st century, our eating habits are directly related to how convenient food is. When we're hungry, we race to a drive-thru. Wandering up and down the aisles of the grocery store, we confront products we would never have imagined eating if they weren't so cheap and readily available. Shopping and diet discipline means analyzing how, where, and why we shop.

How We Shop for Food

When we buy something, we're telling the creator, seller, or original owner, "Thank you, you're doing a great job, keep up the good work," regardless of how we actually feel about the product. Our purchase triggers the supplier to make more. Altering how we shop for food means making conscious decisions about avoiding ingredients we know are not healthy. Here are some suggestions for food shopping as a simplist.

❑ Buy food when it's in season. Purchasing off-season produce encourages markets to continue to stock the product, forcing produce to be shipped thousands of miles. It also pushes farmers to manipulate nature. Nature has cycles that usually work best without human interference. Chemicals are used to trick fruits and vegetables into ripening at the same time, making harvesting easier. But produce will lose vitamins, especially vitamins A and C, the longer it sits on a truck or in the produce section at the store. Americans demand internationally grown food, and because we have more money than smaller economies, other cultures will cut the product out of their own diet and sell it to us. It's better to buy canned products during the winter months rather than purchase fresh fruits or vegetables that were flown in from other countries.

❑ Read labels. Learn to recognize chemical additives, even by their aliases.

❑ Educate yourself about additives and GE and other issues and let your legislators know how you feel.

❑ Call the company and express your opinions if you don't like the packaging your favorite food comes in. Companies do listen to consumer requests. Ask if they sell it in different packaging, such as larger quantity for restaurant supply.

❑ Talk to the produce manager where you shop and express your concerns about pesticides, organics, seasonal, and regional produce. Ask the butcher what type of farms the meat and poultry they stock are raised on. If they don't know, ask them to find out for you.

❑ Learn to read produce cards at the market. They will often tell us where an apple or a stalk of broccoli or whatever was grown, how it was grown, and whether it's organic or waxed. The cards also give nutritional information and suggestions for cooking.

❑ Ask for it. If you can't find a particular product at your favorite supermarket, ask the manager to stock it for you. Supermarkets often keep in stock an item that's been asked for by only a couple people. Getting to know employees at your local supermarket fosters a relationship and proves you are a loyal customer.

Dining Out

We want fast food because we know exactly what we're getting—a highly researched taste and olfactory sensation created by combining flavor additives to make the most desirable beef patty. We're comfortable with fast food. It has become a constant in our lives. And, really, who wants to chance that roadside diner off the interstate when a familiar sign across the street tells us "cheap, easy, fast and familiar"?

In 1970, Americans spent $6 billion on fast food. By 2005, our fast food budget had ballooned to over $130 billion,[79] which is more than we spend on movies, books, magazines, newspapers, videos, and music combined. During this time we have also seen the rates of childhood obesity and diabetes double. Well over half our food dollars are spent on restaurant meals, ready-to-eat store-bought meals, and convenience foods.

Most people have no concern for nutrition when they eat out; they usually make eating out an excuse to treat themselves to something expensive or ignore their diets. The nutritional value of fast food is questionable at best and when we eat out, we have little knowledge of the fat, sugar, and salt contained in the meals we order.

Let's dine out by patronizing restaurants with a commitment to healthy and sustainable food preparation. For a start, look for restaurants that specialize in vegetarian and organic dishes. Ask natural and health food stores for recommendations.

Thinking outside the box: A few good meals with good karma

✓ *O'Naturals* was started by Gary Hirschberg of Stonyfield Farms as a natural and organic alternative to fast food. They serve soups, sandwiches, and noodles at locations in Maine, Massachusetts, North Carolina, Florida and Kansas. (See www.onaturals.com.)

✓ *The White Dog Café* of Philadelphia encourages diners to patronize other local ethnic restaurants, sponsors annual multicultural events and community tours, and has sister relationships with restaurants all over the globe. (See www.whitedog.com.)

✓ *Chez Panisse* in Berkeley, California, is chef Alice Waters' organic restaurant. It supports the Chez Panisse Foundation, which teaches local school children what it preaches about sustainable agriculture and integrates lessons into school lunch programs. (See www.chezpanisse.com.)

Picture this: Italy, 1986. We rush to the McDonalds counter and order our Royale with Cheese. Three minutes later, we're back sightseeing at the Coliseum. What? Wait a minute—*this is Italy?* Where spaghetti comes from? And scaloppini, rigatoni, lasagna, gnocchi, fettuccini alfredo, calzone, bruschetta, eggplant parmesan, not to mention pizza. This is not the land of the instant hamburger!

It was this type of experience that led Carlo Petrini to realize that the introduction of the fast food culture was threatening not only the landscape of his country, but its eating habits as well. *Slow Food* is more than just resisting the temptations of the ever-present Golden Arches; the organization promotes mindful eating as a way to bring us into the present. With more than 80,000 members worldwide, Slow Food's manifesto describes itself as "a movement for the protection of the right to taste." More than just supplying our bodies with sustenance, they want us to be conscious of the "meal" as a force that brings people together, strengthening families and communities and fostering a slower, simpler pace of life. (See www.slowfood.com.)

Where We Shop for Food

The local big box grocery store may appear to be well stocked, but let's look more closely. What we see is evidence of our society's insistence on convenience. The big chains are influenced by the big money; the top twenty food processors control 53 percent of the revenues of top 100.[80] These are the products that get the most face time. To find the diet, health, and organic sections in these gargantuan grocery stores, we must hunt down four-foot sections hidden among thousands of processed products. For shopping without having to scrutinize every label with a magnifying glass, try the following suggestions.

❑ Try specialty health food stores such as Trader Joe's, Whole Foods (Bread & Circus), or Wild Oats. The stores stock a wide variety of natural, organic, and vegetarian products and their sales people are usually knowledgeable and enthusiastic about the products they carry.

❑ See the National Cooperative Business Association (www.ncba.org) for lists of food co-ops. Co-ops are groups of people who organize large purchases of grocery goods through a wholesale catalog to be shared among members.

❑ Find out who's farming in your area. Farmers' markets are usually held on a regular basis and can be found by checking newspapers for community events. The money spent here goes directly to the farmer, eliminating the middleman costs of transportation and retailing.

❑ Support local organic farmers. The average pound of food in America travels between 1,300 and 2,500 miles before it reaches the dinner plate, with local produce, not only is it fresher because it has less distance to travel, but it also spends less time on a truck and requires less energy and fuel for transport.

❑ Patronize restaurants that develop relationships with local farmers and work with natural growing seasons.

❑ Community Supported Agriculture (CSA) is based on the teachings of British economist E.F. Schumacher, who urges "a return to small-scale local and regional economies as a means of promoting prosperity, local self-reliance, and democracy; of preserving the environment and restoring civic responsibility."[81] Farms are relatively small and members pay the farmer up front for a share of the produce, then share in the successes and the failures of the farm. If CSA doesn't exist in your area, try placing a classified ad or talk to local produce growers about offering to help harvest for a share of the crop.

❑ Grow it yourself by planting a garden or helping out with a school garden. Gardening is one of Americans' favorite outdoor pastimes, but even if we're stuck in a small apartment with a brown thumb, we can plant pots of herbs or chili peppers in window boxes and pots on the patio. If you have room for an outdoor plot, start small, and pick up a gardening book to get to know your climate zone and what types of plants are well suited to your area. You're more likely to be successful if you stick with proven methods and plants. When you are finally producing a product, consider saving seeds from your best efforts. If you get really good, make up seed packets for friends telling them how you nurtured your plants.

Why We Shop for Food

Do you wonder why we have one of the most obese societies with the highest number of eating disorders in history? The diet industry is a $40 billion industry. This is shocking, considering the fact that 95 percent of all dieters will regain their lost weight within one to five years.[82] It seems that half the population is too fat and doesn't know it, while the other half thinks they they're too fat when they really aren't. Processed food, minimal exercise, red meat consumption, and ambivalence are the curses of the overweight, while self-image, mediated ideals of perfection, and self-control are the curses of the underweights and "just rights."

"Fat" is seen as a sickness, but in order to lose weight (and keep it off) we must change how we view food and simplify our eating habits. Man is the only creature that eats when not hungry and, more often than not, will continue to eat after full. Other animals instinctively feed themselves when their bodies need energy to a point where they are physically satisfied. For most animals, eating is only a method of survival, whereas humans eat out of a response to satisfy emotional needs: to alleviate anxiety, to fill inner emptiness, to anesthetize against emotional pain, to fill time, to distract. Like any addiction, we use overeating (or undereating) to compensate for something else lacking in our lives.

Domesticated animals (meaning any animal that has been trained by humans: dogs, cats, pigeons, squirrels, even our children) have been taught to beg for food. Food is treated as a reward. It's compensation for something done correctly. Food withheld is a punishment. Mom always said, "Finish what's on your plate, there are starving children in [insert Third World country here])" and "If you don't eat all your peas, you won't get dessert."

In 1985, we sang, "We are the world," but famine conditions continue in Africa as a result of the greenhouse effect. There's plenty of food to feed the world's people—if it were distributed evenly. Americans must learn to consider how our lifestyle affects the global food supply, specifically, those less fortunate than us. Polluted water and air are global problems. Keeping the environment clean will allow everyone to have a chance to eat safe food.

"There's nothing to eat," though the refrigerator is full and the cupboards are stocked. "I'm starving," I say as it nears lunchtime, though I ate breakfast only a few hours ago. Most of us don't know what it's like to live and not know where or when—or if—our next meal is coming. An even sadder thought is the amount of food we waste while people in our own towns struggle to provide food for their families. What can we do to ease the food burden of our neighbors and our community?

- ❏ What if all grocery stores and restaurants were required to donate leftover perishable food or compost it rather than just throwing it away?
- ❏ Test your love affair with (excess) food. Try going without food for a day. Donate the money you would have spent on food to a soup kitchen.
- ❏ Make food incidental by filling your life with so many other meaningful things that you don't have time to think about food all the time.
- ❏ Serve smaller portions and serve meals in stages to slow down eating speeds. Remember, your stomach fills up faster than your brain can tell you it's no longer hungry.
- ❏ Freeze-ahead meals are a great way to cut back on food waste and cut preparation and clean up time for meals. Be sure to write what's in the container and when you made it in permanent ink before storing it. Mom always said, "Air is the enemy of food," so use airtight containers and plastic bags to double seal your meal.

Sometimes simplicity really is just ordering a pizza, but in the long run, changing your eating habits can improve your health and the health of the planet. Do the best you can and if you can't go completely organic right away, start by switching to simpler ingredients.

Do it today
What would it take for you to stop eating meat?

ADDITIONAL RESOURCES

HEALTHY EATING

Earth Save (www.EarthSave.org) promotes food choices that are healthy for people and the planet and advocates a shift toward a plant-based diet and compassionate action for all life on earth. Howard Lyman, president of Earth Save International, was the co-defendant with Oprah Winfrey in the lawsuit filed by the Texas cattlemen.

Lappé, Frances Moore. *Diet for a Small Planet.* New York: Ballantine Books, 1991 (originally published in 1971). Lappé has updated her classic on the social significance of changing the way we eat.

Renders, Eileen, N.D. *Food Additives, Nutrients & Supplements A to Z: A Shopper's Guide.* Santa Fe: Clear Light Publishers, 1999. A dictionary to help decipher food additives.

Schlosser, Eric. *Fast Food Nation: The Dark Side of the All-American Meal.* Boston: Houghton Mifflin, 2001. Commentary on the effects of fast food on our society.

Steinman, David and Samuel S. Epstein, M.D. *The Safe Shopper's Bible.* New York: Macmillan, 1995. A Consumer's Guide to Nontoxic Household Products, Cosmetics and Food. Contains a list of 161 hazardous ingredients found in household products to reference what's in our favorite soup, cleanser, and eye shadow. Also rates products for their safety in terms of carcinogens, neurotoxins, and irritants.

GENETICALLY ENGINEERED FOOD

Cooper, Ann. *Bitter Harvest: A Chef's Perspective on the Hidden Danger in the Foods We Eat and What You Can Do About It.* New York: Routledge, 2000.

Cummins, Ronnie and Ben Lilliston. *Genetically Engineered Food: A Self Defense Guide for Consumers.* New York: Marlow & Company, 1999.

Lappé, Marc and Britt Bailey. *Against the Grain: Biotechnology and the Corporate Takeover of Your Food.* Monroe, ME: Common Courage Press, 1998.

Shiva, Vandana. *Tomorrow's Biodiversity.* New York: Thames & Hudson, Inc., 2000.

EATING LOCAL

Kingsolver, Barbara. *Animal, Vegetable, Miracle: A Year of Food Life*. New York: Harper Collins, 2007. Kingsolver and her family spend a year on their Kentucky farmhouse with the goal of eating only either what they can grow themselves or what was created locally.

Smith, Alisa and J.B. MacKinnon. *Plenty: Eating Locally on The 100-Mile Diet*. New York: Three Rivers Press, 2007. Couple Smith and Mackinnon try eating only ingredients that were produced within a 100-mile radius of wherever they were for an entire year.

The American Community Gardening Association (www.communitygarden.org) is a support group for the estimated 10,000 community gardeners throughout the world. The ACGA offers education, networking, publications, and solutions to challenges that face programs, and hosts an annual conference for anyone who wants to garden.

ORGANICS

The Organic Consumers Association (www.organicconsumers.org) promotes food safety, organic farming, and sustainable agriculture practices. They publish one print newsletter (*Organic View*) and two electronic newsletters (*BioDemocracy News* and *Organic Bytes*).

The Organic Trade Association (www.ota.com) is a membership organization for the North American organics industry with news and information about organics.

For a listing of Farmers' Markets in your area see the USDA's locator page(www.ams.usda.gov/farmersmarkets).

chapter 7

transporting

Why devote an entire chapter to the car? In 2006, there were over 800 million vehicles on the planet. Of these, more than 260 million were cars and light trucks used in the U.S.[83] Worldwide, the number of cars increases five times as fast as the number of humans, but, remarkably, 92 percent of the world's population will never own a car.

The importance of the car in our lives comes with a hefty monetary and ecological price tag. We like to believe that the expense, pollution, and traffic problems are easily compensated by the freedom and mobility that owning a car affords us. Even considering all the reasons we can find against auto ownership, we continue to depend on our cars. Has the automobile truly made our lives more simple? Or will we find that their environmental impact has made them not very convenient at all?

THE TRUE COST OF CAR OWNERSHIP

How much does our car really cost us? The *fixed costs* of car ownership are set amounts that don't depend on how much or how far we drive. Whether we have a hundred-mile daily commute or only use our car to drive our grandmother to church once a week, we still pay auto insurance, routine maintenance (such as oil and filter changes), license fees, smog tests, vehicle registration, and monthly car payment including finance charges.

There are also hidden expenses. The *variable costs* of car ownership are the expenses that are dependent on how much we drive. Gasoline, new tires, emergency maintenance charges (towing, repairs, labor costs), parking fees (for garages, lots, and street meters), tolls for bridges and toll roads, and tickets (parking, speeding, and other moving violations) are all costs that fluctuate according to how much or how little we drive.

What's your per mile fuel cost of driving?

M = Average of how many miles between fill-ups (e.g., 300 miles)

G = How many gallons of gas your tank holds (e.g., 14)

M ÷ G = mpg (how many miles per gallon your car gets, e.g., 21.4)

H = How much gas costs right now = (e.g., $3.29 per gallon in Los Angeles)

H ÷ mpg = How much it costs to drive one mile. (It costs 15 cents to drive a mile in this gas-guzzler.) ·

Unnecessary car-related purchases is a category of charges that may be luxury items. Still, these expenditures can add up—car washes, detailing, and a million miscellaneous accessories like car stereos, alarm systems, and fuzzy dice to hang from the rearview mirror.

Stop & think: Mileage-based driving

Why should we have to pay to build a bridge in Indianapolis if we never leave Muncie? Mileage-based driving is a fair system that taxes the people who drive the most and removes the burden from those who have found alternative methods of transport. There are currently several companies trying institute mileage-based driving insurance plans, where drivers will be charged according to how much they actually drive.

Cars can also be equipped with a sensor that easily charges drivers for the roads, bridges, tunnels and parking lots they actually use. These automatic toll systems are already effective in areas like Massachusetts, New York, and Washington, D.C. They save commuters collectively thousands of hours a year in time lost to traffic at tollbooths.

We can add up the totals of these three categories to get a preliminary estimate of yearly operating costs for our car. But wait—there's still more.

We forget to consider the *hidden costs* of driving, many of which are paid by non-drivers. Fuel taxes charged at the pump give only a clue about how much it costs to drive. Included in our yearly state and federal taxes is funding for road building and development, street cleaning, accident services (emergency and rescue crews, ambulances, fire crews), policing (the highway patrol) and parking enforcement (meter maids). Non-drivers should keep their eyes open for legislation that supports a tax reduction for those without cars.

"Free parking" is never free. A parking lot or garage located in an urban setting takes up valuable real estate. Owners attempt to recover their costs by hiding fees in the prices of the goods and services we buy *after* we've parked our car. Even when we walk to a shopping mall, anything we buy includes a fee that helps pay for the 3,000-car parking lot.

Another forgotten expense—how much is our time worth? We lose time and money when we're stuck in traffic. Multiply your hourly salary by the amount of time you spent stopped in traffic this week and you'll get an idea of how much money you actually waste in your car. But don't bother submitting this time sheet to Accounting.

Each year, American drivers are responsible for over 40,000 deaths and three million injuries,[84] creating a monetary cost that can hardly be estimated and an emotional toll that is incalculable. Those who drive less get in fewer car accidents and require less money to be spent on emergency services and medical coverage. Why should we pay for someone else's whiplash?

> One may whimsically note that these arteries—of concrete or asphalt—are hardened arteries, and that they are subject to clotting (especially at rush hour), a phenomenon which in turn raises the blood pressure in the more vulnerable arteries of drivers.
>
> –Paul L. Wachtel, *The Poverty of Affluence*[85]

The cost of auto ownership is not just financial. Our health is also an important consideration. Breathing problems are caused by poor air quality and a sedentary lifestyle that arises from car dependence. Stress and aggravation lead to road rage. We deal with traffic, maintenance problems, being late, finding legal parking places, and a free-floating anxiety that comes with owning a highly "stealable" vehicle.

Our car dependence also separates us from something we need, a connection to our community. The car is a shell that insulates us from our neighborhood and our neighbors. In our car, though we can isolate ourselves from the problems of the world and feel protected, we never know when we're going to need one of those neighbors to help us change a tire.

The *ecological impact* of driving goes far beyond the visible effects of smog and sprawl. Cars affect every environment, not just those we are allowed to drive through.

Air is vital to our existence, but cars are a leading contributor to its pollution. Gases released by automobiles influence global temperatures and daily weather. Cars add a considerable contribution to three million air pollution-related deaths worldwide each year.[86]

Any time carbon is burned, whether from gasoline, wood, coal, or garbage, it binds with oxygen. When it binds with only one atom of oxygen it becomes carbon monoxide [CO]; with two atoms, carbon dioxide [CO_2]. Carbon monoxide, a colorless, odorless gas, is formed as car exhaust. When we breathe CO, it replaces the oxygen in our red blood cells, making us dizzy. Carbon monoxide poisoning manifests as lethargy, nausea, and tingling; too much carbon monoxide, and we become unconscious. A large enough dose can kill. The gas slows reaction time and affects brain function. Studies reveal that often drivers responsible for accidents have much higher levels of carbon monoxide in their blood.

One gallon of gasoline weighs around eight pounds, six pounds of which is carbon. When that gallon of gasoline is burned, the carbon combines with oxygen to create twenty-two pounds of atmospheric carbon dioxide. In a year, one typical North American car can add five tons of CO_2 to the atmosphere. These tons contribute greatly to the greenhouse effect and global warming.[87]

On the other hand: Just plant more trees?

Why can't we just plant more trees to deal with the carbon dioxide? It sounds like a nifty idea, but there's just too much pollution and not enough unoccupied land space to hold the number of trees needed to counteract the damage carbon dioxide does every day. Author and naturalist Bill McKibben notes, for example, that planting "enough American Sycamores to soak up fifty years of the world's output of carbon dioxide from fossil fuel burning would cover a land area the size of Europe."[88] Even if there were enough available space to plant these trees, there's nothing to say that they would survive until maturity where they would be able to be most effective. Trees would absorb carbon, but only temporarily, because after they die, the carbon is released as they burn or rot.

Ozone [O_3] is another critical air polluter. It's important to note that there are actually two types of ozone. Stratospheric ozone, located between twelve and thirty miles above the earth's surface, shields us from the sun's harmful ultraviolet radiation and maintains earth's hospitable climate. This is the ozone that has been depleted by the chlorofluorocarbons (CFCs) found in aerosol propellants and refrigerating and air conditioning units.

The second type is ground ozone, more commonly referred to and recognized as *smog*. This ozone is formed when exhaust pollutants, nitrogen oxides, and hydrocarbons from gasoline-powered vehicles (and industry) cook in sunlight. The result is that thick brown haze hanging over heavily populated cities that creates not only poor visibility but also a reduction in crop yields. Smog can lead to breathing problems, coughing, and temporary loss of lung function, especially in children, the elderly, and those with previously diagnosed asthma and bronchitis.

After dark

A tip from the National Safety Council: if you must get gasoline during warm weather, try to refuel after the sun goes down. This reduces the chance of the volatile organic compounds and ozone vapors reacting with sunlight and becoming ground-level ozone.

Nitrogen dioxide [NO$_2$] is a light brown gas created by high combustion processes. It causes chemical and structural changes in the lungs, lowers our resistance to respiratory infections, and yellows the healthy leaves of trees. The catalytic converter was invented in the 1970s to be a smog control device that would break down nitrogen and oxygen in car exhaust. Unfortunately, as the quality of the converter improves, sometimes it rearranges the nitrogen oxygen compounds and forms nitrous oxide, (aka laughing gas), which is 300 times more damaging than carbon dioxide in exacerbating the greenhouse effect. In 1998, the EPA showed that 7.2 percent of greenhouse gas is nitrous oxide, half of which is emitted by cars and trucks.[89]

Even gassing up has plenty of hazards. Unleaded gas is anywhere from one to five percent benzene, and up to 80 percent of the benzene in the air we breathe is released at gas pumps when we're refueling our cars. Chronic exposure to benzene can cause chromosomal damage in animals and blood diseases such as leukemia in humans.

In-car air pollution

The air quality inside our car is worse during the winter when we're unable to roll down the windows without suffering from hypothermia. To reduce pollution levels inside your car, consider buying an air filter or ion generator that plugs into your car's cigarette lighter. Be sure to get a model that uses activated carbon to remove both particles and toxic gases.

While air pollution is the first harmful byproduct of car use most of us think of, ground pollution can often be much more hazardous. Chemicals that leach into the ground can destroy entire supplies of drinking water and wildlife habitats.

Antifreeze can leak into soil from roadway runoff. One of the first California condors released into wild was found dead 9 months later after it had drunk from a puddle of antifreeze containing ethylene glycol. If ethylene glycol gets inside your car or is tracked into the house on your shoes, it can cause headaches, asthmatic symptoms, fatigue, muscle soreness, depression, and one-sided pupil dilation. Because the sweet taste of ethylene glycol makes it a poisoning threat, always keep antifreeze locked away from children and pets and repair coolant leaks immediately. Consider using propylene glycol, which is far less toxic if accidentally ingested, instead of ethylene glycol as antifreeze in your car.

Phosphate soaps used by car washes flow down into storm drains, introducing phosphates into lakes and rivers, which leads to algae bloom. Patronize car washes that use only phosphate-free soaps. Wash your own car with castile soap or vinegar.

De-icing with road salt can contaminate the groundwater, reduce soil permeability, and damage wildlife and trees. To melt the ice on your driveway or sidewalk, switch to sand. Lobby your community to switch to safer alternatives, such as calcium magnesium acetate.

Oil and water really don't mix. Every year, people who change their own oil illegally dispose of two hundred million gallons of motor oil. That equals about 120 Exxon Valdez spills.[90] Used oils contain hydrocarbons and heavy metals and are flammable and toxic. Thirty-seven percent of ocean oil pollution is motor oil, and a single gallon of oil can contaminate about a million gallons of water. A rule of thumb: whenever you take any fluid out of the car, never dispose of it yourself. Take it to a recycling facility.

Eighty percent of car batteries are recycled, but each one of the 20 percent that are disposed of improperly and illegally can leak about nineteen pounds of lead and a gallon of sulfuric acid into soil and groundwater. Batteries are fairly easy to recycle. The sulfuric acid and lead are either reprocessed for reuse or sent to a hazardous waste dump. If the garage where you buy your new battery doesn't accept the old one for recycling, Sears Automotive locations will take it free of charge.

Mercury is used in high-intensity headlights, anti-lock brake systems, global positioning screens, and trunk or hood-mounted light switches. It takes only minute amounts of mercury to contaminate water and wildlife. While the automobile industry has agreed to phase out most uses of mercury in switches, it also claims that it would be nearly impossible to remove existing switches because of their widespread use.

A car uses up approximately one tire per year. Two to three billion tires currently lie exposed in landfills and scrap yards. These tires create disposal problems and fire hazards. When they are burned, they are difficult to extinguish, and the smoke from a burning tire releases toxins into the air and the ground. Tires do not biodegrade in any reasonable period of time. Because of their strange shape, they trap rainwater, which makes pools that are breeding grounds for mosquitoes and all the lovely diseases they spread.

On the other hand

Retreading old tires by applying a new tread coating saves 75 percent of the old tire material and 70 percent of the energy needed to make a new tire. They also cost between one third and one half the price of a new tire. In 1993, President Clinton signed an executive order mandating use of retreaded tires on all government vehicles. Although mechanics still don't commonly suggest retreading, slowly but surely retreads are gaining acceptance. See Retreader's World (www.rubber.com/retread/index.html) and the Tire Retread Information Bureau (www.retread.org) for more information.

So far, we've counted up the monetary cost, the medical cost, and the ecological cost of car use ... and yet we're still not done tallying up the total cost. Additional kinds of pollution, such as noise, heat, oil, waste, and sprawl, add their "fees" to the price tag on that new car we're eyeing.

Cars are loud, and I'm not just referring to old junkers with holes in their mufflers. The faster a car goes, the louder it is. But we have become used to the level of noise of never-ending traffic. In Los Angeles we joke, "If you close your eyes, you can almost pretend the sound of a nearby freeway is the ocean." As more cars hit the road, noise pollution adds up even more. The decibel level of engines, car alarms, horns, and subwoofer stereo systems can be damaging to our ears.

Wonder why it's so much hotter in the city? If you can't stand the heat, get out of the car. When we're sitting in a summer traffic jam, the heat buildup can become unbearable. Not only do concrete and asphalt trap solar heat, they also trap the heat created by car engines, moving parts, burning gasoline, tires gripping the pavement, exhaust, and heat displaced by radiator coolant. Each little bit of heat from each car in the parking lot we call a rush hour freeway contributes to raising the surface temperature of the entire planet.

On hot August afternoons, many of us relax in the front seat of the car to cool off as we tool down the freeway. In order to cool us, our car air conditioners must use energy that generates even more heat outside the car. Instead of turning on the car air conditioner, consider buying a car with a lighter interior and exterior that reflects heat instead of absorbing it, keeping the car cooler in the summer. Tinted windows and shades can also reflect solar heat away from the car.

The oil crisis in the world today is much greater than our anger about paying more at the pump. The real crisis is the connection to degraded water supplies and forests due to exploration, extraction, and transportation of the oil we want to be cheap and convenient. We rarely consider the military budget required to defend oil supplies in the Middle East and West Africa. The big oil spills from tanker ships are not the only way "black gold" destroys the ecology. Pipelines and underground service station tanks collectively hold billions of gallons of oil, which can leak and contaminate groundwater and soil.

> It wasn't his driving that caused the Alaskan oil spill. It was yours.
>
> −1989   Greenpeace advertisement picturing *Exxon Valdez* Captain Joseph Hazelwood

---

Oh, those wacky '70s

The early 1970s saw a major gasoline shortage in the U.S. In November of 1973, President Nixon asked gas stations to voluntarily close on Sundays. By February, 1974, drivers whose license plates ended in odd numbers could only buy gas on odd numbered days. People often spent hours waiting in line to buy only a few gallons of gas, but waiting was no guarantee you'd get served, as the gas sometimes ran out before you got to the head of the line.

Car manufacturing in the U.S. creates seven billion pounds of unrecycled scrap materials and waste every year.[91] Producing just one giant SUV also releases four tons of carbon and 700 pounds of pollutants into air.[92] We must continue to develop sustainable ways to make sure the materials used to build our endless car lot of new vehicles don't go to waste. Fortunately cars have been routinely recycled for many years. Materials like steel and aluminum are already routinely recycled into cars. Plastic can be recycled into bumpers, and discarded textiles are chopped up to become filler for car seats.

Most of our concerns about urban sprawl are another direct result of automobile dependence. They paved paradise and put up a parking lot ... and a Megalo-Mart, a new car dealership, a suburban subdivision, and an eight-lane superhighway. Many malls and stores provide enough space for parking as if every day they expected the same number of shoppers as the busiest shopping day of the year. Ninety percent of all car trips end in "free" parking areas. This "free" parking suffocates the land. Paving land without consideration for excess water runoff can lead to flooding and soil erosion. Sprawl also converts farmland to roads, which forces food and goods to travel further. (More on sprawl in the *Balancing* chapter, page 112.)

Parkinson's Law of Garbage applies again. Bigger freeways rarely fix traffic problems. "If you build it, he will come," the movie *Field of Dreams* whispered. The ethereal voice of motoring America also sounds familiar. *If we build the interstate, they will drive it.*

HOPE FOR THE FUTURE

A world where we all give up our cars isn't likely to happen. But, hopefully, seeing the true cost of car ownership will lead us to be more conscious of how much we drive and how we take care of our cars. We can focus on ways to limit our driving, explore alternative forms of transport, and work on being the best driver we can be.

Reclaiming the streets

It's time to start supporting initiatives that encourage car drivers to get out from behind the wheel. The more attractive and convenient walking and mass transit are, the more chances that people will get out of their gas guzzlers and hit the streets. We can make streets safer and encourage more people to walk by adopting simple measures. Make sidewalks wider and better lit. Create more bike lanes and bike parking to support riders. Centralize town centers for convenience of shopping, government services, and entertainment. Lobby for devices that calm traffic and reduce speed—islands, landscaped medians, angled parking, speed bumps, and narrower roads to protect the safety of pedestrians.

Promote car-free days in your community. These days not only reduce car use but also encourage neighbors to mingle. On car-free Sundays in Bogotá, Colombia, two million residents come out each weekend to enjoy 100 miles of major streets that are closed to traffic.

Adopt a stretch of highway (or any public road) and beautify it

Your local transportation department can tell you what areas are available for adoption. The cost of adopting a mile of a road is minimal (like buying a pair of work gloves); everything else you need is usually provided. Start by noticing areas on your commute that have been neglected. If you notice an already adopted area that needs more attention, consider joining an established adoption group. Start a group in your company to get coworkers involved. Often there's free publicity from having the company name or logo on a beautification sign. If official adoption isn't an option, find a public stretch of land and do it unofficially. Of course, you may get strange looks from passers-by, but you can feel good about making a difference in your community and making back a few bucks from can and plastic bottle deposits.

Human-Powered Transport

Worldwide, the bicycle is the most widely used form of transport, but in America, our bikes get pushed to the back of the garage to make more room for our cars.

The Top Reasons to Take the Bike Instead

✓ Increased awareness of our community. When we travel by bike, we're more apt to notice the types of businesses located in our neighborhood. We're also more likely to patronize the local hardware store than to chance riding a bike along twenty miles of fifty mile per hour, two-lane highway to get to the big box store.

✓ Heightened awareness of pedestrians and other non-motorists. When we get back into the car after being on the bike for a while, we appreciate those who don't travel by car. We're conscious of how difficult it is to share the road with motorized vehicles.

✓ Sexy biker legs and biker butt. Biking works every muscle in our legs, front to back, top to bottom. Your gluteus maximus never looked so toned.

✓ Freedom from oil companies. Every gallon of gas we save is another dollar (or two, or—yikes—three or—egad—four) that doesn't go into the pocket of those who control the world's oil supply, specifically those with whom we're often at war.

✓ Saving shopping bags by having to carry our purchases in a backpack or bike bag. Biking or walking to the store also means purchasing smaller quantities and fresher food.

✓ Connection to motion. We spend our lives shuttling between places in time-travel mechanisms: cars and airplanes. When we use our own body to power a bicycle, we can connect to both movement and real-time progression.

✓ Stronger bones and heart. Bikers' lungs are also better at expelling pollution particles. Riding a bike also helps you lose weight.

On the other hand

Cyclists are especially vulnerable to air pollution because they breathe very deeply while riding. Some authorities recommend wearing a facemask to filter airborne particles.

✓ Lower stress levels. Releasing endorphins while exercising helps lower stress levels.

✓ Easier parking. Parking can be quicker when we don't need to spend twenty minutes trying to find a parking space, and then a half hour walking from where we finally parked. Bike racks (formal or improvised) are often closer to or even inside our destination. Before chaining up, though, make sure there are no laws against what you're chaining to.

Biking Safety

Biking can be a fun and easy way to get where we're going, but we need to take certain precautions as we ride. Approximately 750 deaths a year are considered bicycle accidents. The majority of these are caused by negligence or rider error, usually because the rider is not wearing a helmet. No one wants to be draped over the hood of a car (except in the good Whitesnake video kind of way). Apply the following cautions to other small vehicles, too—electric scooters, Segues, skateboards.

- ❑ *Never assume a driver can see you.* Potentially, every driveway has a car ready to pull out and every parked car has a door ready to open. Use lights and reflectors after dark. Make yourself as visible as possible and double check your batteries before you get on the road.
- ❑ Always wear an ANSI or SNELL certified helmet that fits properly. In many communities, helmet laws are mandatory. Replace your helmet every two years or after an accident.
- ❑ Bring water, a snack, and sunscreen with you on long trips.
- ❑ Ride with motor vehicle traffic. Pedestrians walk against traffic. Bikers ride with it.
- ❑ Do not ride on sidewalks, which are for pedestrians. If you're in danger and feel that the sidewalk is the only option, get off your bike and walk it on the sidewalk until it's safe to return to the roadway.
- ❑ Follow the rules of the road. You may feel high and mighty up on your bicycle seat, but no one is exempt from traffic laws.

Know your hand signals and use them.
LEFT TURN: left arm straight out, parallel to the ground
RIGHT TURN: left arm straight out but bent at elbow, forearm perpendicular to ground
SLOW DOWN AND STOP: start with left arm out bent at elbow, then bend forearm 180 degrees toward the ground

---

- ❑ Stay humble. Just because your mode of transportation is better for the environment than a car, you do not own the road and you're not superior to motorists. Like it or not, everyone has just as much right to the road as you do. Arrogance can be met with the bumper of a Chevy.
- ❑ Be comfortable where you ride. If there's a stretch of roadway that makes you white-knuckle the handlebars every time you traverse it, seek an alternate route. Don't wait for your luck to run out.
- ❑ Keep your bike in good working order. Riders can outfit their bikes for any type of weather, even rain or snow by attaching fenders to prevent spray from tires.

Biker's wish list

✓ Showers at work
✓ Paved shoulders on the roads
✓ Direct routes
✓ Tax incentives
✓ Thorn-proof tires
✓ Padded shorts that don't make us look like we're wearing a diaper.

Car Alternatives

Wouldn't you like to...

✓ Not sit in traffic?
✓ Not have to feed the meter?
✓ Avoid parking tickets?
✓ Not worry about where you parked?
✓ Create less airborne pollutants?
✓ Have more money?

A crucial problem with automobiles is not the cars themselves but the dependency they have engendered in us. Simplifying our lives doesn't have to involve sacrificing our cars, though, after careful consideration of how complicated they can be to pay for and clean up after, we may just want to.

We like the convenience of having our own vehicle. We like being able to make a quick getaway whenever we want. More than a quarter of the car trips we make are a mile or less, but how often do we even consider finding another way to get where we're going? Rethinking our dependence on the car should start small and work its way up.

Okay, here's my dirty little secret ... I love to drive. And not just short little trips. I love cross-country driving. I love the freedom of owning my own car. I love knowing that I have the power to go wherever, whenever I want. I hear the call of the open road and next thing you know, I'm on I-40 headed east, windows down, Van Halen blaring. What's a girl with Neal Cassady's soul but a need to save the planet to do? If you're like me, here are some suggestions.

❑ Switch to hybrid. Renting (or buying) a hybrid vehicle can almost double your highway mpg.

❑ Don't want to put the extra miles on your own car? Try drive-away companies. If you can prove you're trustworthy, they'll hire you to drive someone else's car to a prearranged destination.

❑ Get some friends together and combine your road trip with another reason for traveling (Heading home for the holidays? Moving? On the world's best scavenger hunt?). By splitting the time and the cost of driving, you may make up some money otherwise spent on a plane ticket.

Just for a moment, let's overlook the usual annoyances of airline travel: substandard food, exposure to cosmic radiation, poor air quality, lack of blood circulation, dehydration, anxiety from late arrivals, lost luggage, not to mention the high stress that accompanies being security checked and searched.

Instead, let's focus on a dirty little secret of airline travel, which is not so nice to the friendly skies. Airplanes account for 13 percent of transportation-related carbon dioxide emissions. In addition to the nitrogen oxides and sulfur dioxide released at higher altitudes, CO_2 greatly exacerbates global warming and the destruction of the ozone layer in higher quantities than when it's released at ground level. Based on data from the EPA, over one pound of CO_2 is produced as a result of each air mile traveled per person,[93] as opposed to about one third of a pound released by hybrid cars getting over 50 miles per gallon and just under one pound for cars getting 20 mpg. Let's do the cross-country math on my route from Los Angeles to Boston:

✓ On a plane: 2,606 pounds of CO_2 released
✓ In a small SUV (getting 25 mpg): 2,390 pounds of CO_2 are released
✓ In a hybrid compact (averaging 50 mpg): only 1,200 pounds of CO_2 released.

(Check out www.cleanairconservancy.org/calculator_air.php to calculate the pollution created by your airline travel.)

Mass Transit: Leave the driving to them?

Bus systems in many American communities are in a state of disrepair. Routes are long and schedules are unreliable. New routes to dispersed suburbs are difficult and expensive to implement. Many bus systems use alternative fuels to cut pollution and save money, but axle loads can still be as heavy as eighteen-wheel trucks. The car-privileged often fear mass transit with dread. "Take the bus? What if some crazy person touches me?" (Relax, we're not going to get SARS from public transportation.)

So why advocate mass transit? For millions, bus and light rail routes are a necessity of life. For various reasons, one out of three people in the U.S. and Canada cannot drive a car. Even if you can drive, there are reasons to give the bus or train a try. Traveling by mass transit gives us time for meditation, reading, or socializing during the commute. Riding the bus or the train creates an interdependence on community-supported travel. Sure, we may need a secret decoder ring to figure out the New York City subway system, but millions do it daily, and if a Yankee fan can do it, anyone can.

Stop & think:

And you thought Who Framed Roger Rabbit? *was just a movie…*

In the 1930s, auto manufacturers, oil, tire, and other related industries formed a holding company called National City Lines. This company bought up trolley car lines, then dismantled them (when patronage was already low) to create a dependency on cars. They closed approximately one hundred lines in forty-five cities, effectively destroying the American electric rail system.

Alternatively Fueled Vehicles

Most people, when they hear the term *"alternatively fueled vehicles"* (AFV) think no further than the electric car. There are, however, at least a dozen different types of automobiles not solely powered by petroleum-based gasoline. Not only do these cars create less environmental pollution, but their owners are also given tax incentives and are often allowed to use carpool lanes with fewer passengers than normally required. The unfortunate status of AFVs is that there still isn't a clear "winner"; they all offer both advantages and disadvantages, forcing the consumer to decide which is best for their lifestyle.

✓ Diesel-powered vehicles are highly efficient compared to gasoline engines, but release more particulates and nitrogen oxide. Newer diesel fuels are cleaner than older versions and can provide better gas mileage, but they still contribute to air pollution.

✓ Ethanol fuels are produced from renewable, domestic sources like wood, barley, rye, wheat, and corn (though ethanol made from corn is the least efficient as it requires 3 barrels of oil to make 4 barrels of ethanol in this manner). Ethanol produced from sugar cane, sugar beet and hemp are the most efficient, and in fact Brazil no longer imports any foreign oil and instead grows their own sugar cane to create E85 ethanol fuel. While the fuel is renewable, there is a high cost to switch over gasoline vehicles, the driving range is shorter, and fuel is more expensive and not as prevalent as petroleum.

✓ Gasohol is a mixture of gas and alcohol, usually derived from corn and 10 percent ethanol. Its use is prevalent in Mid-Western states where corn is plentiful. Gasohol can be used in cars that use petroleum and doesn't require changing to a special system.

Thinking outside the box

Q: What weighs three tons, goes seventy miles per hour, and smells like French fries?

A: The Veggie Van, the motor home that runs on vegetable oil.

Josh Tickell transformed an ordinary motor home into the Veggie Van, which runs on a biodiesel fuel made mostly from used vegetable oil collected from fast food restaurants. During the summers of 1997 and 1998, the Veggie Van crossed America, logging over 25,000 miles and appearing on national news programs. After the trek, Josh wrote the book *From the Fryer to the Fuel Tank* about his adventures and how he made fuel from vegetable oil. He continues to educate Americans about the benefits of renewable energy through hands-on demonstrations, road tours, the web site, www.biodieselamerica.org, and his documentary *FUEL*.

✓ Compressed Natural Gas (CNG) burns cleanly, emitting 80 percent fewer hydrocarbons, 90 percent less carbon monoxide, and 22 percent fewer nitrous oxides than gasoline-powered vehicles. CNG can be used in modified gasoline engines, but retrofitting existing vehicles is costly (up to several thousand dollars) and standard automobile fuel tanks can only hold the equivalent of about five gallons of gas. Per gallon, CNG fuel costs about a third less than gasoline. Currently, CNG is used by the government vehicles and public buses. The real setback to CNG is obtaining the natural gas; it's not readily available in all areas, and making it from burning coal creates its own carbon dioxide emissions.

✓ Hybrid gas and electric automotive technology switches between a self-contained battery charge and gasoline to power the vehicle without the need to plug into an electric source. Energy is harnessed when braking to regenerate the battery. The technology can cut fuel expenses in half, and some hybrid vehicles can reduce carbon monoxide emissions by up to 90 percent.

In the early 21st century, hybrid gas and electric cars became readily available and affordable for mass consumption. Noting the success of Honda's Civic Hybrid and Toyota's Prius, other manufacturers are now racing to get in the game. There are five types of hybrid technology available to car makers: (1) idle-off capability, (2) regenerative braking, (3) power assist and engine downsizing, (4) electric-only drive (electricity powers the car when first starting up and at low speeds), and (5) extended battery-electric range (will solely use battery power for up to 60 miles of driving and requires plugging into a power source). "Mild" hybrids (like the Honda Civic Hybrid) use the first three technologies. "Full" hybrids (like the Toyota Prius and Ford Escape Hybrid) cover the first four technologies. Currently, no passenger vehicles available use all five technologies.[94]

Advice from a hybrid owner

I bought my first hybrid when my Hyundai (nicknamed "Attila the Hyun"), which had carried me on nine cross-country trips, decided she had had enough and cashed out on Interstate 40 in the unpopulated northeast corner of Arizona. I had waited as long as I could, but faced with having to buy a new car, I wanted fifty miles per gallon and super ultra low emissions.

What have I learned in the past few years of hybrid ownership? Hybrids aren't sports cars. Driving my hybrid has made me a much more conservative driver. You think twice about chancing a yellow light. You become more patient with the slow lane and try not to yell, "Sure, I'll offset your emissions for you," to passing SUVs.

But it's also fun. Driving a hybrid car is slightly like playing a video game: you glance at the dials to see if you're using gas power and find yourself slipping your foot off the accelerator to get back to battery power. You find yourself challenging your best gas mileage and seeing how long you can go before filling up the tank again. You start to wonder why everyone doesn't have one and what society could do with all that gas station property if everyone went hybrid. And I always make a sure to polish up the word hybrid on the trunk and my carpool lane access stickers.

✓ Electric vehicles are virtually maintenance free, give off no exhaust, and produce very little noise. But due to a combination of auto industry strong-arming, oil industry lobbying, and supposed lack of consumer demand, the only electric cars sold by major auto companies in the U.S. were taken off the market before they made it out of the driveway. Their brief availability to the public was chronicled in the documentary *Who Killed the Electric Car?*, an inquisitive look at the reasons why the electric car never made it to mass distribution.

✓ While hydrogen fuel cells are touted as the "next big thing" in automotive history … the reality is their arrival on the consumer market is at least a decade away. Instead of running on gasoline, these cars will run on hydrogen and instead of hazardous emissions, hydrogen powered cars will release only water. Manufacturers are actively pursuing it as a viable option but extracting hydrogen from sources such as natural gas is prohibitively expensive.

> *On the other hand*
> While AFVs may be more beneficial to the environment in terms of hazardous emissions and lowered dependence on non-renewable fossil fuels, they still contribute to the problems of sprawl, traffic, and accidents.

IF WE MUST DRIVE, LET'S KEEP OUR CARS HAPPY AND HEALTHY

We've established that driving is convenient and satisfying. Driving makes us feel safer when we're in control. It means freedom and independence. And though we may want to, many of us just can't give up our cars at this time. How can we learn to minimize our impact without having to put the El Camino up on blocks in the front yard?

It's just this simple: when we *drive less*, we use less gas and spend less money. Fewer natural resources are depleted and less CO_2 is released into the air. Rather than advocating fuel conservation by driving less, however, we have rationalized and validated our driving by working for efficiency in the auto industry. Follow these tips to start driving less:

❑ Start by challenging yourself to do at least one day of errands by foot or bike each week. Say you'll do your grocery shopping without the car. It may mean more trips because we can only carry smaller loads in a backpack or canvas sacks in each hand, but this will also increase the amount of exercise we get. Invest in a "carry-all" cart (a two wheeled luggage cart or a four wheeled standing cart), which can be a lifesaver on the back and which you can take on the bus. Unless you're training to hike the Appalachian Trail, carrying thirty-five pounds of groceries on your back isn't the most fun you can have. Saddlebags for bicycles make errands easier, but a sturdy backpack is also fine for carrying small amounts of groceries home from the store.

❑ Avoid traffic by changing your work hours so that you arrive and leave during less congested traffic times and avoid rush hour tie-ups.

❑ Ponder your dependency on the car. What if you didn't have a car for a day? A week? How would you get where you needed to go?

❑ Combine driving or mass transit with walking or biking. Getting out of the car for even part of your trip is better than not getting out at all. Call the local transit authority to find out what the rules are for taking your bicycle on the train or bus. Some communities allow you to travel with your bike during off-peak hours and some buses are equipped with pull-down storage racks.

❑ Eliminate unnecessary trips, reduce lengths of trips, combine trips, and shop locally. Americans use their vehicles for 82 percent of trips, whereas many Europeans use theirs for well under 50 percent. This is not just because of better-organized mass transit, but because European cities are often more conveniently designed.

❑ Look into ride sharing, carpools, employer sponsored vanpools, and High Occupancy Vehicle (HOV) lanes. Car pools let you drive in the HOV lanes on the freeway, give tax breaks to commuters, and raise a sense of community among riders. Don't just carpool on the way to work. Think of anyone else who may be going your way, even if you have to meet up at an equidistant location. To encourage carpooling during World War II, rationing stickers were placed on car windshields asking, "Is this trip really necessary?"

Thinking outside the box: Zipcar

Why own a car if you only drive a couple times a month? Why order a rental car when you only need it for a few hours? Zipcar offers the freedom and mobility of car ownership without the hassle of maintenance, repairs, or parking. Zipcar's mission: to offer affordable access to vehicles for short-term use as a complement to public transportation.

Paying only for what you use, you can reserve a Zipcar for as little as one hour. Reservations are sent wirelessly to the car so it will open only for the right person at the right car at the right time. The vehicles are parked in dedicated spots located near transit stops and in neighborhoods. A few of the areas that Zipcars are currently available are Boston, New York, Washington, D.C., Chicago, and San Francisco. (See www.zipcar.com)

Another way to reduce gas consumption is to *drive smaller*. In Los Angeles, the home of the free and land of the excess ... the thought of performing *Monkey Wrench Gang* tactics on the thousands of SUVs I see everyday has crossed my mind. Only the threat of instant karma keeps me resisting the urge to throw the one finger salute to the Hummer drivers in the neighborhood.

So, I ask myself, why do I feel such hostility toward these people? Why has the SUV become the symbol of all that is evil, while minivans, which are just as big and gas guzzling, are immune? Why are SUVs exempt from the fuel efficiency standards of smaller vehicles? For one thing, SUVs are not used for the purpose they were designed for: transporting large loads and numerous people off-road.

The commercials proudly advertise room for *seven. Eight. Twenty-five!* But I can't tell you how many people I pass on freeways in the morning driving their SUV solo and usually while talking on the cell phone (but that's another matter). No passengers. No baby seat in the back. Nothing. Just the SUV driver all alone in his or her wheeled ocean liner. Do we ever see more than one or two passengers in these vehicles? No. SUVs are not minivans, which are not "fun." SUVs are status symbols. Car makers have seen the public's desire for these urban assault vehicles skyrocket, and so every car company has introduced their own version to the market (in several sizes—large, extra-large, and Sherman tank), never mind the fact that rarely will any of these vehicles ever be used in any sport utility capacity.

Scary stats: How your SUV becomes my problem
The SUV ticket

In 2002, the comic strip *Doonesbury* ran a segment about "ticketing" SUVs with ecological infractions. You can buy your own SUV tickets at Earth on Empty (www.earthonempty.com), or create your own tickets with these stats.

✓ A sixty-mile trip in an SUV will cost approximately $15.
✓ During hotter months, SUVs can contribute an additional 5,000 tons per day of smog-forming pollutants to the air.[95]
✓ The highest incidence of fatal rollover accidents is involves drivers of small SUVs.[96]
✓ A Hummer averages 6.8 mpg, a Toyota Prius Hybrid, 52 mpg.

Ask yourself: do you really need that SUV? Will you be towing anything? Camping? For that one day a year it snows? Going off-roading? Going on safari? Hauling freight? Barely 10 percent of all SUVs ever venture off road, quite a difference from nearly 100 percent of advertising that shows the SUV "conquering" the wilderness. Concerned that your new car will be too small to carry everything you'll need? Ask yourself how often you really need to carry large loads. If you make your living in construction, the pickup makes more sense. But if you use the SUV bed only once a month to carry things, consider buying a smaller, more economical, more ecologically friendly car. Rent or borrow a truck for the times you need to haul larger loads.

And when renting, always rent the smallest car that meets your needs. If you need to drive a long distance, consider renting a newer car with better gas mileage than your own. Then the wear and tear won't be on your own vehicle. Many companies have begun to even offer hybrid rentals.

Improving *fuel economy* is another way we can reduce our gasoline consumption. If you haven't been able to outfit your Dodge Neon like the Veggie Van, try these tips to get the most for your mpg:

❑ Carry items inside the car or in the trunk rather than on roof racks. Get bodywork done and wash and wax your car to improve aerodynamics. Like the roof rack, surface dirt can increase drag.

❑ In the winter, keep the snow off your car. The weight of snow dramatically increases wind resistance and fuel consumption.

❑ For pickup trucks, when the bed is empty, remove the tailgate and use a mesh gate instead.

❑ At high speeds, drive with the windows closed.

❑ Avoid carrying the extra weight of unneeded items in the trunk.

❑ Keep the tires properly inflated and aligned. It's estimated that half of the cars on the road have underinflated tires, which increases rolling resistance and gas consumption, thus reducing the life of engine and tires. Check tire pressure when the tire is cold and keep tires inflated to the specifications recommended in the owner's manual or on the driver's door.

❑ Check your tires every few weeks in cold weather. Changes in temperature affect tire pressure.

❑ Improve fuel economy by switching to radial tires that meet the manufacturer's specifications.

❑ Test the tread on your tires by putting a penny in the groove. If you can see the top of Lincoln's head, it's time for new tires.

❑ Don't be idle. A quarter of gasoline use occurs when the car isn't even moving forward. When you have to stop for longer than a minute (as at a train crossing with a long freight train), turn the car off.

❑ Get in and go. Don't bother warming up the car, just drive easier during the first few miles.

❑ Avoid using the car for short trips. Half the hydrocarbons released are done so during the first three to four miles.

❑ Drive gently. Try not to brake hard and quickly accelerate. Cars use the least amount of gas when they maintain a consistent speed. To optimize the car's performance, use cruise control when driving long distances.

❑ Drive slower. When we double our speed, we quadruple our air resistance. Fuel economy decreases as much as 25 percent when a vehicle is driven at 65 miles per hour instead of 55.

❑ Support fuel efficiency legislation. Call your legislators and express your feelings on SUVs, fuel exemptions, public transportation, gasoline taxes, or whatever else puts a bee in your bonnet.

Help your car be all it can be. *Proper maintenance* is an easy way to prevent automotive troubles: a well-tuned car can use up to 10 percent less gas and will help the engine last longer.

❑ Extend your car's life with regular preventive maintenance and avoid being that guy who breaks down in the fast lane during rush hour. Read the owner's manual and schedule checkups based on its recommendations.

❑ When visiting the mechanic, bring a list of problems you've been experiencing, so that when you get there you won't forget anything. (This tip also works for visits to the doctor, as long as you try not to mix up the lists.)

❑ Keep a notebook or diary about your car, detailing all services including the date and the mileage. ("Dear Diary, today I turned over to 110,000 miles...")

❑ Look into getting a lifetime alignment service. The quality of today's roads requires cars to be routinely checked for alignment.

Mr. Fix-It-Right

Finding a good mechanic can be as tricky as locating Red Sox tickets on Yankee game day. If you're concerned about the reputation of the person you've brought your car to, call your city's Consumer Affairs department to check for filed grievances. Get second opinions and price quotes in writing.

Keeping Safe on the Road

The car is tuned. She's purring like a kitten. And she's about as fuel-efficient as she's gonna get. We're ready to get our motors running and head out on the highways. But wait! Before we pull out of the driveway, there's one last thing. It's time for *the talk*. Driving is a privilege, not a right. It should be taken away whenever it's abused.

There's rage everywhere these days, but it's most important to acknowledge it when we're behind the wheel. We often forget that a car is a loaded weapon, that in a fraction of an instant, a close encounter can escalate into a situation of grave danger. The majority of accidents are caused by driver negligence or distraction, but all too often these days we hear about incidents where uncontrollable anger is the precursor to tragedy.

When we're angry, our judgment becomes impaired. When we're preoccupied by a negative situation, we become tense. We become fixated on "we're right" and "they're wrong." When the emotions of irritation and impatience become exaggerated, we tend not to notice traffic signs, other cars, and pedestrians.

According to John Larson, author of *Road Rage to Road-Wise*, road ragers suffer from a Jekyll and Hyde Syndrome.[97] They are not usually criminals, not usually violent, and they often feel like a victim. They often say their actions were in self-defense. This means that almost anyone could find themselves in the grip of a road rage attack.

Road Rage Causes and Solutions

✓ Lateness and traffic. I can't think of one event, barring a true medical emergency, when being late is a life or death experience. Allow extra time and be early, but when you find yourself running behind, relax and settle into your lateness. In the grand scheme of things, it's not worth speeding to shave only two minutes off your arrival.

✓ Revenge and retaliation. *They did something to me, I'm going to make them pay for it.* Don't use the horn or finger gestures, don't yell or mouth derogatory or offensive remarks, don't switch on your high beams. Be polite and sincere, even if the other driver isn't. Relax and repeat this mantra: *It's not worth it.*

✓ Feeling that *I'm better than they are. No one else knows how to drive.* Practice "car-ma." It's neither your job nor your responsibility to punish bad drivers.

✓ Tailgaters. You look in the rearview mirror and all you can see is the windshield of the car behind you. Keep your speed constant. Don't tap your brakes. Turn your blinker on to signal that you'll change lanes as soon as it's safe to do so.

✓ Challenges. Accept things that are out of your control: construction, traffic, and other drivers who just don't get it. Slow down. Then get away from the situation. Don't be bullied, but don't stoop to their level.

Thinking outside the box: www.roadragers.com

Roadragers.com is an on-line "confessional community" where you can make a road rage report. Despite the fact that the reports aren't monitored by a legal agency, it can be a cathartic experience to express your anger on the computer instead of on the road. You can even search for your offender's license plate number (or your own, just to be sure).

Driver Courtesy List

I like to think I'm a fairly good driver. But then again, everyone thinks that, and we can't all be right. I paid attention in Mr. Dooley's Driver's Ed class, so I couldn't have possibly done anything that would cause that tractor-trailer behind me to flash his lights and blare his horn. *They're* the jerk. Right? The sound of the automobile horn now has little meaning beyond showing other drivers how upset we are with them.

I know you paid attention in Driver's Ed, too, but just to be sure, how about a mini-refresher. I promise it will be short, and afterwards, we'll go for ice cream.

❑ Use the turn signal, and please, please for the love of Pete, turn your blinker off once you've made your lane change or turn.

❑ Wipers on, lights on. Even on a sunny day, headlights make you more visible to other drivers. In inclement conditions, if visibility changes without warning, your headlights can save your life. Here's a trick I learned driving through torrential rains of Texas: in heavy storms, use your emergency flashers. The blinking red lights are easier to see. Or pull over and wait for the rain to pass. It's never worth taking a chance driving when you can't see past the hood of your own car.

❑ Pass only on the left.

❑ Pedestrians have the right of way. *Always.*

❑ Pay attention to roadway signs. Our commercialized society gives us information-overload. Everywhere we look, there's another billboard, trying even harder than the last one to capture our attention. With so much to take in, we tend to miss the important signs, the ones that say *Stop, One Way,* and *Yield.* Instead, we gaze as if hypnotized at the picture of the half-naked supermodel on the side of a bus.

❑ Know the right of way. At a four-way stop, the driver that arrives first has the right of way. At a traffic light, the driver going straight has the right of way over the driver who is turning. I'm talking to you, drivers of the Northeast…

❑ Watch for emergency vehicles with their sirens and lights on. They have precedence over any other vehicle. As soon as you hear or see an emergency vehicle, *pull over to the right and stop.* Remain there until you're sure all the ambulances and fire trucks have passed.

Stop & think

What if lifelong driver education was mandatory and testing was required after accidents?

❑ There's absolutely no reason to tailgate.

❑ Your dad told you this one: Keep both hands on the wheel, which means putting down the cell phone and the breakfast burrito.

❑ Save the coffee until you get to work. Drink water instead to keep alert but not wired.

Emergency Car Safety List

Keeping the following items in your car may help save you from getting stuck. It can also make you someone else's hero for a day. Be sure to keep a list so you can easily check to see what's missing.

❑ Carry a cell phone and a charger that plugs into your car's auxiliary power port.

❑ Check to make sure you have a spare tire and a jack that works for your car.

❑ Join a roadside assistance club. This is one type of insurance you should never leave the house without.

Thinking outside the box: The Better World Club

Say "road-side assistance," and most of us instantly think the hundred-year-old AAA. Why would we need another organization, especially when forty-five million Americans already belong to AAA? How about the fact that AAA uses membership dollars to lobby against federal environmental issues like clean air standards, public transit funding, and auto safety laws.

There's a more sustainable option on the market: the Better World Club. They offer routine auto services like emergency towing, roadside assistance, insurance, and travel services like maps, travelers' checks and vacation planning. What's not so routine is how the BWC is trying to attract customers, labeling itself the first "socially responsible and environmentally friendly travel resource."

Coverage is nationwide and membership dues are comparable to the AAA. The BWC also offers free carbon offsets to reduce environmental impact on the road, discounts on hybrid and electric cars, green lodging, and eco-travel services. It now even offers a roadside assistance plan for cyclists. BWC also donates one percent of all revenues to environmental clean-up efforts and supports green transportation policies. (See www.betterworldclub.com.)

- ❏ Pack a simple car care bag and include:
  - ✓ Jumper cables
  - ✓ Extra windshield wiper fluid
  - ✓ Quart of motor oil
  - ✓ Transmission fluid and antifreeze (only if driving long distances)
  - ✓ A gallon of non-potable water to put in the radiator if the car overheats
  - ✓ Window scraper
  - ✓ Cleaning rags
- ❏ A basic road-side safety kit
  - ✓ Road flares
  - ✓ Flashlight with working batteries
  - ✓ Whistle
  - ✓ Rope
  - ✓ Duct tape
- ❏ Keep a simple tool kit in the in the trunk:
  - ✓ An adjustable wrench
  - ✓ Screw drivers
  - ✓ Pliers

- ✓ A funnel
- ✓ Socket wrench set
- ✓ Industrial rubber gloves (available at pool supply stores)
❑ Make sure you have a first aid kit that includes:
  - ✓ Basic first aid manual
  - ✓ CPR mouthpiece (and knowledge how to use it)
  - ✓ Thermometer
  - ✓ Non-latex gloves
  - ✓ Scissors and tweezers
  - ✓ Safety pins
  - ✓ Gauze pads
  - ✓ Adhesive tape
  - ✓ Band-Aids
  - ✓ Large square piece of cloth to make a sling (fold it in half to make a triangle)
  - ✓ Ace bandage
  - ✓ Ice pack
  - ✓ Hydrogen peroxide and rubbing alcohol for sterilizing instruments and cleaning wounds
  - ✓ Pain reliever: acetaminophen, aspirin, ibuprofen, depending on preference
  - ✓ Antihistamine for allergic reactions and bee stings
  - ✓ Hydrocortisone cream

Disaster Preparedness (or *"Stuff to keep in trunk to reduce stressful situations"*)

Living in an area prone to earthquakes, I prefer to keep a bag of these items in my car as well as my house. Hopefully, none of us will have to use this disaster kit, but think of a time you were stranded (for whatever reason: car breaks down, having to wait for someone who was late, a change in plans) and what would have made that time less of an aggravation.

Play this quick game every so often: You have 10 minutes to get out of your house for good. What do you take with you? In an emergency situation, every second counts and preparing ahead saves precious time. Think: copies of identification, extra keys, and medications. Remember to consider your furry friends in your evacuation plans, packing pet food, dishes and carrying cases. (This exercise usually scares me into backing up my computer files as well.)

Check list for your disaster preparedness bag:
- ✓ Several bottles of clean drinking water
- ✓ A sweater or jacket
- ✓ A hat
- ✓ Book or magazine
- ✓ Pens (with caps!)
- ✓ Tissues
- ✓ Hand sanitizer or rubbing alcohol
- ✓ Swiss army knife
- ✓ Sturdy comfortable shoes (It's a lot easier hiking to the nearest gas station in a prom dress if you've got a pair of sneakers on.)
- ✓ Compass
- ✓ Candles and matches
- ✓ Can opener
- ✓ Umbrella
- ✓ Water disinfectant tablets
- ✓ Mylar emergency blanket
- ✓ Battery or solar powered radio
- ✓ Energy bars that have a shelf life of more than a few months, such as Clif Bars or Power Bars. Non-chocolate versions, in case they melt.
- ✓ Sunscreen and bug spray
- ✓ A simple cosmetic improvement kit, including a hairbrush, face wipes, and tooth brush.
- ✓ Clean pair of undies. (At least this way when mom asks you if you left the house with clean underpants, you can always say "yes.")

At this time in our society, oil-based fuel is a necessity. But in the near future, we will need to rethink how our transportation needs truly affect this fragile planet. When we fully realize the true costs of operating gasoline powered automobiles, the inconvenience of simplifying our transportation needs will become immaterial.

Do it today
How high do gasoline prices have to go before you get fed up with your car?

Take a look at your emergency and first aid kits. Replace all expired items and refill anything missing.

ADDITIONAL RESOURCES

Alvord, Katie T. *Divorce Your Car!* Gabriola Island, B.C.: New Society Publishers, 2000. A great resource for alternatives to driving that offers lots of options and statistics on why we should all reduce car trips.

Balish, Chris. *How to Live Well Without Owning a Car: Save Money, Breathe Easier and Get More Mileage Out of Life.* Berkeley: Ten Speed Press, 2006. Great tips on all types of auto-commuting alternatives.

Makower, Joel. *The Green Commuter.* Washington, D.C.: National Press Books, 1992. Keep your journey to and from work ecologically sound.

Check out an automobile emission calculator at http://airhead.cnt.org/Calculator/.

ALTERNATIVE VEHICLES
Melville, Greg. *Greasy Rider: Two Dudes, One Fry-Oil-Powered Car, and A Cross-Country Search For A Greener Future.* Chapel Hill, NC: Algonquin Books of Chapel Hill, 2008. Melville and a friend convert an old Mercedes sedan to run on vegetable oil and head off on a cross-country trip just to prove they can.

The Electric Drive Transportation Association (www.electricdrive.org) not only covers electric cars but also monitors news on any other alternatively fueled vehicle from across the globe.

The U.S. Government Fuel Economy site (www.fueleconomy.gov) includes gas mileage tips and a searchable function to compare cars.

Greener Cars.com (www.greenercars.com) is an online rating site for green vehicles.

The Car Sharing Network (www.carsharing.net) connects riders with car sharing options around the globe.

ACTIVISM
The National Center for Bicycling & Walking (www.bikewalk.org) gives advice on how we can help to create walking and bicycling communities. Not just sidewalks, bike lanes, and trails, but finding new opportunities to make walking and bicycling safe, easy and convenient.

The League of American Bicyclists League of American Bicyclists (www.bikeleague.org) works for a "bicycle friendly America". See their website for bike-related community programs, advocacy and education.

On the last Friday of every month, in over 100 cities around the world, Critical Mass brings anyone who wants to reduce auto dependency together for a festive rolling celebration. Called an "unorganized coincidence" by participants, there's no leader and no set agenda. People come together for many reasons: to assert their right to cleaner air, less congestion, safer roads, and to celebrate and ride in solidarity with other cyclists and like-minded individuals. There's no official Critical Mass web page, (which would defeat the purpose of being "unorganized"), but a web search will lead you to list of unofficial pages.

chapter 8

working

Before we get into professional simplicity, let's do a little background research on our attitude toward our employment.

1. On a workday, when you wake up in the morning, what is your first thought?
2. How about on your day off?
3. How much you like your job?
4. How much do you enjoy what you do at your job?
5. Do you feel you're working at the job you're most compatible with?
6. Are you satisfied with your contribution to the world?
7. In your current job, what is your long-term intention?
8. Are you working at a career just because you think you should be? Just because it follows the course of study you chose in college?
9. Do you work too much? Define "too much."
10. Do you find yourself needing to "unwind" more than three times a week?
11. When you finish the workweek, do you feel as if the only way to relax is by drinking?
12. What hobbies do you have? How do they relate to your job?
13. What is the most aggravating part of your workday?
14. If you didn't have to work, what would you do with your time?
15. If you didn't have to work for the money, what new twist could you put on your job? Would you donate your time or services to do what you do now? Would you do something completely different?
16. What other things in your life would you like to get paid to do?
17. If you got laid off, would you see it as a crisis or an opportunity?
18. If you were suddenly told that you couldn't have your job anymore, what would your reaction be?
19. What kind of work would you do if you only had six months to live?
20. What if you could work because you wanted to, not because you had to? What would you choose to do?
21. What are all your passions?
22. What are your strengths?
23. Who are your heroes and why?
24. What do you want to discover or learn?
25. What impact do you want to have on the world? What do you want to create in the world?
26. There's only one you. How do you want to be remembered?

There are, of course, no right or wrong answers to these questions, but putting our responses down on paper helps us see what we really think and what our true passions are. Since we spend so much of our lives working, it's crucial that we're honest with ourselves about what we love to do. We need to find what rejuvenates us and incorporate it into our working lives.

Get Passionate

Is there any word more beautiful than "passion"? Its sexual connotations notwithstanding, the word "passion" conjures up ideas of fire and intensity and living life to the fullest. When we're passionate about something, we're doing what we love and telling the world what we support. It's our passions that focus our attention on our goals and dreams. Develop your own sense of passion and suddenly you'll notice a change in how you interact with the world.

Imagine having a typical nine-to-five job that is also an outlet for our passion. We awake in the morning, eager to get to our desks. We return home energized and refreshed. Our coworkers become a community of friends, a loving support group.

When work and passions coincide, a simpler life reveals itself. By changing the way we make money, we can redefine our job so that it's a path to emotional accomplishment and personal pride, not just economic success.

What are you passionate about? Are you honest enough with yourself to tell the people you love how you feel? Do you respect the passion in others? What makes your blood boil? What spurs you to the point of action? What do you fight for?

But what if you are unsure of your passions? How do we find what we love? Look at what fires your spirit. Seek out others who are passionate. Watch Bruce Springsteen sing. Lance Armstrong ride. Al Sharpton for inspiration. Look for the conviction of the heart.

Brother can you spare a hand?

A personal connection helps to put a human face on problems but there is never a shortage of worthy causes to stand up for. Once we can identify our passions, we can learn to incorporate them into our occupation, we can start programs, relate our business to their causes. If our enthusiasm is strong enough, we can even switch careers. At a loss for what to care about? Here are some issues to focus your altruistic tendencies upon:

✓ Education: 67 percent of New York City fourth graders can't read; one child in 8 won't graduate from high school.
✓ Poverty: 36 million Americans live below the poverty line.
✓ Health care: 46 million Americans are without health insurance.

(cont'd)

✓ Hunger: 13 million American children go hungry each day.

✓ Homelessness and low-income housing: while 10 million Americans have two or more homes, there are an estimated 300,000 homeless people.

✓ Reproductive planning: Of the one million pregnancies that will begin today, half will probably be unintentional.

✓ Rights of the disabled or mentally ill: almost 300,000 people with mental illnesses are incarcerated in American prisons.

✓ Environment: the 70,000 manmade chemicals in use worldwide contribute to staggering rates of cancer, asthma, and endocrine disruption.

✓ Suicide prevention: 15 million Americans are clinically depressed. The U.S. has a higher rate of depression than almost every other country; as other countries Americanize, their rates of depression increase.

We must discover what work drains the soul and what work nourishes it. When we analyze our answers to the quiz that opens this chapter, we can start to refocus our energies on things that are truly important to us.

If you notice a pattern of negative thoughts emerging about your current job, it's definitely time to reevaluate what you do. Consider this. Does the amount of money you're being paid compensate you for the stress you're under? The notoriously overworked Japanese had to create a word for working yourself to death (*karoshi*) because over 10,000 people were dying each year from work related stress. If you think you're in danger of *karoshi*, you can make a conscious decision to leave a job that does not serve your needs.

But even if you hate your current job, perhaps it contains seeds of what you really want to do. Something drew you to this experience. If you hate your job because of the physical pain (sleep deprivation, repetitive motion injury, or emotional stress that leads to physical pain) it puts you in, work to make yourself stronger or get the business to change some of its methods.

There's hope. People who live simply tend to think outside the box when it comes to redefining the traditional successful working life. Simplists prefer to work in jobs that reflect their beliefs. They tend to work on a smaller scale with more customer interaction. Even if the job they have is not an ideal match, simplists know that their identity doesn't come exclusively from how they earn their living. Simplists also know that when they're happy, it often doesn't matter how much money they earn.

> It doesn't interest me what you do for a living. I want to know what you ache for, and if you dare to dream of meeting your heart's longing.
>
> –Oriah Mountain Dreamer,
> *The Invitation*

DECIDING WHAT WE REALLY, REALLY, <u>REALLY</u> WANT TO DO

Finding out what we really want to do with our lives can be either the hardest thing to do or the easiest. Doing what we love expresses our soul. Explore this formula for success:

1. Discover what you're best at.
2. Discover what you love.
3. Create a combination of the two, and you'll not merely work for a living, but work at something that's truly important to you.

Is your career your calling? We all have passions that complete us, activities that consume our thoughts and make us lose track of time. How can we take what we love to do and make a living at it? That's the tricky part. We distinguish between work and play because we feel they need to be separate, but when we figure out what we truly love (baseball, fashion, early childhood education), we've taken the first step to earning a living from our passion.

There are careers related to all our seemingly childish pursuits or pipe dreams. Your dreams of becoming an Olympic figure skater may have been dashed when you spent more time with your butt on the ice than in the air, but you can find a related career. Analyze the part of your dream about ice skating that was the most satisfying. Maybe you liked the grace and beauty of the sport. Maybe it was helping younger students with their routines. What other related careers could give you the same feeling as performing? Maybe you don't need to be the best in the world; maybe a weekend warrior could be enough for you.

On the other hand

What we're best at may still not be what we *want* to do. Brainstorm with the people who know you best and ask them to tell you honestly what your strengths are. Find a coach to help discover your passions.

The hardest part is to take that first step once you realize what you truly want to do. But don't fear taking action to get on the path to your goal. Look into going back to school if the job requires special training. Consider correspondence courses for a less expensive way of gaining new knowledge. Talk with people who have been working in your dream job. Offer to volunteer or shadow them if they're willing. Find a career coach who can emphasize your talents and motivate you toward success.

Staying Where You Are

In the interest of full disclosure, I confess that I once worked for a Ubiquitous Mall Store—their managerial guidance was summed up in the directive to "sell as much as you possibly can." Currently I work in freelance television production where I am routinely compensated by the same Madison Avenue I railed against in the *Shopping* chapter, yet I love my work. How do we reconcile our jobs and their ecological and sociological harms?

Work is such an enormous part of our lives that it's crucial to do what supports our soul. I like what I do, but I don't derive my entire personal identity from it. I know that if it ever gets unbearable I will leave and investigate a new career path. If you enjoy the job you already have, stick with it. If it increasingly conflicts with what you believe in, take the time to thoroughly investigate changing jobs. Don't be the vegetarian working at a hamburger stand.

If you don't want to change your job because you still enjoy it, perhaps you need to change your motivation to work. How can we use our jobs to become better people? How can we incorporate our personal beliefs on the environment and society into how our companies do business?

How to Make Where We Work More Palatable

> Human beings weren't meant to sit in little cubicles, staring at computer screens all day, filling out useless forms and listening to eight different bosses drone on about mission statements.
>
> –Mike Judge, *Office Space* (spoken by Peter Gibbons, the personal messiah of the lowly cubicle drone)

In a perfect world, we would all have the perfect job. In Utopia, I'd probably choose to work down at the bar in Key West putting the lime in the coconut. But life isn't that easy. Reality indicates that as the average life span increases and Social Security disappears, we'll be working later and later in life. Here are some tips on how to make our current work situation more palatable, even if you're not the boss.

Evaluate *why you work*. Do you use your job solely for monetary support? The majority of us are required to work to provide an income for our lifestyles. But are you working to pay basic living expenses or to keep up with those Joneses? If it's the latter, it's time to reevaluate your perception of *rich*. Go back to the *Budgeting* chapter and see if there's anything you missed the first time around.

Once we simplify our idea about how much money we truly need to survive, we realize we don't need a million dollars to be an authentically rich person. This realization will change how much money we want in our lives. We'll transform how we work and what we do. When we don't feel the need to make a lot of money just to be making the money, our options will increase and we'll be able to do what we want: charity, non-profit, working for friends or family, doing startup work, or doing things that don't pay a lot but have other rewards. (Consider Kevin Spacey's stint as a drive-thru window clerk in *American Beauty*.)

If you use your job to support only a basic standard of living, learn to pare your bills down to a minimum and increase your investments to a maximum return. This may not happen overnight, but focusing on a goal to make your income sustain your expenses will keep you on track to become self-sufficient and weed out unnecessary purchases.

For those few people out there who don't have to work as a means of support, we applaud their dedication to Denny's counter service. But why are they still in the game? For most people, work provides personal emotional growth, experiences to learn from, and an outlet for expression. No matter where we work, or for whatever reason, we can always develop and apply new skills.

> Work spares us from three great evils:
> boredom, vice, and need.
> –Voltaire

Take This Job and Shove It?

Why don't you like where you currently work? If you don't like the job, analyze your reasons for keeping it. You may not know what else you want to do, but you can eliminate things you don't want to do. Maybe you haven't even realized that you don't like your job. Look at your work habits. Are you frequently late? Do you do your job in a half-assed manner? Do you use work time to do personal business? These are signals that what you're doing isn't fulfilling enough.

Even if we're in the "wrong job," we can use our skills and our desires to shape our experience. Always take lessons with you when you leave, even if it's only collecting research on kooky characters to include in your screenplay on the fast food industry.

Sometimes we feel that our true calling never bothered to contact us, so instead we've settled for the next best thing: a job that's "not too bad" and pays the bills. That's fine … as long as we're happy and can handle not exploring our full potential.

There's no shame in changing careers. There's no law that says we have to continue to do what we're doing now forever. (Well, unless you signed that contract with the devil. If that's the case, then you're on your own.) Some of us decide on a career path and think once we get on it, there's no exit until retirement. We feel obligated to follow the path we've chosen, whether it fulfills a family duty ("All sons in our family have always been lawyers.") or impressing someone else ("People respect police officers." "If I make a hundred grand a year, I can buy that car all the chicks dig."). The career we choose should have *less* to do with proving ourselves to others and more to do with personal dreams and satisfaction.

We've got the best job in the world—a corner office, an expense account, benefits, a free massage after lunch, and a make-your-own sundae bar in the break room. But the deal breaker is the hour-long commute in both directions. The national commuting average is nine hours per week. What can you do so you can keep this job? You can change your hours to miss heavy traffic times, join a carpool, or face the decision about which location is more important, where you live or where you work.

Do you feel like just another worker bee? The work is satisfying, you may say, but where do I fit into the grand scheme? Corporate drones are more likely to enjoy their job if they have a personal stake in the success of the company. Personal growth and empowerment give employees ways to be active participants as a part of the team. Participation raises morale and productivity.

Stop and think

What if the biggies in corporate management had to work at least one day a month (or week) in the lowest level position? How about the CEO of the Four Seasons working as a chambermaid, Mobil executives pumping gas, and the president of Target stocking shelves on Friday nights?

Do you feel that the speed of business is too fast for you? Why do the sleep-deprived and super-stressed seem more productive? Time and speed equal money. Everything has to be done *now*. Any delay is a loss. Although bosses reward workaholics (who often use work as an excuse to avoid other parts of their lives), you don't have to succumb to the pressure (or temptation) to spend your whole life working. Learn to work smarter, not harder. Abandon the Puritan work ethic and the pressure to climb the corporate ladder.

Could you be happier just working indefinitely at the same position?

Twenty-odd years ago, Dolly Parton sang about the hassles of working nine to five, but today a mere forty-hour workweek would be a welcome change for many of us. The average American works eight weeks a year longer than the average Western European. As a way to cut unemployment, the French government has implemented a thirty-five-hour workweek. In Norway and Sweden, ordinary workers get four to six weeks of *paid* vacation. Plus holidays. Okay, before you go searching for your passport and learning to say "You want fries with that?" in German, know that you have the power to increase your leisure time right here in the good ol' U.S. of A.

Top Five Ways to Work Less

1. Switch to part time. Employers can make part-time work more attractive by offering benefits and keeping salaries at a financially feasible level.
2. Work in your jammies. Telecommuting has come a long way, baby. Some businesses today are eager to have employees working from home, as telecommuting saves the space and money of having to provide another desk and computer. Telecommuters can be more productive because their work can be done without the distractions of coworkers. Sick days are kept to a minimum. Not every job is suited to telecommuting (sorry, air traffic controllers), but if you work a job that has flexible hours and deadlines, it may be right for you.
3. Take a sabbatical. No, haughty Ivy League professors aren't the only ones who can take a sabbatical; you, too, can have six months (or more) off. From the ancient Judean concept of having one year of rest for every seven worked, today a sabbatical refers to any leave of absence, usually used for research, travel, or rest.

How to ask for a sabbatical

✓ Find out who can approve your request.
✓ Find out if anyone has been granted such a leave in the past.
✓ If the company has no official sabbatical policy, what is their *unofficial* policy?
✓ What kinds of sabbaticals do companies similar to yours offer?
✓ What were the terms of the sabbaticals offered in the past? Look for paid leave, health insurance maintained, job security, continued accumulation of vacation and sick days.
✓ In lieu of overtime pay, could you bank up comp time to be used for time off?
✓ Are you flexible as to when you want to leave? Could you suggest that you leave at a time of the year that is slow for your company?

---

4. Flex. There's no law that states that everyone must work from nine to five, Monday through Friday. Some people try job sharing with another employee, where each of you works half shifts or alternate days so that each of you can accommodate other priorities in your schedules. Many people would take a pay cut in order to have more time off. What if people cared so much about the company they worked for that they would volunteer to work less time when they knew the company was doing less business? We should find ways to share jobs so unneeded goods aren't produced just to provide jobs for people.

5. Make life less stressful and save time by doing what you love. When we spend our days enjoying what we do, we come home feeling refreshed. We don't have to go through the necessary relaxation techniques of vegging out with the latest Fox reality show and a six pack. Coming home refreshed frees up this time after work to do what needs to be done.

On the other hand

Once you get that free time, don't waste it in a mediated TV reality or in a Ubiquitous Mall Store. Get out and live! When some of us are handed free time, we don't know what to do with it. Remember the Jack Nicholson in *About Schmidt*, the retiree who found himself back at the office after only a week of retirement? Unexpected leisure time can seem overwhelming. Start with the "What to Do When You're at a Loss" list on page 47.

Change the Nature of Business

> You must be the change you want to see
> in the world.
>
> –Gandhi

We've all worked at jobs just to earn money. We've all had jobs where we had no idea what the corporate entity thought of the worker bees. We punched in, did our eight-hour shift as instructed, and collected our paycheck at the end of the week.

But we've all (hopefully) also had at least one job that inspired us to make a difference. When we want the company to succeed, we think of suggestions that would make our workday easier, things we think would improve our performance and make us proud of where we work. Each of us has the ability to help the company shift the focus away from profits and back to human and environmental rights.

Many of the following tips may seem "boss specific," but they are important for the worker bees, too. Someday the worker bees may become queens of the hives; you will be bosses and these tips are meant for inspiration at every level. And even if you're never the boss, you can always have a hand in shaping how your company behaves.

❑ Create not just an office or a business, but a *community*.

❑ Have some fun. Go beyond the ordinary casual Fridays and the once-a-year company picnic.

❑ Develop your feeling of social and ecological accountability. Ben Cohen, co-founder of Ben & Jerry's has said, "Businesses have created most of our social and environmental problems. If business were instead trying to solve these problems, they would be solved in short order."[98] Companies need to realize that their responsibility doesn't end with the manufacture or selling of their product. Companies like Hewlett Packard are implementing recycling programs for their unsold or used computer products to help keep hazardous materials out of the waste stream. Shoe and clothing manufacturer Timberland has created "Path of Service", an in-house volunteer program where employees are given up to 40 hours a year of paid time off to devote to volunteer service.

❑ Practice *true* human resources and employee relations. People will love to come to work if they take pride in what they do. When they feel the company respects them and truly cares about their well-being, results will show in productivity and loyalty. An understanding that not all managers are overpaid bureaucrats and that union members are not lazy and uneducated fosters a positive working community. If companies took a pro-worker attitude to begin with, workers wouldn't even need unions.

❑ Learn to balance solitary work with team work. Creating a healthy balance between being able to complete tasks alone and working with others makes for a well-rounded work environment.

❑ Mix it up. Repetitive tasks can rob us of our desire to succeed and make us feel powerless and bored. Learn new tasks, look for new opportunities, and keep your mind and body refreshed.

❑ Beef up the fringe benefits. Stock options, 401K or retirement pension plans, health and dental insurance, continuing education reimbursement, and onsite subsidized childcare are a few options offered by progressive companies today. Beyond medical insurance, there are additional incentives to keep workers healthy: onsite medical facilities, smoking cessation clinics, gym memberships, etc. The Centers for Disease Control notes that companies with wellness programs report $7 in ultimate savings for every dollar invested in company sponsored exercise programs.[99] Worker-owners are created when owners share the success of company with workers by giving them annual bonuses based on a percentage of sales increase.

❑ Support your team. Show disabled employees or those who cannot do their original job any longer their value to the company by training them for new positions within the company and providing rehabilitation services.

❑ Look for a "perfect fit." Instead of hiring just "anyone," create a workplace and employees that need each other. Reward employees' potential by promoting from within.

Unemployment

I once watched a friend loading my bicycle onto the roof rack of her car. "But what if it falls off?" I asked her. She turned to me and with a straight face replied, "Then we'll turn around, pick it up, and put it back on." I had to laugh at my paranoia. It was, after all, just a bike. And though the bike didn't fall off, since then, we've adopted this as our employment mantra. If you haven't lost a job yet, you're fortunate, but you're also in the minority. When you do lose a job, pick the bike up.

We've outsourced jobs to other countries. We've made tasks easier. And we continue to create trivial products (like Happy Meal toys) that don't serve our needs (like better housing). Unemployment is high because as American jobs become extinct, American workers are left to fend for themselves.

It's time for American companies to find alternatives to laying people off: relocation services, retraining, generous severance packages, and employee exchange (partnering with another company during layoff threats and temporarily transferring your employees over to their business). In the 1930's FDR's New Deal was created to get the country working again after the Great Depression. New Deal projects were both creative and restorative. What if today's America offered work building public housing? What if jobs were created to save our National Parks? What if there was comprehensive public training for any job?

Hopefully, job extinction could someday be a reality for the tobacco farmer, the logger, the gas station attendant, and the nuclear technician. But what right do we have to tell them to just get another job? We must build bridges with the industries that harm the environment. We need to work together to find solutions to make these industries more ecologically healthy and show these workers that there is more work than just the job in front of them.

Here's a little secret: *there's no such thing as job security*. No matter how much we love our job, no matter how much we love our manager, change is the nature of business. This is especially true if we're not our own bosses. No matter how good we are at what we do, we need to learn to pack our own parachute. Keep your options open and always keep your resume updated. Here are a few more tips to make unemployment easier:

❑ Don't attach your whole identity to your job. Being only what you do sets us up for a double loss—the sense of identity plus the source of income. Get your sense of accomplishment from both your leisure activities and your work.

❑ Look for the good, even in being laid off or fired. Was the job not serving your ultimate goal? Was it taking time away from your family or other things you want to do? Trust that everything happens for a reason.

❑ During time off, read up on subjects and learn new skills that will make you more marketable. Seek out free courses at libraries and community centers. See time off as an opportunity to test yourself for survival.

❑ Use the time you're not working to your advantage. Be productive. Whatever you do, import your experience onto your resume.

❑ Focus less on the fact that money is not coming in and more on relaxing and refreshing your soul.

> Beware of all enterprises that require new clothes.
> –Henry David Thoreau

ORGANIZING AND SIMPLIFYING YOUR WORKPLACE

We become so focused on whatever task is immediately at hand that we often overlook organizing, simplifying, and recycling opportunities in our work environment. It's a fact, however, that our cubicles and offices waste even more energy and materials than our homes do. This section will address how to minimize pollution and maximize the efficiency of the resources we use where we work. Bringing our beliefs about sustainable living into the office (or school, restaurant or wherever we work) we can change our emotional and physical health.

Initially, it may be difficult to implement a plan or overcome managerial restrictions. Be patient. Do your research and make a detailed list of ways you can solve problems. Present the problem and your solutions as you would any project. Show your manager the bottom line. If your plan is economically feasible—better yet, if it saves time or money—chances are you'll have that employee-of-the-month parking spot in no time. If there's a more serious issue, like something that causes health problems for employees, consider turning to government agencies like the Occupational Safety and Health Administration (OSHA) and the National Institute for Occupational Safety and Health (NIOSH), which provide protection for workers.

Keeping Work Clutter-Free

The tips listed in the first chapter on organizing our lives and homes can be easily adapted to fit our offices. Use your finely honed decluttering skills to keep your work area organized:

❑ Encourage a company wide cleanup in lieu of a weekly staff meeting.

❑ Learn to file and then take the time to file correctly. A lot of time is wasted looking for misfiled and mislaid papers.

❑ If the mountain of work on your desk is overwhelming, take a Saturday or other time when you won't be distracted to catch up. It's much easier to clean out your in box when the phone isn't ringing and coworkers aren't barging in with questions or giving you new items to add to your to-do list.

❑ Make sure a recycling program is in place and encourage others to use it.

Test yourself

Suggest an office trash competition. Ask your office manager if the company pays a fee for a trash hauling service. Rally coworkers into seeing if you can cut company waste in half. Take away coworkers' individual trashcans and place one bin in the middle of the room. This will make everyone more conscious of what they throw away.

❑ Bring your own coffee mug. Pack a lunch. Reuse a sack or a lunchbox. Bring silverware, plates, bowls and cloth napkins from home. (Reuse plastic containers when you bring your lunch.)

❑ Encourage incentives for employees that car pool or take alternative forms of transit to work.

Paper

While using recycled paper is a start, it's much more important to reduce our overall consumption of paper. "Cutting Paper," a web site sponsored by the U.S. Department of Energy, tells us that the average office worker in the U.S. uses about 10,000 sheets of copy paper each year.[100] The naïve idea that we would have "paperless offices" and that e-mail would reduce the amount of paper we use has obviously backfired; paper use steadily grows.

The term "recycled paper" is misleading. Unless the percentage of post-consumer paper is given, the percentage of recycled content is almost meaningless. "Pre-consumer" means unused paper (scraps left over from printers and paper mills) is recycled into new paper. "Post-consumer" means paper that is recycled from the public's paper supply. This is paper that would have been disposed in a landfill if it hadn't been sent to be recycled into new paper. The higher the post-consumer waste content (100 percent post-consumer is ideal), the more eco-friendly the paper is. One hundred percent post-consumer paper guarantees that no trees were specifically cut to make the piece of paper you're holding.

> ### On the other hand
>
> Buying 100 percent post-consumer paper doesn't do much if that paper isn't recycled again. Many products add an amount of virgin paper to give the product strength, and new paper must still be deinked and bleached. A tremendous amount of waste is generated in the process of making any paper. Trees are cut down, thousands of gallons of water are used, and inks and bleaches create contamination.

❑ Reuse the back sides of paper for printing drafts, pages that will be faxed, or items that people outside the company won't see. How about doing the office football pool on previously used paper?

❑ Consider using narrower margins on letters, memos, and other documents. You get more words per page and reduce the number of pages.

❑ Copy on both sides of paper when making multiple-page copies.

❑ Avoid using stick-on labels on envelopes. Because of insoluble adhesive that can clog papermaking equipment, these envelopes cannot be recycled.

❑ Consider using tree-free paper made from hemp, fabric, and kenaf (a hibiscus-type plant) for special projects.

Office Supplies

Everyone loves office supply delivery day. I've seen grown adults act like children on Christmas morning when they get a new tape dispenser. But few of us realize the connection between the cancellation of their annual bonus and how much money is wasted on stocking up on supplies. How to save some of that money:

❑ Save and separate everything. Keep bins of different products in the supply room: paper clips, rubber bands, thumbtacks, pens. You'd be amazed how much stuff accumulates in desk drawers.

❑ Switch to refillable pens and pencils. It seems we can never find a pen when we need one, which probably accounts for the 1.6 billion ballpoint pens lost every year.

❑ Use shredded paper as packing material instead of foam peanuts.

❑ Hunt for going-out-of-business sales and "fire sales," which are listed in the classified section of the newspaper. Even if you don't need desks or computers, you can often find office supplies for sale at prices that would make Office Depot weep.

❑ Look for reusable products, such as recycled copier toner and laser printer cartridges. When the plastic components aren't recycled, they add an average of four pounds to the waste stream and they may not biodegrade for 300 years.

❑ Use the "draft" setting when printing documents to use less ink and toner.

❑ Simplify your digital needs. Every month, forty-five tons of digital media (CDs, CD-ROMS, and DVDs) are disposed of. Switch from one-time-use to re-writeable versions and investigate recycling options offered through companies such as Washington-based GreenDisk (www.greendisk.com), which recycles products without violating company security.

Equipment

- ❑ Be sure to dispose of office and computer equipment properly, even if there's a fee to do so. It's said that for every computer sold, another becomes obsolete. Each of these computers contains lead, beryllium, mercury, chromium, cadmium, and brominated flame retardant. These computers sit in the back of a closet or are tossed out with the trash. The average monitor contains eight to ten pounds of lead in the cathode ray tubes. It may protect us from radiation, but it can also leak into the ground when the monitor is dumped in a landfill. Currently, Massachusetts and California are the only states that require the recycling of television and computer monitors but see www.earth911.org for additional solutions.
- ❑ Ask the recycler what will happen to your computer when it's recycled. Some companies have been exporting older computers out of the country to be dismantled in places where recycling practices are often not monitored by any safety organization. Approximately 15 percent of computer equipment dropped off at authorized recycling centers is salvageable. These computers can be fixed and sent back for resale. Outdated models are often shipped to developing countries for use in schools. The other 85 percent of equipment is either harvested for parts or recycled.

Thinking outside the box: UsedComputer.com

Since 1995, UsedComputer.com has been a clearinghouse of links and resources with one goal in mind: to help everyone responsibly recycle and dispose of used computer equipment and other high tech toys. Since it's common now to have to pay for proper disposal of electronics, they want to help your gadgets find one last chance at salvation. They put the consumer in touch with nonprofit organizations that accept donations of old computer equipment and even old cell phones that can be reused as emergency lifelines for victims of domestic violence. They also provide lists of recycling outlets for electronics and old diskettes and CDs.

You can also create your own classified ad on the site to sell your equipment yourself or to request the missing piece that will finally make that flight simulation game work on your precious Commodore 64. Ads are viewed not only by the usual technophiles, but also by dealers who resell to a wider public.

❑ Buy only necessary computer and electronic products and try to upgrade components instead of purchasing an entirely new computer.

❑ If you do buy new, look for computers that are lead-free and halogen-free and use recycled plastics in their components.

❑ Consider donating your old computer to an educational, community, or non-profit organization.

❑ Consider purchasing a liquid crystal display (LCD) instead of a standard computer monitor, which give off more radiation. LCDs are the displays found on laptop computers and "flat screen" computers. They produce radiation, too, but it extends for a shorter distance and operates on a less powerful voltage than standard video monitors. The cost is significantly higher, but the radiation is significantly less.

❑ Turn off all computer equipment when you leave the office. Monitors and printers are among the largest energy consumers. Many of America's PCs are left running overnight or over the weekend, still consuming energy while we're off eating Sunday brunch. When we power off, we can greatly reduce energy costs to our companies. Be aware that screen savers also waste energy by tricking us into thinking that because our computer is "asleep" it's not using electricity. Not true.

❑ Hang onto that phone. Today cell phones are used for an average of just eighteen months before being replaced by newer models. Do you really need all those bells and whistles? When you get a new phone, remember to recycle your old phone. Currently, certain Staples office supply stores offer drop boxes where patrons can donate old cell phone equipment to be recycled or donated to charities.

Eco-design

Eco-design is not just about choosing "recycled" copy paper. Eco-design looks at brochures, mailings, advertising, marketing materials, store fixtures, and office furniture for environmental responsibility. There are ways to be artistic and creative without excessive waste of materials and harmful finishing techniques.

✓ Ask yourself, what will happen to this product once it has served its purpose? Will it break down in a landfill? Can it be recycled? Can we save it and use it for something else?

✓ Instead of petroleum-based inks, try soy or vegetable inks made from corn, walnut, and coconut oils. Patronize companies that will recycle waste ink into new ink. These inks require additional drying time, but they also emit fewer volatile organic compounds, are less toxic when dumped in landfills, and are more water-soluble than petroleum-based inks. About 90 percent of daily newspapers (with a circulation larger than 1,500) already use soy inks.

✓ Decide which clients you really want to work with. It's said that the client is always right, but what if they only care about the bottom line and nothing about the recycled content of your paper? When you tell clients about how you're changing toward social responsibility, some will only see dollar signs. It's time to decide if you really want to work with these people.

✓ Think smaller. Renovating seems imperative when you move your business into someone else's space. How can you keep the basic framework, but put your own look on the space?

HEALTH HAZARDS OF THE WORKPLACE

Sometimes the aggravations of our jobs are not all that's damaging to our health. The cause of indoor air pollution can be physical, chemical, or microbiological agents, and it's made worse by poor ventilation. Our offices may be full of ozone, airborne particulates, static, radiation, carbon dioxide and heat generated by computers, laser printers, copiers, and fax machines.

Air quality problems happen in any type of building. In newer or recently renovated office structures, the problems are most often due to construction materials, especially new carpeting, paint, or wallboard. In older buildings that haven't been properly maintained, problems are usually related to bacteria growth. Regardless of the age of the building, if ventilation is inadequate, chemical and biological contaminants will build up and the air conditioning system will simply circulate this hazardous air. Here are some tips for making your workplace healthier.

❑ Rehydrate. If people are being shocked by static electricity around the office, this is an indication that humidity is too low. Dry air leads to dehydration of mucous membranes in the nose, sinuses, throat, and lungs. To rehydrate your office and eliminate static, open the windows, introduce several leafy plants to the space, or purchase a negative ion generator to disperse positive ions generated by the office machines.

❑ Get the air circulating. If the windows open, open them. If you suspect filtered air is unclean, hang a sheet of white paper in front of the vent—after a few days see how dirty the blowing air has made it. This visual can convince anyone to have the vents cleaned.

❑ Use a portable air filter. Pick a conversion unit that can be plugged into either a car cigarette lighter or an electrical outlet.

> *Poor Ventilation + Inadequate Filtration + Multiple Chemical Sensitivity =*
> *Sick Building Syndrome*
>
> In 1983, the World Health Organization published a list symptoms that characterize Sick Building Syndrome (SBS), including irritated eyes, nose and throat; dry mucous membranes and skin; mental fatigue, dizziness and headaches; respiratory infections and cough; hoarseness of voice and wheezing; hypersensitivity reactions; and nausea.[101] As the quantity of volatile organic compounds rise and ventilation decreases, SBS manifests itself.
>
> Conditions are not easily traced to a specific substance, but are perceived as a result of a combination of unidentified contaminants. Very little is known about the long-term effects of these chemicals and the cause of 75 percent of cases remain unknown.

There are other working conditions that affect the senses that we may not otherwise consider. Sensory deprivation or overload, for example, can cause potentially severe problems for office workers. It's crucial to find a healthy balance between too much and too little.

✓ Hearing is affected by unnerving or repetitive noise or music. The body responds to continual noise with high blood pressure, headaches, tension, hyperactivity, poor digestion, ulcers, fatigue, cardiovascular disease, decreased immunity, neurological disorders, disturbed sleep, irritability, moodiness, poor work performance, and mental disturbance. OSHA recommends that workers exposed to eighty-five decibels or louder (roughly the level of rush-hour traffic) every day have an annual hearing test.

✓ Bad lighting leads to poor eyesight. The spectrum of light provided by most fluorescents is not the same as the light produced by the sun. When we're confined indoors with either incandescent or fluorescent lighting all day (especially in the winter when the days are shorter), our bodies suffer from a lack of natural light. Artificial light has also been blamed for changing the body's natural rhythms, causing hyperactivity as well as fatigue. Some fluorescents also produce a distracting audible hum and a visible flicker. Be sure the lighting in your workplace is adequate for the type of task being done.

✓ Toxic chemicals used in office supplies and building materials can affect taste and smell. If you're unable to switch to healthier alternatives, at least improve the ventilation in the office or (especially) the break room.

✓ People need a healthy personal space, that is, a balance between crowding too many people into too small a workspace and the solitary confinement of having to work alone. Everyone has a right to elbow room.

✓ Vibration numbs our senses to hidden dangers. Vibrating energy and sounds that we absorb without knowing it have a negative effect on the cells of our bodies.

✓ Become conscious of how much fresh air you get. Highly energy efficient office buildings insulate us from the outdoors. Such buildings have either windows that don't open or no windows at all.

✓ Workers need adequate bathroom breaks. The office water supply should not have to be regulated by a schedule. Take a break and leave the office when you can.

✓ Poor ergonomics leads to bad posture. Many jobs require workers to be in the same position for eight hours, which can lead to injury and illness.

Office Ergonomics

✓ Stretch often. Do a few laps around the office while your document is printing.

✓ Don't forget to hydrate. A glass of water an hour is a good ratio; a cup of coffee an hour is not.

✓ Set your computer screen at eye level. Looking up or down at it strains your neck, shoulders, and upper back.

✓ Keep your elbows at a ninety-degree angle and rest your hands gently on the keyboard.

✓ Your chair should be adjustable so that you can easily change its position throughout the day. It should support your back, legs, arms, and butt. To find your correct chair height, both of your feet should rest easily on the floor or footrest and the backs of your knees should be slightly higher than the seat of the chair. This allows the blood in your legs to circulate freely. Armrests should support your forearms but not interfere with movement.

✓ Remember to blink. Constant looking at your monitor can lead to fatigued and dry eyes. Rest your eyes periodically by focusing on an object at least twenty feet away.

How do you want to be remembered? By the title listed on your pay stub or by the conviction of your heart? Have the confidence to create the change you want in your own life. You can recognize when your job doesn't serve your passions any longer. You have the power to become who you want to be. You can bring your beliefs about the environment to your workplace. When we simplify our professional lives, we can create a career from doing what we love.

Do it today
How's your job treating you? What changes can you make tomorrow?

ADDITIONAL RESOURCES

Ballard, Chris, *The Butterfly Hunter: Adventures of People Who Found Their True Calling Way Off The Beaten Path.* New York: Broadway Books, c2006.

Batstone, David. Saving the *Corporate Soul: & (Who Knows) Maybe Your Own.* San Francisco: Jossey-Bass, 2003. Eight principles for creating and preserving integrity and profitability without selling out.

Dass, Ram and Paul Gorman. *How Can I Help? Stories and Reflections on Service.* New York: Knopf, 1985.

de Graff, John, ed. *Take Back Your Time: Fighting Overwork and Time Poverty in America.* San Francisco: Berrett-Koehler, 2003.

Dlugozima, Hope, James Scott, and David Sharp. *Six Months Off: The Sabbatical Book.* New York: Henry Holt and Company, 1996.

The Environmental Careers Organization, *The Eco Guide to Careers that Make a Difference.* Washington, D.C.: Island Press, 2004. Environmental Work for a Sustainable World.

Reder, Alan. *75 Best Business Practices for Socially Responsible Companies.* New York: Jeremy P. Tarcher, 1995.

Schor, Juliet B. *The Overworked American: The Unexpected Decline of Leisure.* New York: Basic Books, 1992.

Sher, Barbara. *I Could Do Anything If I Only Knew What It Was.* New York: Dell Publishing, 1994.

St. James, Elaine. *Simplify Your Work Life.* New York: Hyperion, 2001.

Zelinski, Ernie. *The Joy of Not Working.* Berkeley, CA: Ten Speed Press, 1997.

SustainableBusiness.com offers advice on everything from renewable energy, organic products, and social investing to green building. You'll meet the movers and shakers who are taking us to a greener economy. Click on Green Dream Jobs to find satisfying work with an environmentally conscious nonprofit or business or help find top-notch employees.

Vocation Vacations® is a service that allows you to "test-drive your dream job". More than just fantasy camp, they pair you with mentors that get you elbow deep into the profession—a great way to live out your dreams or to see if making the leap to change careers is a better idea than you expected. You can choose from hundreds of dream job packages that vary from chocolatier to pit crew member, from sports announcer to dude rancher. (www.vocationvacations.com)

chapter 9

healing

For some of us, staying healthy may be anything but simple. But the connection between environmental health and our personal physical, mental and emotional wellbeing is critical. It's never possible to achieve perfect health. If anyone tries to promise this unattainable goal, it should raise a red flag for us. Our health changes every day, but if we monitor our body's responses to environmental factors, we can learn to regulate our physical and emotional condition. To enhance the performance of our body's natural healing ability, we must look at the *whole picture of health*. We must consider not only our physical well-being, but also a balanced combination of the physical, psychological, and spiritual health.

Medical science has cured or been able to vaccinate for many of the deadly diseases of the past, but good health has not inevitably followed these advances. Instead, the so-called progress of the Industrial Age has unleashed chronic and persistent disorders such as heart disease, asthma, diabetes, and cancer. Between 1935 and 1987, the number of Americans living with one or more chronic diseases doubled from 22 percent to 45 percent.[102] Now more than 90 million Americans live with chronic illness, which accounts for 70 percent of all deaths.[103]

Every single day, we are exposed to toxins. Many have adopted a "damned if you do, damned if you don't" attitude toward trying to keep healthy. But why do we live in a society that resigns itself to cancer as an inevitability?

Even those who consciously eat healthily and monitor their exposure to environmental pollutants have no clue as to which toxins are flowing through their bodies. We could be dealing with any combination of up to 500 toxic chemicals, including some found readily in household products and food. Many of these chemicals didn't even exist before World War I and some, such as DDT, have been banned in the U.S. for over thirty years. All of this toxic intake adds up. How much is enough? How much does it take to contribute to the climbing rates of cancers, asthma, heart disease, pesticide and chemical poisonings, infertility, allergic reactions, multiple chemical sensitivity and other environmental illnesses?

It's estimated that 15 percent of the population now suffers from what is being called "the 21st century disease"—environmental illnesses and multiple chemical sensitivity (EI/MCS). Many of us do not even realize that we suffer from these conditions. Onset of these symptoms can be an unexplained headache or an allergic reaction. The sufferer can be suddenly knocked down by a strong initial trigger of fragrance or vapor. After this initial hit, exposure to almost any chemical can set off symptoms. The fact that the number of cases of multiple chemical sensitivity continues to rise should be a warning sign that we must regulate and reduce our use of all chemicals.

Symptoms that may accompany EI/MCS

Headaches, disorientation, inability to concentrate, mental confusion, dizziness, severe chest pains, fainting, stomach pains, body aches, convulsions, vomiting, rashes, sleeplessness, nausea, allergic symptoms, conjunctivitis and other eye and vision problems, watery eyes, diarrhea, amenorrhea, photosensitivity, weakness, fatigue, incoherent speech, anxiety, tingling sensation in extremities, muscle twitches, numbness, facial burning, upper respiratory problems (colds, earaches, sneezing, shortness of breath, closed airways, sore throat), metallic taste in mouth, depression.

Triggers are countless. We can suffer reactions when we are exposed to newspaper inks, perfumes, fragranced cosmetic products, gasoline fumes and auto exhaust, mold, cigarette smoke, charcoal, scented candles, office supplies like correction fluid and markers, cleaning products, laundry detergent and fabric softener, dry cleaning solvent, pesticides, plastic off-gassing, "new car smell," and even highly fragrant flowers.

MCS is often labeled a psychological condition because its cause cannot be easily located, and some "experts" dismiss people who cannot function out of their plastic bubble-type homes as crazy. As Mom used to say, "Show me blood, show me broken bones, show me vomit." Those were examples of concrete evidence that proved we were sick. With MCS, however, we often don't look sick to others. We cannot provide *visible symptoms* as proof of illness. Uninformed medical professionals who attempt to treat us tell us to avoid the source of the irritant. But how can we avoid products that are so pervasive in our lives?

When environmental illnesses are present, chemicals usually affect each sufferer differently. There are only patterns, not a clear, consistent path leading from cause to effect. While a certain chemical may cause one person to develop cancer, other members of that person's family who consume the same foods, drink the same water, and breathe the same air may not have any symptoms at all.

Thanks to genetic differences, our bodies vary in their abilities to break down or eliminate certain chemicals. Diet, illness, pregnancy, and medicinal or recreational drug use can also affect a person's sensitivity or immunity to chemicals in the environment. Age is another factor. Young children are often more sensitive because their bodies are still developing and they breathe more air. The kidneys and livers of the elderly begin deteriorating and are less able to manage environmental toxins.

Attack of the household chemicals

Have you ever used a cleaning product and then spent the afternoon laid up with a headache? Has a co-worker's hand lotion caused you breathing problems? Have you felt lightheaded after flipping through a magazine laden with perfume samples?

If you have, call the manufacturer of the product and express your sensitivity complaints.

There's no shield against chemicals today. Environmentalists get cancer. Activists get EI/MCS. Doctors have breathing problems related to air pollution. We have all become lab rats upon which the hazards of the twenty-first century are being tested. Disorders can manifest themselves at any time, but there's no "cure" and new causes are being created and released daily. Trying to avoid the barrage of chemicals that exist outside our personal living space can make us feel helpless.

How can we protect ourselves against unseen chemical enemies as we go through our daily lives? The only way to shield ourselves is to lessen our exposure to chemicals on a continual basis. Since there are nontoxic alternatives readily available for most products, why do we feel the need to take so many chances?

KEEPING HEALTHY

The most dangerous diseases and conditions are the ones that compromise our immunity. Our body's immune system is an automatic process that fixes what's broken down. How successful we are at keeping healthy has a lot to do with how strong our immune system is. When immunity is lowered or compromised, we become less tolerant to pollutants and more susceptible to illness.

Visualize your immune system as an army of protectors, with white blood cells as the soldiers. When immunity is compromised, however, this army slows down and its weapons lose their effectiveness.

All armies have weaknesses. Our immune system is pretty good at fending off small attacks, but the stronger and more prolonged the attack, the harder it gets to win the war. When we keep our immune system strong and healthy, we give our body a fighting chance against illness.

Bacteria are everywhere—they were around long before humans even existed and will exist long after we're gone. Even when we're clean and in good health, there's still about a hundred thousand bacteria living on just one square centimeter of our skin ... and that's just on the outside of us.

Despite our fear of bacteria, they are an integral part of the web of life. Since the middle of the 20th century, we've been using antibiotics to fight them, but antibiotics merely reduce the number of invading germs to a point where the immune system can take over and heal the body. Even when an infection is present, the healing comes from the immune system, not the antibiotic. When we indiscriminately kill bacteria—the good ones along with the bad ones—we weaken our immune system. We don't realize that tiny bacterial infections are necessary to help strengthen our immunity against larger attacks.

It's not the presence of microorganisms that causes infection, but our immune system's inability to fight off the right number of bad microorganisms. When antibacterial products end up in the waste stream, bacteria are forced to do what comes naturally. They learn to defend themselves. Eventually, they evolve into Super Bugs.

Some believe it's our insistence on always being squeaky clean that causes our immune system to not function to its full potential. In the past, our homes and lifestyles (and the microscopic germs and critters that lived with us) were "dirty" enough to allow us to build up natural immunities. But now, supermarket and pharmacy shelves are lined with antibacterial hand sanitizers, body washes, disinfectants, bathroom cleansers, mouthwashes, even articles of workout clothing. Everything comes complete with bacteria-killing chemicals. With our newly acquired germ phobia and the arsenal of industrial strength cleaners, we're no longer able to produce the same antibodies that used to fight an overgrowth of bad bacteria.

What if 75 percent of all antibiotics prescribed were unneeded? When they were first introduced, antibiotics were seen as "miracle cures," so much that even now they are taken for health problems on which they have no effect. Americans have developed a psychological addiction to antibiotics and doctors legally prescribe them without second-guessing their patients' requests for them. Antibiotics should be prescribed *only when a bacterial infection is present.* They have no effect on the flu or the common cold, which are caused by viruses.

We can learn to strengthen our immune system and keep ourselves healthy with simple natural methods. We can build immunity by balancing antibiotics with good biotics, releasing toxins, eating right, managing our stress, and getting a good night's sleep.

Releasing Toxins

Ridding our bodies of toxins is the first important way to keep our immune system functioning properly and our bodies healthy and happy. Try these simple tips for releasing toxins.

❑ Sweat heavily. Any type of sweating is good because toxins are being eliminated. Be sure to replenish your electrolytes as you go since sweating will excrete salt. Note that you perspire about a cup per sleep cycle, so drink a glass of water before bed to wake up hydrated.

❑ Use the sauna regularly. Hot baths or saunas deeply cleanse and rejuvenate the body. They relax the body and stimulate the immune system. They help fight off viral and bacterial infections. A wet sauna, more commonly referred to as a steam room, has lower temperatures (around 115 °F) than a traditional dry Scandinavian sauna, which keeps humidity low and temperature high (between 160 and 210 °F). A rinse with cold water after the sauna stimulates circulation, reduces inflammation, closes pores, and produces a healthy afterglow.

❑ Try dry skin brushing. Brushing is said to not only help immunity but also to decrease cellulite by improving blood circulation and muscle tone. Once a week, for about ten minutes, use a dry brush with natural bristles to brush your skin in circular motions (always toward the heart), avoiding only your face and broken or irritated skin. Brushing removes dead skin and opens clogged pores. Afterwards jump in a shower or bath to wash away the dead skin cells. Hot water opens the pores, increasing blood circulation and drawing out body wastes and toxins.

❑ Take a sea salt or Epsom salts bath. Salt stimulates warming in the body. The minerals in Epsom salts will draw toxins and sweat away from pores.

❑ Try a fast. Fasting gives us the chance to build a healthier body from the ground up, as new cells are created from scratch rather than by a system that is burdened by toxins. Fasting is not easy and first-timers should always follow a pre-tested regimen.

Tips for fasting

✓ Ease in and out of your fast. Several days beforehand, start limiting your intake of sugars and meats. Wait a few days after the end of the fast before devouring that pepperoni pizza.

✓ Do not drink caffeinated beverages during the fast. Drink herbal teas instead.

✓ For juice fasting, follow Pamela Serure's book *3-Day Energy Fast*. Fresh squeeze juices yourself or look for bottled juices without added sugar or preservatives.

✓ Drink lots of water.

✓ Eliminate the use of refined sugars.

✓ Don't overdo exercise. If possible, fast when you've got little to do. Take time off from work if you can, and try to include some time for meditation or introspection. Strange emotions come up when we change our eating patterns, possibly revealing our real relationship to food. Notice if you feel the need to eat when you're bored, anxious, or sad.

✓ Consult a doctor before you begin any fast over seven days or if you have a serious medical condition.

❑ Drink lots of filtered water, at least eight to ten eight-ounce glasses daily. If we don't replenish our personal water supply, cells start to draw water from the bloodstream. This causes our blood to get sludgy, which means our heart has to work harder, which means blood gets redirected away from less vital areas, and, well ... we can see where this is going. Increasing our fluid intake to up to a gallon of water a day can wash bacteria out of our system, combat daytime fatigue, and improve ability to focus.

❑ Try the Big "E." Americans fear getting an enema (or colonic) as much as they dread an IRS audit, but Europeans continue to swear by its benefits. Use the juice of half a lemon with one quart of warm water. The benefits of a clean colon include feeling better and thinner and looking healthier.

❑ Regulate your intake of B_6, B_{12}, D, and E: the vitamins that help release toxins.

❑ Schedule a massage. Massage stimulates circulation and accelerates the flow of lymphatic fluid, which promotes the release of body toxins from muscles. Massage also increases the flexibility of muscles, ligaments, and other soft tissues. It's good to visit a massage therapist to relieve pain or to relax and reduce stress, but an added benefit is well-nourished and healthy skin. Always massage in the direction of blood flow toward the heart.

❑ Use regular soap instead of antibacterial products that eliminate both the good and bad germs that help strengthen our immunity.

❑ Keep your kidneys and liver happy. Both clean blood of the hundreds of chemicals we encounter every day. The liver is a resilient organ, capable of adapting and repairing itself under normal circumstances, but many chemicals can slow its function down. The more chemicals we're exposed to, the more overworked the immune system becomes, and when blood cells become damaged, illness and disease can set in. Signs of toxic overload of the liver include many of the symptoms associated with environmental illness. If caught early, these symptoms can be alleviated through lifestyle changes like diet, exercise, and reduced chemical exposure. However, if early warning symptoms are not acknowledged, the body can suffer permanent damage or permanent sensitivity to all toxins.

❑ Ask your doctor to test your body fat for toxins. This will answer questions if you're seriously concerned about your chemical burden. It can cost several thousands of dollars to test for 250 chemical contaminants, but these tests can reveal how heavy your toxin load really is.

❑ Seek a supervised detoxification program. There are weekend (or longer) retreats that teach us to monitor our eating habits, keep us isolated from chemicals, and train us how to keep our toxic exposure to a minimum.

Eating Right

Eliminating certain foods from our diet can improve our health, but vitamin reinforcement can protect us from getting sick in the first place. When taking vitamins, however, do so intelligently and within reason. Try to take vitamins in their simplest form, as they are found naturally in fresh fruits and vegetables, and only supplement with tablets if absolutely necessary. Prolonged consumption and increasing dosages of mineral and vitamin supplements can be harmful, so always read labels, as you would any medicine. If you have questions, consult a health care professional.

Enrich your diet with phytomins

Phytomins (also known as phytonutrients, phytochemicals, or just plain "phytos") are natural plant chemicals that have specific health applications. Since most of our medicines originate from plants, instead of taking a vitamin pill, look to fruits and vegetables to find all the nutrients you need to help the body prevent and fight disease.

According to askdrsears.com, the top twelve phyto foods are soy, tomatoes, broccoli, garlic, flax seeds, citrus fruits, melons (cantaloupe and watermelon), pink grapefruit, blueberries, sweet potatoes, chili peppers, and legumes (beans and lentils).[104]

On the other hand

"Nutraceuticals" (or "functional foods") is the term that describes replacing our food with chemicals that contain all the nutrients we need. And coming soon are "pharma crops": plants that are genetically engineered to produce pharmaceuticals and industrial chemicals.

There's no governmental regulatory agency that monitors herbal supplements, alternative medicines, and homeopathic remedies. Be alert for warning labels and always consult a professional if you have any questions about an herb or other supplement or if you're pregnant. Always tell your doctor about any herbal medicines you're taking, as they may interact with prescription medication.

When taking supplements, know that the pill form is the least beneficial because pills require large amounts of water to be metabolized. Gelatin capsules, extracts, sprays, and teas are preferable.

You can release toxins, balance your vitamins, and supplement your diet with these immunity-boosting foods:

❑ Mince up some garlic. Exactly how garlic works is unclear, but it's continually praised for its antibiotic and antiviral effects and protection against infection. The strong odor is due to its most potent chemical, allicin, which is only released if exposed to air when the garlic clove is cut or mashed. A whole clove can be swallowed per day, and as long as it's whole (not cut or nicked) it won't cause you to produce its odor. Dried garlic can offer some benefits, but doesn't preserve the full activity of the fresh herb. Garlic also has cardiovascular effects, lowering blood pressure and cholesterol and inhibiting blood clotting. Use garlic with caution, however, if you're on anticoagulant medication or if you notice stomach problems.

❑ Eat yogurt with active cultures (that's the non-frozen versions; when yogurt is frozen the good bacteria die). This increases production of gamma interferon, which is important in fighting certain allergies and viral infections. Yogurt cultures help the body digest food, manufacture essential vitamins, combat overgrowth of yeast, and prevent constipation. It is especially important to take a probiotic culture when taking antibiotics to balance your system. Beneficial cultures include: *Lactobacillus acidophilus, L. casei, L. reuteri,* and *Bifidobacterium bifidum.*

❑ Take vitamin F. It goes by many names: essential fatty acids, polyunsaturated fats, and omega-3/alpha-linoleic and omega-6/linoleic acid. Whatever we call it, EFAs are the building blocks of every human cell; EFAs create new cells and repair damaged ones. They prevent buildup of fatty deposits in tissues, transport oxygen to cells, make blood coagulate, and prohibit the growth of bacteria. EFAs work with vitamin D to provide calcium to tissues. But with all they do, they are usually monitored the least of all vitamins.

These acids are difficult to get naturally and are not manufactured by the body. We get plenty of omega-6 from safflower oil, soy oil, sunflower seeds, pumpkin seeds, corn oil, sesame oil, and wheat germ oil, but our intake of omega-3s (found in oily fish such as cod, salmon, sardines, and mackerel) often is lower than it should be. The purest form of omega-3 is cold-pressed flaxseed oil (also called linseed oil). It's not an easily acquired taste, but small doses can be added to salad dressings, pasta, smoothies or stirred into yogurt. Be sure to watch "use by" dates because flaxseed oil deteriorates quickly. Preparations of flaxseed oil must be stored properly in a dark bottle in the refrigerator to avoid spoilage.

Researchers say that omega-3 oils may also help treat depression and arthritis. In addition, they lubricate the body, promoting smoother skin, hair, and nails and healthy mucous membranes. Dry skin and "chicken skin bumps" are indicators that we may need more omega-3 oils. By inhibiting the clotting tendency of the blood, they also reduce excessive inflammation, lower cholesterol, and help reduce risk of heart attacks. There is even some research that shows that fish oils might help prevent cancer.

❑ Eat immunity-boosting mushrooms. These include maitake, shiitake, and reishi mushrooms, which produce many beneficial compounds, including polysaccharides that can protect us against invading germs or cancer. Reishi mushrooms have also helped with altitude sickness, fatigue, and high blood pressure. For centuries, traditional Chinese medicine has used mushrooms to treat general fatigue and weakness, asthma, insomnia, and coughing.

On the other hand

Mushrooms can be dangerous, especially if you try to pick them yourself. Do not, I repeat, *do not* stray outside the produce section for your mushrooms.

❑ Reduce sugar intake. When you eat or drink 100 grams of sugar (about twenty-one teaspoons, about a can and a half of regular soda), this can reduce your white blood cells' ability to kill germs by 40 percent. This decrease in immunity starts in less than thirty minutes after ingestion and can last up to five hours.

❑ Reduce alcohol intake. The body consumes valuable nutrients when it's processing the alcohol you drink. High doses of alcohol stop white blood cells from multiplying, which makes them less effective at destroying cancer cells and other invaders.

❑ Grind up some wheatgrass. This is another taste may take some getting used to, but the chlorophyll content in wheatgrass acts as a magnet to draw toxins out of the body. A two-ounce shot is equal to four pounds of organic green vegetables.

❑ Indulge in antioxidants. These are necessary to help prevent damage from toxins. Antioxidants are present in bananas, onions, peas, beans, lentils, and all other leafy dark green vegetables (such as broccoli and cabbage). Blueberries have one of the highest levels of antioxidants. Milk thistle, which protects and repairs liver tissue, is a good antioxidant for treating environmental sensitivities.

❑ Take ginseng. Ginseng has been known to both boost energy and stimulate immune function.

❑ Try echinacea. This herb is one of the best known herbal immunity boosters. Although its effects are not yet fully understood, it stimulates the immune system and counters both bacterial and viral infections. Use it only while you're ill and only the dose recommended. Studies don't report much success with people using it as a preventive measure.

❑ Boost your resistance to colds and flu with astragalus root. This herb stimulates production of immune system cells and promotes the production of interferon, which prevents viruses from reproducing.

> ### On the other hand
> *Caution:* Even though both echinacea and astragalus show promise for boosting the immune system, do not take them on an extended basis (more than two weeks at a time).

Stress Management

Healing the soul is as important as healing the body. It may be even more important, because when the mind is stressed, the body often falls victim to illness. Runners often get colds after a marathon, the flu runs rampant through the office after a busy season at work, and traumatic experiences such as a car accident can lay us up for days with exhaustion.

While we all cope with stress differently, there are some common ways to handle it. It's not stress itself that is always bad. It's *our reaction to it* that determines its effect on our bodies. When stress fills our mind, it slows our reflexes, which means our chances of having an accident drastically increases. Stress and anxiety cause wrinkles and poor skin, which give us a rundown appearance. Eventually stress can lead to more serious illnesses. Health hazards of stress include ulcers, high blood pressure, headaches, and alcohol or drug dependency.

The constant stress of our society is a combination of personal and social factors, but most stress is of our own creation. We can trace the feelings related to stress back to the presence and amount of three basic emotions: joy, fear, and anger. When we can recognize these emotions and what causes them, we can control what kind of effect they have on our stress levels.

Joy: C'mon, Get Happy

Life being what it is these days, a surplus of happiness is not usually an issue. We can feel like we can never have enough joy in our life, but we can also become addicted to it, chasing the emotion and needing more and more of it to get high.

Why are we so unhappy? We allow physical and emotional pain rule our lives. We reject the past and apologize for the way we live. We don't see the peace and love in the here and now. We compare ourselves to others. We feel sorry for ourselves. We expect a Fairy Godmother to swoop down and magically solve all our problems.

A big part of happiness is perception. People spend too much time doing things because they think they should because of peer pressure or what they believe society thinks is right. You want to know the real secret to life? Life is much easier when we realize that:

I AM NOT, NOR WILL I EVER BE, WHAT OTHER PEOPLE THINK I AM.

Even more so:

I AM NOT, NOR WILL I EVER BE
WHAT I *PERCEIVE* OTHER PEOPLE THINK I AM.

Woah, man, that's pretty heavy.

Wait, let me get this straight. Just because that boy in fourth grade called me "chubby," that doesn't mean it's true? And when I thought my boss hated me because I was out sick the day of our big presentation it doesn't mean he actually thought that at all?

Who is that voice in our head? Who is that voice that tells us what to do? How we should look and act? Is it God? Madison Avenue? Mom? Society? The media? Hollywood? Friends? Someone we look up to? We fill our lives with purchases that we hope will show our status and how "cool" we are. How often do we purchase something we really like instead of something we think other people will approve of or react favorably to?

We may not even notice that this distortion of reality is actually in our mind. We may think that we're immune to peer pressures, but, like it or not, we want to be popular, and this desire to be liked causes us to pick up on nonverbal cues, take insults personally, and overanalyze offhand comments.

But what if none of it mattered?

On the other hand: chemically unhappy

The U.S. has higher rate of depression than almost every other country. This becomes more obvious as Asian countries become more Americanized and their depression rates increase. Unfortunately, as much as we want to be happy, our body chemistry sometimes prevents it. The pharmaceutical industry is happy to sell us a handy cure-all, chemical panacea that will make all our troubles go away. While these fixes have provided millions with a brighter outlook on life, are they only the loose patch that covers the hole?

We all have the capability to be extraordinary. Even when we think we're at our lowest, we can give back love and encouragement.

> Your playing small does not serve the world. Who are you not to be great?
> –Nelson Mandela
> (paraphrasing Marianne Faithfull)

Well, then, how exactly do we get happy? How do we fight back against that voice inside that says, "I suck"? What can we turn to in times when we're feeling bluer than blue? What will get us out of the doldrums?

❑ Get busy. When we're absorbed in a task, the work becomes a form of meditation. We lose track of time. We feel fulfilled and at peace and endlessly creative.

❑ Nurture your passions and express yourself. Listen to your own "wants."

❑ Rent *Airplane!* Laughter releases endorphins, the naturally occurring feel-good substances that are produced in the brain. Studies show that laughter helps to fight disease, lowers blood pressure, reduces stress hormones, and increases muscle flexibility. Laughter is even used in pain management for terminally ill patients.

❑ Try one (or more) of these: pets, music, pampering, friends.

❑ Go out for Mexican food. Some people swear by hot and spicy foods to perk them up mentally.

❑ Read *14,000 Things to be Happy About* by Barbara Ann Kipfer. Mark up your copy with notes and ideas, changes you can make in your life.

❑ Create your own sanctuary. Find a space where you can hide from the everyday world, if only for a while.

❑ Get up and exercise. Norepinephrine, serotonin, and dopamine (the brain chemicals that transmit messages between nerves) are low in depressed people. Physical activity boosts these chemicals and endorphins. Even if it's just a twenty-minute walk, try to do a little exercise every day. It also stimulates creative thinking and helps you release tension, frustration, and anger.

If you want to live a life of simplicity, it helps to have a sense of humor. Laughter naturally accompanies being relaxed. It can help lower stress levels in almost any situation. Once our lives have become organized and simplified, we'll find we have more time to decide, see, realize, or discover what we truly love and enjoy doing. Happiness often naturally follows finding our passions.

On the other hand

Don't forget your dreams while you're on your way to reaching your goals. While organizing and simplifying, be sure to recognize your dreams and reward yourself for working so hard. Don't focus so intently on achieving your goals that you neglect to have fun along the way.

> When one door of happiness closes, another opens, but often we look so long at the closed door that we do not see the one that has been opened before us.
> –Helen Keller

If Helen Keller could find light in her life, what's our excuse?

Fear

The bottom line of all fear is "I can't handle it." Fear arises from low self-esteem and lack of trust in our abilities. The only way to overcome it is to meet it head on and do it anyway. Remember—everyone gets scared. To overcome fears, try these steps:

- ❏ Stay busy. If you have a lot to get done without a lot of time, you're more likely to jump in and just get things over with.
- ❏ Recognize that power is a sure cure for fear.
- ❏ Change how you think from passive to active, from negative to positive. Instead of, "Maybe I will try to do it," say, "It will be done today."
- ❏ Know that many things are only difficult because we haven't experienced them before (or enough).
- ❏ When you say, "I can't," think about your life and the most difficult thing you've ever done. Know that a girl who ran a marathon can do this, or that a guy who saved the company $500,000 last year can do that.
- ❏ Break daunting tasks down into manageable chunks.
- ❏ Banish resistance to some task or event by writing down how you want the situation to turn out. Write down the "baby steps" for achieving your goal.
- ❏ Learn to accept yourself just the way you are. Mr. Rogers was right.
- ❏ Recite and believe the serenity prayer written by Reinhold Niebuhr: "God grant me the serenity to accept the things I cannot change, the courage to change the things I can, and the wisdom to know the difference."

Knowing that we can handle anything is the key to allowing ourselves to take risks. Mom always said, "That which does not kill us can only make us stronger." Another wise man once said, "Anticipation of death is worse than death itself." The power to face fear and survive is available to us—we can surmount its effects and come out a stronger person.

Test yourself: Journey outside your zone of comfort

What do you fear? Do you want to something more for yourself, but can't seem to go for it? Remember, you can only grow as big as the pot you're planted in.

Anger

Rage is an emotion with a mind all of its own. We feel we can't control it. We're afraid that when we're under its spell it's too easy to become irrational and even dangerous. Anger management has become a necessity for many people in the 21st century because stress levels can be uncontrollable. We're frustrated with what we don't have power over and our frustration manifests itself in heart conditions, high blood pressure, and strokes. To help cope with anger, try these solutions:

❑ Pick your battles.
❑ Direct your anger at the right person, in the right place, at the right time. Don't displace anger onto an innocent party.
❑ Don't get mad at inanimate objects. What good does it do? Instead, figure out who or what the inanimate object represents.

How to get sick

✓ Don't pay attention to your body.
✓ Do only the things you don't like to do. Avoid what you do like to do.
✓ Worry constantly.
✓ Blame others.
✓ Bottle up your feelings.
✓ Avoid change.
✓ Dwell on bad things and past mistakes.
✓ Sulk.
✓ Read, watch, and listen to things that reinforce your idea that there's no hope.
✓ Isolate yourself from those who love you.
✓ Complain a lot.
✓ Wear T-shirt that says "Life sucks and then you die."

❑ Don't use anger to retaliate. Use it to explain the harm done and to correct the situation.

❑ Keep your anger in proportion to its cause.

❑ Let anger go when the situation is corrected or you have received an apology.

Stress Reduction Tips

When not kept in check, stress can be deadly. It's said more Americans die at 9 a.m. on Mondays than at any other time.[105] Just remember, we're never too young to start working on that heart attack.

❑ Relax and keep your stress level low. Don't underestimate the value of doing nothing. Be sure to take a break every day. Establish a private space and some quiet time when you don't have to do anything.

❑ Meditate. Meditation aims to relax the mind and body as well as to achieve a heightened state of awareness. Buddhists have been using meditation not only for stress relief but also for pain management for 2,500 years. They believe a calm mind is the key to health. Health benefits of meditation include regulating blood pressure, stimulating circulation, alleviating pain, and reducing muscular tension. It slows hormonal activity and helps migraines, anxiety attacks, sinus problems, asthma, and cardiac rhythms. It can improve performance in sports, business, and arts. It also helps in building self-confidence and increasing energy and efficiency.

Meditation is neither as time consuming nor as difficult as it appears. It can be as simple as a quiet walk. If you don't want to try a walking meditation, find a quiet spot, get into comfortable seated position, and clear your thoughts. The trick to meditation is to acknowledge any thought that creeps into your head and then let it go. If you drift off, you lose the focus of the exercise. Focus with detachment, but stay aware. Be here now. Stay present in the moment. Don't think ahead or back. For a more intense meditation experience, seek out classes, books or CDs to help get you to that higher plane.

❑ Practice yoga. Yoga is an ancient Indian science that is not just stretching poses, but also breathing disciplines that help students achieve higher consciousness and a relaxed state. You don't have to be able to put both of your legs behind your head to give yoga a try, but you may find it deceptively simple. A word of caution to first-timers: the postures may look easy, but you'll have a few days of "yoga remorse" if you overdo it. Classes can be found at neighborhood health clubs, the YMCA, or community centers. Private teachers often offer classes in yoga studios or in homes.

❑ Change how you perceive stress. Do you get frustrated at things beyond your control? Or do you face them head on as challenges to conquer?

❑ Get your hands dirty. The relaxing pace of gardening has been shown to be an excellent way to lower stress and raise your level of patience as you wait for seeds to sprout or plants to bloom.

❑ Leave your baggage at the door. Learn to let go of things. Stop criticizing, judging, complaining, whining, gossiping, worrying, and thinking negatively. Just let it go. Forgive yourself and accept what has happened as a learning experience. When we cling to the past, we cannot live fully in the present.

❑ Stop reading or watching a movie if you don't like where it's going. You can turn off the TV. You can put down the magazine. You have the power to decide what you want to view.

❑ Limit your news intake. "News" in its many forms—televised, printed, electronic, or word of mouth—can produce different feelings. Negative stories produce mainly anxiety, rage, and depression. Taking a break from too much information keeps unnecessary stress out of our lives.

❑ Escape the two-dimensional world. The television, the computer screen, even the windshield of our car separates us from reality.

❑ Be honest. Express your feelings. Unexpressed emotions become internal obstacles.

❑ Learn to ask for and accept support without fear, remorse, or obligation.

❑ Eliminate toxic relationships with poisonous people who don't support or encourage your growth. Do you feel worse after seeing certain people? Do you give more than you get back? How do you feel when that friend cancels on you again? Is there someone who belittles you or doesn't support your dreams? Reevaluate your acquaintances and ask yourself how your life would be without them in it.

❑ Learn to say no. Two letters can save so much time and aggravation.

❑ Curb your indecision. When we don't choose, we deprive ourselves of something. Not choosing keeps us stuck in ambivalence. Is the problem that there aren't enough good choices? Gain clarity in the situation by making a scale to weigh the pros and cons. Move things around to see them in a new light.

❑ Bring on the Beethoven. When you're stuck in a traffic jam, try changing the radio dial to a classical music station. Studies show a lowered heart rate and leveled emotional state while subjects listened to classical music. It also changes our perception of space, which is especially helpful when trapped within the confines of the car. If you can't handle Bach or Mozart, at least switch off the Limp Bizkit.

❑ Acknowledge that you may have Seasonal Affect Disorder (aptly anagrammed as SAD). Spending all day indoors without natural light manifests itself in depression, lethargy, weight gain, and carbohydrate craving, not to mention peaking suicide rates in late winter. Treatment studies have found that full spectrum light helps support the endocrine system, aids in concentration, and improves moods. In full spectrum light (which mimics the balance of color found in natural sunlight), colors appear more vibrant with sharper contrast. Get out of the house when you can.

❑ Exercise. Kick your endorphins into high gear.

Make your own gym

Health clubs are tremendous energy wasters, having to provide extra cooling in the summer and power for lights and machines all year. Air quality is poor due to chemicals from disinfectants and bleach, EMFs from equipment, and hundreds of sweaty bodies confined to poorly ventilated areas.

Okay, maybe the gym isn't all that bad, once we get past the sweaty air, the funky showers, and the muscle man with the thirty-inch neck, but our ancestors didn't need 24 Hour Fitness. Their daily lives provided more than enough of a workout. We avoid physical labor, but spend hundreds of hours and dollars a year trying to get buff.

E.F. Schumacher wrote that "The amount of genuine leisure available in a society is generally in inverse proportion to the amount of labor-saving machinery it employs."

Instead:

✓ Take the stairs instead of the escalator or elevator.

✓ Rake leaves, use a push lawnmower, shovel snow with a real shovel. (Each has the added bonus of lessening air and noise pollution as well.)

✓ Carry buckets of "waiting to heat up" water from your shower to your plants.

✓ Forego a shopping cart at the supermarket.

✓ Park your car closer to the exit of the parking lot, but further from the entrance of the store. You gain a little walk and save the hassle of circling until you find and empty spot.

✓ Walk or bike to work or errands. Don't have enough errands to do by foot or bike? Consider saving the price of a stamp and delivering your utility bills by hand. Most companies have a drop box and some have alternate locations where you can make payments in person.

✓ Forgo the slick high-pressured sales pitch of corporate gyms, in favor of joining your local YMCA. Not just a place to burn some calories, but members support a community minded organization. Many locations offer you the option of being able to use Y facilities nationwide.

❑ Reduce stress with food. Serotonin-producing foods include bananas, tomatoes, pineapples, avocados, eggplant, dates, walnuts, figs, and passion fruit. Even small amounts of chocolate are okay if you choose good, high quality chocolate. Darker is better because it contains more theobromine, a chemical that stimulates the release of endorphins.

- Cut out caffeine. Too much caffeine can lead to chronic anxiety. Simpler alternatives to that cuppa Joe include herbal teas, water, color therapy (reds, oranges, and yellows can brighten our day by changing light energy), aromatherapy (eucalyptus, rosemary, geranium, peppermint and lemon scents are invigorating), and—my personal favorite—more sleep.
- Try a little wort. St. John's Wort capsules (or drops of tinctures in tea) can be taken for anxiety, irritability, or emotional upsets. It can lighten our mood and lift our spirits.
- View yourself as healthy. Keep a positive attitude. Guard yourself against cynicism and hostility.
- Take life less seriously. Laugh as much as you can. A depressed mind can depress a body. Laughter actually increases production of an antibody that is responsible for our first line of defense against bacterial infections.
- Keep a journal. Write. It doesn't matter if anyone ever reads what you write, not even yourself. Write to clear your mind of negative and stressful thoughts and experiences. Julia Cameron, author of *The Artists' Way*, recommends "morning pages," a writing exercise that asks you to write three pages first thing every morning as a way to unlock creative blocks and release stress. While we may find solutions to problems in our writing, sometimes answers may elude us for months. Don't despair, and whatever you do, don't stop writing. Even mundane observations (such as commenting on the weather, your physical appearance, or what you need to do that day) can lead to insight when you least expect it. According to *Writing Your Authentic Self*, writing about your deepest feelings for twenty minutes a day increases the efficiency of the immune system.
- Find a sense of meaning in your life, even if it's just for the day at hand. When we're happy with what we do and who we are, stress can seem insignificant.

Sleep

> Fatigue makes cowards of all of us.
> –Vince Lombardi

If you're feeling cranky, confused, or clumsy, if your body is run down, if your hair is weak and your mouth and skin are dry—maybe what you really need is just a good night's rest. Tips to help us sleep:

- Respect the body's natural rhythms. When does your body tell you to go to sleep or wake up? If you need an alarm clock to wake up, you're probably sleeping too little.
- Relish your bath time. Three bathing ideas to promote sleep:

✓   Take warm bath one to two hours before bed.

✓   Take a cold two minute footbath.

✓   Kneel or sit in cold water for three to five minutes. This will regulate circulation and help you fall asleep.

❑ Skip the soda and the coffee or tea. Don't drink caffeine after 2 p.m.

❑ Avoid large meals before bed. Instead, try sleepy snacks: banana, lemon water with honey, warm skim milk with honey, or wheat germ.

❑ Try autosuggestion. Lie still and mentally tell each part of your body to go to sleep.

❑ Drink mineral water before bed. A Native American custom is to drink a glass of water before sleeping to help you wake up more easily in the morning.

❑ Exercise regularly, but not less than two hours before bedtime. I know people who are able to fall asleep soundly after a workout and big meal, but if you're having trouble sleeping, change your workout pattern and see if you notice a difference.

❑ Sleep with an herbal pillow next to your regular pillow. Chamomile and lavender are good relaxing herbs.

❑ Breathe in relaxing essential oils from an infuser: allspice, anise, basil, cedarwood, dill, fennel, lemon, marjoram, orange, sandalwood, or vanilla.

❑ Try herbal sleep remedies. Melatonin is a brain hormone that is a nontoxic regulator of the sleep cycle. Valerian is another natural sleep aid that has proven effective. You can buy tinctures in health food stores or pharmacies. Take these only occasionally for situational insomnia or to regulate sleep cycle after traveling across time zones.

❑ Make your bedroom as healthy as possible. Open windows during the day to air out pollutants (including dust mites) and refresh the air.

❑ Simplify with natural fibers. Bedding made of polyester blends can be treated with formaldehyde to prevent wrinkles, but formaldehyde is known to cause insomnia. Off-gassing can occur from mattresses and box springs made with chemically-treated foams, plastics, artificial fibers, treated wood, and chemical adhesives. Consider a bed made from healthier natural materials like untreated wood and organic cotton bedding.

❑ Don't let the bedbugs bite. Protect yourself from dust mites, the microscopic creatures that live in pillows (about 40,000 there) and mattresses (approximately two million there!) by washing bedding weekly in hot water and using covers designed to prevent exposure to the mite fragments and waste that cause allergies.

❑ Don't sleep in the wrong bed in the wrong location. According to the principles of feng shui, there are no bad directions to sleep in. But if you have trouble sleeping, try reorienting your bed for a few weeks to see if you notice a change. Is your mattress too hard or too soft? Is the air too stuffy in your bedroom? Get out your bagua and refocus your ch'i. (More on feng shui on page 311).

❑ Quiet down where you sleep. Not-so sound sleeper? Is there too much ambient noise? If outside sounds disturb you, add seals to windows and doors to block them or muffle windows with heavy drapes. If noise continues to creep in, consider a "white noise" machine or CD that simulates the ocean, forests, rain, or other soothing sounds.

❑ Get away from electromagnetic fields that can disturb your body's natural rhythms. Take the television, the computer, and other electrical distractions out of the bedroom.

❑ Avoid pre-bedtime worry caused by pain, depression, or stress. These can do as much damage as caffeine in keeping you awake.

❑ If all else fails and you can't fall asleep, get up and do something. Keep it simple. It won't kill you if you miss an occasional night of sleep, and you might even finally get that 5,000-piece jigsaw puzzle finished.

A DIFFERENT WAY TO HEALTH: ALTERNATIVE HEALTH PATHS

Conventional Western Medicine is what most of us have relied on to keep us healthy. Until fairly recently, in the United States, there has been little alternative to the "get sick, go to doctor, take prescription, hope to get better" approach to health care. With deepening understanding of other cultures, we have begun to accept their healing systems. The National Center for Complementary and Alternative Medicine classifies these healing systems in five categories:

✓ Biologically based therapies use herbal supplements as well as the foods and vitamins to treat ailments.

✓ Energy therapies involve either the manipulating energy *within* the body using magnets and other electric impulses like sound and light therapy; or balancing the energy *around* the body (also referred to as ch'i or aura) using practices such as the Chinese art of *qi gong, Reiki* and *laying-on of hands*.

✓ Manipulation and body based practices: *osteopaths, chiropractors,* and *massage therapists* are all examples of practitioners who use physical manipulation to keep bones and muscles aligned.

✓ Mind-Body Medicine uses the power of the human mind to overcome illness and maintain a healthy body. Examples are the use of *placeboes, meditation,* and *relaxation*.

✓ Whole Medical Systems are complete systems where practitioners look at the totality of symptoms to determine a diagnosis. *Homeopathy* is based on the concept of The Law of Similars: like cures like. Administering a highly diluted form of the substance causing the illness will stimulate the body to recover its health. It is the same methodology that is exhibited when choosing radiation to treat people with cancer, prescribing Ritalin for hyperactive children or vaccines to prevent disease. *Naturopathy* is a drugless approach to medicine based on the principle that the body can heal itself. By treating the patient, not just the symptoms and instead of focusing on the disease, the practitioner focuses on encouraging the healing process and avoiding anything that might interfere with it. *Ayurveda* dates back to 2,500 BC and says that everything a person eats, thinks, and experiences has an impact—positive or negative, on physical and mental health. Illness is instability and herbs and dietary control can be used to restore balance. *Traditional Chinese Medicine* uses the five elements (wood, water, earth, fire, metal) to explain interaction between people and their environment. Even though it is almost 5,000 years old, the same information is still being used today. Illness is seen as disharmony with the whole person, when balance and harmony are restored, healing mechanisms work more efficiently.

SIMPLE TIPS FOR HEALING BEFORE POPPING A PILL

When we're feeling under the weather, the knee jerk reaction is to medicate. Health care being what it is, we turn away from doctors and self-prescribe over-the-counter medications instead. These drugs are formulated to relieve symptoms but they do not cure the underlying disease. They are used when we think we need them, often without a physician's guidance. By making us less miserable, they allow us to go about our daily routine while the body works on curing itself. OTC drugs are meant for temporary relief of occasional symptoms, not for use on a regular basis.

Worse yet, prescription drug companies now spend billions of dollars on television and magazine advertising to a paranoid public, so that we can self diagnose and then have the name of what will fix it, all, in under 60 seconds.

Scary stats: Prescription drugs

✓ In 2002, Americans made an estimated 890 million visits to office-based doctors and filled 1.3 billion prescriptions.

✓ Ninety-one percent of Americans report that they take prescription drugs.

✓ More than half (54 percent) say they take prescription drugs on a regular basis, and one-fourth (24 percent) say that they take three or more drugs regularly.[106]

✓ One hundred thousand people will die from the side effects of prescription drugs this year.[107]

Some medications are truly revolutionary—insulin and others that make a normal existence possible for so many that suffer. Others have had to be created to solve the problems we've created—high blood pressure and heartburn medications, all formulated to combat the results of a highly stressed lifestyle. No one is telling you to stop taking your insulin. If a medication makes your life simpler because it gets you through the day, by all means keep taking it. It is a very personal decision to medicate or not, but many of us have become dependent on medications without investigating alternatives.

"The gods visit us through illness," said Carl Jung. What are our bodies trying to tell us when they get sick? A cough clears out the lungs, a fever fights infection, and a headache may be a sign of stress. Pay attention to your body. Listen to what it's telling you. Learn to attend to and trust symptoms as signals that something is wrong. Ignoring them could lead to bigger problems down the road.

Headaches

The American Gastroenterological Association states that, "NSAIDs [non-steroidal anti-inflammatory drugs] are taken by more than thirty million Americans every day for a swift and easy solution to discomfort caused by everything from headaches to arthritis."[108] Headaches are caused by blood vessels swelling in the head, and analgesics—aspirin (Bayer), ibuprofen (Advil), and acetaminophen (Tylenol)—work by blocking the transmission of pain impulses to the brain. Nine out of ten headaches are the result of worry, anxiety, depression, and other emotional states; the other ten percent are headaches caused by migraines, fever, high blood pressure, and drinking too much. Try these tricks instead for relieving headache pain:

- ❑ Put your feet in a bucket of the hottest water you can stand. This causes a reflex action that narrows the blood vessels in your head. Adding a cold compress to your head helps the blood flow away from the head to the extremities.
- ❑ Try fresh air coupled with a quick walk.
- ❑ Try a dab of peppermint or eucalyptus aromatherapy applied to the temples and forehead.
- ❑ Try acupressure. This is therapeutic foot massage based on the physiological and neurological study of the body. For headaches, there are specific pressure techniques on the feet that correspond to certain areas of the body. Squeeze or massage one of these pressure points: webbing of hand between thumb and index finger; the base of the thumb on the top of the hand; or pinch your earlobe.
- ❑ Sex it up. In spite of that timeless joke, "Not tonight honey, I have a headache," who knew that sex could actually be a pain reliever? The hormone oxytocin (which creates orgasms) is secreted in your body whenever you engage in sexual activity. It causes the release of endorphins, the body's natural pain reliever.

❑ Go lie down and take a nap. Most headaches will pass even if you don't take anything.

Skin

Our skin goes through a lot to keep our bodies protected. Keep it healthy and happy with these tips:

❑ To ease sunburn pain, try one these remedies:
  ✓ Spread yogurt on the affected area. Let it sit for twenty minutes, then rinse with warm water.
  ✓ Apply cider vinegar directly on the burn.
  ✓ Apply aloe to stop the itching and ease pain.
  ✓ For more serious sunburns, spread real honey on the burn to seal the wound against infection. Honey is a natural healer that can act as a mild painkiller. It will also reduce tissue damage to the area.
  ✓ Spread mayonnaise on your skin as a soothing skin cream for sunburns.
❑ To relieve poison oak or ivy itches:
  ✓ Apply calamine lotion, which is made from zinc oxide and iron oxide and is generally regarded as safe.
  ✓ If you catch the infection before blisters form, clean the affected area with rubbing alcohol.
  ✓ Apply vinegar to restore the pH balance of the skin and soothe the itch.
  ✓ Submerge the affected area in the hottest water you can stand. The heat will release and deplete the cells of histamines, giving you several hours of relief from itching.
❑ Make a paste with water and baking soda or Epsom salt and apply it to insect bites.
❑ Moisten a bar of soap and rub it on insect bites. When it dries, your skin will feel numb.
❑ Keep mosquitoes at bay, while avoiding commercial formulas that contain DEET (diethyl toluamide), which is an irritant to sensitive skin, respiratory tissues, and the central nervous system. Instead, try citronella (made from lemon balm), pennyroyal mint, eucalyptus, cloves, geranium, peppermint, rosemary, onions, garlic, or feverfew. Plant basil to keep them out of the yard and home, and serve lots of garlicky food at backyard barbecues.
❑ Treat athlete's foot with simple cider vinegar, which is antifungal. After washing your feet, douse the affected area with vinegar, then rinse and dry well.

Colds and Flu

The common cold is a mystery that has plagued scientists for ages and has accounted for uncountable unnecessary visits to the doctor's office. It doesn't help that there are hundreds of different strains of the condition. Good general health is our best defense against getting either a cold or the flu, and the best way to maintain good health is to stay rested and stress free and get moderate exercise.

❑ Fix up a sore throat with these remedies:
  ✓ Gargle with salt water.
  ✓ Drink a mixture of three tablespoons of cider vinegar in a cup of water and add a pinch of cayenne pepper. This mixture will act as an antibacterial and loosen up the sinuses. Vinegar kills the nasty bacteria that are causing the irritation.
  ✓ Try a mixture of lemon juice, honey, and hot water to soothe the throat and loosen mucus.

❑ Clear your clogged-up sinuses by hanging upside down. Use alternating cold and hot cloths on your face to stimulate circulation. Increase the humidity in dry rooms to keep your nasal passages from drying out. Sinus problems can be aggravated by eating too many mucus-generating foods (dairy) or histamine-releasing foods (alcohol, eggs, tomatoes, fish, shellfish, bananas, and chocolate).

❑ Try nasal douching to relieve nasal congestion. Rinse nasal passages using a bulb syringe or neti pot containing a mixture of a quarter teaspoon of salt in a cup of lukewarm water.

❑ Cough when you need to. Coughing is the body's way of getting rid of phlegm and clearing foreign material from air passages. Studies show that commercial cough remedies are often ineffective. Ginger tea stimulates circulation and helps clear sinuses and lungs of mucus.

❑ Put a hat and gloves on if your hands or feet are cold. It may be August, but it still works.

❑ Pay attention to fever. A fever is your body fighting an infection. Because it's a natural defense cycle, it's not always the best thing to lower a fever. Sometimes it's better to just let it run its course. Cool yourself by sponging the skin with lukewarm water.

❑ Start taking vitamin C as soon as cold symptoms begin. Monitor dosages. Chewable tabs can erode teeth enamel, and anything over 1000 mg will be eliminated quickly.

❑ Take goldenseal (*Hydrastis canadensis*), a drying, mucus-reducing remedy, if you have a cold. Use it as mouthwash for mouth ulcers, sore throats and mucus conditions.

❑ See echinacea and astragalus, as described above (page 232).

Stomach

Not feeling so hot? Chances are, that uncomfortable feeling resides around the stomach area. Antacids are generally deemed as safe for heartburn and indigestion, but taken habitually over long periods of time, they can become dangerous. Many antacids contain aluminum compounds, which have been suspected of contributing to the development of Alzheimer's disease. Instead of the usual chewables, try these tips:

❑ Dilute to one to two tablespoons of cider vinegar in a glass of water and drink it. Vinegar can be a soothing mixture for the stomach. It even helps fight food poisoning by acting as an antibacterial in the stomach.

❑ Watch what you eat. If something "doesn't agree with you," your body is probably trying to tell you something. Like, if you eat chili again, pardner, you're gonna regret it.

❑ Use baking soda as an easy antacid. Dissolve a half-teaspoon in a half-cup of water and drink it. Use this for quick relief, but not for repeated use.

❑ To ease nausea, try chewing a piece of crystallized ginger.

❑ Take Pepto-Bismol (bismuth subsalicylate), which is generally recognized as having no side effects or lasting health implications. It's a good portable remedy for stomach problems. (Watch out for the black tongue, though.) It also offers a good indication that if it doesn't solve what ails us, there's possibly a more severe problem at hand.

❑ For a good laxative, try Epsom salts, an FDA approved laxative. Directions are on the carton, but the Epsom Salt Council suggests consulting a doctor first.

Boo-Boos

First aid for cuts, sprains, bruises, swelling, aches, and pains does not always have to involve a trip to the drug store. Try these simple multipurpose remedies that can be found within your kitchen cabinets.

❑ Stock up on more vinegar. As recently as World War I, vinegar was commonly being used to treat wounds. Today it's recommended for treatment of rashes, bites and other minor ailments when camping.

❑ Epsom salts ease swollen ankles and feet and relieve early symptoms of colds. Add two cups to a warm bath, and soak.

❑ Soaking in Epsom salts will also draw a splinter to the skin's surface.

❑ Tea tree oil is also a good natural antibiotic for cleaning wounds.

What to keep in the medicine cabinet

A pain reliever
An antiseptic
Hydrogen peroxide
Rubbing alcohol
Tweezers

Non-mercury thermometer
Band aids and bandages
Pepto Bismol type product
An antacid

HEALING AND THE MIND

Americans rely on medications to fix almost anything, but we forget to realize that we need to allow our mind to work on healing our body, too. Because thoughts have a biochemical effect on our bodies, our minds need to be an active part of the healing process. Our attitude makes a real difference, and our immune system is not "immune" to feelings and thoughts. When you're ill, whether it's as minor as a boo-boo or as life altering as cancer, never underestimate the power of positive thinking, creative visualization, and attitudinal healing. Without emotional support, the time it takes the body to recover increases significantly.

❑ Avoid negative mind-body effects. Feelings of "giving up," helplessness, and hopelessness are counterproductive to healing. Stress wears a body down.

❑ Move away from the idea that you're only your condition. Sickness is not personal failure.

❑ Ask your doctor or nurse to show you your chart. Doctors should give patients the option to see their charts and teach the patient whatever they want to know about their body. Some of us may choose not to learn, but others will want to know the relationship between our illness and our emotions. Studies have shown patients who are taught about their condition heal faster.

❑ Don't internalize your feelings. When you speak up and emote (cry, laugh, scream, or yell), this can have a more positive result than not expressing your emotions (being depressed, lethargic, or apathetic). If a treatment hurts or makes you uncomfortable, express your emotions. Tell somebody how you feel.

❑ Never underestimate the power of the placebo. Auto-responses from tastes, smells, or sounds, "spontaneous healing," faith in healers, hope, belief, and the "fighting spirit" may seem imaginary or coincidental, but they are often credited with recovery.

❑ Find out what illness trying to get you to learn about yourself. Sometimes a cold is just a cold, but sometimes health problems are more than symbolic. They can be manifestations of other things that are wrong in our lives. What are our bodies trying to tell us? Are we eating too much sugar? Do we need more exercise? Should we find another way to lower stress levels?

❑ Let your body choose its own medicine. Some of us will be cured by natural therapies, but others won't. Accept the fact that not every cure works for everyone.

❑ Learn to accept illness. There is importance and value in sickness, which can be an opportunity to reevaluate our lives and accept a challenge presented. We can decide if our illness is a gift and see it as a source of growth and a redirection of life.

❑ Do not let the limitations of your body (sickness or disability) limit your ability to be loved or to love yourself. Learn self-love and peace of mind, and the body will respond.

HEALTH INSURANCE

While staying in the pink is never as easy at it sounds, it truly is more expensive to *become* sick than it is to remain healthy. Know that when less money is put into the health care system (a system that fewer and fewer Americans can afford to be insured for), it helps to drive down costs for everyone. Until universal comprehensive care is available for all, keep these guidelines in mind:

❑ Don't visit a doctor for problems you can easily manage yourself. Invest in a self-care book that describes most common symptoms and how to treat them.

❑ Build a trusting relationship with your doctor. Make him or her someone you can call for simple problems and get free advice over the phone.

❑ Guarantee you're paying reasonable rates for services by contacting your insurance company or local medical board to find out typical prices for certain procedures.

❑ Try to stay out of the hospital. Only go to the emergency room when you have a true life-threatening emergency. If possible, get treatments and procedures done in a doctor's office or an outpatient clinic. Treatment in a hospital can be far too expensive.

❑ Bring your own medications if you're in the hospital. You'll be charged for something as simple as one aspirin or a bandage, and what you pay can be 150 percent more than you'd pay at a drug store.

❑ Keep track of every procedure you have done in the hospital. List times, dates, and medications received. These records will prove invaluable when you're reviewing your bill.

❑ Review your hospital bill with a fine-tooth comb. Much more often than not, you'll find an error in your favor. You can easily be overcharged hundreds of dollars and not realize it until it's too late.

❑ Get a second opinion when a doctor recommends an expensive medical treatment.

- ❑ Prepare yourself mentally before surgery. Patients have used creative visualization to imagine themselves healthy to control their bleeding and speed up recovery time.
- ❑ Ask for the generic version of your prescription. Almost half the generic medications on the market are made by the same company that developed the brand name product. Independent companies must prove to the FDA that their medications work in the same manner as the brand name.
- ❑ Get a copy of your eyeglass prescription and shop around for the frames you like and can afford.
- ❑ Take preventive measures: Wash your hands with soap. Keep cuts covered. Stay buckled up and fully alert while driving. Wear a helmet when riding your bike. Don't join Fight Club.
- ❑ Practice health karma. What goes around comes around. Learn CPR, donate blood, take care of someone when they're sick.
- ❑ Take advantage of free tests and screenings, whether they're offered by your employer or sponsored by local organizations, hospitals, or public health agencies or clinics. These can be considerably cheaper than going to the doctor's office. Check listings in the phone book are under the county government section.
- ❑ Allow yourself to take mental health days. These are just as important as sick days, if not more important.

Hospitals

The physical environment around us can assist or detract from the healing process. The typical hospital is, alas, often cold, impersonal, and technical. The Hippocratic oath states, "First do no harm," but chemicals used in hospitals can indeed conflict with the goals of healing.

Fortunately, hospital managers are beginning to rethink hospital construction. Several health management organizations are, for example, phasing out the use of PVC in medical devices and pipes in the construction of new hospitals. Green health centers are being created with natural wood and windows that open to fresh air. Toxic cleaning products are being banished.

While cosmetic changes are very important, they're not enough unless they're combined with changing how doctors and nurses administer care to patients. Doctors tend to feel guilty that they can't fix the patient in front of them, so they rush off to another patient in hopes that they'll be more successful. It's human nature to feel this way and this emotional pain should be addressed. Doctors can treat patients and still acknowledge their own humanity and human shortcomings. Because they carry a weight of many illnesses on their shoulders, caregivers need touch and stress relief just as much as patients do.

Thinking outside the box: Planetree

We can trust our doctors, but we can also feel in control of our own hospital experience. Planetree is a health management organization that is rethinking how hospitals serve patients by offering unlimited visiting hours, providing kitchens for visitors to cook their loved ones a meal, and furnishing pull-out beds in every room for family or friends to stay with the patient. Knowing the soothing benefits of classical music and massage, Planetree offers both to patients. Because it has been found that when loved ones are anxious, their anxiety can adversely affect the patient, these "perks" are as much for loved ones as they are for the patients. See www.planetree.org.

Try these tips to remain in control of your health care:

- Write lists before you go to the doctor. Make a list of your symptoms. Write out the questions you want to ask. Some of us get shy or nervous and forget things when we've been kept waiting. Be specific about your problem. When did it start? Describe the pain or symptom, any changes, and what makes you better or worse. Write down the doctor's answers so you can remember what you need to do once you get home. Ask for a copy of the doctor's notes. It's our right to have this information. Trying to get it at a later time may be expensive.
- Be assertive. Bring along your own ideas. Speak up.
- Talk about what worries you most, even if it's the cost of a procedure. Explain your financial restrictions.
- Tell the truth. Help the doctor help you by communicating honestly, especially if you have bad habits that affect your health directly. If you can't, or won't, follow doctor's orders, say so.
- Ask for information and translation, if necessary. No matter what language we speak, we have a right to informed consent—the right to understand and agree to procedures. If you feel overwhelmed and intimidated by your doctor, maybe it's time to find a new one.
- Don't ignore your intuition. Find out about referrals or tests and alternatives. Don't assume that there aren't alternatives to the treatment or tests that a doctor prescribes.
- If a doctor is not meeting your needs, seek someone new. When looking for a new doctor, discuss with them what you'd like from the partnership. Ask them about their approach to health care. Ask any question you want answers to. If you don't want to wait three months for a check-up appointment and this doctor has a large number of patients, maybe you should consider someone else.
- Don't be afraid to ask for credentials. The word "specializes" doesn't have a legal definition. Ask for "Board Certification" instead.

It's time to fully understand the connections our lifestyles have had on our physical, mental and emotional health. We can take control of our well-being by limiting exposure to chemicals and rethinking how we medicate ourselves. We can simplify health care when we lessen the burden upon our bodies and the environment.

Do it today

Open your medicine cabinet and get rid of everything that's expired or that you don't use.

ADDITIONAL RESOURCES

ENVIRONMENTAL ILLNESS

Health Care Without Harm (www.noharm.org) is an international coalition of health, environmental, and religious groups devoted to transforming the health care industry worldwide to make it ecologically sustainable and no longer a source of harm to public health and the environment.

Lawson, Lynn. *Staying Well in a Toxic World.* Chicago: The Noble Press, 1993. Understanding environmental illness, multiple chemical sensitivities, chemical injuries, and Sick Building Syndrome.

National Organization of the Chemically Sensitive and the Human Ecology Action League, Inc. (HEAL, www.healnatl.org)

Steinman, David and R. Michael Wisner. *Living Healthy in a Toxic World.* New York: Berkeley Publishing Group, 1996. Simple steps to protect you and your family from everyday chemicals, poisons, and pollution.

PHYSICAL HEALTH

Ody, Penelope. *The Complete Medicinal Herbal.* New York: Dorling Kindersley, 1993. A practical guide to the healing properties of herbs, with more than 250 remedies for common ailments.

Serure, Pamela. *3-Day Energy Fast.* New York: HarperCollins, 1997.

Schmidt, Michael, Lendon Smith, and Keith Sehnert. *Beyond Antibiotics.* Berkeley, CA: North Atlantic Books, 1993.

Weil, Andrew, *Eight Weeks to Optimum Health.* New York: Alfred A. Knopf, 1997.
His website (www.drweil.com) is a popular online community where Dr. Weil offers advice on alternative therapies.

EMOTIONAL HEALTH
Jeffers, Susan. *Feel the Fear and Do It Anyway.* New York: Fawcett Columbine, 1987.

Kabat-Zinn, John. *Wherever You Go, There You Are.* New York: Hyperion, 1994.

Siegel, Bernie S. *Peace Love and Healing.* New York: Harper and Row Publishers, 1989.

chapter 10

beautifying

> The beauty myth moves for men as a mirage; its power lies in its ever-receding nature. When the gap is closed, the lover embraces only his own disillusion.
>
> –Naomi Wolf,
> *The Beauty Myth*

The cosmetics industry is fueled by what has been called *the beauty myth*, beauty being that elusive quality we chase, believing that we'll be loved and admired if only we could capture it. The quest is global; worldwide, $124 billion is spent every year on beauty products.[109] When we find simplicity in our lives, we realize that true beauty is much less expensive, if not free.

We feel we need synthetic products to achieve an artificial appearance in an attempt to conform to a societal ideal of beauty. But by definition, cosmetics are added for decorative purposes rather than for any real function, making them unnecessary. They are used to alter, preserve, enhance, or downplay features. Most are designed and marketed to appeal to and appease our sense of aesthetics and to pamper our weary bodies; they are thus used as a matter of personal preference rather than any intrinsic need.

The myth of image

When we buy cosmetics, we pay for much more than what we put in our shopping basket. We pay for the package that will be thrown away before the ingredients are read, the salary of the spokesmodel who will advertise the product on TV, the salary of the other model who will advertise the product in magazines, the marketing and research to find out if the proper demographic (the one with the most buying power) has enough desire for the product, the image of sexuality or cleanliness we hope to achieve, and, of course, the 30 cents worth of actual ingredients.

We may be using upwards of twenty cosmetic products a day. We rub, pour, sprinkle, spray, and otherwise apply them to our hair, skin, face, cheeks, lips, teeth, ears, eyes, hands, legs, feet, nails, underarms, even "down there." These personal care products come in contact with very sensitive and delicate parts of our bodies and we repeatedly expose ourselves to their ingredients in daily doses.

What we put *on* our body is truly as important as what we put in it. The chemicals contained in cosmetics can be absorbed through the skin, mucous membranes, or nails, bypassing the liver, the body's detoxifying organ, and flowing directly into the bloodstream. It's estimated that women absorb up to four pounds of chemicals through cosmetics every year.[110]

Animal Testing

Animals sacrifice their health in the testing of products for human consumption. Between ten and fifteen million animals are tortured and killed every year in American laboratories in trials to determine the safety of cosmetics and household products. These chemical-filled products are often administered to test animals without benefit of pain relievers that might interfere with test results. For example, the notorious Draize Eye-Irritancy Test, in use since 1959, binds albino rabbits in restraining devices so that a substance can be administered to their eyes. The eyes can swell and redden until the animals go blind. Another test is LD-50 (lethal dose 50 percent), which feeds chemicals to animals to determine how much is required to kill half the test animals.

The Leaping Bunny

Seven animal protection groups banded together to create CCIC: The Coalition for Consumer Information on Cosmetics, which provides consumers with a simple but internationally recognized standard. Companies whose products bear the leaping bunny logo agree to not test on animals and to comply with on-site audits. Instead of testing on animals, they test using artificial skin systems, human volunteers, and utilize known safety data of the 8,000 ingredients deemed safe for cosmetics. See their web site (www.leapingbunny.org) for a list of certified participants.

Although the U.S. Food and Drug Administration (FDA) does not regulate cosmetics, cosmetic companies try to claim that they have tested their products thoroughly for consumer safety. Of the approximately 5,500 substances approved for use in cosmetic products, the U.S. National Institute of Occupational Safety and Health has found 884 chemicals used in personal care products and cosmetics that are known to be toxic.[111]

Health problems associated with cosmetics fall into two main categories: carcinogens (which cause cancer) and allergens (which are irritants and sensitizers). But just because one substance by itself doesn't cause cancer or allergies, that isn't to say that it cannot become a risk when it is mixed with other products.

Cosmetics are a top contributor to multiple chemical sensitivities. The two leading causes of cosmetic allergy reaction are from fragrances and preservatives. Some allergic reactions caused by cosmetic products have led only to mild skin irritation, whereas other reactions are strong enough to induce hives and/or restrict breathing.

But wait—there's more. Some of the ingredients in products we use daily are hormone disrupters. Some are neurotoxins. Some can cause organ damage and it's the unknown combinations of products that ultimately can create health issues.

Government Regulation

The FDA oversees the regulation of the food we eat and every drug on the market, but the personal care industry is left to police itself. All the FDA does is supervise a voluntary registration program that manufacturers can participate in; this voluntary program is understaffed and plagued by budget cuts. Cosmetics are not required to have warning labels, and the FDA doesn't have the authority to ban the sale of products that have caused harm. Even if a company is found guilty of wrongdoing, there are few standards for negligence or penalties for fraud. It has been only since the late 1970s that ingredient labeling has been required on cosmetics. If the government won't protect us from allergens and carcinogens in cosmetic products, it's up to us to educate ourselves to recognize the hazards in what we put on our bodies. An advanced degree in organic chemistry might be helpful, but we can learn to recognize red flags when we're shopping for cosmetics.

On the other hand

The FDA regulates the colors and dyes used in cosmetics, but only because they are used specifically for the purpose of altering color.

CHEMICAL WATCHWORDS

Alkyl sulfates—with the code names Sodium dodecylsulfate (SDS), sodium laureth sulfate (SLES), or ammonium laurel sulfate (and watch out: "laurel" is also spelled "lauryl")—are foaming agents used in cosmetic and cleaning products. Almost all commercial liquid soap products use a detergent called sodium laurel sulfate (SLS), which can be derived naturally from coconut oil but can also be manufactured synthetically. Both methods create the same substance: a harsh detergent and aggressive cleanser that also works well in brake fluid, engine degreasers, and anti-freeze. Because of its low cost, SLS is found in many products.

In large doses, SLS can destroy delicate tissues in the eye, leading to improper eye development in children and cataracts in adults. It slows the healing time of wounds, irritates the skin, and permeates the heart, liver, lungs, and brain. When used on lab animals, it has penetrated the skin and killed cells. Even though it has been implicated in corroding hair follicles and impairing the ability of hair to grow, SLS is commonly found in shampoo. SLS can react with *alkyloamides* (see below) in products or packaging to create NDELA, a *nitrosamine* and potent carcinogen.

Not all SLS users, however, are out for the quick, cheap, and easy route. Environmentally conscious companies (like Tom's of Maine) defend their use of SLS in toothpaste by citing federal approval and long-term use as proof of safety. By itself, SLS is probably not carcinogenic, but when it is combined with other ingredients, it forms nitrates, which are potential carcinogens. Two mild and generally regarded as safe alternatives to SLS are ammonium cocoyl isethionate and olefin sulfonate.

Alkyl sulfates are found in shampoos, body washes, personal cleansers, dish detergents, toothpastes, mouthwashes, bathroom cleaners, infant-care products, and almost every other product that makes big, fluffy, soapy bubbles.

Scary stat

It's especially important to go natural in the bath because the hot water increases the permeability of skin, allowing products to be more readily absorbed. The fine mist created by showering also makes it easy to inhale particles from cosmetic products.

It's recommended that we avoid products containing *alkyloamides*—the "amines": monoethanolamine (MEA), diethanolamine (DEA), and triethanolamine (TEA)—because they can react with nitrates (often present in preservatives) inside the shampoo bottle to form nitrosamines, potent carcinogens. This reaction can occur during manufacturing or storage. Risk of this reaction is higher if the shampoo contains bronopol (another preservative that is a nitrosamine precursor).

Alkyloamides lurk in makeup, hair colors, shampoos (DEA is the wetting agent used to create thick lather), liquid soaps, and bath and shower gels. To help protect yourself against nitrosamine contamination, you can add antioxidants (two teaspoons of vitamin C powder and a half teaspoon of vitamin A powder) to a sixteen-ounce bottle of shampoo.

Coal tar colors (CTCs) are synthetic coloring agents made from the distillation process of bituminous coal. Ingredients in CTCs vary, but include toxins like *benzene, xylene,* and *naphthalene.* These toxins were grandfathered under the 1938 Food, Drug & Cosmetic Act and are still in widespread use. CTCs are regulated and categorized by the FDA in three ways:

- ✓ FD&C: deemed safe for use in foods, drugs, & cosmetics
- ✓ D&C: safe for use in drugs and cosmetics, okay to ingest or come in contact with mucous membranes
- ✓ Ext. D&C: not safe for foods, but deemed safe enough for external use cosmetics, though not around mucous membranes.[112]

Colors are found in all types of cosmetic, food, and drug products. Colors derived from coal tars are frequent sources of allergic reactions, including rashes and hives. Some colors have been implicated in causing cancer in lab animals. What is referred to as "lake" coloring is a solid form of dye made by mixing the color with an insoluble powder, like aluminum oxide, to make a coloring that is insoluble. Aluminum oxide is not friendly to the body and won't dissolve when absorbed by the skin.

Color danger

David Steinman, the author of *The Safe Shopper's Bible*, suggests avoiding the following colorings:[113]

- ✓ FD&C Blue 1 and FD&C Green 3 (carcinogenic)
- ✓ FD&C Red 4
- ✓ FD&C Red 40
- ✓ FD&C Yellow 5, FD&C Yellow 6, and D&C Red 33 (Impurities in these colors have been shown to cause cancer when applied to the skin.)
- ✓ D&C Green 5
- ✓ D&C Orange 17
- ✓ D&C Red 19

Preservatives

Preservatives are used to protect a product's shelf life by killing microorganisms and preventing them from "going bad." But the chemicals used in preservatives can react with other ingredients (or even the packaging) to create hazardous substances. Safer natural preservatives options include vitamin A (retinyl), vitamin C (ascorbic acid), vitamin E (tocopherol), vitamin F, and citrus seed extracts.

Parabens are the most commonly used preservatives. Look out for *methylparaben, propylparaben, butyl paraben* (a widely used antifungal), and *parahydroxybenzoate.* They have a broad range of antimicrobial properties, but they can also be allergenic, and there's preliminary evidence that parabens mimic estrogen and disrupt normal hormone functions. Parabens, which are found in cosmetics, shampoos, skin cream, and deodorants, have been discovered in many breast tumors.[114] Ironically, many cosmetic companies support breast cancer awareness and charities, yet some ingredients in their products could actually be culprits in creating the disease.

Butylated hydroxyanisole (BHA) and *butylated hydroxytoluene* (BHT) are color preservatives that are synthetic antioxidant compounds often added to lipstick and eye shadow to preserve color. They are also added to food to preserve fats, food odor, color, and flavor. (See *Eating* chapter for food uses of BHA/BHT, page 149).

While BHA and BHT may have antiviral and antimicrobial activities, there is also evidence that some people have difficulty metabolizing these compounds, resulting in health and behavior changes. Research is also underway concerning the use of BHT in the treatment of herpes simplex and AIDS.

Formaldehyde, a common preservative and disinfectant, is also a volatile organic compound found in the following cosmetic ingredients: *hydantoins* (*DMDM hydantoin*), *diazolidinyl urea, imidazolidinyl urea, quaternium-15*, and *bronopol*. Formaldehyde can cause nausea, coughing, wheezing, and burning sensations in the eyes, nose, throat, and skin at air levels as low as 0.1 parts per million. The EPA has classified formaldehyde as a "probable human carcinogen."[115]

Formaldehyde is used in nail polish and hardeners, some eye shadows and mascaras, and as a preservative in some shampoos, conditioners, and hair growth products. (See *Housing & Decorating* chapter, page 306, for more hazards of formaldehyde.)

Quaternary ammonium compounds are preservatives, germicides, sanitizers, water repellants, fabric softeners, antistatic agents, emulsifiers, corrosion inhibitors, and surfactants (or detergents) all at once. They are used in cosmetic products such as hair dyes, shampoos, hair conditioners, cream rinses, and lotions for making hair and skin feel softer immediately after use. Also called *quaternary ammonium salts* (QACs or "quats"), they hide behind such names as *bezalkonium chloride, cetrimonium bromide, stearalkonium chloride, cocotrimonium chloride*, and *quaternium 1-29, 15, 22, 26*, etc.

Despite the initial softening, repeated application causes the skin to lose moisture and leaves it dry and flaky. Quats can be very toxic, depending on concentration and exposure. Ingestion can be fatal. According to the American Dermatological Association, quaternium-15 is the number one cause of preservative-related contact dermatitis.[116]

Fragrance

Everything seems to smell these days—everything is "mountain fresh" or "sun kissed" or full of "April rain" and "all natural fragrances." Marketers use images of nature to suggest that their products contain natural ingredients when, in actuality, the scents were probably created in a lab from petroleum derivatives.

Some fragranced products can desensitize the nose. We might easily notice the smell the first few times we use a product, but repeated exposure to the same odor can cause our sense of smell to become overwhelmed or lost even as the effects of the chemicals remain unchanged or get worse. The longer a person uses the same fragrance, the greater the likelihood that they cease to actually smell it on themselves. (Let's not even talk about how much cologne Grandpa pours on.) This leads to increased doses that can aggravate multiple chemical sensitivity symptoms in those who have to breathe around them.

Phthalates are a family of chemical plasticizers, solvents, and fixatives used to make plastic soft and pliable; they are also commonly used in perfumes and fragrances. Because they don't bond with plastic, they can easily leach from packaging into products. Don't expect to find the word *phthalates* on labels, however; these chemicals usually fall into the cracks as part of that mysterious "fragrance" ingredient listed on cosmetic and household products.

Phthalates are easily absorbed through the skin and accumulate in body fat and organs. Long-term exposure has been implicated in kidney, liver, and reproductive organ damage. A Harvard research study found a correlation between sperm damage in men and the levels of diethyl phthalate.[117] High levels of phthalates have also been found in cases of premature development.[118]

To help avoid hidden phthalates, choose unscented products or those whose labels state how they are scented. Although much of our exposure to phthalates comes from plastic leaching into food products from packaging, they are also used in hair spray, perfume, shampoo, and in nail polish to reduce brittleness. They are used in lotions to help penetrate the skin.

Scary stats

The main thrust of marketing a scent is the creation of an image. Customers buy based on a name, a feeling, a promise: beauty, elegance, sexuality, sophistication, youth.

✓ 45 percent of cosmetic sales are perfumes.[119]

✓ Fragrance manufacturers use more than 5,000 different chemicals.

✓ A single scent can contain hundreds of chemicals, 95 percent of which are derived from petroleum.

✓ The perfume industry is unregulated. There is, in fact, no way for us to know whether the chemicals in our perfume contain carcinogens because the FDA protects "fragrance" ingredients as confidential trade secrets.

But even if we use products labeled "fragrance-free" and "unscented," we still may not be home free. These terms have no legal definition. Products claiming to be either fragrance-free or unscented may contain raw fragrance ingredients or may add masking fragrances to hide unpleasant odors. The fact is that usually these odors have nothing to do with the effectiveness of the product, and when we smell anything, molecules of that substance are drawn into our lungs and absorbed through our skin.

Hope for the Future: Simple Tips for Protecting Ourselves

Chemical ingredients and synthetic fragrances are prevalent in cosmetics because they are cheap and easy to use. Many of these ingredients are petroleum-based products whose synergistic effects have not thoroughly been studied. Keeping them out of our medicine chest is a preventive measure worth taking. Here's where to start:

❑ Read labels to find and avoid toxins. If an ingredient has an unpronounceable, chemical-sounding name of six syllables or more (e.g., *octyldodecyl myristate*) or a code name (e.g., FD&C Red no. 40), nine times out of ten, it isn't natural.

❑ Research the ingredients on the Internet or through customer service numbers before buying a product. If you're serious about decoding ingredient lists, invest in a chemical dictionary. Try Aubrey Hampton's *Natural Organic Hair and Skin Care*, which includes an A-to-Z guide of natural and synthetic chemicals in cosmetics.

❑ Remember that cosmetics usually come "double packaged." Most of the time we throw away the part of the package (a box, a wrapper, etc.) that contains the list of ingredients as soon as we get home.

❑ If you find cutting out all synthetic products too difficult, begin by cutting out scented beauty and hygiene products.

❑ Handle all cosmetics (even natural ones) with the awareness that bacterial contamination can occur. If you notice a cream separating (where it pulls away from the side of the jar), this indicates contamination. Do not share cosmetics with anyone, especially eye products such as eye shadow, eyeliner, and mascara. If you feel an infection (the dreaded conjunctivitis) coming on, throw the suspected product away immediately. When applying cosmetics, use a clean spoon to take products out of their containers to avoid contamination from your hands.

❑ Try using natural products with fewer ingredients.

❑ Be cautious of products that advertise their "natural"-ness but still continue to include the same chemical concoctions that are in their "unnatural" versions. Don't be fooled by words like "botanical," "essences," "herbal," "organically," "simply," and "pure." Just because something smells "lemony" doesn't mean it actually contains lemons. Just because a company makes one natural product, don't assume that all of its products are natural.

> **Terms to trust**
>
> ✓ *All Natural.* No hormones, artificial flavorings, colors, or preservatives.
> ✓ *Chemical Sensitivity Safe.* No synthetic dyes, fragrances, or chemicals.
> ✓ *Cruelty-free.* Not tested on animals.
> ✓ *Fair trade.* Ethical treatment of workers.
> ✓ *Fragrance-free.* The product is considered to have no perceptible odor.
> ✓ *Hypoallergenic.* Common allergens, such as fragrances, lanolin, cocoa butter, cornstarch, and cottonseed oils, have been removed from the product.
> ✓ *Organic.* While the U.S. Department of Agriculture oversees organic food labeling, there's no agency yet that monitors personal care products and regulates the term "organic" for use on cosmetic labels. Reputable companies adhere to standards set by the USDA for organic ingredients.
> ✓ *Vegan.* Contains no ingredients derived from animals.

❑ Make your own cosmetics. There are no preservatives in homemade remedies unless you put them there yourself. Another cool thing about making your own is that many natural products made with fruits and vegetables can be used on many parts of your body. Just try using that commercial foot soak on your hair or that nail treatment on your face. When mixing, always use glass or stainless steel bowls and jars because plastics can alter the chemicals while you're mixing or storing your preparation. Read on for easy tips and see the end of this chapter for some great cosmetic cookbooks.

SIMPLER ALTERNATIVES

The secret to simple beauty? Surprise, surprise ... the best beauty tips are many of the same tips that help boost our immunity and reduce stress.

✓ Exfoliate.
✓ Drink lots of water, at least eight 8-ounce glasses daily.
✓ Sweat.
✓ Sleep.
✓ Relax.
✓ Get vitamins naturally through a well balanced diet.
✓ Regulate sun exposure.
✓ Exercise regularly.

But it's been a long hard week, even at our dream job at the eco-widget factory. Despite the gallon of water we've drunk today, every-day environmental conditions have left our bodies a little worse for wear. Some days, we all want to feel a little bit better about ourselves and enjoy a little pampering. This is where homemade natural alternatives come in.

Smelling "Good" And The Deodorant Myth

Another innovation of the chemical revolution, deodorant, did not become commonplace in the American medicine cabinet until after World War II, when body odor suddenly became offensive.

It's advertising that tries to tell us that sweat is unhealthy. Perspiration itself is normally odorless, and sweating is a natural and necessary process that regulates body temperature and helps cool us off. Some body odor is the result of the bacterial breakdown of sweat, but other strong odors can be indicative of an underlying health problem.

Body odor can also be affected by what we eat and drink. As we improve our diet, we'll notice our natural smell changing. Ever wake up after a night of partying smelling like the floor of the bar you were at? That's because alcohol and other toxins are released through sweating. Caffeine also contributes to body odor by increasing sweat gland activity.

What we commonly call "deodorant" is usually an antiperspirant/deodorant combination. Antiperspirants, which use chemicals (zinc or aluminum salts) to clog pores, stop us from sweating and prevent toxins from being excreted. Deodorant changes the smell of our secretions by inhibiting the growth of bacteria. Like any antibacterial, deodorants can also destroy beneficial protective skin flora. Germ phobia harms the earth because all the chemicals we put on or in our bodies eventually end up in the environment, where they can break down the ecosystem.

Other harmful ingredients of deodorants are propylene glycol, aluminum chloride, aerosol propellants, ammonia, formaldehyde, parabens, and antibacterials, like triclosan. In order to avoid these chemicals, try the following instead:

❑ Let yourself sweat. Sweating is one way the body releases toxins, relieving some of the burden on our kidneys and liver, which usually take care of detoxifying us.

❑ Buy deodorant only, as opposed to antiperspirant and deodorant combinations that contain aluminum.

❑ Spritz your feet and armpits with rubbing alcohol to keep them cool and eliminate odor by reducing the amount of bacteria that grow there.

❑ Try natural crystals (available in health and natural food stores) that are made from naturally formed mineral salts that won't block pores when applied.

❑ Use baking soda alone or prepare this simple mixture:

Home made deodorizing powder

1/2-cup baking soda

1/2-cup cornstarch

Add a few drops of an antibacterial essential oil: tea tree, lavender, or rosemary. Place in a clean jar, mix thoroughly and cover. To use, dampen a powder puff, and dab into the mixture.

❑ Say, "Clean enough." Most of us are too clean already. Try showering or washing your hair every other day and use deodorant sparingly, especially when you're home alone.

❑ Ladies (and especially men), stay away from the feminine deodorant sprays. If there's an odor that shouldn't be there, it's a sign that something is wrong and you should see a doctor. Covering it up with chemicals is about the worst thing you can do.

❑ Make your own blends of scents using essential oils instead of buying high priced perfumes.

On the other hand: Essential cautions for essential oils

Essential oils are flammable and volatile and will evaporate quickly. Even though they are natural, use caution when handling them because they can burn tender skin or mucous membranes.

✓ Seek guidance when using essential oils. Study a comprehensive book.

✓ Do not use more than recommended amount.

✓ Do not use oils around the eyes.

✓ Mix oils thoroughly and dilute them before applying any oil directly to skin.

✓ Exercise special caution using essential oils on pregnant women, babies, children, and the elderly.

Skin

Our body's largest organ was once considered an impermeable armor that protected our insides from all harm. In fact, our skin is pretty much like a screen door that lets in anything applied to it. (Think of broken or damaged skin as a big gaping hole in that screen.)

While soap and toners are designed to rebalance the skin's natural pH and purify pores, they can actually upset our pH balance, leaving us vulnerable to germs and chemical toxins. What's more, many cleansers, toners, and moisturizers actually contain alcohol or petroleum products, which are drying agents.

Even though the skin can let in harmful elements, it also absorbs vitamins. Remember, what we put *on* our bodies truly is as important as what we put *in* them. See the *Healing* chapter for information about vitamins to eat for healthy skin and hair from the inside out, but also follow these tips for keeping healthy on the outside:

Scrubs and Cleansers

Foods for our skin include glycerin, honey, mangoes, strawberries, avocados, bananas, papaya, eggs, oatmeal, and yogurt. Use them to make facial masks or add sea salt or sugar to make scrubs. Here's how to feed your skin:

- Combine baking soda and water to make a good simple facial cleanser.
- Use Epsom salts to make a good body scrub that smoothes and softens skin and draws out toxins.
- Cleanse and tone your face with witch hazel. It can also be used to treat stings, bites, burns and irritation. Rub it into sore muscles for soreness relief.
- Pamper yourself with a clay mask. Pure clay is usually available at natural food stores and can be mixed with water to form a thin paste.

Wonderful world of clay

Bentonite clay is a medicinal white-to-gray clay found in Midwestern states (it's named for Benton, Montana) that is derived from volcanic ash. Also known as "Indian Healing Clay," or *montmorillonite*, it absorbs moisture and used in blemish masks to draw toxins out of the skin. It's also used as an intestinal detoxifier (but seek professional advice before attempting this process).

Kaolin, also known as China clay, comes from Mt. Kaolin in China. It's the pure white clay that was used to powder faces and wigs in eighteenth century England and is now used in powdering cosmetics and soaps. It mixes well, has absorbing and dehydrating power, and is an emollient and an astringent.

Fuller's Earth is another type of clay that works well for both blemishes and oily skin. Originally used for removing oil from sheep's wool, it's now also used to clean up spilled oils.

Banishing Blemishes

- Mash a banana with tablespoon of real honey and pat on your face as a mask for fifteen minutes.
- Melt real honey (but please *let it cool* before applying it to your skin) and spread it over your face for blackheads. Leave it on for fifteen minutes, then rinse with water.

- ❑ Apply warm mashed potatoes in cheesecloth several times a day to remove stubborn blackheads.
- ❑ Tame oily skin with peppermint oil steam or tea.
- ❑ Apply lemon juice over blackheads and other facial blemishes before bed.

Tea Tree Oil (Melaleuca alternifolia)

Tea trees are grown mainly in Australia and create an oil that has antibacterial and antifungal properties that make it well suited for many purposes, including medicinal, cosmetic, and cleaning. (See *Healing* chapter for health uses and *Cleaning* chapter for disinfecting uses.) Cosmetically, tea tree oil can be used to treat skin blemishes, but it should only be used in tiny diluted amounts because at full strength it can burn the skin. It works against vaginal infections, athlete's foot, stings, toothaches, gum infections, and helps to heal abrasions.

Too Much Sun

Some sun is good for us, providing vitamin D that the body needs but often we put too much faith in sun care solutions. Believing we are immune to all rays, we slather on some cream and then hit the beach, where we overexpose ourselves to the sun. The best preventive measure is to wear a large hat and limit outdoor time during the hours between 11 a.m. and 2 p.m.

- ❑ Try a light coating of sesame seed oil, which reputedly screens out 30 percent of the sun's rays,[120] for simple protection from the sun.
- ❑ Wear sunglasses to protect your eyes and the delicate skin around them from the getting burnt and wrinkled.

To makeup, or not to makeup...

One of the main reasons we use makeup is to make ourselves look younger, but, ironically, many makeup products can actually speed the skin's aging process. As our eating and sleeping habits improve, we'll begin to notice a change in our skin quality. As the change occurs, we may find it no longer necessary to apply the war paint every morning.

Bathing

Water can be so rejuvenating, not only to our soul but also to our skin. Why ruin a bath or shower with toxins? Here are some tips for a good bath:

- ❑ Use a natural sea sponge, loofah, sisal cloth, or a natural bristle brush to exfoliate dead skin.

❑ Soften your skin using one cup of cider vinegar in your bath. Vinegar can also be used as a straight toner and is great at cleansing oils from hair. Keep a bottle of cider vinegar in the bathtub for personal cleansing, but use white vinegar for household cleaning.

Epsom salts

Magnesium sulfate (commonly known as Epsom salts) is like Dead Sea salts, which contain the highest concentration of minerals on earth. When Epsom salts are absorbed through the skin in a bath, they have the following effects:

✓ Induce detoxification by promoting heavy sweating.

✓ Sedate the nervous system.

✓ Are a natural emollient and exfoliater, great for softening skin.

✓ Reduce swelling and relaxes and soothes sore muscles. (The magnesium in Epsom salts is thought to cause a gentle drawing action that reduces inflammation in and around swollen and/or bruised tissues.) It is believed that the magnesium can be absorbed through the skin, helping the body to heal.

(Adapted from the Epsom Salt Industry Council www.epsomsaltcouncil.org)[121]

❑ Try this basic bath soak:

1/4-cup sea salts

1/2-cup baking soda

1/4 cup Epsom salts

5 drops of your favorite essential oil: rosemary, lavender, peppermint, eucalyptus, orange oil.

Mix in a glass jar with a tight lid. Pour mixture under running water to dissolve salts, then soak until skin is pruny.

❑ Whip up an herbal aromatherapy bath:

Make your own herbal bath using your favorite scents. Pour boiling water over leaves and flowers and allow them to steep for 6 to 8 hours; strain and discard the plant matter. Add 1 quart of this herb water to your bath. Try lavender, mint, lemon balm, sage, rose, chamomile, rosemary, or calendula.

Hair

Shampoos are mostly water, foaming agents, and fragrances. With frequent use, the chemicals in shampoo can strip the hair of the natural oils that keep it shiny and healthy. Conditioners are often nothing more than fabric softeners and perfume. Many hair helpers can be found in the kitchen. Beer, eggs, mayonnaise, yogurt, cider vinegar, lemon, and red wine are great for hair repair. Additional hair care tips include:

For Damaged and Dry Hair

- ❑ Add pure aloe to an herbal shampoo to naturally soften hair. Aloe cleans by bringing impurities to the surface so they can be easily washed away.
- ❑ Take one tablespoon of flax seed oil once a day for omega-3 fatty acids.
- ❑ Massage honey (for light hair) or blackstrap molasses (for darker hair) into dry hair. This isn't as easy as it sounds, but it works great. Cover your hair and read a book for an hour, then rinse your hair thoroughly.
- ❑ If you have damaged or dry hair, massage one to two tablespoons of jojoba oil into your hair and your scalp when they are dry. Cover and leave on for one hour or up to overnight. Then shampoo as usual.
- ❑ Consider using a sunscreen for your hair or rub a small amount of sesame oil on your hair to protect it from the sun.
- ❑ Apply mayonnaise to dry hair once a week as a conditioner. Leave it on for thirty minutes, then shampoo out.

For Oily Hair

- ❑ Swab your scalp with cotton balls soaked in cider vinegar before shampooing.
- ❑ Soak up excess oil from hair with Epsom salts. Mix a tablespoon of Epsom salt with your normal amount of oily hair shampoo. Apply to hair when it's dry, then rinse with cold water. Will promote body and restore curls.

For Body Building

- ❑ Try keeping a variety of shampoos and switch brands every few days.
- ❑ Eat more protein: eggs, lean meat and fish, beans and seeds, whole grains, and low-fat dairy or soy products.
- ❑ Use a mashed avocado with regular shampoo to counteract frizz and dryness.
- ❑ Mix an egg into shampoo for bounce and protein.
- ❑ Rinse your hair with flat beer. A bottle might not bring life to the party, but it will bring life back to your hair.
- ❑ Pour lemon juice or organic apple cider vinegar through your hair to revitalize hair of any color, leave on for five to ten minutes, and then rinse.
- ❑ Promote hair growth with a scalp massage.

For Cleansing

- ❑ Rinse your hair with club soda.
- ❑ Rinse your hair with a tablespoon of baking soda dissolved in water to remove residues of styling products.

❏ Apply plain yogurt to your hair for ten minutes before shampooing for dandruff problems.

For Hair Dyes

We want a change. Something different, something bold. Maybe a new hair color will change our outlook on life. Blondes have more fun, right? Before you head to the drugstore, you should know that long-term use of dark hair dye increases the risk of non-Hodgkin's lymphoma by up to four times and that ingredients contained in hair dyes have been implicated in cases of breast cancer, multiple myeloma, and Hodgkin's disease.[122]

If you must dye your hair, you can make it safer and simplify the process by trying a natural alternative, using lighter shades, or by putting it off for as long as you can. Studies show that women who start dyeing at age forty have less of a risk than those who start at age thirty or twenty.

Hair dyes contain surfactants, coal tar colors, solvents, preservatives, and chemicals that pollute wastewater and are often tested on animals. Lead acetate is found in certain hair dyes, especially those that change hair color gradually. Another common ingredient, *phenylenediamine* (PPD), has been banned in Europe because of its status as a "probable human carcinogen."

There are natural alternatives, but as with any dye, always cover your hands when dyeing your hair unless you want your hands to match your head.

Tips for Blondes

For blondes or to lighten other colors, rinse your hair with the juice of a lemon. Rinse with flat champagne to bring out blonde highlights. Pour two cups of boiling water over 1/4 cup of dried chamomile flowers and leaves, dandelion flowers, sunflower petals, or onion skins. Let the mixture cool. Strain it, and use the liquid to color your hair. Rinse with orange pekoe tea for golden highlights. After any of these treatments, dry your hair out in the sun for further lightening.

Tips for Carrot Tops

Henna is a nontoxic red dye that has been used for centuries, but many of today's henna products are mixed with other natural ingredients to produce different shades. While chemical dyes penetrate hair, henna wraps around individual strands, sealing in oils with a reflective coating to give hair more shine. Commonly found in natural food stores, henna shampoos offer highlighting effects.

On the other hand

Mixing henna applications in a metal bowl or with metal utensils can cause adverse reactions. Never use henna on facial hair, eyebrows, or eyelashes or on chemically dyed or treated hair. Be aware that some individuals are allergic to henna. Before using any hair dye, test it on a small, inconspicuous part of your arm or leg and a strand of hidden hair before applying it all over your scalp. Start with a small of amount color. You can always go darker later if you want, but going lighter is much more difficult. No one wants to be called Bozo the Clown.

Other red dyes include paprika, beet juice, hibiscus flowers, and cranberries. Mix henna with black tea for a brown-red, cider vinegar for copper or golden highlights, ground cloves or red wine for a darker red, or a strong chamomile flower infusion for an auburn color.

Temporary tattoo

Henna is also used to make *mehndi* tattoos, an Indian tradition where designs are painted on a bride's hands and feet before her wedding. Egyptian mummies have been found with their fingers toes, palms, and soles of their feet colored with henna dyes. Like any cosmetic dye, test a small amount of henna on your skin and choose your design carefully. It will wear off, but it often takes several weeks to do so.

Tips for Brunettes

Pour 2 cups of boiling water over 2 teaspoons dried sage leaves. Allow to steep and cool, then strain out leaves and pour the liquid over your hair after your regular shampoo. Also try ground ginger, allspice, nutmeg, cinnamon, coffee, lavender or marigold flowers for other browns.

Tips for the Grays

You can help prevent graying by using apple cider vinegar, sage tea, or boiled crushed walnut shells.

Tips for Getting Out the Green

A summer spent by the pool can leave hair a brittle, and dried out, a green mer-mess. Make a mixture of baking soda and lemon juice and massage into wet hair and scalp. Leave on for 30 minutes then rinse hair and shampoo as usual. Rinsing with 1/4-cup tomato juice also works well for both chlorine and heavy odors like skunk.

Treat Your Feet

Though they are two of the hardest working parts of our bodies, our feet are often the most neglected. The American Podiatric Medical Association says that the average person takes 8,000 to 10,000 steps a day, which adds up to about 115,000 miles in a lifetime ... more than four times the circumference of the globe.[123] There are times when we're walking that the pressure on our feet exceeds our body weight. When we're running, the pressure can be three or four times our weight, but how often do we treat ourselves to a foot massage?

❑ Mix up your own arthritis foot rub:

1-cup beach sand

1 to 2 teaspoons of olive oil

10 to 20 drops of rosemary essential oil.

Combine ingredients, apply to feet, massage it in.

❑ Try a relaxing soak: soak feet in 1/2-cup Epsom or sea salts dissolved in a gallon of warm water.

❑ Make an antibacterial soak: warm water with 2 drops of tea tree and 2 drops of lavender oil.

❑ For stinky feet, dust them with baking soda before putting on your shoes.

❑ For softer feet, massage them with apple cider vinegar.

❑ Rub rough spots with a pumice stone or emery board instead of using chemicals.

Teeth and Mouth

Major brand fluoride toothpastes all have similar formulas, which are usually tested on animals. Consider how much fluoride we get daily: the fluoridation many communities add to their drinking water, water that's used in store-bought beverages, and the fluoride that naturally occurs in food. Long-term use of fluoride may cause fluorosis, or white splotches on teeth that indicate weak enamel. Consider switching to non-fluoride toothpaste at least every other day.

Stop & think

Fluoride was originally sold as a bug and rat poison. It's more toxic than lead. On toothpaste packaging, you'll find this warning: *In case of accidental ingestion, contact poison control.* And you want to put this in your mouth?

❑ Try natural non-fluoride brands such as Tom's of Maine, Desert Essence, and Peelu, available at health food stores and mail order sites.

❑ Make a foaming toothpaste using baking soda and hydrogen peroxide. Be sure to spit it all out, as hydrogen peroxide can upset your stomach if swallowed.

- ❏ Make your own toothpaste using one part crushed salt and 2 parts baking soda. Sprinkled on a toothbrush, this natural remedy whitens teeth, encourages healthy gums, and removes plaque. A drop of peppermint essential oil can be added for taste.

- ❏ Brush naked. Well, your toothbrush can be naked, you might want to wear your jammies. Dentists state that it's the brushing action that removes most of the organisms that cause tooth decay. Take a small gulp of water, and brush for at least two minutes. (This trick is really helpful when you're camping.)

- ❏ Decrease your intake of foods with a highly refined sugar content, which can lead to bad breath.

- ❏ Eat a sprig of fresh parsley. Thanks to its high chlorophyll content, it will freshen your breath.

- ❏ Flossing doesn't just make your time in the dentist chair a little easier, it's a tried and true way to freshen your breath.

- ❏ Drink water (as if you needed another reason). It helps to flush food particles out of teeth.

Finger and Toenails

Nail polish contains a high percentage of solvents, including the formaldehyde resin glue that helps the polish adhere to nails better. It's effective at penetrating and strengthening the nail plate, but it's also carcinogenic and toxic and can be absorbed through the skin or inhaled when nail polish is still wet. More chemical watchwords: other chemicals used in nail polish are *ethyl acetate, phenol, xylene,* and *dibutyl phthalate* (the toxic plasticizer which is also a developmental toxin). *Toluene,* another toxic ingredient, is a petroleum derivative that is flammable and explosive and can affect the central nervous system.

Nail polish remover contains acetone, which is flammable, moderately toxic, and a narcotic; it has caused cancer in laboratory animals. It's also poisonous if swallowed and can cause blindness if splashed in the eyes. Always use non-acetone nail polish remover.

Keep your nails strong and healthy with these natural tips:

- ❏ Stick with a good diet, which is the key to healthy fingernails. Balance proteins, calcium, and essential fatty acids.

- ❏ Wear rubber gloves when working in the garden, doing the dishes, or handling cleaning supplies.

- ❏ Don't use your fingernails as tools. Don't use them to pick teeth, scratch off a lottery ticket, pry open the skin on that orange, or practice kitty-boxing with the cat.

- ❏ Give your fingernails a chance to breathe by leaving them unpolished at least one day a week or one week a month.

- ☐ Use warmed milk to soften and smooth skin and cuticles.
- ☐ Apply nail polish in a well-ventilated area, preferably outdoors. Wash your hands thoroughly after application and keep your fingers away from your face.
- ☐ Make nail polish last longer by soaking your fingers in a 1:1 solution of warm water and cider vinegar before applying.
- ☐ Mix two to three vitamin E capsules and 1/4-cup olive oil and soak your nails in this mixture for 5 to 10 minutes daily to strengthen them.
- ☐ Massage a small amount of sweet almond oil into your nails several times a week to fortify them.
- ☐ Check natural food stores for natural alternatives to chemical nail polish such as Honeybee Gardens' earth-friendly versions.

Sanitary Products

Marketing in the sanitary protection industry is cloaked in secrecy, sterility, and purity. We want convenience, comfort, and price, but most of all we really don't want to get our hands dirty. We associate the whiteness of these products with cleanliness, sanitary-ness, and freshness, but tampons and pads are not sterile.

We should probably be most concerned about the process of manufacturing these products. Since we're subjected to forty or more years of up close and personal exposure to sanitary napkins and tampons, plus disposable diapers for infants and older adults, we should be apprehensive about the safety of these products. The chlorine bleaching process of rayon and cotton for sanitary protection is not only unnecessary but causes the formation of dioxin.

Ecologically, we probably don't give a damn where these products go when we're done with them. We want to believe that once they're out of the house, it's not our problem. In reality, the environmental impact of the disposal of these objects is not yet huge, but over the course of our potential forty years of menstruating, the numbers add up. Pads and diapers are made from fluff pulp, a type of paper that dissolves fairly easily; it's the plastic waste created by individual wrappers, plastic coverings, plastic backing, sticky tape, and packaging that makes for a bigger mess in the landfill.

Plastic tampon applicators, which have earned the nicknames "New Jersey seashells" and "beach whistles," threaten marine life, beach goers, and waste treatment workers. Don't flush anything away, including applicators and the actual used tampon, since they can circumvent screens at waste treatment facilities, clog mechanisms, damage equipment, and put the safety of workers at risk.

Look for these safer alternatives:

- Switch to organic cotton pads and tampons that do not use chlorine to bleach and support sustainable farming. Organic Essentials (www.organicessentials.com) creates not only organic cotton personal care products, but also cotton swabs and cotton balls.
- Try pads made of cotton and flannel. Gladrags, Lunapads, and Sisterly Works make pads that can be washed and reused.
- The Keeper is a rubber menstrual cup the size and shape of an egg cup that can be reused every day of your cycle, every month of the year.
- Bring back the menstrual hut! I certainly wouldn't mind taking three days off each month to rejuvenate myself and hang out in a clubhouse with my girlfriends. Anything's better than having to watch commercials about wearing white pants to a party "during that time" or talking about freshness with my mother.

> I want to know if you can see beauty, even when it's not pretty, every day, and if you can source your own life from its presence.
>
> –Oriah Mountain Dreamer,
> *The Invitation*

A mediated and perfected ideal of beauty is nothing new, and we can all fall victim to peer pressure every once in a while. A new shade of lip gloss, a hair treatment that promises fuller bouncier hair, bath gel that assures smoother skin. We can step back from these mediated messages and realize that true beauty truly does come from within. Eating simply, lessening toxic burden, lowering stress levels and finding emotional confidence is all it really takes to make us look and feel fabulous.

Do it today
Take this week to detox your body. Don't use hair products, makeup, and other unnecessary cosmetics. Be sure to drink your 8 to 10 glasses of water every day.

ADDITIONAL RESOURCES

Armstrong, Liz and Adrienne Scott. *Whitewash: Exposing the Health and Environmental Dangers of Women's Sanitary Products and Disposable Diapers—What You Can Do About It.* Toronto: Harper Perennial, 1992.

Erickson, Kim. *Drop-Dead Gorgeous: Protecting Yourself from the Hidden Dangers of Cosmetics.* New York: Contemporary Books, 2002.

The Campaign for Safe Cosmetics (www.safecosmetics.org) is an on-line resource created by a coalition of public health, educational, religious, labor, women's, environmental, and consumer groups. They are working to better the safety of health and beauty aids by asking companies to phase out their use of toxic chemicals.

CREATING YOUR OWN COSMETICS

Here are some great books on natural beauty tips with simple recipes that are easy to make and really do work.

Byers, Dorie. *Natural Beauty Basics: Create Your Own Cosmetics and Body Care Products.* Bloomington, IL: Vital Health Publishing, 2001.

Cox, Janice. *Natural Beauty at Home.* New York: Henry Holt and Co., 2002.

Gallagher, Dawn. *Naturally Beautiful.* New York: Universe Publishing, 1999.

chapter 11

cleaning

If cleanliness is next to godliness, then dirt and germs must be evil, right? But even the fear of sin is not enough to get us to enjoy cleaning. And cleaning can often be anything but simple. Once we've got sufficient disposable income, the maid's the first person we add to our payroll. If we have to do it ourselves, we want to done fast and easy. The household product industry knows how much we hate to clean. They focus their advertising on how their product can help us get our chores out of the way quickly and easily. If the product gets the job done, we'll gladly overlook the harmful chemicals.

We often have little or no control over the toxins to which we're exposed. We organize protests, boycotts, and other legal actions when we find that a local company has been polluting the watershed, but we knowingly allow similar toxins into our home every day. Chemicals found in household cleaning supplies are sent into wastewater, where they break down slowly, and where they can be ingested and stored in the fat of animals we eat and live with, to say nothing of the amounts that get in our own bodies.

Know Your Ingredients

While many cleaners contain unnecessary additives such as fragrances and colors, it's the active ingredients that are usually the most dangerous. Knowing what's in a product can help us decide whether the risk of using it is worth taking.

Accidental ingestion is not the only thing to be concerned about when we use chemical cleaning products. Chemicals can also enter the body through inhalation and absorption through skin, eyes, and mucous membranes. Small, toxic, airborne drops of cleaning products can be inhaled or land on surfaces throughout our home. We then can continue to be exposed to chemicals even after we're finished using them. These toxins cause headaches, confusion, and breathing problems. They can also be carcinogenic.

Where cleaning supplies are concerned, effective performance builds brand loyalty. We'll purchase the same product again and again as long as it continues to satisfy our cleaning needs. This loyalty brings repeated exposure to toxic chemicals, which can accumulate in our body even if the product is used to exact specifications.

Think the only problems our favorite cleanser gives us are itchy eyes and a slight headache? Research is now indicating that fumes released from chemical-based household cleaners and aerosol propellants may be responsible for creating smoggy skies. Could this container of furniture polish be the reason why I can't see the

Hollywood sign anymore when I visit Los Angeles? According to *The Los Angeles Times*, chemical household cleaning products send out about twice as many hydrocarbons as all of the SUVs and light trucks driven in California, three times more smog-forming compounds than all the factories in L.A., and five times more than all the gas stations.[124]

Stop & think

Don't you just love those ladies in the commercials who take a big long deep whiff of their chemical cleaning product to revel in its "pine-freshness", from a bottle that recommends that you use the product in a well-ventilated area? Know that *any time* you can smell something (good or bad) you are inhaling particles of that substance.

Dangerous Cleaners

Companies wouldn't put something on the market if it weren't completely safe ... right? Wouldn't they get sued if someone died from using their product? The government will protect us. That's why we pay taxes—to fund the FDA and EPA ... right? Sadly, the answer to all of these questions is no. Products released to the public are innocent until proven guilty. Implicating a certain chemical in disease or death and finding it guilty requires years and years of documented exposure and eliminating any other possible cause.

Let's start with *chlorine*. The use of chlorine has serious risks to both human and environmental health. It whitens well, but its strong chemicals weaken fabrics over time, even when used sparingly. Never allow acids (such as ammonia or vinegar) to be mixed with chlorine bleach; the combination creates a deadly toxic gas.

Realize that chlorine is often hidden among the listed ingredients of cleaning products. Without reading the labels carefully, we may not realize that we're mixing them. Look for "chlor-" in compound names, including: sodium hypochlorite, calcium hypochlorite, and chloramines.

Chlorine is found commonly in chlorine bleach, cleansers, mildew removers, and toilet bowl cleaners. Automatic chlorinated dishwashing detergents are especially dangerous because tiny particles of chlorine are released in the steamy mist when the door is opened, and we breathe that steamy, chlorinated mist right into our lungs. Other uses of chlorine (besides household cleaners) include bleached paper products, PVC (polyvinyl chloride plastic), insecticides, refrigerants, and air conditioning units.

Chlorine fumes alone are irritating enough to eyes and nose, but liquid chlorine is highly corrosive when it contacts the skin, eyes, and mucous membranes. Bleach can cause nausea and vomiting and has been known to burn throat tissue. If you swallow liquid chlorine, call Poison Control (800-222-1222) *immediately*. When flushed down the toilet or drain, bleach will continue to kill bacteria and react with other chemicals it meets down there.

Thinking outside of the box: becoming chlorine-free

With all the dangers of chlorine, why do we feel the need to submerge ourselves in a pool of it when summer rolls around? Chlorinated swimming pools may cool us off when it gets hot, but are the side effects worth the swim? Dry skin, bloodshot eyes, green and brittle hair, increased mucus production—where's the fun in that?

Besides recreating the set for *Swamp Thing* (not very conducive to backyard barbecues), there are non-chlorine alternatives for use in swimming pools and hot tubs. These systems first use ultra-violet light or ozone generation to filter and eliminate organic material, chlorine, bacteria and viruses and algae. A second stage usually involves treatment with natural substances to keep your cement pond clean and clear.

Triclosan, which is found in antibacterial products, is marketed as an ingredient that increases personal health by killing bacteria and germs. It's a member of the compound family called *chlorophenols*, which are related to dioxin (see page 104). New research says that in the presence of sunlight, triclosan breaks down into dioxin. It readily survives conventional wastewater treatment methods and easily reenters the environment. Scientists have found triclosan in human breast milk and suspect that it causes liver damage.

Antibacterials that often contain triclosan are popping up everywhere. Thanks to heavy marketing pressure, they're found in soaps, cleansers, toothpaste, deodorants, kitchen implements (like cutting boards), clothing, and even some meats. Supermarkets in Britain have banned the sale of antibacterial products containing triclosan. For a safer antibacterial, try rubbing alcohol or hydrogen peroxide.

Ammonia, which is made from a natural gas through a complex heat intensive process that pollutes air and water, is natural and biodegradable, but also flammable. It's a powerful irritant to lungs, eyes, and skin and causes rashes, redness, or chemical burn. Ammonia can change into cancer-causing nitrates when it reacts with elements in soil and water. It is commonly found in commercial glass cleaners and fertilizers.

Pesticide is a term that encompasses a worldwide-industry whose sales exceed $30 billion annually and include herbicides, bacteriacides, fungicides, insecticides, rodenticides, acaricides, avicides, algaecides, nematicides, and mildewcides. These products not only kill what they're meant to kill, but can also destroy other organisms in the soil, water, and air.

We may not think we're using weed killers or pesticides ... but we are. Every time we buy a product that has been manufactured from a crop that was treated with pesticides, go to a ballgame at a park with a lush green lawn, or shop at a non-organic florist, we perpetuate the system of chemical industry-supported agriculture. Precipitation and winds disperse these chemicals over a larger area. Although the insecticide DDT was banned for use in the U.S. in 1972, as of 2005 it was still produced in India and China and sold to the world market where more than twenty-five countries continue to use it. America routinely imports fabrics and produce from these countries.

"Inert" chemicals

Look at the back of a container of weed killer and read the list of ingredients. You'll find that 0.4 percent of the product is a twelve syllable chemical, while 99.6 percent is "other inert ingredients." You think it's probably safe, considering such a small amount is the unknown chemical, right? Newsflash: *Inert does not mean harmless.* Ingredients are considered inert if they do not specifically help to kill the particular insects or weeds as stated on the label of the product, but they may be just as harmful as the active ingredients. According to the EPA, of the 1,400 chemicals allowed to be inert, forty are carcinogenic or cause brain damage or other chronic effects. Sixty-four, including benzene, asbestos, formaldehyde, and xylene, are potentially toxic.[125]

According to the clause in the Federal Insecticide, Fungicide, and Rodenticide Act regarding trade secrets, chemical companies are not required to disclose what the inert ingredients really are.

We expect pesticides to be used in agriculture, but should we find it in schools and paper grocery bags? Golf courses and athletic fields and other highly manicured parks and gardens are covered with chemicals that destroy weeds. Latex paints and carpeting also contain chemicals that resist pests.

Insect and weed killers can be endocrine disrupters that can cause miscarriages in both domestic and wild animals. Some are carcinogenic. Some toxins included in pesticides produce multiple chemical sensitivities, compromise immunity, or can cause damage to the nervous system. Some pesticides are rapidly eliminated from the body, while others are stored in body fat. A pesticide also may become more poisonous in the presence of other chemicals.

In order to stop the devastating effects of these chemicals, we need to be aware of how often they are used. Knowledge of where pesticides are used and what harm they cause is the first step to eliminating hidden uses. Take back control of your kids' health by monitoring pesticides and cleaning products used in schools. When we support the trend toward organic products, we lessen our dependence on pesticides.

Perchloroethylene (or *perc*), which was first used as a metal degreaser in Germany during 1920s, is still used by most American dry cleaners. A solvent of perc (a manufacturing byproduct of CFCs and HCFCs) and other chemicals (benzene, formaldehyde, naphthalene, trichloroethylene, and xylene) is poured into a rotating drum along with the clothing. The drum spins out most of the solvent and hot air evaporates the remaining fluid before the garments are pressed and bagged.

The solvents are excellent at dissolving soils and removing stains without damage to the fabric. Unfortunately, they can also make us sick. Perc has been linked to cancer, damage to the liver and nervous system, infertility, hormonal disruption, and a host of less serious conditions from nausea to dizziness.

At least *fifty-seven million pounds* of perc are used every year by over 34,000 dry cleaners.[126] Around twelve million pounds of the chemical are released into the atmosphere. Because of its persistence, it turns up everywhere in the environment: in rainwater, seawater, ground water, rivers, and lakes. It has been identified in breast milk, cow's milk, meat, cooking oil, fruit, fish, shellfish, even algae. High levels of perc have even been found in butter and other fatty items in grocery and convenience stores located next to dry-cleaning establishments.

Hope for the Future of Safer Dry Cleaning

- ☐ Take control of your community by banning perc machines from new dry cleaning businesses.
- ☐ Protect the environment by siding with the perc manufacturers who have been urging dry cleaners to switch to newer equipment that recycles perc and therefore uses less of it. The bad news here, however, is that it locks the dry cleaners into continuous use of perc, rather than allowing them to explore alternative methods.
- ☐ Simplify your life by buying clothes that don't need to be dry-cleaned. Almost every closet contains tiny advertisements for perc: they're on those labels that say 'Dry Clean Only'. Advertisers play off our fears of harming delicate fabrics. Instead of getting them dry cleaned, try hand-washing delicates with shampoo or dishwashing liquid.
- ☐ When I gave up dry cleaning, I decided to try to wash my dry clean only clothing in the washer. I don't recommend trying this with your favorite items of clothing or your ball gowns, but with other items you don't mind experimenting with, saving $50 over the life of the garment can be enough incentive to give up the cleaners.

❑ Hunt down wet cleaners. Wet cleaning is the alternative to dry cleaning that cleans clothing using biodegradable detergents and water. Computer technology has made wet cleaning easier. The cleaner doesn't have to monitor the machine as closely as before, while the computer controls temperature, agitation, and drying.

❑ Other types of environmentally friendly dry cleaning are silicone-based and carbon dioxide-based dry-cleaning. For locations check www.greenearthcleaning.com.

❑ If you must dry clean, try to find a cleaner that is non- or low-polluting. Ask them not to bag your clothes so chemicals can thoroughly dissipate. (This also saves using a plastic bag.) Air your clothes in a well-ventilated area or outdoors before wearing them.

COMMON USES FOR COMMON ITEMS:
TEN MUST-HAVE CLEANING INGREDIENTS

So the hazards of toxic chemicals have you a bit worried and you'd rather not take a chance with the products you're not sure of. What's next? While the ten items listed below might not all be edible, they're all much safer and able to clean almost everything in the house. They have the added bonus of being dirt (pun intended) cheap.

1. *Hydrogen Peroxide* (3 percent solution) easily breaks down into oxygen and water, leaving behind no toxic residues. It's an oxygen bleach that works against many bacteria, viruses, and molds. If you do not want bleaching properties, use it with caution. Be sure to keep peroxide in a dark bottle and remember it becomes inactive in nine months to one year, so note the expiration date on the bottle. It's a best buy because it also has medicinal uses.

2. *Baking Soda* can be used as a mild scouring powder and multi-purpose deodorizer. Since it's a base, mixing it with acids (such as vinegar) will cause a foaming reaction. Check out www.armandhammer.com for hundreds of uses.

3. *Borax*, most often used as a laundry booster, has similar uses to vinegar: disinfecting, deodorizing, and inhibiting the growth of mold. It also can be used to put out grease fires and polish silver. Note that borax is slightly toxic and should be handled with care and stored safely. It is safe for use around pets, but if large quantities are ingested, seek medical or veterinary help. For more borax tips see www.purex.com.

4. *Rubbing alcohol* (or *isopropyl alcohol*) is a disinfectant that removes dirt and grime from a variety of surfaces, such as vertical blinds and candles. Caution: it is highly flammable.

5. *Vinegar* is a mild acid that cleans and shines. Because of its acidity, it also kills molds and mildews. H.J. Heinz Company references numerous studies that their ordinary supermarket-bought vinegar can kill 99 percent of bacteria, 82 percent of molds, and 80 percent of germs.[127] Don't look for these hints on the bottle, however, because they cannot claim that vinegar is a disinfectant on the packaging unless they register it as a pesticide with the Environmental Protection Agency.

Vinegar also cuts grease, dissolves adhesives, and removes mineral deposits and stains. Vinegar removes soapy films from clothing, porcelain, skin, and hair. Despite its distinctive odor, vinegar will act as a neutralizing air freshener.

In vinegar we trust...

It may be hidden on the bottom shelf of the condiment aisle, but vinegar was first discovered more than 10,000 years ago when someone opened a cask of wine accidentally gone sour. Through the centuries, vinegar has been produced from molasses, sorghum, fruits, coconut, honey, beer, maple syrup, potatoes, beets, malt, grains, and whey. The principle behind the production of vinegar is two biochemical processes: first, the fermentation of sugar to alcohol under controlled conditions, and then the bacterial conversion of alcohol to acid. Voilà—vinegar.

Vinegar is self-preserving. It doesn't need refrigeration and its shelf life is almost indefinite. While its color may change or haze and sediment may develop, these are only an aesthetic change; the strength remains the same. Vinegar works well hot or cold. Use white vinegar for cleaning purposes and cider vinegar for cosmetic purposes. For more on vinegar, check out www.versatilevinegar.org.

---

6. *Bon Ami*—*en français*, it's our "good friend"; when found in the cleaning aisle, it's a gentle scouring powder that doesn't contain chlorine, phosphate, perfumes, or dyes. It's made from feldspar and calcite and can be used on porcelain, stainless steel, ceramic tile, cookware, chrome, tile, even fiberglass and imitation marble. It keeps white paint and shoes white, and it can be used to remove residual candle wax—all without harsh chemicals or gritty residue.

7. *Lemon juice* is an all-purpose natural acid that acts as an air freshener. Heat lemons in a microwave for thirty seconds to squeeze more juice from them.

8. *Salt* can be used as a mild but effective abrasive. It's a natural preservative that inhibits the growth of bacteria, yeast, and molds.

9. *Club soda* is an all-purpose stain remover for fabric and stainless steel.

10. *Tea tree oil* (also known as melaleuca oil) is a fungicide and bactericide that also has antiseptic medicinal and cosmetic uses.

Read on for specific applications for all these ingredients.

Laundry

Laundry detergents, fabric softeners and anti-static sheets used to clean clothing can damage the ecology and greatly affect those with chemical sensitivities. Why chance it when there are many safer and cheaper alternatives available?

❑ Use baking soda to help remove chemical odors from new clothing. Soak new clothes overnight in the washer with a cup of baking soda, then launder as usual.

❑ Do not use chlorine bleach. The safest way to avoid exposure to chlorine is to make sure chlorine bleaches never enter your house. Instead, try oxygen bleaches like hydrogen peroxide. (Use 8 ounces of per wash load.)

❑ Brighten dingy white cottons such as socks and underwear, by washing them first, then boiling them in water containing several slices of lemon.

❑ Clean out soap scum in the washing machine by running a load with a gallon of vinegar through one cycle.

❑ Soften fabric in hard water areas by using a half to a full cup of (pick one) baking soda, borax, vinegar, or washing soda. Because everyone's water quality is different, you might want to experiment with different amounts and combinations.

❑ The best solution for removing most food and drink stains is club soda, which can be especially helpful when stains arise while dining out. Lemon is another natural stain remover that also works well on most stains.

❑ Reduce the charge. With the introduction of synthetic fabrics after World War II, fabric softeners were developed to prevent the static cling. To control static, they leave a highly scented residue on clothing that is highly nauseating to the chemically sensitive and can be toxic when released into the home through poorly vented dryers. If you must use fabric softener, know that even if it doesn't affect you, you can affect chemically sensitive people you meet just by wearing something that has washed or dried with fabric softener. Look for fragrance-free versions. Half a dryer sheet or less will usually do the same job.

Thinking outside the box: laundry disks

While concentrated detergents may save packaging with their condensed size, they can cause skin reactions if they are not properly used. A natural alternative to harsh and over-fragranced detergents are laundry disks, cone shaped disks filled with ionizing ceramic beads to be used with an all-natural papaya enzyme cleaner. Three disks cost about $50, but they can be used to wash up to 700 loads. Using laundry boosters such as white vinegar or borax won't damage the ceramic beads. Disks are available through www.gaiam.com.

The 6,000 items that the typical household washes each year add up to considerable energy and water usage. With the washer using one percent of total household energy use, the dryer using eight percent, and hot water using 40 percent, laundry becomes one of the greediest energy consumers in the house.

❑ Wash in warm water. Most of the energy used by washing machines is to heat the water. Washing in warm or cold water for normal clothing loads is just as effective as washing in hot water, which accelerates chemical reactions, locks chemicals into fabric, and breaks down fibers.

❑ Switch to a front-loading washer that uses less water than top loaders. Clothes also require less drying time because the spin cycle is faster.

❑ Dry your clothing in sunlight, which acts as a natural sanitizing and bleaching agent and uses 100 percent less energy than the dryer!

Ninety percent of washed clothing is dried in the dryer, which puts almost a ton of CO_2 into the atmosphere each year. The dryer is one of our clothing's natural enemies, causing shrinkage and generating static electricity. Clothes will last longer when they aren't exposed to high dryer temperatures. (Just look what's left in the lint trap.) If you do use the dryer, follow these suggestions:

❑ Dry two or more loads in a row, taking advantage of the heat still in the dryer from the first load.

❑ Don't underload, but don't overload either. Because overloading restricts the air from circulating freely, it leads to uneven drying and wrinkled clothes that will have to be ironed later.

❑ Take clothes out of the dryer when they are just slightly damp. If you hang them up promptly, they may need little or no ironing.

❑ Read labels and sort clothes by fabrics and colors before washing.

❑ Wash clothes inside out to preserve fabric and color.

❑ Fasten all zippers, buttons, snaps, hooks and clasps to maintain shape and prevent snags.

❑ Decrease visible pilling, by drying clothing inside out. If pilling still occurs, invest in an electric pill shaver to gently remove the little balls of fuzz.

❑ I have a friend swears by using dryer lint as a fire starter when camping. This may be a resourceful recycling tip, but don't follow it if you use fabric softener, bleach or dry a lot of synthetic fabrics unless you want to create toxic fumes in the fire pit.

But what's wrong with the clothesline on breezy, sunny days? Line drying allows air to flow through fabrics, lifting out odors, while the sunlight acts as a natural bleaching agent. Outdoor air gives clothing a fresh smell. It's strange but true that apartment complexes and even some residential communities prohibit the use of outdoor clotheslines, claiming they ruin the visual appeal of neighborhoods. If your landlord or neighbors have set up a neighborhood watch against outdoor line drying, try these alternatives:

❏ Use hotel style clotheslines that can be affixed to walls and retracted when not in use.

❏ Buy an inexpensive drying rack that can be folded up after the clothes are dry.

❏ Hang wet clothes on hangers on your shower curtain rod or near the ceiling where warmer air will help to dry them faster.

❏ Hang damp clothes in the house during the drier and colder months of winter. The clothes become a humidifier, returning moisture to the air.

❏ Suspend pants by their cuffs, smoothing and creasing as you hang them. This often reduces your need to iron them.

❏ Use safety pins to connect socks to each other before washing. This cuts down on the time you spend hunting for mates that get sucked into the laundry vortex and makes them easier to dry on the bar of a hanger.

❏ Lay damp sweaters flat on towels and block them to original shape.

Antibacterials: Germs, Molds, and Other Icky Stuff

Everywhere we turn, we see ads for another product with special "antibacterial" abilities. The companies are playing off our germ phobias (which they usually created) and other fears by creating soaps, mouthwashes, hand sanitizers, even clothing containing disinfectants.

We must first remember that *not all bacteria are bad* and that when we use antibacterial products, we often kill beneficial bacteria as well as harmful ones. Beneficial bacteria help us maintain the balance of health and strengthen our immunity. A few friendly germs can be a good thing.

Because disinfectants are considered to be pesticides, the FDA regulates those used on the body or in food. The EPA regulates all other uses. If you must use antibacterial products, use them only when truly necessary—not every day. Follow these tips for antibacterials that are less toxic to humans.

❏ Use ultraviolet light to kill mold. (Do not look directly at the light.)

❏ Mix two teaspoons of tea tree oil with two cups of water in a spray bottle. Applying this mixture to moldy areas will kill both mold and bacteria. This mixture will last indefinitely if kept in a glass bottle. (Tea tree oil will dissolve plastic.)

❏ Use vinegar or hydrogen peroxide instead, which have antibacterial and antifungal properties.

❏ Keep a spray bottle of rubbing alcohol to spritz and disinfect kitchen items, such as knives and cutting boards.

❏ Replace chemically based cleaning products with lavender, which naturally contains the antibiotic phenol. Make a spray using water and a teaspoon of lavender essential oil.

❏ Sterilize wood and metal items by placing them in boiling water. Note that submerging plastic in boiling water can weaken its structure and cause it to off gas.

❏ Keep things dry. Without moisture, bacteria, viruses, mildew, and mold generally cannot survive. Squeegee, squeegee, squeegee!

Cleansers

In addition to killing germs, cleansers also remove dirt, grime and odor. This is mostly for a sense of aesthetics, the most disinfected surface in the world doesn't appeal to us if it's stained. Elbow grease is often your number one weapon against dirt.

In the Kitchen

❏ To clean the fridge, rub the walls and shelves with moist baking soda, cornstarch, or vinegar. Use heated vinegar to dissolve stuck-on foodstuffs of anything unidentifiable. Use rubbing alcohol (alcohol doesn't freeze) to clean freezer shelves.

❏ Don't use liquid drain clog removers that contain lye, a caustic toxin that pollutes water, destroys beneficial bacteria in sewers and drains, and eats through pretty much anything. Before you pick up that commercial drain product, think about your skin and mucous membranes. Instead:

✓ Try pouring baking soda or salt down the drain, followed by a pot of boiling water.

✓ If that doesn't work, try mixing one cup baking soda, one cup salt, and one quarter cup cream of tartar. Once a week, pour a half-cup of this mixture down the drain, followed by one quart of boiling water.

✓ You can also boil three cups of vinegar and pour that down the drain.

✓ Pouring boiling water down the drain usually dissolves grease, which is cause of many clogs.

✓ A preventive measure is to pour a cup of vinegar down the drain once a month just to keep things moving along.

❏ Use a spray of vinegar to clean the oven instead of commercial oven cleaners that contain lye and other strong chemicals that can irritate and burn skin and eyes. For easy results, start when the oven has cooled down, but is still warm to the touch. For baked on food, sprinkle on baking soda and add a little vinegar, then gently scrub with a sponge. Rinse with water. An ounce of prevention works well in the oven: always use drip catchers under dishes that may bubble over.

❑ Work away stovetop grease spots with a cotton cloth dipped in vinegar and/or borax.

Washing the Dishes

Many newer dishwashers are more efficient than washing by hand, saving more water and using less electricity (to heat the hot water). On average, a dishwasher uses only about ten gallons of water, as opposed to hand washing which uses between fifteen to seventeen gallons. (I wish all my apartment dwelling friends luck in trying to convince their landlords that this is a great reason to install a dishwasher.)

Thinking outside the box: The little dishwasher that could

The landlord has shot you down again and you're sick of your dishpan hands. A solution? The countertop dishwasher: portable, affordable, energy efficient, and it attaches to almost any tap. Turn on the hot water and it does the work for you. It's less than two feet high and washes about a meal's worth of dishes (more if you've only got one plate). See www.countertopdishwasher.com.

Automatic dishwashing detergents often contain chlorine that is released into kitchen air as the water heats into mist. Phosphates are also a concern. Liquid dish detergents have agents that are added to increase foaming for aesthetic reasons. We have other options:

❑ Make a homemade automatic dishwashing detergent, by using equal amounts of borax and washing soda.

❑ Use baking soda or vinegar. Both clean effectively with the high temperatures of automatic dishwashers.

❑ Wash pots and pans by filling a large pot with a mixture of a half-cup of water, a half-cup of vinegar, and two tablespoons of baking soda. Cover, bring to a boil, then soak the pans for thirty minutes.

❑ Remove stuck-on food by filling the pot or dish with vinegar for a half hour, then rinsing in hot soapy water.

❑ Cut grease in the dishwasher by adding a few lemon slices or few tablespoons of vinegar. Vinegar can also be used to clean the oil residue from peanut butter, mayonnaise, and salad dressing jars.

❑ Clean stained aluminum by boiling the item in a pot of water with grapefruit or lemon rinds for a half hour. Or fill the aluminum pot with water, add two tablespoons of cream of tartar, and boil for five to ten minutes.

❑ To eliminate odors in plastic containers, seal a lemon wedge, a sheet of newspaper, or a piece of bread moistened with vinegar in the container for a few days, then rewash it.

❑ Add borax or vinegar to rinse water to avoid water spots on glassware.

❑ Sprinkle baking soda or a 1:1 salt and vinegar solution on coffee and tea stains in china cups.

Most of the energy used by the dishwasher is used to heat the water. To avoid a bit of unnecessary energy usage, allow your dishes to air dry. If you dry them by hand, be sure the towel is thoroughly clean and pick up a new one when the first gets too damp. A towel with only a small amount of bacteria on it can manage to contaminate an entire load of dishes.

For the Bathroom

Mold and mildew thrive in moist conditions. To keep them out of your bathroom, provide adequate ventilation and sunlight and squeegee the tiles around the tub dry after every bath. Since water flows freely in the bathroom, the best way to clean is to first find out about the hardness of your water. Everything in the "Ten Best Cleaners List" will help you clean your bathroom, but if you experiment with combinations you can probably create one cleaner to clean the tub, toilet, tile, sink and flooring.

❑ Water high in mineral content (calcium, magnesium, iron, lime, copper, etc.) can stain porcelain and metal. Conquer these stains by wrapping towels soaked in vinegar on the faucet head for a couple hours to remove mineral deposits.

❑ Use soft scrubs for tiles, porcelain, and countertops. Baking soda, salt, Epsom salts, and borax are mild abrasives. Use these alone or mix them with vinegar, cream of tartar, or hydrogen peroxide. Experiment to find the best solution for your water and soap combinations.

❑ To remove stubborn rust stains from porcelain or ceramic without scratching, scrub with a pumice stone.

❑ Switch to a cotton or hemp shower curtain that can be easily washed and won't off gas like the PVC plastic versions do. When you wash your shower curtain, add a cup vinegar, borax, or baking soda in the rinse cycle.

Furniture

Most commercial furniture polishes contain phenol and a nice little chemical called nitrobenzene that can cause skin discoloration, shallow breathing, vomiting, and death.[128] Both phenol and nitrobenzene are associated with cancer and birth defects. Aerosol sprays increase chances of ingestion by allowing particulates to spread through the air, and exposure can continue once the product is applied to wood, as the chemicals continue to off gas. To contain the stream, spray the polish directly onto your dust cloth. (Note: Always test these furniture polishes in an inconspicuous area first.)

❑ Make a basic furniture cleaner and polish with one teaspoon of lemon juice in one-pint mineral oil, or a 1:1 ratio of olive oil and vinegar. For either mixture, mix the solution until it is well blended. Apply it lightly to furniture with a clean soft cloth, work it in well, and wipe off the excess.

❑ Remove white rings from wood furniture by using small mixture of olive oil and salt. A light coating of mayonnaise on the ring also works well; let it stand for an hour, then wipe off.

❑ Get rid of wax on wood by putting a paper bag or four paper towels over the stained wood and holding a hot iron an inch above the wax. Do not touch the paper with the iron, as this will only soften the wax. Pressing the paper to the stain will lift up the melted wax.

❑ Eliminate water stains on wood with one tablespoon of vegetable oil and enough salt to make a paste. Make the paste only as grainy as you feel comfortable using on your furniture.

❑ Erase scratches on wood by gently rubbing the scratch with the meat of a walnut or pecan or a brown crayon.

Floors

Carpet cleaners often contain perchloroethylene, that notorious villain from the dry cleaning industry. They also contain naphthalene, another nasty chemical that is toxic merely by inhalation and causes anemia, liver damage, convulsions, and the possibility of coma. Our best defense against dirty carpets is a quick recovery. Clean spills right away. Regular vacuuming of floors helps keep dirt from getting ground in. If all else fails, throw down a tarp while you're eating in front of the TV.

❑ Mop linoleum or tiles with mixture of three quarters of a cup of vinegar and one gallon of hot water. There's no need to rinse. Remove scuffmarks on linoleum with toothpaste.

❑ Clean wood floors by mopping with warm water every week or so. Mop a dirty wood floor with a quarter cup of vinegar in one gallon of warm water.

❑ Try hydrogen peroxide or club soda for carpet stains. For recent wet spills, sprinkling either salt or cornstarch directly on the liquid will absorb the stain. Wait until dry, then vacuum.

❑ Deodorize carpets by sprinkling baking soda or borax over the rug. Leave it on for a few hours then vacuum. To be safe, lock pets out of the room until after you vacuum.

Windows and Glass

When we consider the fact that the bulk of most commercial window cleaners is water, why should we pay money for something we have readily available in our homes? The ingredient that does the dirty work is ammonia, but that provides its own hazards.

❑ Make your own all-purpose glass cleaner: a solution of 1:1 vinegar and water. Don't get discouraged if you notice messy streaks when you use plain vinegar. It's probably wax buildup residue left over from the commercial cleaners. Clean the glass thoroughly with soap, vinegar, and water, then wipe down with newsprint.

❑ Clean your car's windshield wipers and windshield with vinegar and water.

❑ Spray hairspray or spread some peanut butter to remove something sticky from glass.

❑ Peel labels easily from glass (or plastic) containers, by applying a thick coat of vegetable oil to the label, letting it soak in for a day, then peeling the label off. If it doesn't come off easily, reapply the oil and wait another day.

Air Freshening

Many commercial "deodorizers" are misnamed. They don't remove odors; they merely replace one scent with another. Yes, the funky smell is gone, but what's causing the smell probably still remains. As an alternative to costly chemical air fresheners (which can contain formaldehyde and/or phenol), try these easy and safe alternatives.

❑ Place bowls of vinegar in corners of recently painted or smoky rooms. Boil a pot of vinegar to remove unpleasant kitchen odors.

❑ Set bowls of baking soda in the refrigerator and freezer, in cabinets, and in corners of rooms to absorb odors.

❑ Put small mesh bags filled with dried orange or lemon peel in drawers and closets.

❑ Freshen drains by grinding lemon rinds in the disposal.

❑ Place newspaper between musty books to deodorize them. Or place them in a bag with a cup of cat litter or a mesh bag of activated charcoal.

❑ Put cloves in the vacuum cleaner bag to sweeten the smell of your carpets.

❑ Try silica gel for other moisture absorbing needs. It's available at camera supply stores and is often found in little packets in shoeboxes or vitamins to absorb moisture. It will change color when it's saturated, but heating it in an oven to dry it out will reactivate it.

❑ Freshen the air in other ways, including lighting matches for a minute or two, opening the windows to let in some fresh air, setting out bowls of hydrogen peroxide in corners of the room (if you don't have pets or children that can get into them), putting sachets in closets and drawers, or daubing essential oils on the undersides of furniture. Plants also make great air fresheners; see page 90.

On the other hand: candles

Candle sales have skyrocketed in recent years, (even necessitating their own Ubiquitous Mall Store), but almost every part of the candle can cause a sensitivity problem. Many candles are made from nonrenewable paraffin and contain artificial scents and dyes that can easily aggravate MCS, even when they're not being burned. There are at least seven toxins in paraffin candle wax, including benzene, which is a carcinogen.

Choose only non-petroleum candles made from natural beeswax or vegetable wax that burns cleaner and does not emit unhealthy fumes and soot.

Make sure the wick doesn't contain a thin metal core (which is often lead) to help it stand upright. Ensure that the wick burns down evenly with the wax. Avoid multiple wick candles that burn faster and release more soot. Choose candles with thin braided cloth wicks that curl over when burned.

Most fragrance oils used for candle making are petroleum-based synthetics. Buy candles with scents that are specifically formulated for candles. Avoid candles that contain volatile aromatic hydrocarbons.

Soot is partially burned particles that become airborne and settle as dust or are inhaled. Soot from petroleum wax and fragrances can contain carcinogens, neurotoxins, and reproductive toxins. A flame without soot will burn blue, like the flame of a gas stove.

Increase ventilation in rooms where candles are burning, but avoid placing a candle in line of a direct draft. The goal is a low and even flame. Candles should only be burned for one hour at a time. Allow them to cool before relighting them.

Pests

Not many things are creepier than the sight of insects dancing in the pantry or scurrying across the floor when we turn on the light at three a.m. Our first reaction is, "I want that dead. *Now.*" First thing in the morning, we run to the store and grab the first twelve cans of insecticide we can find. But pesticides are dangerous concoctions and finding pesticides that use safe chemicals is a job worthy of someone with a doctorate in organic chemistry. The rest of us don't have the time or the energy to devote to this task, especially when the ant trail is making a conga line through the kitchen. There are two steps to solving a pest problem, and if you're successful at both, chemical intervention won't be necessary.

Step 1: Figure out where the critters are coming from. Step 2: Figure out why they're staying. The first step requires a little detective work. Find the point of entry and close it off. A dab of white glue makes a good tight seal. Check screens for holes and doorways for a tight fit.

Next, look at your living conditions. *Clean up.* Like us, insects are naturally attracted to food. Tightly seal all containers and packages, sweep the floors regularly, wipe down the counters, take out the trash, and put a small pile of borax underneath the liner bag. If these ounces of prevention fail, try these steps:

- ❑ Know your pest. Find out what it eats, where it sleeps and hides, and how long it normally lives. Sometimes your bug problem will cure itself when the insect reaches the end of its life span. To identify critters I've been known to bring specimens to my local home and garden center.

- ❑ Deter ants by pouring a bit of lemon juice or vinegar at point of entry. A sprinkling of cinnamon also works. Spray soapy water or rubbing alcohol directly on the ants you can see. (It will neutralize the odor that the ants produce.) If you have outdoor ant problems, pour a pot of boiling water down an anthill. Small trays (about the size of a jar lid) of borax will also kill ants. Despite their need to bring everyone in their extended family with them wherever they go, ants are harmless. They don't carry disease or bacteria and they generally end up leaving shortly after arriving. They also eat the eggs and larvae of fleas and can keep termites from establishing colonies. Consider their parade across the kitchen retribution for your failed childhood ant farm.

- ❑ Discourage cockroaches with boric acid. Spread some at the baseboards, under the sink, behind the refrigerator. It can irritate mucous membranes when inhaled and is toxic when ingested, so if you have pets, use caution. As long as it's kept dry, it's effective indefinitely.

- ❑ Use salt and borax to repel fleas. Try sprinkling either one on your carpets to dissolve the waxy coating on the fleas, their eggs and larvae. Vacuum often, then remove the vacuum bag and place it in the sun where extreme heat will kill the rest.

- ❑ Understand that while arachnophobia is the most common fear, the most important thing to know about spiders is that *they are some of the most beneficial creatures on earth.* Spiders eat flies, moths, grasshoppers, bedbugs, and even cockroaches. And fear not—of the 3,000 species of spiders in the U.S., only two are dangerous to humans, the black widow and the brown recluse. (By the way, the urban legend that we unconsciously eat spiders while we sleep is just that.)

- ❑ Use cedar as a natural moth repellant. The chemicals in mothballs are toxic to the brain, liver, and blood. They also accumulate in our body and irritate our lungs and respiratory functions. Use blocks of cedar in your dresser drawers or make sachets from chips to hang in your closet. Sachets filled with lavender, cloves, rosemary, or dried lemon peels have also proven to be effective.

❏ Debug your houseplants by spraying the plant with plain ice water or a mixture of one-quart water mixed with one to two tablespoons of skim milk or beer. Repeat every two to three days.

❏ Control mealy bugs by spraying rubbing alcohol on infested plants.

❏ Seek out natural alternatives to pesticides, including *Bacillus thuringiensis*, a microorganism that attacks beetles, caterpillars, fungus gnats, and mosquitoes. Insects such as ladybugs attack aphids. Safe chemical solutions are diatomaceous earth, which acts against ants and aphids, and sulfur, which combats fungus, mites, mildew, and rust.

❏ Learn to love bugs. Understand that *many insects are beneficial*. They act as pollinators, decomposers, regulators of pests, and are food for other beneficial animals like birds and fish. Accept them for what they are and try to live peacefully with them.

Safety for Cleaning Products and Pesticides, If You Must Use Them

Unfortunately for us, the consumer, the Consumer Product Safety Commission doesn't require cleaning products to list their ingredients on their labels. The information that is given will often refer only to the immediate health effects of the product and the reaction to only the dosage specified. Labels do not factor long-term cumulative effects from prolonged exposure during typical repeated use, by absorption through the skin, inhalation from particles suspended in the air, and from residues the product left behind.

Companies are protected by "label as shield" laws that allow them to print "it's a violation of federal law not to use this product accordingly" on labels to warn the user that if we use more than the company recommends, the company assumes no responsibility for whatever happens. Always read labels carefully. Follow instructions and never use more than recommended.

What do they mean?

✓ *Irritant:* product can cause skin rashes or irritate mucous membranes.

✓ *Strong sensitizer:* product can cause an allergic reaction.

✓ *Toxic:* poisonous if eaten, inhaled, or absorbed through the skin.

✓ *Caution:* lethal dose is one ounce to one pint. Slightly toxic.

✓ *Warning:* lethal dose is one teaspoon to one tablespoon. Moderately toxic.

✓ *Danger or Poison:* lethal dose is one taste to one teaspoon. Highly toxic.

✓ *Inflammable* or *flammable* (these words mean the same thing), *ignitable*, or *combustible:* product catches fire easily.

✓ *Chemically reactive:* product could possibly react with other substances, including water and air.

✓ *Corrosive:* product can eat away your skin.

Use even "natural" cleansers with caution. Follow directions as you would any cleanser.

❏ Buy the least toxic product available and select fragrance-free products.

❏ Store solutions you've created yourself well labeled and in new containers. Never mix homemade cleaners with store-bought cleaners.

❏ Leave all store-bought cleaners in their original containers and do not mix them with other solutions.

❏ Avoid inhaling fumes by using cleaners in well-ventilated areas. Open all windows and redirect fumes outside with a fan.

❏ Wear protective gear (rubber gloves, face mask, biohazard suit) if possible. If chemicals spill on your clothing, change immediately to limit exposure and consider your jeans and T-shirt contaminated.

Science has built a better paper towel! Tools for cleaning

Not only are our daytime TV shows cluttered with commercials for every type of cleaning product imaginable, but now the cleaning tool revolution has also begun. Rags, mops, dusters, suckers, grabbers—all newly designed to bring cleaning into the 21st century. But there are still old fashioned, all natural tools you can use to keep your chores as simple as the rest of your life.

✓ Bypass paper towels. Use rags instead. Old T-shirts, cotton, terry cloth, and cloth diapers work best.

✓ Use a razor blade to scrape stuck-on macaroni and cheese, leg wax, or gum off surfaces.

✓ Use an old toothbrush to scrub in those hard-to-reach places. I find that toothbrushes belonging to ex-boyfriends work best.

✓ Scrub larger areas with natural bristle brushes.

✓ Keep your hands safe, clean, and soft with a durable pair of rubber gloves. Natural latex will biodegrade completely and still protect you from dishpan hands.

❏ Spray cleaners directly into a rag to keep chemical particulates from being released into the air.

❏ Keep cleaners out of reach of children and pets and away from food preparation and consumption areas. If possible, keep them in a locked cabinet. If ingestion or exposure occurs, call Poison Control (800-222-1222) first before heading to the emergency room. They may be able to give you an immediate antidote over the phone.

Thinking outside the box: Seventh Generation

The name is based on a Native American ethic: living by taking into account how our actions will affect the next seven generations. Seventh Generation, based in Vermont for over twenty years, has worked to make the most ecologically sustainable and healthy household paper and cleaning products—free of chlorine, phosphates, genetically modified organisms. Their products are derived from vegetables and biodegradable and are not tested on animals.

Seventh Generation is dedicated to providing competitively priced, high quality, environmentally conscious household products that work as well or better than leading brands. But their commitment doesn't stop with their products. They also aim to educate consumers about why we should all be concerned about the dangers hidden in products that seem to innocently line the shelves at our local grocery stores. See www.seventhgeneration.com for products and a monthly online newsletter and blog that alert readers to the latest on health and environmental topics written by founder and CEO, Jeffrey Hollender.

❑ Buy only the amount that you need, use what you have in its intended dosage, then don't buy any more. Use as little as necessary to get the job done. Try borrowing cleaning products from a friend so there will be less material left for storage or disposal. The best way to dispose of old paint is to use it all. If you can't use it yourself, donate it to a theater production company. If that fails, paint an old piece of wood with it, allow it to dry and then dispose of the wood.

Decluttering Your Cleaning Product Cabinet

❑ Take inventory of the chemicals you have in your home. Cleaners hide in closets and garages, in cabinets, in the trunk of your car, under your kitchen sink. (Why anyone would store cleaning products in proximity to food preparation is beyond me.)

❑ Do not assume that you can just throw something in the trash or dump the remaining product down the drain. Call your local or county water, sanitation, or health department or the EPA for advice on proper disposal. Think before you throw these products away. You may be breaking the law by disposing of them improperly.

Many communities have hazardous waste pickup (or drop-off) days, where you can bring unused products and they will dispose of them properly for you. Although hazardous waste pickup can be expensive to set up (over $10,000 for even small communities and proof of residency is required), for the safety of the earth, lobby for your town to allocate tax money for this worthy venture.

Just what is "hazardous waste"?

Paints, cleaning solvents, mothballs, all pesticides (see page 279 for a full description of pesticides), automotive products, pool chemicals, acids, medications, mercury thermometers, smoke detectors, fluorescent light bulbs, glues and cements, craft supplies (including adhesives, paints, and photographic chemicals), paint thinners, aerosol cans, hair dyes and permanent solutions, nail polish and remover, flea powders or shampoos, shoe polishes, lighter fluid, or anything with a cautionary label on it.

When in doubt, consider it hazardous.

We willingly bring unnecessary toxins into our homes, but with a little research into water type, a little trial and error, and a little extra elbow grease, we can eliminate the need for these dangerous cleaning chemicals. When we make simpler cleaning product choices we can stop the cycle of chemical dependency.

Do it today

Are there any chemical products still lurking beneath your sink or in the garage? Find out when the next hazardous waste drop-off day in your community is and clean out the last of your toxic cleaning products.

ADDITIONAL RESOURCES

Berthold-Bond, Annie. *Clean and Green*. Ceres Press: Woodstock, NY, 1994.

_____. *Better Basics for the Home*. Ceres Press: Woodstock, NY, 1999. Two complete guides to environmentally safe housekeeping. Berthold-Bond is a nontoxic guru as well as a multiple chemical sensitivity sufferer. Her web site, www.anniebbond.com, is searchable for household tips and offers an e-mail newsletter.

Dadd, Debra Lynn. *Nontoxic, Natural and Earthwise: How to Protect Yourself and Your Family from Harmful Products and Live In Harmony with the Earth*. Los Angeles: Jeremy P. Tarcher, 1990. Another guide to nontoxic living with information on cleaners, water purity, cosmetics, office and art supplies, building materials, clothing, and food. See also www.debraslist.com.

Sandbeck, Ellen. *Slug Bread & Beheaded Thistles: Amusing & Useful Techniques for Nontoxic Housekeeping & Gardening*. New York: Broadway Books, 2000. Strange but true remedies for naturally removing creepy crawlies from your home and garden. If you need to get rid of armyworms, harlequin bugs, or Braconid wasps, this guide's for you.

Winter, Ruth. *A Consumer's Dictionary of Household, Yard and Office Chemicals*. New York: Crown Publishers, Inc., 1992. Defines the chemicals found in everyday products and their effects on humans. An essential guide to helping us understand what's in that bottle of furniture polish, shampoo, or toilet bowl cleaner.

Project Laundry List (www.LaundryList.org) is an online community based in Vermont, a simple group with a simple message: to provide information about how simple lifestyle modifications, like how air drying one's clothes and washing with cold water can significantly decrease dependence on electricity. They sponsor "National Hanging Out Day" every April 19th to raise awareness for clotheslines.

chapter 12

housing & decorating

A recent trend of design and decorating shows has Americans rushing to their local big box stores to stock up on the necessary supplies in an attempt to turn their money pits into their own castles. We spend thousands of dollars and hours on decorating, but all this money and energy may be for naught if where we've built our castles and what we've used to improve them are dangerous to our health.

And where we live is just as important as *how* we live. The location, structure, and what we use to embellish our home can have a profound effect on both our physical and emotional health. How can we ensure that where we've decided to live is the best location and how can we simplify renovations?

RIGHT HOME, RIGHT NOW?

Let's start evaluating where we live right now. How do you like your home? How much of your life do you spend there? The more time you spend in your home, the more important it is to have it be safe, comfortable, and spirit enhancing.

Maybe it's time for a change. Start by asking these questions, either about where you live now or about the space you're considering moving to.

- ✓ How does climate affect you? Do the changing of the seasons, the weather, and the environment help or hinder your health?
- ✓ Do the design and layout of your home provide enough natural light?
- ✓ Is the location of your home convenient for your lifestyle?
- ✓ How simple or difficult does the location and structure of your home make your life?
- ✓ Do you live near a high voltage power station?
- ✓ Are there golf courses, nurseries, parks, farms, or heavily landscaped areas nearby that may be potential sources of pesticide runoff?
- ✓ What is the quality of the water where you live? Can you drink water straight from your kitchen tap? Does your local water discolor the porcelain and fixtures?
- ✓ If you live in an apartment, is it above a laundry room or the garage?
- ✓ What is the noise pollution like where you live? Is there a busy freeway or train within sight and earshot? Is there a nearby airport or are you in the path of the flight pattern?

✓ Are there bad memories attached to your home? Some believe that a house will hold the negative energy of previous occupants, not to mention energies that arise from our own experiences.

✓ How big is your home? Is it too small? Too large? Just right?

✓ What is the quality of building you live in? Of the local transportation? Of the culture of the neighborhood, community, or city?

✓ Are there security problems on your street? In your neighborhood?

✓ What is the character of the people who live nearby?

✓ How closely is your home located to your work? To the center of your social life? To your friends and family?

Location, Location, Location

It's a misconception that the only way to minimize our impact on the planet is to live in a rural area. Simple living can and *must* be adapted to fit any environment. Each of the three environments—rural, urban, and suburban—can be modified to fit the simple lifestyle. Each has its own benefits. Each can be improved in some way. Deciding which location is best for you should involve analyzing what is most important in your life and what role you want your home to play in how you live.

Rural Living

Is Green Acres the place for *you*? When we choose to live out in the sticks, there are many housing options. A dollar seems to stretch further in the country, and we can be in better control of our water, soil and air. There are usually fewer variables contributing to environmental harm.

Isolation can be either a blessing or a curse. Whereas the peace and solitude of not having close neighbors and fewer options for work can be a dream come true for some, it can be disheartening for others. Removing ourselves from a bustling city society may make it more difficult to get the goods and services we're used to in the city, though with a few clicks, the Internet can often deliver most of what we want to our door.

To live simply in the country, get yourself in tune with the roots of bucolic simplicity. Continue to reevaluate what modern conveniences do for you. Decide truthfully what you can and cannot live without.

Urban Living

City living may seem like the antithesis of simple living. Sometimes the city is too social, leading to overcommitted schedules. Crime, pollution, overcrowding, and traffic all stem from too many people living in too little space. City dwellers have to deal with close neighbors, the possible lack of privacy, noise at all hours.

High housing costs in the city are a result of greater demand and fewer locations. Because the ground around them is usually covered in concrete, urbanites also seem to forget that the environment sustains them, unlike those who are in direct contact with land and water, who know how important it is to protect these elements of the environment.

Despite all this, however, city life can be very simple. City dwellers are often better at adapting their personal spheres to the convenience of busy streets and mass transit. And life in the city gives us all kinds of cultural and social experiences unique to the urban location. Businesses that support the eco-lifestyle (e.g., natural grocery stores and pharmacies) continue to crop up in urban locations—often more so than in the country or 'burbs.

To keep it simple in the city, rethink your disposable lifestyle. What can you substitute for the things you throw away every day? Stop using plastic shopping bags and switch to cloth bags; instead of plastic or Styrofoam, ask Starbucks to pour your coffee into your own mug. Keep your emergency preparedness kit (see page 199) at work to be ready for anything that might come up.

Always consider what you throw away. Remember—what goes down the drain becomes part of your city's ecology. More difficult is the quantity and quality of cleaning products used to keep city businesses clean. Being an EI/MCS sufferer in the city can be very difficult.

When shopping for a new home in the city, visit it at different times of the day. What do you hear? You may not notice the twenty eight-year-olds at the bus stop below your bedroom window if you only visit at night. Conversely, you may not notice the ladies of the evening who set up shop at 9 p.m. if you only stop by during the day.

Suburban Living

The cookie-cutter housing developments midway between the city and the country embody the proverbial American dream. The suburb has become the symbol of success and excess. Becoming a suburban simplist requires deprogramming yourself of the ideas of always wanting and needing more. Living simply in the suburbs takes the most discipline, because everything about the design of suburbs mitigates against simple living.

To stay simple in the suburbs, you have to think of new ways to reduce consumption. Think twice about every purchase. Step back and reevaluate what is truly important to help gain a new perspective on simplicity.

The major detriment to living in the 'burbs is that they are almost solely residential—we must transport ourselves to work, to school, and to the big box department or outlet stores down on Route 20. Transportation to and from the suburbs can lead to one of our greatest monetary and ecological expenses. To reduce car use from the suburbs, we can telecommute, carpool, combine driving with mass transit use and diligently plan our errands (once a week, paired up with friends or neighbors).

Housing Costs

Housing is probably the single largest expenditure we make in our lives. Many decide to go it alone, and then we find that housing costs can be overwhelming. But there are many options besides just getting a roommate to help offset the cost of rent or mortgage. Consider some of these housing alternatives:

❑ Consider cohousing (which sometimes looks like an old-fashioned boarding house). This is much like college dorm living—you have your own private space, but there are also communal areas like the kitchen, dining room, and living or recreation room. Cohousing helps us conserve resources and construction materials: one shared refrigerator, washer, and dryer are certainly better than four. Living with others also creates a built-in community. The Cohousing Association of the United States (www.cohousing.org) helps likeminded citizens create "intentional neighborhoods" where residents plan the development and maintenance of the community. They focus on forming leaderless groups where members are represented equally and they recommend that the community not be the primary source of income for its residents.

❑ Look for shared housing. Not all time-shares require having to listen to a two-hour presentation for a free weekend in Tahoe. Legitimate shared housing experiences involve house swapping with someone who also wants to spend time in another part of the country. See the listings at www.nationalsharedhousing.org.

❑ Try working off your rent as a nanny or caretaker. Check out www.caretaker.org to subscribe to *The Caretaker Gazette*, a resource that provides advertisements for caretakers needed and situations wanted. They also offer advice on living the life of a caretaker.

The Property

In the 1950s, the size of the average house was less than 800 square feet for the typical family of four. By 1989, the house had grown to 2,000 square feet, with fewer people living in it.[129] On my mornings off, when I walk the dog past these huge, beautiful, well-manicured homes, the driveways are empty. Who's sitting outside, taking pleasure in the lush lawn? Who's inside, enjoying the splendor? No one. This lifestyle requires homeowners to work all the time to afford the upkeep of the McManor. Living in a larger house means having to work longer hours to pay for more maintenance, cleaning, utilities, protection (insurance, food for big guard dog), not to mention a much larger mortgage. These larger houses built deep in the suburbs frequently mean an even longer commute, which can add even more stress to our overworked lives.

When considering what kind of space you want to move into, look beyond the price tag and consider the size, the amenities, and what is included. Do they furnish appliances? Maybe you'd rather supply your own or borrow a fridge or a washer. If you're renting, who pays for utilities and parking? Are laundry facilities provided? Factor these costs into your overall payment and you may come to find out that rent is lower than it seems.

Finally, never forget to evaluate and factor in the quality and condition of the building? Is it worth what you're paying to move into a place that could potentially be damaging to your health?

HAZARDOUS HOME

Creating a nontoxic building will usually be more expensive, but how much is our health worth? Developed in Germany during the 1960s, *Bau-biologie* is "building biology," or creating a healthy physical structure. This is a holistic approach to building that focuses not only on how living environments affect our health, but also on putting everything about the building in harmony with how we live. Our house can be considered our "third skin," and unhealthy living spaces can lead to long-lasting health problems.

Architect, author, and planner David Pearson compiled the Gaia House Charter, which says that houses should be designed to be in harmony with the planet, at peace with the spirit, and healthy for the body.[130] What can you do to bring your home up to Gaia code? When building or moving, consider these recommendations for the planet, spirit and health:

✓ The house is placed to make the best use of renewable resources. The sun is used for heating; Light and shade are used for cooling and privacy. The house is situated to minimize the loss of water, soil, and air. Use of daylight is maximized, the need for artificial lighting is minimized.

✓ Nonpolluting natural materials are used in construction and decorating to create safe indoor and outdoor environments.

✓ The house is integrated into the local ecosystem. Local plants are grown in an organic garden, food and yard waste are composted, and gray water is recycled.

✓ The house is sited away from power lines and electromagnetic fields.

✓ Indoor air quality allows the inhabitants to breathe comfortably and safely.

✓ As lives of the residents develop, the house continues to be in total harmony with the environment.

✓ Owners take an active responsibility in how their house is shaped into a home, creating a space that reflects their ideas and beliefs.

✓ The environment surrounding the home is quiet and peaceful.

Indoor Air

One of the most crucial components of a healthy home is the quality of the indoor air. Most of today's buildings are sealed boxes that trap the chemicals used in construction and renovation inside, where we have no choice but to breathe them. An older, drafty house—which may waste heat and electricity—may actually be better for residents because it allows the exchange of indoor and outdoor air. Replenishing air is especially important in newly constructed buildings that can contain toxic volatile organic compounds from paint fumes, new carpeting, and plastics.

Get to know your home's volatile organic compounds (VOCs), that toxic stew of substances that readily become volatile at room temperature and create unstable particles that are released into the atmosphere that you're inhaling. Chances are, if you can smell a chemical odor, it's a VOC.

Natural gas is used for gas-powered stoves, furnaces, water heaters, and fireplaces. Natural gas contains benzene, which is destroyed when the gas is burned, but when gas appliances aren't working properly, the benzene can be released into the air. Soot, formaldehyde, carbon monoxide, and nitrogen dioxide are also produced when natural gas is burned. Even in vented kitchens, levels of these toxins can become dangerously high. Prolonged exposure to natural gas can cause headaches, dizziness, and fatigue and induce chemical sensitivities.

Keep areas where natural gas is used properly ventilated and ensure that all gas appliances are working properly. Orange flames (as opposed to blue) denote gas that is not being burned correctly. Most public gas utilities will do complimentary home visits to check burners.

Paint and *paint fumes* can cause eye and respiratory irritation. All skin contact with paint should be avoided. Although latex paints stopped containing lead in 1977 and mercury in 1990, many paints still contain toxic volatile solvents like toluene, xylene, and benzene. Painters have been found to have a twenty percent higher rate of cancer than the nation's average, specifically, a forty percent higher rate of lung cancer.[131] Other effects include nausea, dizziness, headaches, disorientation, and increased violent behavior.

Hope for the Future

❑ Seek out nontoxic alternatives, which are paints based on linseed oils, milk, and water and containing chalk, lime, and natural earth and mineral pigments. (For some options see www.bioshieldpaint.com.)

❑ While painting or using solvents, always wear a facemask and thoroughly ventilate the area. Painting outside is best, but if the work requires being indoors, make sure at least two windows are open to create a cross current and use a fan to carry fumes outside. If possible, wait at least a week to move back into a newly painted room.

❑ Use only as much paint as you need to cover the surface. Take careful measurements and buy only the amount of paint you'll need. Are you sure you need more than one coat on that wall?

❑ When using a chemical varnish, first ask yourself ... *do I really need it?* Instead use shellac, which is a natural varnish.

❑ Patronize stores that give expert help and will take back unopened cans of paint.

❑ Note that while recycled latex paint does help reuse a product that would normally be thrown away, it doesn't mean that the product is any better for the environment.

❑ Look for paint products specifically designed for those with chemical or environmental sensitivities. Formaldehyde-free, "no odor," or zero VOC paints are nontoxic and formulated with a consideration of human health. Be warned, however, that "zero VOC" doesn't necessarily mean "nontoxic."

Wall to wall *carpeting* is generally not recommended for the chemically sensitive because carpet is usually backed with toxic synthetic materials that release VOCs. Carpet fibers are fashioned from a mix of plastics (often acrylic, polyester, and nylon) and treated with chemical fire retardants, insecticides, and mildewcides. In addition to vapors, carpets can also generate a static charge, trap dust and dirt, and (if the floor or room is damp) harbor mold. Even though carpets are heavily treated with insecticides, dust mites can still take up residence in them. Instead of carpets made from petroleum products, try these healthy and ecologically sound alternatives:

❑ Install natural fiber carpets. Coir (from the husk of coconut palms), jute (fibers from an Asian plant), and sisal (strong fibers from a Mexican agave species) are plant fibers that work well for indoor carpeting, area rugs, and mats.

❑ Switch to cork. Cork flooring has been used for over three thousand years. It's moisture resistant, so it won't mold or rot, and it also absorbs vibration and sound well.

❑ Don't confuse real linoleum, which is entirely made of natural ingredients and safe, with what is commonly called "linoleum," which is actually made from polyvinyl chloride (PVC) and can release VOCs. The U.S. hasn't manufactured real linoleum since the 1970s; if you want linoleum, you'll have to look to Europe, where several companies still produce it.

❑ Tile that floor. Ceramic or terracotta tile is one of the healthiest flooring choices. Tiles of slate, limestone, or sandstone will also help keep the house cool from the ground up.

❑ Leave your floors bare. Untreated wood flooring made from recycled hardwood and salvaged flooring is a healthier option than carpeting.

❑ Ask landlord not to replace the carpet before you move in. Explain that this will save his money and your health. Ask them to deep clean the carpets (and come prepared with the name a local eco-cleaner).

❑ Allow maximum ventilation before, during, and at least two to three days after installation of any flooring.

❑ Avoid latex or rubber padding.

❑ Before buying carpet, try living with a small sample for a few days. To gauge your reaction to it, sleep with it under your pillow.

❑ Live as the Asians do. Take off your street shoes before entering the house. When we come in, we may have particles of dirt, gasoline, and antifreeze on our shoes, and these particles sink into the fibers of our carpets. Anyone with pets or children (especially the kind that crawl on the floor) would be wise to leave the Buster Browns by the front door.

Formaldehyde, which is made by Borden (the kind folks who also bring us Elmer's Glue and condensed milk), has an unmistakable irritating odor that calls to mind Anatomy 101 or a funeral home. Formaldehyde is created by heating methanol, a petroleum byproduct, and mixing it with the chemical urea to form a glue used to hold wood chips and sawdust together. This mixture is used to create almost all of the familiar composition wood products (particleboard, plywood, medium density fiberboard, and veneer) that are turned into all sorts of cheap furniture.

Even though formaldehyde's toxicity has been known since the 1920s, billions of pounds of it are produced every year at a very low cost. On the one hand, without formaldehyde, sawdust and wood chips would revert to waste instead of being transformed into valuable building materials. On the other hand, unstable particles are released, or off gassed, into the atmosphere. There's no way to get rid of formaldehyde gas except to let it dissipate over time, and dissipation may take up to three years before all the fumes have been released.

Formaldehyde is an irritant to the skin, eyes, nose, and throat. It's associated with breathing difficulties, nosebleeds, and headaches. It causes flu-like symptoms, from fatigue and nausea to rashes and neurological illnesses. It acts as a sensitizer, both to itself and to other chemicals, thus lowering our threshold to allergic reactions. While some are unaffected by the gas, others can have severe reactions. According to the National Toxicology Program's *Ninth Report on Carcinogens* and the EPA, formaldehyde is "reasonably anticipated to be a human carcinogen."[132]

Uncovering formaldehyde

In addition to the hundreds of daily encounters we have with wood composition products, we also run into formaldehyde in many other common household products. According to the Formaldehyde Institute, some of these other products are:

- ✓ Air fresheners and mildew preventives
- ✓ Some paints
- ✓ Household cleaners
- ✓ Electronic equipment
- ✓ Lawn and garden equipment
- ✓ Toilet seats
- ✓ Wax and butcher wet-strength paper
- ✓ Garbage bags
- ✓ Housings for electric shavers and mixers
- ✓ Cosmetics like lipsticks, shampoos, toothpaste, and nail hardeners
- ✓ Medical products such as bandages and casts, prescription drugs, and antihistamines
- ✓ Foam pillows and cushions, foam insulation; diaper liners
- ✓ Fabrics like rayon, acrylic, and the wrinkle-resistant fabrics used to make drapes, sheets, and permanent-press clothing
- ✓ Reformulated gasoline
- ✓ Cigarette smoke
- ✓ Explosives
- ✓ When mixed with soap, formaldehyde creates foam that was once used as an insulation product.

Hope for the Future

- ❑ Whenever possible, choose unfinished solid wood products or other natural materials as substitutes for particleboard, plywood, fiberboard, and veneer. Look for natural fiberfill and fabrics such as cotton and wool.
- ❑ Buy "previously-loved" furniture or drapes that have had several years of out gassing behind them.
- ❑ Ventilate. Even in the dead of winter, open the windows for a little air circulation at least once a week.

❑ Test for formaldehyde in your home. Look online for industrial health and safety supply companies that sell monitors for under $100 that can detect ballpark levels of formaldehyde. For more accurate results, seek out a professional testing company.

❑ For more on VOCs—including radon—see the *Balancing* chapter, page 87.)

DECORATING

The majority of us who live in rented spaces have little or no say in terms of carpeting, painting, major appliances, and heating and cooling units. Regardless of whether or not we're on good terms with our landlord, they're often reluctant to let us make long-term cosmetic or structural changes to their property. Besides, even if we're allowed to make changes to a rented space, what is our incentive to do so? Many of us remain in these temporary living situations for less than five years. How do we convince building owners that ecology is a good investment?

Talk to the landlord and explain in detail why you want to make a change. If you can convince him that the change will increase the value of the property or improve the lives of all tenants, they will probably be somewhat more eager to agree to your ideas. Whether you want to repaint the walls with nontoxic paint or install a hardwood floor instead of new carpeting, explain the hazards and the physical, emotional, sociological effects of renovation materials. Convince them that renovations without attention to environmental health set us—and them—up for future problems.

The ideal situation, of course, is where the landlord thinks our ideas are great and offers to pay for everything. If (and probably when) that fails, you might consider offering to pay for the renovations yourself or barter the rent or partial reimbursement for the costs that you incur. The last resort is to offer to make the repairs without any reimbursement. You'll need to weigh the pros and cons of making these changes against the amount of time you expect to remain in that space.

I'd love to put in a skylight, solar panels, a roof garden and a tankless water heater around my apartment building, but these options are unlikely to be accepted by my landlord. Nevertheless, I continue to weigh these options and pick and choose my battles with him. This is when it's time to get creative. Here are some tips:

❑ Adapt the gutters on the roof to catch and store rain water. Use that water in the garden, on the lawn, around the trees.

❑ Remodel with reclaimed fixtures salvaged from demolition sites: windows, doors, doorknobs, handles, light switches, sinks, and bathtubs. Check the yellow pages or the classified section of the newspaper for salvage or auctions.

❑ Instead of using the clothes dryer, lower the energy bill of the entire building by hanging an outdoor clothesline (if you've got the space).

❑ Foster relationships among neighbors with a community garden.

❑ Compost organic garbage to reduce trash volume and provide homemade fertilizer for your garden.

❑ Research recycling initiatives in the community.

❑ Install solar hot water collectors and photovoltaic panels on the roof to harness solar energy and help cut energy bills.

❑ Take advantage of southern exposure to help heat your building. Keep south facing window shades open during the day in winter months to warm your home and closed during the summer months to keep it cooler. Talk about the effects of landscaping on building temperature. Removing a tree from southern exposure can increase solar heating.

❑ If you're painting the outside of the building, remember that light colors reflect and dark colors absorb heat.

❑ Insulate against the cold in winter and absorb heat in summer with a roof garden. The garden also invites local wildlife, birds, and insects to visit, absorbs rainwater, and shields and protects the roof from the sun's damaging rays. See www.greenroofs.com for more information.

Questions to ask when buying remodeling materials

✓ How far did this product have to travel?

✓ How much destruction of the environment occurred during its production?

✓ How much virgin material will be consumed in production? How much of it is non-renewable?

✓ What kinds of pollution (water, air, soil, noise) are created during production?

✓ How much waste is created during production?

✓ How durable is the product?

✓ What kind of cleaning and maintenance will it require during its life span?

✓ What are the health risks associated with using this product?

✓ How were the workers that produced this product treated?

Cheap and Easy Tips for Feeling at Home in a Rented Space

Our homes have a greater effect on our emotional and physical states than we may realize. In the 1950s, human behaviorist Abraham Maslow studied how we subconsciously react to the quality of our living spaces. He showed photographs of ugly, beautiful, and average rooms to test subjects and asked them to describe the people in the photos. Their responses were closely related to the appearance of the rooms.

When we rent, we're often at the mercy of someone else's taste and talent for home design. Decorating is one of the few ways we can exert some control over living in a space someone else owns. Decorating organically by using natural materials not only helps keep us healthy while we're at home, but it also keeps the environment safe when the décor is changed and the old stuff is thrown away. Try these tips:

❑ Start with curtains. For some reason (probably a monetary one), landlords believe that plastic vertical blinds are the classiest home decorating idea ever. A simple trick is to unclip (carefully so that you don't break the plastic top) the plastic slat, and replace it with curtain clips or a butterfly clip (the small ones sold in office supply stores). This will allow you to hang your own curtains using the previously installed hardware and re-hang the plastic verticals when you move out.

❑ Replace handles, knobs, and faceplates with elements that match your style.

❑ Add area rugs and a welcome mat to catch dirt before you track it in.

❑ Plant window boxes with flowers or herbs to keep a little nature close at hand.

❑ Get rid of furniture that doesn't fit your current lifestyle or cover outdated styles with slipcovers or tablecloths. Fix up or repaint used furniture you find at yard sales, antique malls, or flea markets. Have worn furniture reupholstered.

❑ Put up photographs that make you feel like the best days of your life are only in the next room.

❑ Use light and mirrors to make a small space seem larger.

❑ To lower a high ceiling, paint it two or three shades darker than the walls. To make a low ceiling seem higher, paint it a pale cool color.

❑ Vacuum the furniture regularly to stop dust and dirt buildup.

What exactly is "dust"?

Those big fluffy dust bunnies you find hopping around under your bed are composed of molds, bacteria, mites, pollen, human and animal hair, skin and dandruff, textile fragments, leftover food, and various decomposed materials. Sweet dreams!

❑ Let form follow function. What will you be doing in that room? Just because the last tenant used it as a dining room, that doesn't mean you have to. How about your own yoga studio, dog bedroom, or home office?

❑ Learn to make your home your sanctuary, both indoors and whatever outdoors you can claim. Mythologist Joseph Campbell said that sanctuaries are for inducing a state of mind that is not centered in the self. Thanks to sensory overload, creating a sanctuary is especially important if you live in a big city or with several other people. Make where you live a place you can relax in, a place you don't have to spend your whole life working for, a place you truly enjoy being at home in. An easy way to start is to adopt feng shui practices to keep your ch'i balanced and flowing.

Simple Feng Shui: Getting to Know Our Ch'i

Feng shui (Chinese words that mean "wind" and "water") is used to determine the correct placement and spatial arrangement of objects in your living and working surroundings. It's a philosophy of seeing the world and using *ch'i*, life force or energy, to improve our living conditions wherever we live. The Chinese have believed for over 3,000 years that to ignore the laws of feng shui is to invite bad luck and to misdirect natural energy fields.

Feng shui examines how the structure of the building and the placement of furnishings affect our ch'i. Placement can determine success or failure. We can, for example, implement feng shui "cures" to compensate for the "unlucky" placement of doors, windows, plumbing, individual rooms, or the entire house. It may seem like superstition at first, but the more we work with feng shui, the more we notice patterns emerging and elements of our lives changing.

To give your home a feng shui overhaul, I recommend picking up a comprehensive guide (see the *Additional Resources* at the end of this chapter), which will give you some basic background on the subject. Since the essential idea of feng shui is to keep ch'i moving, one of the simplest ways to do so is to *eliminate clutter*. Fortunately, we don't have to fully understand the hows and whys of feng shui to benefit from the cures. Some simple feng shui cures (tricks that are considered lucky) and energy cleansers include the following:

❑ Favorable cures include bamboo, jade plants, Chinese coins, brass bells, wind chimes, red ribbons, and candles.

❑ Water signifies life and good fortune. Fountains and other sources of running water keep ch'i flowing. Fish are also good luck.

❑ The running—flushing—water in your bathroom can cause your good luck to flow right down the drain. Keep the toilet cover down and the door closed when not in use. Place a mirror on the outside of the door.

❑ Use mirrors to reflect good things, doubling their effects. Mirrors can be also used to create more space in smaller areas. Get rid of all cracked and faded mirrors.

❑ Living objects are beneficial to energy. Stimulate activity and growth with plants. Activate energy with crystals.

❑ Get rid of dead plants, and items that are broken, damaged or don't work properly. They represent failure and steal productive energy. Remove old calendars and clocks that don't work. They keep us living in the past and stop time.

❑ Remove objects that remind of us of poisonous people or negative influences. Such objects can subconsciously affect us, both what they represent and who gave them to us.

❑ Remove barriers to entrances or paths to keep ch'i unobstructed. Is there a table you always hit your hip on as you come into the house? Is the back door difficult to open or close? Wonder why you're stuck in that dead-end job? Poles, exposed beams, and sharp corners can also cause ch'i to get trapped or reflected in the wrong direction.

❑ Reorient where you work or sleep. Can't concentrate at your desk? Too antsy in your meditation spot? Have trouble falling asleep? Move your desk or pillow or bed to face a different direction. When your life seems stuck to be in a rut, move twenty-seven objects you haven't moved in a year.

❑ Create your own type of sacred space. Find a quiet area and set up a small table. Place objects that you enjoy looking at: photographs, inspirational messages, pictures of places to escape to. You don't need to take an up entire room; instead, close off an area with Japanese shoji screens. Whatever you do, make *your space* hallowed and private. Don't allow negative thoughts or people to enter it.

❑ Bring the sounds of nature inside. Wind chimes will connect us to the breezes, but also try a bubbling fountain or play nature CDs with sounds of the forest, the ocean, or a summer night.

❑ Visualize success. Use feng shui cures to invite prosperity into your life. Think about how you want your life to be. A promotion at work? Finding your soul mate? Moving into your dream house? What do you want these successes to look like?

❑ Find more cures in a good book, but don't overdo it and clutter up your house all over again. And remember that old saying: "If it's not broke, don't fix it."

❑ Be aware of responses to color. Color arouses emotional and aesthetic reactions that affect our moods, impulses, heart rate, respiration, muscular tension, and brain wave activity. Knowing how colors affect us can help us place them where they will be most beneficial. Use your instincts. The colors we like best will probably do us the most good, whereas just putting up with colors we don't like can drain energy, no matter how healing anyone tells us they might be. When used correctly, color can help us balance the role we want a room to have in our life.

Let a Little Color In

Although color wisdom is related to feng shui, it's also a science of its own. The colors around us affect our moods, invite growth and prosperity into our lives, and alter our perceptions of the size and shape of rooms. Color therapy doesn't have to mean painting every wall. Carefully chosen accents can provide an emotional boost.

❑ In feng shui *red* means luck. It's used as an accent in many cures to stimulate good ch'i. Red also signifies anger, passion, power, strength, fire, and vitality; those who are outgoing and optimistic often choose to wear or decorate with red. It increases blood pressure, respiration rate and heart rate, causing an excited state and encouraging physical energy. Because it's stimulating and invigorating and makes rooms look smaller, red is not recommended for anxious people and should be avoided in meditation rooms or healing areas where calm and rest are desired. In an activity or exercise room, however, red would be energizing. Using red for a bedroom would not be restful, although red accents can be used to enhance sensuality. Red can be overpowering and stressful; if that's the case for you, use it in small doses.

❑ *Orange* signifies optimism, independence, fearlessness, curiosity, courage, happiness, enthusiasm, and confidence. It is considered a social color that dispels anxiety, depression, and stress disorders. It is good for use in areas of creative study and spaces for social gatherings. It also improves digestion, so painting the dining room orange can stimulate the appetite and communication; this is probably the main reason why the Brady Bunch always seemed so happy in the kitchen.

❑ *Yellow* signifies intellect, logic, imagination, tolerance, patience, loyalty, and perspective. It vitalizes, accelerates mental activity and feelings of joy, fosters introspection, and creates enlightenment, happiness, mental creativity, and inspiration. Yellow is good for use in healing rooms, creative spaces, kitchens, home offices, and rooms that are the center of activity for the house.

❑ *Green* symbolizes balance, nature, harmony, tranquility, growth, development, healing, love, peace, and hope. It's both calm and active at the same time, and its properties of balance can be used to help people who are troubled or in need of refreshment. Thanks to its restful and rejuvenating qualities, green can be good for bedrooms, bathrooms, and hospital rooms. Try varying hues to represent the many greens found in nature.

❑ *Blue* can be positive or negative and can symbolize inspiration, creativity, spirituality, truth, revelation, wisdom, serenity, loyalty, and harmony. Since Asians consider blue a secondary mourning color they seldom use it. Blue has the opposite effects of red. Blue is often chosen for bedrooms and meditation rooms because its cool energy is very calming and spiritual and helps to inspire quiet and soothing sleep. Color therapy with blue has been found to reduce blood pressure.

❑ *Purple* signifies intuition, inspiration for creativity and uniqueness, richness, power, and loyalty. It induces relaxation and sleep, lowers the body temperature, and decreases sensitivity to pain. Since it's a combination of blue and red, purple is also a stimulant. It's a rich color that inspires faith. A purple room can be overpowering, but accents or lighter shades create a healing and calming atmosphere. Those who choose purple tend to be unconventional.

❑ *White* symbolizes innocence, optimism, coolness, and simplicity. It's purifying, uplifting, and cleansing and focuses the imagination. Since white carries the qualities of all colors, white rooms can work anywhere if other colors are used as accents. Too much white, however, can create a sterile and isolating environment, something akin to a hospital operating room. Ceilings painted white will reflect light and brighten rooms. White is good for welcoming areas, like foyers and kitchens.

❑ *Black* suggests dignity and spiritual and intellectual strength, but in the West it also carries negative connotations of death and depression, whereas in Asia, white is the color of death. Black absorbs and restores energy, it restricts and protects. When combined with white, black accents are good for bathrooms.

❑ *Brown* symbolizes the earth, stability, and elegance. It is a color of balance that aids concentration, although it can also have a heavy effect. Use brown when you need to be more in control of your passions. Since brown is the natural color of many woods, it's probably already in use in many of our rooms.

Housecleaning

"Housework" seems to be a dirty word—it conjures up the 1950s housewife spending her days making the home spotless. Housework can also mean spring cleaning, fighting a year's worth of dust and clutter, losing an entire weekend to the vacuum cleaner, the dust mop, the scrub brush. We put off housework until the last minute and then we have to bribe family members to help us tackle the job, when we'd all just rather be at the beach.

In *Simple Abundance*, Sarah Ban Breathnach talks about changing our perception of "housework" to "home caring."[133] Just as we pamper our bodies and souls, we also need to care for our homes, which are an extension of our skins and souls. The walls and roof protect us from the elements, and we find security and safety behind the door. But just as we need to breathe, we also need to let our homes breathe. Open the windows, move the furniture, shake out the rugs, wash the curtains. Spring is a perfect time to schedule total "home caring" projects. The freshness of the new spring air can rejuvenate any stale room and enliven our stale life. When your home feels fusty and boring, maybe all that's needed is a thorough cleaning.

Regardless of where we live, "home caring" is essential to our well-being. Notice how your home affects your moods and emotions. A clean home can influence our energy and renew the clarity of our lives.

Gaining back some time from housework

Since hours spent doing housework have not significantly changed in fifty years, despite the introduction of labor saving devices and space age products, we should look at new ways to simplify housework and cut back on our chores.

- ✓ Laundry: Go nudist. No more clothes to wash.
- ✓ Cooking: Visit the local junior high lunch ladies for tips on cooking for 300. Freeze the leftovers, and you've got food for almost a year.
- ✓ Cleaning: Become a home economics teacher and give students "real world experience" by allowing them to use your home as a case study in cleaning.
- ✓ Gardening: Ask the lunch ladies for recipes featuring dandelion greens and acorns.
- ✓ Dusting: Learn to love dirt.
- ✓ Vacuuming: Wear shoes with sticky bottoms.
- ✓ Shopping: Ask the lunch ladies for their catalog and buy in bulk.
- ✓ Childcare: Bring back the papoose.

Eliminating the Middleman and Fixing It Up

Every time we give a task over to another person, we give up a bit of our personal power. Can you wash your own car? Clean your own apartment? Pump your own septic tank? What services do you employ that do the odd jobs you can learn to do yourself?

Don't be intimidated by professionals. They're providing a service, and if you suspect they're overcharging you or you don't understand what you're paying for, ask questions or talk to a supervisor. The marketing men have finally caught on that we want to do it ourselves. This is evidenced by the fact that do-it-yourself (DIY) has become a multi-million dollar industry, complete with big box stores and cable networks for the eager Mr./Ms. Fix-it. The knowledge we gain when we learn to do simple household repairs can not only save us money, but also encourage us to take more responsibility for our lives. When doing it on your own:

- ❏ Always shop around for price, service, and value.
- ❏ Consider starting a tool "lending library" in your building or community. Instead of buying, rent from large hardware stores such as Home Depot.
- ❏ Start an online community or bulletin board among friends to share tools and expertise.
- ❏ Get started. It's that first step that's the hardest. Once we get used to doing projects, we'll find ourselves taking on things we never would have considered trying before. (Mom started with installing her own hardwood floors, worked up to re-siding the garage last year, and then borrowed a tile saw to finish two bathrooms this year.)

❏ Ask for help. Someone out there knows how to do what we need done. Who's got a backhoe? Anyone need someone to install a shower door? If your local listserve can't help, it's time to head to the Internet for research.

❏ Stock your toolbox. These are the tools you want on your belt: hammer, pliers, adjustable wrench, screwdrivers (at least one Phillips head, one flat head, and one on the rocks—for later), tape measure, utility blade. Anything else, you can rent or borrow.

How to fix your toilet

Few household problems are as instantly annoying as a broken toilet. Before sending for the all-night plumber, get to know how your toilet works. Simple problems are often easy to fix.

Here's how the toilet works. Pushing the handle (or flush lever) lifts the flapper in the bottom of the tank. While the flapper is up, water empties into the toilet bowl, which forces the contents out and away. When the flapper goes back down, the water supply refills the tank. As the water pours in, the float ball or cup will rise. When it reaches the top, the water shuts off. If the train gets derailed at any of these steps, here are some quick fixes:

✓ Use an unfolded coat hanger as a snake (keep the hook intact) to fish out whatever might be clogging the drain.

✓ Invest a couple of bucks in a plunger. Do this *before* the toilet clogs for the first time.

✓ For continuously running toilets, sometimes the rubber stopper in the tank doesn't rest snugly over the hole. First jiggle the handle. If that stops it, the handle is too loose (and can easily be tightened by adjusting the nut that holds it in place). If that's not it, check for knots in the chain. If both those fail, shut off the water, then remove and replace the stopper.

Plants Are Furnishings, Too

Creating an indoor jungle with houseplants can provide a bit of nature that our urban lives (especially during the housebound winter months) often lack. Plants freshen the air we breathe by increasing the oxygen content. They act as humidifiers. They improve air quality by removing hazardous chemicals. And unlike the dog, they won't mock us for our karaoke and air guitar skills.

> ### *On the other hand*
> Humidity may be good for plants, but it also can cause mold and algae to grow and spread. Those with sensitivities can stick to low humidity plants, such as succulents like cacti or anything that doesn't need to be watered very often. Pet owners should also beware that certain houseplants can be dangerous (or, at the very worst, fatal) to animals. If you have pets or children, check for toxicity before integrating any plant into your home.

Gardening, which is one of America's favorite pastimes, can be both relaxing and rewarding. The Surgeon General even agrees and says that thirty minutes of daily gardening is a "moderate activity" that can reduce the risk of many chronic diseases.[134] An outdoor garden is a place where we can commune with nature. With a little labor, we can also reap what we sowed: our own fruit (or veggies).

But everything doesn't always come up roses, and those with brown thumbs can see why so many gardeners turn to chemical fertilizers and pesticides to get the job done more quickly and easily. Getting our garden to flourish organically may not be simple, but keeping chemicals out of the soil and air is worth the sacrifice of time and energy. See organic farming tips in *Eating*, page 158 and try these tips:

❑ Get some fertile friends. If you're without your own outdoor plot, seek out like-minded individuals in your neighborhood and start a community garden. Cities sometimes donate otherwise unused space for such purposes.

❑ Think about the space you have. Before you start digging, plan out on paper what you want to plant and where you want to plant it.

❑ Talk to employees at local home and garden centers. They love to talk plants and can help you to find your soil type and pH. They'll probably also recommend some good plants to start your garden.

❑ Start easy. For guaranteed success, try planting zucchini, strawberries, or beans. They're highly prolific and almost foolproof.

❑ Start small. You may just surprise yourself and find out you have a green thumb. You may wind up with more zucchinis, strawberries, or beans than you know what to do with.

❑ Keep your garden as far away from the street as possible. Be conscious that run off from the road can include antifreeze, gasoline, and other hazardous chemicals that can make their way into your new food supply.

❑ Strengthen your plants with Epsom salts, which are magnesium sulfate, a mineral plants need for a stronger root structure and to facilitate the uptake of chlorophyll. Epsom salts act like a multivitamin for plants and prevent weak stalks and yellow leaves. For specific tips, see www.epsomsaltcouncil.org.

❑ Allow a corner of your garden to "return to the wild" and be come a mini-habitat for local wildflowers, insects, and birds.

❑ Fresh supermarket herbs cost approximately the same as a packet of seeds. Dried spices can be three to four times as expensive. Their convenience doesn't begin to make up for the taste. Once you've tried your own fresh basil, you'll never go back to dried and boxed.

❑ Balance out the universe. If you cut something down, be sure to replace it somewhere. But check before starting up the chain saw. In some communities, it is illegal to remove native trees that are past a certain age.

Living simply begins at home. We can become conscious of the products we bring into our homes and eliminate those that are harmful to our physical, spiritual and emotional health. When you surround yourself with environmentally safe furnishings, when you determine the best energy flow for your living space; when you realize how much space you truly need to be happy, soon your home will become your sanctuary.

Do it today
When's the last time you opened all the windows and freshened your indoor air? Shake out the throw rugs, wash the curtains, vacuum those hard to reach corners.

ADDITIONAL RESOURCES

DECORATING
Parikh, Anoop. *Making the Most of Small Spaces.* New York: Rizzoli International Publications, 1994. Ideas for making the best of having to live in a shoebox-sized apartment. Oh, those efficient Europeans!

CREATING A HEALTHY HOME
Pearson, David. *The New Natural House Book.* New York: Simon & Schuster, 1998. Creating a healthy, harmonious, and ecologically sound home.

Tanqueray, Rebecca. *Eco Chic: Organic Living.* London: Carlton Books, 2000.

Schultz, Warren. *The Organic Suburbanite.* Emmaus, PA: Rodale Press, 2001.

CREATING YOUR SANCTUARY
Kahn, Lloyd. *Home Work: Handbuilt Shelter.* Bolinas, CA: Shelter Publishing, Inc., 2004.

Linn, Denise. *Sacred Space: Clearing and Enhancing the Energy of Your Home.* (New York: Ballantine Books) 1995.

Moran, Victoria. *Shelter for the Spirit: Create your own haven in a hectic world.* New York: Harper Perennial, 1998.

Stang, Alanna and Christopher Hawthorne. *The Green House: New Directions in Sustainable Architecture.* New York: Princeton Architectural Press, 2005.

Venolia, Carol. *Healing Environments.* Berkeley, CA: Celestial Arts, 1988.

FENG SHUI
Lazenby, Gina. *The Feng Shui House Book.* New York: Watson-Guptill, 1998.

Rossbach, Sarah. *Interior Design with Feng Shui.* New York: Arkana, 2000.

Spear, William. *Feng Shui Made Easy.* San Francisco: Harper Publishing, 1995. An introduction to the Chinese art of placement.

Too, Lillian. *The Complete Illustrated Guide To Feng Shui.* Boston: Element, 1998.

DO IT YOURSELF
Keville, Kathi. *Herbs: An Illustrated Encyclopedia.* New York: Friedman/Fairfax Publishers, 1994. A beautiful full-color guide to over 140 herbs you can grow yourself, with their cosmetic, culinary, medicinal, and other uses.

Reader's Digest Practical Problem Solver: Substitutes, shortcuts, and ingenious solutions for making life easier. Pleasantville, NY: Reader's Digest Association, 1991.

Proulx, Earl. *Yankee Magazine's Practical Problem Solver.* Yankee Books: Dublin, NH, 1998.

chapter 13

disposing

> Hi. Welcome to City Hall. By the way, you have no place to put the trash.
>
> –A note left by New York City Sanitation Commissioner for newly elected mayor David Dinkins in 1989.

In 1960, U.S. residents, businesses, and institutions produced only 2.7 pounds of trash per person per day. By 2005, it had almost doubled to 4.5 pounds of waste per person per day (with a 60 percent higher population). This is more than 254 million tons of municipal solid waste per year.[135]

What is all this trash? A quarter of America's trash comes from the forty days between Thanksgiving and New Year's Day.[136] Cat litter alone contributes to two million tons of all garbage.[137] But our trash is more than just gift-wrapping and cat poop. It is the result of our consumer culture, our insistence on convenience and our desire to have everything newer and better all the time.

If Chemistry 101 has taught us anything, it's that matter cannot be destroyed completely and that everything has to go somewhere. So what is the solution to America's disposal problem?

Going After the Big-Time Dumpers and Toxic Bad Asses

Our weekly Hefty bag at the curb is nothing, compared to the millions of tons of refuse that corporations create each year. In 1998, 200 million tons of hazardous waste was produced by American industries.[138] Hazardous waste is any substance or byproduct that (1) is toxic, poisonous, corrosive, ignitable, or chemically reactive and (2) poses a threat to plants, animals, and humans. Toxic waste can stimulate or suppress the normal metabolic functions of organs. Other types of toxic waste accumulate and create health problems that appear later in our lives long after we've taken out the trash.

Toxic waste is not just the green glowing nuclear waste we see in movies. It's the products we use every day, such as household cleansers, prescription drugs, gasoline, pesticides, and cosmetics. Under certain conditions, almost any chemical can be toxic or harmful.

Some states, believing that the more solid waste we make, the more we should pay, charge a landfill tax per ton of waste disposed. Other states offer tax credits to businesses that pollute less. But these efforts often do little to lessen the quantity of trash produced. Most corporations just pay the extra fees while others sell their tax credits to those who pollute more.

What is a Superfund site?

A Superfund site is any uncontrolled or abandoned land in the U.S. that has been contaminated by hazardous waste and poses a risk to human health and the environment. The EPA prioritizes these sites so that the most dangerous can be addressed. To check for cleanup efforts in your neck of the woods, see the National Priorities List: www.epa.gov/superfund.

Another effect of the Big Time Dumpers is what has led to a majority of factories, dumping grounds, incinerators and smoke stacks, and toxic waste Superfund sites in the U.S. being located in poor and minority communities, a practice activists call "environmental racism."

Sixty percent of all Hispanics and African-Americans live in communities with one or more toxic waste sites, leading to environmental pollution and health hazards.[139] But the reason these facilities end up in minority communities isn't always the result of outright racist attitudes. It often happens because these neighborhoods are just the easiest places to locate such facilities. In lower-income communities, resources and energy to fight dump developers are not available. Planning sessions are carefully and quietly conducted so that when the plans finally come to light it's usually too late for the people in the neighborhood to do anything to stop them. Even when it's affordable, those who might try to organize their community find the struggle for daily survival takes precedence.

Try putting that same incinerator near a middle-class (white) suburb and before it even leaves the drawing board, people begin their grassroots campaign to fight city hall and make the corporation change its mind. Every backyard is as important as the next, and everyone should have equal rights to defend against environmental racism. To fight back, we need to empower the powerless and fight for cleaner air and water standards across all economic and social boundaries.

What if all power plant and factory owners were required to live within a five-mile radius of their buildings? Would this change how they treated their waste products? Would oil executives have a different outlook if their mansions were downwind from a refinery? Would manufacturers find new solutions for waste products if that landfill were located in their backyard? Joe Public can recycle all his soda cans but how do we all fight back against those who create 85 percent of the country's waste?

Hope for the future
☐ Patronize companies that take waste generation seriously. The Ford Motor Company, for example, has redesigned their River Rouge factory to treat their wastewater using plants and organisms. Dell Computer asks customers to support their carbon neutral program.
☐ Properly recycle all computer and electronic equipment with reputable dealers. See *Working* chapter, page 217 for solutions.
☐ Fight for legislation that requires companies to retain ownership of their waste. Find out what local businesses are doing to keep their waste out of local landfills.
☐ Support organic ingredients, natural materials, and durable products, all which can lessen the burden on trash production.

The Trash Man Cometh: How We Dispose

Where does your trash go? And what does it do when it gets there? Nationwide, about 10 percent of household trash now ends up being incinerated. In theory, incineration sounds like a pretty good idea: the trash volume is greatly reduced and the heat produced by incinerators can be used to generate electricity. Unfortunately, there's a major side effect: air pollution. Incineration emits smoke that contains particulates, heavy metals, and other toxic compounds. Some materials do not completely burn. Toxic residues and sludge left over from incineration contain most of the toxic pollutants found in garbage, but now in highly concentrated form.

Some states have taken to shipping their trash off to another, less populated state. Imagine how much easier life would be if we just designated, say, Utah as America's landfill. Move all the people out, and all the trash in. But garbage trains are portable toxic waste dumps that are at risk of contaminating massive amounts of farm (and other) land and garbage barges that sail out of our coastal cities are floating toxic waste dumps that can contaminate the oceans.

The Environmental Protection Agency's "Pay as You Throw" program (also known as unit pricing or variable-rate pricing, see www.epa.gov/payt) charges residents a fee per filled garbage bag. In other PAYT communities, participants are charged by the weight of the bags. Either way, it's an adaptable rate, depending how much of the service consumers use. It creates an economic incentive to generate less waste.

Critics argue that PAYT increases illegal dumping, but proponents say it's fair because residents don't have to subsidize their neighbors' wastefulness, garbage production is reduced, and soaring waste management expenses are controlled. It also has resulted in higher recycling rates.

Others debate that there's plenty of room for all the trash we continue to create and that the status quo of waste disposal is acceptable. There may be no physical shortage of landfill space, but it's far from easy to win support of neighborhoods where we wish to dump the trash. 'Not in my backyard' is the cry heard from the suburbs regarding the placement of dumps or landfills. There seems to be no generally acceptable location for our waste. Which would you rather have across the street from your house: a park or a landfill?

Contrarians argue that there is realistically not enough space for trash dumps. There seem to be fewer landfills because a landfill typically operates for fewer than ten years. Half of all landfills in use at any given time will be closed within five years. Each day's load of trash must be covered with a six-inch layer of dirt in order to discourage odors and scavenging by birds, rodents, insects, and dumpster-diving humans. When a landfill is closed for good, it must be capped with a layer of clay or plastic, plus six feet of topsoil to seal the contents from open air. (Who's ready to move into the suburban subdivision that's on top of that?) But while cutting trash off from oxygen may prohibit disease and bacteria from spreading, it also prevents decomposition.

The crucial issue with garbage is not only how much there is and how much space the landfill takes, but *how* it decomposes. Everything will biodegrade ... eventually. Whether or not it happens within any reasonable amount of time often depends upon how the item is disposed of.

Because the term "biodegradable" has no legal definition, manufacturers and marketing men throw it around as if it actually means something. What most plastic products do is "photodegrade"—break down into smaller pieces. Eventually, yes, everything will decompose, but for most organic garbage buried in landfills, biodegradation goes on for a while and then slows almost to a stop. After ten or fifteen years, even organic garbage in the typical American landfill can still be identified. Our dumps are modern-day pyramids mummifying today's trash for tomorrow's archaeologists.

Stop & think: Place your butts here

Remember that cigarette butts are trash, too. As a society, we have ignored the fact that millions of smokers continue to fertilize our environment with chemicals. It takes that one cigarette butt between one and twelve years to biodegrade and during that time, leach trace amounts of chemicals into the ground. If even only one percent of cigarettes smoked yearly are dropped on the ground and stamped out, that's still 4.4 billion cigarette butts littering our landscapes.

It's not just because there are more Americans that there's more trash, but that in the U.S. there's more per capita consumption and resulting waste than anywhere else. Current disposal solutions make only a small ripple on the surface of the real issue. Clearly, something must be done about our overproduction of refuse.

As we've established throughout the book, there's a simple and ecological solution to almost any problem. It's time we started developing more proactive solutions. The rallying cry of environmentalists—and the only rational solution to the garbage problem in this country—is to:

Reduce.

Reuse.

Recycle.

Breakdown of Municipal Solid Waste
(Courtesy: EPA 2007)

Paper – 34.7%	Rubber, Leather & Textiles – 7.6%
Yard Trimmings – 12.8%	Wood – 5.6%
Food Scraps – 12.5%	Glass – 5.3%
Plastics – 12.1%	Other – 3.2%
Metals – 8.2%	

REDUCE

> Saving our planet will require more than recycling bottles and cans. There is something ridiculous about producing unnecessary trinkets and various other products just to keep people busy working.
>
> –Ernie Zelinski, *The Joy of Not Working*

It's simple: the best way to lessen our impact on the environment is to create fewer products that eventually will need to be thrown away. Our mission, should we choose to accept it, is *reduction*. But before we start chucking stuff into the trashbin, we should:

- ❏ Think about your trash consciousness. How often do you take out the trash? How aware of your garbage are you?

- ❏ Analyze your trash. What kind of things do you throw away?

- ❏ Write a list of everything you throw away for one week. See if you can come up with alternative solutions that would eliminate that waste.

- ❏ Make disposing less convenient. Everything the house and home gurus tell us is to make our lives *more convenient*; I say make your trash can *less convenient*. If you had to walk a half-mile to throw something away, how often you would want to make that trip?

- ❏ Reduce your can. Use a smaller receptacle to make yourself more conscious of how often you have to empty it. We can adapt Parkinson's Law to the topic of garbage: "Garbage expands so as to fill the receptacles available for its containment." The bigger the bin, the more trash.

- ❏ Place a sign over the trashcan that makes you stop and think before depositing. Come up with a good slogan or statistic. "Are you sure you want to throw that away?"

How much we toss away isn't the only issue, of course; we should also be more concerned about *how we throw stuff away*. Trash sorting makes us more conscious of what we throw away, and gives us a second chance to reuse things. Since dumpster diving and trash picking are illegal in most communities and many businesses have even taken to locking their trash up (to keep it nice and safe?), we need to prevent things from entering the bin in the first place.

Stop & think: Before you throw it away, ask...	
If it's...	*then:*
Empty...	fill it.
Broken...	fix it.
Torn...	sew it.
Dirty...	wash it.
Too big...	donate it.
Not for you...	pass it on.
Ugly...	spruce it up.
Dying...	revive it.
Dead...	compost it.
Needed...	borrow it.
Beautiful...	treasure it.

Simplifying Personal Consumption

Here's the big one. *This is how we'll save the planet.* When we're conscious of consumption, we begin to focus on how the product will be disposed of when we're finished with it. The less we think we need, the less we buy; the less we use, the less we have to get rid of. The New England Puritan ethic was "use it up, make it do, or do without." Using less also conserves time and money. For specific ideas on lowering consumption and buying for dual function and durability, see the *Budgeting* and *Shopping* chapters.

Reducing Packaging

Since so much of our trash is packaging (by volume, 33 percent[140]), changing *how* we buy things can make a significant decrease in waste production. We can learn to recognize packaging tricks and consider the environmental consequences of how items are packaged.

- Buy products packaged in recycled materials.
- Buy products that use less packaging. When ordering take-out food, ask for it to be unwrapped or without a bag. If eating at home, decline utensils and napkins. What if grocery stores asked or allowed customers to bring their own containers for deli food?
- Buy in bulk and suggest to manufacturers of your favorite products that you'd like to see larger quantities.
- Buy loose products instead of pre-packaged ones.
- Buy returnable and refillable packaging or make it reusable.
- Choose glass and paper packaging over plastic, then always recycle.
- Switch to ecologically conscious packing peanuts that are made from rice or potato starch that will dissolve in water to 5 percent of their volume for packing materials.

Junk Mail

I approach my mail box as I'm sure they must have back done in the days of the Pony Express, even though I know that when I open that little door, I will most likely find four credit card offers, a coupon book for services I couldn't imagine using, and a catalogue of clothing that makes me weep for the people who actually buy them. Yet, I am still optimistic that a card, a check, or a personal response to my 1982 letter to *The Dukes of Hazzard*'s John Schneider might be in there, too.

Junk mail is actually direct mail. When we request information on a product or service, chances are our information is being sold to another company with somewhat similar beliefs. Subscribe to one magazine, and next thing we know, there are four more offers in our mailbox. We also get on mailing lists by entering contests, filling out warranty cards, ordering something by mail, and completing forms on the Internet.

However, one man's *direct* mail is another man's *junk*. Mailing information on the greatest product in the world instantly becomes junk mail when it's sent to the wrong person. In theory, marketers should want to know if we don't want their mail so they can stop wasting money on sending us something we don't want. That's in theory…

Scary stat

It takes 150,000 pieces of direct mail to garner only 1,500 memberships to any given organization.

The Postal Service cannot refuse to deliver mail if it has proper postage. However, there's some hope to breaking the cycle of unwanted mail. It's not enough to simply throw away the information we receive. Unless we request that we be removed from a mailing list, chances are our name and address will be passed on again. And the next company will sell our info to two more companies, and so on and on and on. Tossing junk mail without complaining only encourages the practice to continue. Try these tips to reduce the burden on your mail carrier:

1. *Opt out*. Tell companies that you actively support (including your credit card company) to keep your information private. Whenever you order a product or otherwise share your address, always remember to say, "Please do *not* release, sell, rent, or trade my information." Many companies maintain a database of clients with several contact options. You can call to request that you only receive your bill and not marketing material such as promotional offers.

2. *Leave me alone*. If a phone number is listed on a piece of unsolicited mail, call and ask to be taken off their mailing list. The same goes for telemarketing calls. Hanging up on them doesn't do any good. You need to state clearly that you do not wish to be contacted again. The simple and polite phrase, "Please take me off your marketing list," leaves no room for confusion on either end of the phone line. If you have to leave a message, be specific and speak clearly and slowly.

Do not call

You're just about to sit down to a delicious home-cooked meal with your loved ones. As that first bite of organic vegetarian lasagna heads toward your mouth and little Sally starts to tell you about her field trip to the cruelty-free petting zoo, there it goes. *Ring, ring*. It never fails. A phone call during dinner.

Is it a relative calling to announce a birth in the family? Is it a warning call that a twister is heading to your town? Is it John Schneider (we still haven't gotten his letter)? Sadly, no. It's Roberta, an automated body-less voice with an important message for you. Not a sales call, mind you, but if you just wait on the line a minute, an actual human will be with you to tell you all about it. Inconvenience is the least of it. Marketing calls are frequent and telemarketers are persistent. Finally the government is doing something to help consumers fight back.

Get your name and number on the National Do Not Call List (www.donotcall.gov). This registry gives you the control over telemarketers. Once your home or cell phone number has been listed for three months, you should stop receiving calls and registration will be effective for five years. If continue to receive calls, you can also use the web site to file a complaint.

When sending the mail back to a solicitor, include a sample of the mailing label so the sender can identify how you're listed in their files. Sometimes your name will be listed several different ways. Give the company all versions of how your name has appeared printed on the mail you have received. For example: Susan Jones, Sue Jones, Susan B. Jones, SB Jones, Susan Maidenname, Susan Maidenname-Jones. Some companies include a business reply envelope, where the addressee pays the postage. Use it to mail your removal request back to them.

You can also return junk mail to the sender without additional postage, but only if the envelope is labeled ADDRESS CORRECTION REQUESTED or RETURN POSTAGE GUARANTEED. Mail it back unopened by writing "Refused, return to sender" on the envelope.

3. What to do about that *RESIDENT or OCCUPANT mail*? If a piece of mail has your address on it, the postal service is required to deliver it. To get around this, contact the company directly, by calling or writing and ask to have your address removed from their database. The Mail Preference Service maintains a national marketing list; removal requests must be in writing and will remove your name from their database. See www.dmachoice.org for the current address (it changes every so often) to mail your removal request to.

4. Say *No more cards!* To eliminate unsolicited pre-approved credit card offers, call Experian Opt-Out at (888) 567-8688. Select "remove name permanently" from the voice menu and leave the required information. This free service will send your information to the four credit reporting services, Experian, eNovus, Equifax, and Transunion, and remove your name from the mailing lists that are compiled by credit card companies.

5. *Be patient.* It can take three to six months before you notice a reduction in the amount of junk mail you receive. If you feel like you're still receiving mail from a company you have already requested to be removed from, call them again. Most companies can tell you whether or not you're still in their system.

REUSE

The word "disposable" should be a dirty word, yet in our culture it has become a convenience, a blessing, even a so-called necessity. An easy way to reduce consumption and subsequent disposal is to learn to reuse. When we pass along what we don't need or use, we keep a new product from being manufactured and an old one from being disposed of.

Reuse is already a subtle part of our lives. Think: libraries, video stores, antique malls, consignment stores, and Goodwill and the Salvation Army. In each instance, we're patronizing or donating to an organization that makes the product available to many consumers for reuse. Lately, advertisers have come up with a whole list of euphemisms for the word "used." How about that *Pre-owned* Lexus? A shopping spree at a *consignment boutique*? A *classic* car, *vintage* jeans, *resale* music, *salvaged* fixtures, a *refurbished* computer product, *gently used* books, and my personal favorite, *previously loved* lingerie. Any way we say it, it's a reuse.

The Case for Cloth Towels and Napkins

One of the easiest things to reduce by reusing is our consumption of paper products. It takes about fifteen million trees to produce the paper towels that Americans use every year and which create 556,000 tons of waste.[141] Think of all the paper towels we use in one day. Without a thought, we grab a handful. Many paper towels cannot be recycled because of wet strength additives, and plain paper towel recycling is rarely done.

One forty-five yard cloth towel roll, washed and reused ninety times, can save as many as 30,000 single fold paper towels. Only 5 percent of U.S. public restrooms use cloth towels, while in the United Kingdom, Australia, and Japan, the number is at 60 percent.[142] People seem to be afraid of germs on cloth towels in public restrooms, but as long as the towels are washed regularly, this fear is unwarranted.

330 * the simplicity connection

At home, turning old T-shirts, clothes, napkins, bath towels, or sheets into rags can eliminate our need for paper towels. Cotton and terry cloth fibers work best because they're soft and absorbent, and if we have to eventually throw them away, they don't contain any synthetic fibers to resist breaking down quickly and safely. Along the same lines, reduce paper napkin use by cutting up old sheets, curtains, or fabric samples to make reusable cloth napkins.

Bags

> "Would you like a bag for that?"
> "No, I'd rather have the tree."
> –The EarthWorks Group,
> 50 Simple Things Kids
> Can Do to Save the Earth

We're standing at the checkout, and they ask, "Paper or plastic?" And the debate begins again.

"Paper," we're about to say...

"Oh really?" the voice in our head interrupts. "Most paper bags are made from virgin paper with no recycled content because bags containing recycled content are not as strong."

"Oh," we say, "okay ... plastic?"

"Fine," says the little voice, "fine, if you want to contribute to all those toxic chemicals and use of nonrenewable petroleum that plastic production creates."

"Okay," we say, "I'm taking the paper—at least I can use it to line the cat box."

"Well," the little voice persists, "a fifteen-year-old tree only makes about 700 bags. That's about one hour's worth of bags in a large supermarket."

We're not winning this argument. "Grrr ... plastic," we finally say. "Plastic, fine. I'll take the plastic! I'll bring them back to the store next time and recycle them." (Meanwhile, the mother of four in the line behind us is plotting to follow us to our car and slash our tires...)

"Be sure to get everything out of the bag before you do," the voice advises. "Any substance left in there—a receipt, liquid, a single staple can contaminate an entire batch of recycled plastic."

We're running out of patience with the voice of our conscience. "Paper! No more! I can't take it, I want the paper!"

"Well, for every seven trucks needed to deliver paper grocery bags to the store, only one truck is needed to carry the same number of plastic grocery bags ... and paper used to make brown bags is often contaminated with pesticides."

At this point we give up and stare glassy-eyed at the bag boy, who has automatically handed us the paper-plastic double bag combo.

Which way to go? As long as we start using less, we shouldn't feel guilty about taking an occasional bag from the store. We can completely avoid this debate by bringing our own canvas or string bag or a basket to the store and maybe we'll inspire our fellow shoppers to reconsider their plastic bag loving ways.

Some grocery stores in the U.S. will refund five cents for each bag we reuse, but many European countries have implemented a charge for every bag taken out of the store. When Ireland instituted a ten-cent per-bag tax, shops reduced bag consumption by 90 percent, which translated into a billion fewer bags in the waste stream and raised funds for waste management and environmental initiatives.[143] U.S. retailers have finally caught on that they can make a little extra money, be seen as environmentally friendly, and keep the mini-billboard advertising that store bags provide by selling reusable cloth bags with the company logo on them.

There are other ways to reduce bag use. Each year, more than a billion dry cleaning bags end up in landfills.[144] If you must use dry cleaning, ask for your clothes to be returned uncovered. Ziploc bags are often durable enough to be washed and reused, though for perishable food storage (e.g., meats, produce, and cheeses) it's best to always use new bags. Small gift bags can easily be regifted or make perfect lunch sacks that last for several months' worth of reuse.

Diapers

Okay, let's do some serious talking about baby poop. Every second, Americans throw away 570 disposable diapers.[145] Some disposable diapers (which are now available for children up to four years of age) are so resistant to biodegrading that they may outlive the great-grandchild of the child who wore them.

If the plastic and pulp fiber in diaper trash weren't bad enough, these wrapped bundles hidden in landfills contain 2.8 million tons of excrement and urine. Infant feces can contain over 100 viruses, including live polio and hepatitis residues from vaccines. Instructions on packages of disposable diapers state that we should rinse the disposable in the toilet before throwing the diaper away—but how often does anyone actually do this?

The choice between disposable and cloth diapers is a personal one. Disposables are a habit of convenience, while cloth diapers require extending personal energy to maintain supply. Washing cloth diapers definitely uses more energy, but disposables create a major amount of trash. For parents who use reusable diapers, every two years spent in washable diapers protect about twenty trees and keep about a ton of solid waste from the landfill.[146] A good gift idea for new mothers is to give a gift certificate for a month or more of diaper service. This gives her the option of trying the service without obligation.

And to cut back on those 2 million tons of kitty litter in landfills? Consider switching to litter made from pine or wheat that dissolves in water and can easily biodegrade in gardens.

Creative Ideas for Reuse

Before you throw anything out, always ask yourself, "Who else can use this?" Besides the obvious ideas, consider the following suggestions:

❑ Create a reusable fax transparency that can be written on with wet erase markers then erased and reused. Efax.com offers a free service that allows you to receive faxes directly to your computer (www.efax.com/efax-free).

❑ Donate old furniture and paint to theater groups, the Salvation Army, or Goodwill. In some cases, they will come to your home and haul it away for you. Place an ad in a free paper or post at a grocery store: *free for the taking.*

❑ Melt candle stubs down to make new candles.

❑ Wash and reuse chopsticks like any other utensil.

❑ Eliminate the need for paper coffee filters by purchasing a gold plated version.

❑ Keep Christmas alive. How about instead of heading to the tree lot this year, getting a living tree? Decorate an outdoor tree that is still in the ground. Buy a smaller live tree that can be planted after the holidays. Or (egad!) shop the thrifts for plastic trees from Christmases past.

❑ Lobby for refillable bottles by calling distributors and government representatives. It takes a lot less energy to sterilize a bottle than it does to melt one down and reshape it into a new one. In Canada (Canadians are very serious about their beer), 97 percent of beer bottles are returned for refilling, and in Denmark, an amazing 99 percent of all soda and beer bottles are refilled.[147] More than 200 schools in seven states and Canada, use refillable plastic milk bottles that can be washed, refilled, and reused over 100 times before being recycled. Ask your local grocer to stock milk in returnable and refillable glass or plastic bottles.

❑ Take out your car air filter and vacuum the dirt out of it for extended use.

❑ Give eyeglasses another chance by donating old pairs at LensCrafters (see www.lenscrafters.com or call (800) 541-LENS for locations). They are sent to developing countries by Give the Gift of Sight, a joint venture between Luxottica and Lions Club International, which has been collecting and recycling eyeglasses for over seventy years. By delivering both doctors and glasses, they have helped over two million underprivileged people in the U.S. and in twenty-five developing countries.

❑ Purchase razor blades or reusable razors with disposable heads to cut back on the two billion disposable razors that are sold and disposed of each year.

Thinking outside the box: Play It Again Sports

Remember when you played hockey for a month and then broke your collarbone in a pick-up game against some ex-pros? Or how about when you bought the Rollerblades in hopes of impressing your upstairs neighbor? Or the time you thought for sure that snowboarding was going to be *your* sport and the $500 you shelled out for equipment was going to prove it?

If you came across some unused sporting goods during your journey into decluttering and organizing, Play It Again Sports is the place for you. For over twenty-five years (and in 360 franchised locations), Play It Again has bought, sold, and traded new and used sporting equipment. Resale value depends upon age, condition, and consumer demand for the gear. In addition to turning in your slightly used or outgrown equipment for cash, you can shop for gear for hobbies where you just want to get your feet wet. Sure, golf sounds like great fun, but who has $1000 to know for sure? Most people who drop off their old gear are like you. They tried it a few times, then noticed that the equipment was just collecting dust and decided to recoup some of their investment before it was too late. See: www.playitagainsports.com.

Play It Again is part of the Minneapolis-based, recycling dynasty the Winmark Corporation, which also owns Once Upon a Child (buys and sells quality used and new children's clothing, toys, furniture, and other accessories), Music Go Round (buys, sells, and trades quality used musical instruments and equipment), and Plato's Closet (buys and sells gently used brand name clothing and accessories for teens and young adults).

❑ Donate old magazines to convalescent homes, clubs, hospitals, shelters, libraries, or community centers when you're finished with them. There are also some vintage bookstores (check online) that buy back issues of magazines that are in good condition for resale to collectors.

❑ Use plastic film canisters for storing change, push pins, paper clips, buttons, safety or straight pins, and craft items (glitter, beads, confetti). Ritz Photo stores also accept them for recycling—see www.ritzcamera.com for locations.

❑ Donate old formal dresses or suits to Goodwill or to a high school where lower-income youth can wear them to the prom. If the clothes are in good and stylish condition, try selling them to a consignment shop.

❑ Think about what can be done with the old "stuff" that you're throwing away when the company where you work is changing to a new system. Sell or donate old equipment or supplies to a creative eco-design firm. Pre-schools love to use scrap materials for craft projects. Old books, letterhead paper, rubber stamps, and packing materials are good choices for creative little hands.

❑ Donate cancelled postage stamps to participating Sons of Norway lodges (www.sofn.com). Stamps are sent to Norway to the Tubfrim Society, which processes the stamps to raise money for children's health charities. They accept stamps from any country, as well as old envelopes and used phone cards. Damaged stamps are worthless, so cut the stamp off the envelope and leave approximately a half-inch margin around the stamp to keep the perforation intact.

❑ Recharge your batteries. Americans purchase three billion single-use batteries per year. When we accidentally leave the music player on, there goes another pair of batteries, straight to the landfill. Alkaline rechargeables can charged up to twenty-five times, last longer in devices than nickel cadmium (NiCads), and they hold a charge for up to five years when not in use. They are less expensive and can be disposed of like regular single-use alkaline batteries. NiCad batteries are the most common rechargeables. Each charge only lasts half as long as single-use alkalines, but they can be charged almost a thousand times. Use caution when disposing, however. See the Rechargeable Battery Recycling Corporation (www.rbrc.org) for tips.

RECYCLE

There's a reason why recycling has ended up at last place on our list. Many of us raised in the 1980s were fed a curriculum that extolled the virtues of recycling but ignored reducing and reusing. We felt empowered when we recycled anything. We had made a change in the world. We felt good when we filled the recycle bin, but now we realize we should have felt better when there wasn't anything to put in it. Recycling may prevent us from using untapped resources, but does nothing to combat the already mounting pile of garbage.

We're recycling more than ever before. The average recycling rate ranges from 27 percent to over 60 percent for some materials and has exceeded the EPA's national goal.[148] Over 12,000 communities provide recycling services to 184 million people, and the post-consumer plastics recycling industry provides jobs for more than 52,000 American workers. But in spite of all the success of recycling rates, consumption has also increased. Recycling and consumption essentially cancel each other out.

Recycling is not always the best or most cost-effective answer, but it is at least a step toward slowing the consumption of new resources. Putting out the blue recycling bucket once a week won't save the world, but doing it shows we're conscious that the earth is in trouble because of our consumption habits. Not all changes are easy or painless to implement, but with time and repetition, reducing our needs and reusing things can become just as simple as recycling.

What if products came with "design for disassembly" information, directions for how to break something down into its recyclable components? Products can be constructed to be deconstructed efficiently and completely. We need to design products so that they are able to disappear when we're finished using them; so that their resulting components will be beneficial to the environment.

Some European countries are experimenting with the concept of companies' taking lifetime custody of the materials inside their products. Eco-leasing essentially rents a product to a consumer with the idea that the manufacturer will take the product back once the consumer is done with it, turning it into a new product by breaking down its components and recycling them into something new. Imagine this: if we were done with our car, we could just return it to the dealer for BMW to properly dispose of it, creating new steel from the frame, new plastic from the bumper, and fertilizer from the seat fabric.

Recycle vs. Downcycle

In true recycling, a product (like a glass bottle) is made into the same thing over and over again. Recycling is often confused with *downcycling*, where the item (a plastic soda bottle or white paper) can only become something of lesser quality because the new material picks up part of what it contained before. The more the item is downcycled, the greater reduction in quality of the material over time. Downcycled plastic, such as when soda bottles are turned into fleece or filler, may also contain chemicals that were never originally intended to come in contact with our skin.

Upcycling is recycling a product to create something of higher quality than the original item. A European concept, upcycling adapts discarded objects for new uses in ways so that the new product exceeds the quality of the old. Defective industrial components, discarded products, and production remnants are transformed into marketable products. Unsold computers that have become obsolete while waiting for sale are returned to the manufacturer to be refurbished with new components. The art and design communities have always been very successful at upcycling by turning old LP records into CD covers, making designer handbags out of license plates, turning old trash into new treasure. Upcycler William McDonough talks about the possibility of five-year cars, where all components are recycled into newer models. This provides jobs, alleviates consumer guilt, and give style and progress free reign.[149]

On the other hand, recycling has its downside. It is not always economically feasible. The cost to sort, transport, and reprocess may outweigh any profit or environmental benefit. Contamination of recycling stores is frequent. It takes only one piece of foreign material to ruin an entire batch of recyclable glass, plastic, or paper. Self-service facilities have become rare, as professionals are hired to ensure proper sorting.

Critics also point to the fact that recycled material has to be turned into something new and that even if we save that new thing for many years, eventually it, too, will have to be disposed of. To support recycling, consumers need to create a demand for products made from recycled materials, choosing them over non-recycled goods, even if it means paying a little more.

Of the eighty billion pounds of plastic produced every year, only 5 percent is currently being recycled.[150] Recycled plastic waste has to be refortified with large amounts of virgin plastic, creating a lower quality product that cannot be recycled. Even when we drop plastic containers into the recycle bin, chances are that recyclers will send them on to the landfill because it just costs too much to reprocess them.

Those Little Recycling Numbers

Turn that plastic container over and look at the bottom. What do you see? Most likely there's a tiny little triangle, with an even tinier number in the middle of it. More important than deciding how to recycle these items is looking for these numbers when you're shopping and not purchasing products packaged in anything but numbers 1 or 2, which are in higher demand for recycling on the world market.

✓ Δ1 - Polyethylene terephthalate (PET) is a clear, tough polymer with exceptional gas and moisture barrier properties, making it ideal for use in soft drink bottles and some detergent bottles. It's commonly recycled and can be turned into a wide range of textiles, including polyesters and fiberfills (for carpets, stuffing, and clothing), and deli and bakery trays.

✓ Δ2 - High-density polyethylene (HDPE) has great protective barrier properties and is used for milk jugs and juice and water containers. HDPE makes good containers for household chemicals and detergents. It is commonly recycled into plastic fencing, garden furniture, agricultural pipe, bags, motor oil bottles, decking and marine pilings, toys, bottles for laundry products, milk crates, and recycling bins.

The higher numbers label theoretically recyclable products that may contain toxic components. Avoid purchasing products with the following numbers:

✓ Δ3 – Polyvinyl chloride (PVC) is clear, clings well, and resists puncturing. Uses include garden hoses, plastic flooring, credit cards, shower curtains, toys (for children and pets), vinyl house siding, and some shampoo bottles. PVC is often blamed for toxic off gassing and for leaching endocrine disruptor compounds into the environment so always avoid purchasing. See the *Balancing* chapter, page 111 for more dangers of PVC.

✓   Δ4 - Low-density polyethylene (LDPE) is clear and flexible. Uses include plastic sandwich bags, garbage bags, coating for milk cartons, and plastic grocery bags (which are recycled at many grocery stores). Recycled LDPE becomes new bags, shrink film, and compost bins.

✓   Δ5 – Polypropylene (PP) is a very strong plastic that works well for caps and lids that have to hold tightly on threaded openings, like plastic lids, bottle caps, straws, and some food containers. PP is generally not recyclable, but when it is recycled, it's used in automobile parts, carpets, battery casings, textiles, industrial fibers, and film used for packaging products like candy.

✓   Δ6 – Polystyrene Styrofoam (PS) is the new and improved Styrofoam (the old kind was banned because of CFCs that caused ozone depletion). It has good insulation properties for coffee cups, meat trays, egg cartons, and packing materials and can be recycled into building insulation and office accessories.

✓   Δ7 – This is the "other" category (mixed plastics) and is several types of plastic mixed together. It's commonly used for camping water bottles and other food containers. Recycling is not possible.

There are many other simple ways to use less plastic. If you can find a product in another type of container, always choose that instead. Suggest to restaurants that use plastic utensils to recycle them or to switch to silverware. Look for natural alternatives for one-time use plastic products.

Thinking outside the box: the Durabook

You've had a long day at the eco-widget factory. A nice relaxing bath, a glass of organic wine, and a good book will make all the tension go away. Ploink! Whoops, there goes that mass-market paperback, right into your bubbles.

Melcher Media has created Durabook (patent pending), a paperless book not made from any wood pulp or cotton fiber, but from a mixture of stretched polypropylene resin and inorganic fillers. This "paper" doesn't require bleaching with chlorine, and the inks are nontoxic and can be rinsed off with a polymer to be harnessed for reuse. It's waterproof, extremely durable (the pages are virtually impossible to tear), and if necessary, recyclable.

Durabooks currently in print include *The Amazing Book of Paper Boats*, a collection of cut-out-and-fold boats made of the waterproof paper so they actually float; National Geographic's *The American Road Atlas* and trip planner; and *Cradle to Cradle*, a guide to "remaking the way we make things" by eco-designers William McDonough and Michael Braungart, who are currently working on branding cradle-to-cradle products like Durabook with an upcycling certification logo.

Glass is the easiest and most practical material to recycle because it can't be burned in incinerators and, if left intact, won't break down. Of the twenty billion pounds of glass that enter the municipal solid waste stream every year, 90 percent are bottles and jars that could easily be recycled.[151] When recycling, don't include kitchenware, mirrors, light bulbs, ceramics, windows, or any other glass that has been coated with anything that might ruin an entire batch of recycled glass.

Aluminum is a non-renewable source that is very simple to recycle. Aluminum foil can often be reused (if it hasn't come in contact with meat or cheese), but it should be recycled rather than sent to the landfill. Each recycled aluminum can saves enough energy to run a television for three hours. Currently, only twelve states have beverage deposit laws, yet these states recycle more bottles and cans than the other thirty-eight combined, a fact that proves the success of such a simple incentive.

The Wolverine State

Michigan, which has had a 10¢ aluminum can deposit since 1978, has always had the highest rate in the nation. But don't even think about trying to be a hardcore recycler like *Seinfeld's* Kramer and Newman, filling a truck with empties and heading cross-country. Bringing bottles and cans into Michigan to get that dime is illegal, and machines read barcodes to make sure the product was purchased in the state. Penalties can be a fine of up to $500 or ninety-three days in jail.

We think that because *paper* is made from natural components, it will easily break down and recycle into usable organic matter. Not true. Most white paper is heavily bleached with chlorine, causing it to release dioxins, toxic chemicals, and emissions that threaten air quality during manufacture. When paper is disposed in landfills, these toxins are buried and mummified with it.

In America, we love paper to the tune of using 31 percent of the world's paper products: approximately 31.5 million tons of printing and writing paper each year, an amount requiring over 535 million trees and more than twelve billion gallons of oil to produce.[152] Our switch to electronics has done little to reduce this consumption. But we can always recycle more. See *Working* page 215 for paper recycling tips.

Thinking outside the box: EarthShell

Back at the Davis homestead in Massachusetts, almost every ubiquitous fast-food joint is within a 5-mile radius. Despite the 97.7 inches of snow we got one winter, it's not unusual to see fast food wrappers along the side of the road come spring. When we're finished eating, what if—instead of feeling guilty for throwing a fast food wrapper onto the ground—we could trust that it would quickly decompose and provide nitrogen to the soil? Alas, that's just a crazy pipe dream of a tree-huggin' hippie like myself. But ... what if?

EarthShell plates and bowls make that pipe dream a reality. The technology combines simple, abundant, renewable materials, such as limestone and potato starch, into a plastic-like material that within sixty to ninety days is 100 percent biodegradable.

Nature has always been able to provide its own packaging (peels, skins, shells), but our insistence on transporting food and saving it for later has necessitated more sturdy and secure forms of packaging. EarthShell's answer is a paper and plastic alternative that is high quality and price-competitive. They make hinged-lid sandwich and salad containers and microwavable plates and bowls. Products are hot and cold insulating, easy to ship, stack, store, and use. They resist cutting, staining, and grease; they're flexible, but strong and tear-resistant. Currently, the products are available in over 10,000 stores. See www.earthshellnow.com.

In earlier centuries, the *textile* scrap business was sustainable and lucrative. Ragmen would collect fabric remnants and sell them to paper and textile manufacturers for recycling. Although the introduction of blended fabrics essentially killed the rag trade, creative designers always see potential in fabric waste. Wool and 100 percent polyester fabrics can still be chopped up and dyed into new fabrics. Other companies recycle post-industrial denim to create an insulation that can be installed by the consumer with no protective gear. Still others chop up used fibers for padding filler used in car seats or cushions. Patagonia has started "Common Threads" a program that accepts any Polartec garment for recycling.

Check out your local recycling center to see what other items they accept for recycling. To my surprise, in addition to aluminum, paper, and glass, I learned that my local center accepts tennis shoes, videocassettes, eyeglasses, and various kinds of electronic equipment.

Food Waste: The Case for Composting

Over 25 percent of the garbage we throw away is actually compostable waste. This is not only yard waste like weeds, but also the 35,000 tons of food the U.S. throws away every day. When this food is mixed in with other garbage, it rots, causing bacteria to grow and spread. Organic waste in landfills releases methane gas, which can deplete the ozone layer.

Saving food from the landfill is simple. All we have to do is plan our meals before we go shopping, be conscious of how much food we buy, keep it fresh, and use it before it goes bad. But even so, there will be some remnants we just can't eat—coffee grounds, apple cores, and the pasta that fell on the floor. To eliminate our food waste, we can look at several options:

1. Stop eating (not recommended)
2. Dry all eggshells and lemon rinds and make them into potpourri for Christmas gifts (also not recommended)
3. Start our own compost box or pile (hmmm... option three, you intrigue me...).

Compost is the result of decomposition of organic matter. It is one of the most natural ways to break down organic garbage and if done properly, can be done anywhere to reduce waste. The resulting mixture can be used to fertilize or condition plants.

Keep your garbage out of my dump!

Those who compost create 75 percent less trash than those who don't.[153] Considering that statistic, separating our garbage and composting on a larger scale must become routine. While we may have to wait for mandatory composting to become law, we can start today and take composting into our own hands, so to speak. Find a local composting site by calling your local parks or recycling department or by checking the government listings in your phone book for "composting." If you'd rather keep all that rich black gold compost for yourself, read on.

Stop & think

What if the compost man came around each week like the trash man or the recycling truck to pick up our organic garbage?

The benefits of composting far outweigh the energy expended in maintaining a bin. Composting helps keep organic matter out of the municipal solid waste stream, prevents the production of greenhouse gases, and reduces air pollution caused by incineration.

Humus (the byproduct of composting) and castings (the byproduct of vermiculture, or worm composting) also keep soil in good health by returning essential nutrients and beneficial organisms to the ground. Compost fed to plants improves the texture and water retention capability of the soil, helping prevent erosion and regulate temperature. Composting thus reduces the use of store-bought chemical fertilizers.

Indoor vs. Outdoor? Pile vs. Bin?

Before we decide to leap into composting, we have to make some decisions. Where do we want our pile or bin to be located? How do we want to create our compost? First, measure how much waste you make before choosing the system that is best for you. Plan on one square foot of surface for each pound of garbage per week. Your worm to garbage ratio should be 2:1 (that is, one pound of worms per each half pound of garbage).

Backyard compost piles are as easy as it gets, if you've got the space. Build a pile by adding organic material to it. Turn your outdoor pile several times during the first few months to distribute the organisms.

Most people opt for outdoor composting, but for those perched in the high rise, there are indoor options, too. Indoor vermiculture bins are popular with apartment composters. These bins can be fairly small, there's limited maintenance, and when the bins are cared for properly, odors are not a factor. You can buy a commercial bin or find books to help you design your own bin.

A simple formula for composting:

PILE or BIN

+

BEDDING

+

ACTIVATOR (MICROBES and/or WORMS)

+

FOOD (COMPOSTING MATERIAL)

+

MAINTENANCE

=

COMPOST/HUMUS

Pile or Bin

A pile is pretty straightforward. It's basically just … a pile. Find an out-of-the-way location and just plop down your stuff. If there are animal scavengers in your neighborhood, you need a secure location for your pile. (If you're not sure, just wait. You'll know soon enough…)

Holding bins for vermiculture can be barrels, tumblers, or plastic rectangular buckets. They all work essentially the same way: they allow air in, but the worms do all the work. Usually, they involve trays or shelves where worms can move freely to have easy access to fresh compostable material. Two suppliers of commercial vermiculture bins are: Worm-topia and Can-o-Worms, but visit my friends at Worm's Way (www.wormsway.com) for more options.

Bedding

The bedding in your bin or pile is the base layer, which will hold moisture and allow for ventilation. For pile bedding, start with a layer of material like broken-up twigs, tree or bush prunings, dry leaves, and torn newspaper on the bottom of the heap to allow air to flow. Add a thin layer of rich soil or finished compost from a previous heap and then pour in enough water to make everything moist.

Bin bedding can be peat moss, corrugated cardboard, wood chips, coconut fiber (also called coir), shredded newsprint, or plain white paper. (Avoid colored papers because of the inks.) Processed compost can also be used as a bedding material for a worm bin.

Activators

Your activator is what will get the motor running (so to speak) and your compost cooking. Once the activator is added, composting begins. For an outdoor compost pile, activators cause heat to build up. The mixture cooks and bacteria begin to grow and break down materials. To get microbes and heat started, choose one or two of the following activators:

- ✓ Animal manure
- ✓ Comfrey
- ✓ Nettles
- ✓ Seaweed
- ✓ Grass clippings
- ✓ Compost accelerator powder
- ✓ Soil or compost from a previous heap
- ✓ Shredded newspaper
- ✓ Wood ash, dolomite, or lime.

To get your squirm of worms wriggling, use red wigglers or African night crawlers, which are often available at fishing supply stores, bait shops, and some home and garden centers. (You may have to mail order your worms.) Do not use common earthworms, which will die in a worm bin.

What to Compost

The secret to healthy composting is the ratio of carbon and nitrogen materials that we add to it. According to *The Urban/Suburban Composter*, a ratio of between 20:1 to 30:1 (carbon to nitrogen) is ideal. "Browns" are materials that are high in carbon, whereas "greens" are high in nitrogen.

NITRO-GREENS	CARBO-BROWNS
Rinds, skins and peels (of any vegetable or fruit) or any other vegetable waste	Dead yard waste and flowers
Nuts and their shells	Wood ashes
Clipped hair (avoid chemically treated hair)	Brown paper bags
Coffee grounds and filter (Starbucks locations offer packaged grinds for customers to take home for composting, free of charge)	Old wool and cotton clothing (No chemically treated fabrics) (*Composting only*)
Tea bags	Newsprint (without color photos)
Manure (*Composting only*)	Sawdust (but no chemically treated wood)
Pulverized eggshells (will neutralize acidic materials)	Rice, grains, pasta, bread (*Worms only*)
Plate scrapings	
Recently cut grass and yard waste (avoid bringing older clippings indoors because of microscopic organisms) (*Composting only*)	
Seaweed	

Don't add too much of one type of composting material at once and chop all material into easier-to-digest or inch-sized pieces. A tip to speed up the process is to use an old blender and puree your scraps with a compostable liquid into milkshake form. Cover all waste added to a worm bin with a layer of newspaper to prevent odors, mold, and insects.

What Not to Compost

As important as what we put in our compost piles, it bears repeating what not to put in them:

✓ Meat, fish, or dairy products that will smell and attract pests. (I have heard of people composting meat in bins and piles, but the thought of an animal knocking my bin over isn't one I want to contemplate.)

✓ Bones. Bone meal is okay, if for some reason you have that, but whole bones take a very long time to decompose.

✓ Processed foods. The preservatives and other chemicals added to processed food are what keep that box of cookies tasting fresh months after production. It's best to keep chemicals out of your bin.

✓ Pet feces and litter, which possibly contain antibiotics and pathogens.

✓ Diseased plants and weeds that have gone to seed. Compost helps plants grow naturally, and it's not unusual to find something growing in your bin. Best not to give it a head start.

✓ Coal or charcoal ashes and bleached or colored papers that contain chemicals.

✓ Any plywood or particleboard made from formaldehyde resins.

✓ Any yard waste or vegetable waste that has been chemically treated with pesticides. Putting these materials in your compost pile continues a cycle of adding chemicals back into the soil.

✓ Anything that is not easily biodegradable.

✓ Citrus rinds and tomatoes can be composted, but they take a longer time to decompose. If you don't mind waiting, go for it, but be warned that they mold easily so bury them deep.

If you don't visit the compost pile every day, store compostable scraps in labeled containers in the refrigerator or freezer to prevent bacterial outbreaks, insects, or mold. Two days is about the maximum amount of time that food scraps can be at room temperature before mold starts to grow and the scraps become toxic.

Maintaining Your Pile or Bin

Once you're cooking, you can pretty much let the worms and microorganisms do their job on their own, though you should check on them every once in a while. Here are some maintenance tips:

❑ Allow compost piles and bins to *breathe*. More air means less smell. The most important part of a compost pile is to mix it up. Turn your pile once a week (but not more than that) to aerate and speed up decomposition. Don't worry about turning your worms, though; as long as they're alive, they'll do their own turning.

❑ Keep your bin moist (but not too wet) and filter water for impurities before adding. For a worm bin, you can remoisturize the bin with worm tea, the drained liquid from the bin. To fix moisture problems, add dry bedding to the top layer to absorb excess liquid. Zeolite can be added for moisture and odor control.

❑ Keep acidity in the median range of pH 5-9. pH-testing kits are available at home and garden centers. Adjust alkalinity by varying carbon and nitrogen additives.

❑ Keep it from getting smelly. A compost pile will smell bad only if something is wrong. An ammonia smell reveals that there's too much nitrogen in the pile; you'll want to add more carbon-based material to compensate.

❑ Regulate the temperature. Worms like dark warmer areas, though not too hot. Don't leave them outside in temperatures under 40 °F or over 80 °F. For your compost pile, however, the hotter the better.

❑ Add minerals and control insects. Add a cup of rock dust to the bin once a year. It not only adds minerals to the vermicompost but also helps to control flies.

❑ Prevent pests. The only insects we need to worry about in the worm bin are centipedes, which will eat your worms. Flies and larva won't affect the composting process and are harmless to worms. If ants, cockroaches, or rodents make your pile their home, make sure you're thoroughly covering all waste with a layer of newspaper or soil.

Hummus vs. Humus

Hummus: (Hum-es) Chickpeas, garlic, and lemon juice.

Humus: (Hyoo-mus) Dark rich decomposed organic matter. While it may look like crumbled chocolate cake, you shouldn't eat it.

How to Use Humus or Castings

When you can no longer identify any of the original waste materials you put in the pile, it's time to put your humus or castings to work. Humus should have a fairly uniform dark brown color and the earthlike smell of the floor of a deep forest. If it still smells moldy or rotten, it's not finished and probably needs more air. Its consistency will be crumbly and loose, not clumpy.

When planting your garden, don't use compost as a pure mixture. Take the decomposed mixture and blend it with other soils and use it selectively and sparingly as a treat. Use vermicompost as a top dressing for house plants every forty-five to sixty days.

Magical mushrooms

Another natural recycler is the mushroom network (such as shiitake) that easily decomposes organic matter. Some of these are strong enough to break down petroleum products, pesticides, and herbicides. Some networks have even been used to help clean up toxic waste sites. Mushrooms can inoculate gardens and yards with mycorrhizae, a fungus that enters into beneficial relationships with plant roots. Mushrooms also help trees absorb nutrients while protecting them from drought and disease.

Since we never truly "consume"—we merely borrow—simplifying our disposing habits is critical. If we remember the life cycle of products before purchasing, we can anticipate disposal problems when shopping for all types of products. When we begin to reevaluate how we dispose of materials we use at home, we can implement similar actions in our workplaces; if we all take small steps, they can add up to remarkable change.

Do it today

Leave everything a little neater than you found it. How beautiful would the world be if we all did this small thing?

ADDITIONAL RESOURCES
REDUCING
Lilienfeld, Robert and William Rathje. *Use Less Stuff*. New York: Fawcett Books, 1998. "Smart consumer strategies to reduce consumption, conserve resources, save money, simplify your life."

REUSING
Goldbeck, Nikki and David. *Choose to Reuse*. Woodstock, NY: Ceres Press, 1995. "An Encyclopedia of Services, Businesses, Tools and Charitable Programs That Facilitate Reuse."

RECYCLING

The Grass Roots Recycling Network (www.grrn.org) is a voice for those who want to waste less and go beyond just recycling soup cans. They are advocates for corporate, governmental and individual responsibility for waste. They use grassroots activism to initiate change, and professional expertise to follow through.

Earth 911 (www.earth911.org) is a web site that allows us to search by location for local recycling initiatives, hazardous waste drop-off locations, and sites to which to send that old computer, battery, cell phone, or TV.

The American Plastics Council's web site (www.plasticsresource.com) provides a directory of products made from recycled plastic.

COMPOSTING

Applehof, Mary. *Worms Eat My Garbage.* Kalamazoo, MI: Flower Press, 1997. Everything we need to know about vermiculture from the late great "Worm Lady." (www.wormwoman.com)

Cullen, Mark and Lorraine Johnson. *The Urban/Suburban Composter.* New York: St. Martin's Press: 1992. Composting tips for wherever you live. Gives advice on how to pick the right bin or pile for your home and how to troubleshoot common composting problems.

The Los Angeles Department of Water and Power's web site (www.smartgardening.com) provides good composting information for all types of bins and piles.

How to Compost.org (www.howtocompost.org) is a comprehensive resource for composting.

remembering

> Those who forget history are condemned to repeat it.
>
> –George Santayana

We have emptied our cluttered closets, examined our spending habits, and discovered how to live more organically. But after we've done all this ... now what are we supposed to do with all this information?

First and foremost, we must always remember how hard we've just worked to simplify our lives. If we forget how much we've done to recover from presumptuous consumption, we are more likely to fall back into our old, familiar patterns. We must revisit and reevaluate our simplicity systems to make sure they're always working. And know that it's easier to stay simplified than it is to get simplified.

Second, we must pass on what we've learned. We need to teach others how to simplify their lives. Environmental education should be taught in every school, right beside history and math. Received wisdom teaches us that progress is good and necessary if we are to solve the problems that our culture faces, but very little of our schooling has given us the practical wisdom to face and overcome environmental and technological challenges. We must make a special effort to keep the media and big business accountable for environmental concepts. Instead of gathering for one Earth Day every year, we must realize every day, on a daily basis, that the earth is in crisis.

Third, we should never stop learning what true simplicity is (it's not just a fad or a magazine that sells expensive products). We should never stop expanding our view of simplicity. Technology continues to evolve, and while not all advancements are positive, some will in fact make life simpler and more sustainable. Simplicity looks different for everyone, but the concepts are fundamental foundations for a simple life.

Fourth, we must always continue to explore different paths. No one path is the best or only way, nor is there one all-purpose solution for every problem. What works wonderfully for you may not work for someone you know. Each of us needs to make a personal decision which path is right for us. And always keep one eye on the guy mixing the Kool-Aid.

Some teachings have gotten corrupted along the way. Searching for the truth, we follow a path, and it's easy to find only the simplistic answers we want to hear. They may not, however, be the right answers. We can also learn a lot from the paths that don't work for us.

On the other hand: try the path sampler…You don't have to be a Buddhist to meditate, Chinese to try Tai Chi, or Lee Trevino to try magnet therapy. You don't have to become one of "those people" (whatever they look like in your mind) to follow a certain path.

Labels often make us fear a path. Fearing that the task is too big, we do nothing at all. Instead, take a little from each path to create a system that feels right to you.

Be aware of how your choice might affect your partner, your relatives, and your close friends. Changing your life for the better may create some tension between you and your loved ones. They're used to your old ways, and change is often frightening to people who don't understand why we have to do it.

Let's worry about our own lifestyle choices, and let others work out their issues in their own time. If a change you make leads to something so severe as the other person leaving your life that may be a sign that larger problems were lying beneath the surface. Accept their opinion, but make that difference in opinion an opportunity for reflection rather than a sign to abandon your path. Rather than fighting about it, remember that (just like you) they also have a path they must travel. Staying true to yourself is the only true path to enlightenment.

Keeping Our Beliefs Intact

> I will not let anyone walk through my
> mind with their dirty feet.
>
> –Mahatma Gandhi

Our life-long journey of simplicity can be like wandering into the dark and scary woods. There are certain times when it might seem easier to abandon what we believe:
- ✓ When we're unemployed and worried about paying bills
- ✓ When we're in a rush
- ✓ When there's an emergency in our life
- ✓ When we experience a conflict of interest (one thing we believe in contradicts our belief in something else.)
- ✓ When we succumb to peer pressure and the "cute boy syndrome" ("If I want them to like me, I better do it, too!")
- ✓ During the holidays or on vacation
- ✓ Any time we're distracted.

It is at these times that we must especially be aware of staying true to our conscience. Recognize dangerous times and avoid them if you can. Remember the good of what you have accomplished. Stay strong in your convictions.

It is time to put aside our petty differences and work together to solve the truly important problems of the world. When emergency situations arise (9/11, the Asian tsunami at the end of 2004, the monster hurricane season of 2005), we tend to come together. We change how we treat each other and how we allocate our time and resources. But when these crises fade off the front pages and out of the nightly news, some habits of the old "me and only me" mindset return. Mom was ahead of her time when she used to tell you and your little brother, "Be nice to one another". The Golden Rule still applies in any situation.

The "simple life" is not heiresses gallivanting across the country without their credit cards in hand. Nor is practicing simplicity and sustainability an automatic quick fix. Finding the simple life must be an individual, lifelong pursuit. It can change your life. It can be immensely rewarding. When we seek simplicity in our daily lives, we can prioritize our values and organize our goals. Start thinking about the future in new ways—systemically, holistically, sustainably.

People are constantly looking for ways to complete themselves. We all want to satisfy the desires of a consumer culture while maintaining the comfort of our civilized society. Recycling aluminum cans, walking to work, and eating organic apples alone will not save the world, but simplifying our actions and refocusing our thinking about consumption and production and making sustainable choices just might. A more peaceful life awaits us all when we find *The Simplicity Connection*.

acknowledgements

This book has been a labor of love for a very long time and it could not have been possible without the following people:

To my editor Barbara Ardinger, thank you for helping me keep my thoughts coherent.

To the tireless Carol Holst, for her friendship and amazing dedication to making simplicity a household name.

To my emotional support team: Annemarie Crivelli, Julia Quigley, Chad Murphy, and Brian Hodges for their love and encouragement.

And of course to mom for all that creativity.

index

notes

[1] Duane Elgin, *Voluntary Simplicity: Toward a Way of Life That Is Outwardly Simple, Inwardly Rich* (New York: Morrow, 1981).

[2] Elgin, 31.

[3] Janice Castro, "The Simple Life," *TIME Magazine* 8 April 1991: 58-63.

[4] Arnie Cooper, "Peril and Promise: Duane Elgin on Simplicity and Humanity's Future," *The Sun Magazine* (Aug. 2002) 4 ff.

[5] Jon Kabat-Zinn, *Wherever You Go, There You Are* (New York: Hyperion, 1994), 130.

[6] Paul Roland, *How to Meditate* (Berkeley, CA: Ulysses Press, 2000).

[7] Thich Nhat Hanh and Robert Ellsberg, ed., *Thich Nhat Hanh: Essential Writings (Modern Spiritual Masters Series)* (Maryknoll, NY: Orbis Books, 2001), 19-20.

[8] Rebecca Tanqueray, *Eco Chic: Organic Living* (London: Carlton Books, 2000), 6.

[9] Stephen R. Kellert and Edward O. Wilson, eds., *The Biophilia Hypothesis* (Washington, D.C.: Island Press, 1993), 31.

[10] www.ecopsychology.org.

[11] Joseph Murphy, *Secrets of the I Ching* (Paramus, NJ: Reward Books, 2000), 24.

[12] John De Graaf, et al., *Affluenza: The All-Consuming Epidemic* (San Francisco: Berrett-Koehler Publishers, 2001), 2.

[13] www.simplelivingamerica.org.

[14] Tom Jordan, *Pre: The Story of America's Greatest Running Legend, Steve Prefontaine* (Emmaus, PA: Rodale Press, 1997), 159.

[15] Sarah Ban Breathnach, *Something More: Excavating Your Authentic Self* (New York: Warner Books, 1998), 344.

[16] Ralph Keyes, *Timelock* (New York: Harper Collins, 1991), 111.

[17] Jeffery Kottler, Ph.D., *Private Moments, Secret Selves* (Los Angeles: Jeremy P. Tarcher, Inc, 1990), 18.

[18] Wanda Urbanska and Frank Levering, *Simple Living: One Couple's Search for a Better Life* (New York: Viking Penguin, 1992), 246.

[19] Friends of Peace Pilgrim, *Peace Pilgrim: Her Life and Work in Her Own Words, Compiled by Some of Her Friends* (Santa Fe: Ocean Tree Books, 1991). See also www.peacepilgrim.org.

[20] Carol Venolia, *Healing Environments* (Berkeley: Celestial Arts, 1988), 89.

[21] Steven Halpern, *Sound Health* (San Francisco: Harper & Row, 1985), 9.

[22] Don Campbell, *The Mozart Effect: Tapping the Power of Music to Heal the Body, Strengthen the Mind and Unlock the Creative Spirit* (New York: HarperCollins, 1997), 1, 22, 130.

[23] Paul L. Wachtel, *The Poverty of Affluence: A Psychological Portrait of the American Way of Life* (Gabriola Island, B.C.: New Society, 1983), 71.

[24] Robert J. Hastings, *A Penny's Worth of Minced Ham, Another Look at the Great Depression* (Carbondale, IL: Southern Illinois University Press, 1986), 90-91.

[25] Ernie Zelinski, *The Joy of Not Working* (Berkeley, CA: Ten Speed Press, 1997), 36.

[26] Creditcards.com, "Credit Card Industry Facts and Personal Debt Statistics" 13 March, 2007, http://www.creditcards.com/credit-card-industry-facts-and-personal-debt-statistics.php.

[27] E.F. Schumacher, *Small is Beautiful: Economics as if People Mattered, (25 Years Later ... with commentaries)* (Point Roberts, WA: Hartley & Marks, 1999), 164.

[28] Greenhaven Press, 11 May, 2005, http://www.galegroup.com/greenhaven/about.htm.

[29] Susannah Blake Goodman, *Girls Just Want to Have Funds: How to Spruce Up Your Financial Life and Invest Like a Pro* (New York: Hyperion, 2000), 45.

[30] Oxfam America, "Valentine's Gold Jewelry Sales Generate 34 Million Tons of Mine Waste" 11 February, 2005, http://www.oxfamamerica.org/newsandpublications/press_releases/press_release.2005-02-11.6113995793.

[31] "NOAA Reports 2005 Global Temperature Similar To 1998 Record Warm Year", 30 January, 2006, http://www.publicaffairs.noaa.gov/releases2006/jan06/noaa06-013.html.

[32] Natural Resources Defense Council, "Global Warming and Sudden Climate Change", 10 March, 2004, http://www.nrdc.org/media/pressreleases/040310.asp.

[33] Thomas Homer Dixon, *The Ingenuity Gap* (Toronto: Alfred A. Knopf, 2000), 178.

[34] Hal Kane, *Triumph of the Mundane* (Washington, D.C., Island Press, 2001), 41.

[35] Bill Bryson, *A Short History of Nearly Everything* (New York: Broadway Books, 2003), 159.

[36] Asthma and Allergy Foundation of America, New England Chapter, "Facts and Figures", 15 May 2005, http://www.asthmaandallergies.org/Facts.html.

[37] Susanne Antonetta, *Body Toxic: An Environmental Memoir* (Washington, D.C.: Counterpoint, 2001), 240.

[38] Devra Davis, *When Smoke Ran Like Water* (New York: Basic Books, 2002), 56.

[39] Nikki Goldbeck and David Goldbeck, *Choose to Reuse* (Woodstock, NY: Ceres Press, 1995), 7.

[40] Dr. B.C. Wolverton, *How to Grow Fresh Air: 50 Houseplants That Purify Your Home or Office* (New York: Penguin Books, 1996).

[41] Maude Barlow and Tony Clarke, *Blue Gold* (New York: The New Press, 2002), 142-3.

[42] "Protecting International Waters Sustaining Livelihoods Experiences," GEF-UNDP INTERNATIONAL WATERS PROJECTS (August 2002), 4.

[43] Douglas Frantz, "The EPA Asked to Crack Down on Discharges of Cruise Ships," *American* on-line, March 20, 2000.

[44] "Estimated Use of Water in the United States in 2000," 31 March, 2005, http://water.usgs.gov/pubs/circ/2004/circ1268/htdocs/text-pt.html.

[45] Barlow, 5.

[46] David Pearson, *The New Natural House Book* (New York: Simon & Schuster, 1998), 109.

[47] David Steinman and R. Michael Wisner, *Living Healthy in a Toxic World* (New York: Perigree Books, 1996), 29.

[48] Denis Hayes, *The Official Earth Day Guide to Planet Repair* (Washington, D.C.: Island Press, 2000), 153.

[49] Theo Colborn, et al., *Our Stolen Future: Are We Threatening Our Fertility, Intelligence, and Survival? A Scientific Detective Story* (New York: Dutton Books, 1996), 89-92.

[50] "Agency for Toxic Substances and Disease Registry (ATSDR) Announces the Availability of the Updated Toxicological Profile for Mercury," 19 April, 1999, http://www.atsdr.cdc.gov/press/ma990419.html.

[51] Jim Motavalli, "Heavy Metal Harm" *E / The Environmental Magazine* (May-June, 2002), 5.

[52] Sheldon Rampton and John Stauber, *Trust Us, We're Experts* (New York: Jeremy P. Tarcher, 2001), 97-98.

[53] Bryson, 158.

[54] Andres Duany, et al., *Suburban Nation: The Rise of Sprawl and the Decline of the American Dream* (New York: North Point Press, 2000), 12.

[55] "Sprawl-Busters," 16 March 2005, http://www.sprawl-busters.com/.

[56] Rainforest Action Network, 30 March 2005, http://www.ran.org/info_center/about_rainforests.html.

[57] Rainforest Action Network, 30 March 2005, http://www.ran.org/info_center/about_rainforests.html.

[58] Rainforest Action Network, 30 March 2005, http://www.ran.org/info_center/about_rainforests.html.

[59] Dana Ullman, *Discovering Homeopathy* (Berkeley, CA: North Atlantic Books, 1991), 163.

[60] http://www.mbayaq.org/cr/cr_seafoodwatch/content/media/MBA_SeafoodWatch_ShrimpFactCard.pdf

[61] Christopher Lasch, *The Culture of Narcissism* (New York: W.W. Norton and Company, Inc., 1979), xviii.

[62] John Steinbeck, *Travels with Charley* (New York: Penguin Books, 1961), ix.

[63] Grecia Matos and Lorie Wagner, "Consumption of Materials in the United States, 1900–1995," November, 1998, www.pubs.usgs.gov/annrev/ar-23-107/aerdocnew.pdf, 4.

[64] "BHA and BHT: Why are BHA and BHT in foods? Are they safe?" 20 March, 2003, http://chemistry.about.com/library/weekly/aa082101a.htm.

[65] Mark D. Gold, "Aspartame Summary," 12 January, 2002, http://www.fda.gov/ohrms/dockets/dailys/03/Jan03/012203/02P-0317_emc-000196.txt.

[66] "Global Healing Center," May, 2002, http://www.ghchealth.com/may-02.html.

[67] Ronnie Cummins and Ben Lilliston, *Genetically Engineered Food: A Self-Defense Guide for Consumers* (New York: Marlow & Company, 1999), 40.

[68] Martin Teitel, *Rain Forest in Your Kitchen: The Hidden Connection Between Extinction and Your Supermarket* (Washington, D.C.: Island Press, 1992), 4.

[69] Environmental Working Group, "Teflon Trial Will Be Public," 30 August, 2004, http://www.ewg.org/issues/PFCs/index.php.

[70] Jeffrey Hollender, *The Non-Toxic Times*, Vol. 3, Number 10, August, 2002, http://www.seventhgeneration.com/page.asp?id=1365.

[71] Environmental Working Group, "Highest in Pesticides," 20 November, 2006, http://www.foodnews.org/walletguide.php.

[72] Jim Motavalli, "The Case Against Meat," *E / The Environmental Magazine*, Jan-Feb, 2002, http://www.emagazine.com/view/?142.

[73] Motavalli, http://www.emagazine.com/view/?142.

[74] Dr. Peter J. D'Adamo, *Eat Right 4 Your Type* (New York: G.P. Putnam and Sons, 1996).

[75] Mark Kurlansky, *Cod: A Biography of the Fish That Changed the World* (New York: Walker and Company, 1997), 198.

[76] New American Dream, "Turn the Tide," 13 April, 2005, http://www.newdream.org/TurnTheTide/ActionItems/icons.html.

[77] Kurlansky, 207.

[78] "Salmon, Wild vs. Farm Raised," 13 April, 2005, http://www.american.edu/TED/alaskasalmon.htm.

[79] Matt Helms, "If You Like Your Fries with Your Drive, This Is a Device for You," *Detroit Free Press*, 28 July, 2005, http://www.freep.com/news/driving/helms28e_20050728.htm.

[80] ETC Group, "Oligopoly, Inc. Concentration in Corporate Power: 2003," 5 December, 2003, http://www.etcgroup.org/text/txt_article.asp?newsid=420.

[81] Philip Shabecoff, *Earth Rising* (Washington, D.C.: Island Press, 2000), 78.

[82] Nikki Katz, "Body Image Statistics," 12 April, 2005, http://womensissues.about.com/cs/bodyimage/a/bodyimagestats.htm.

[83] Plunkett Research, Ltd., "Automotive Industry Overview," 2006, http://www.plunkettresearch.com/AutomobilesTrucks/AutomobilesandTrucksStatistics/tabid/90/Default.aspx, February 14, 2007.

[84] Bureau of Transportation Statistics, "Table 2-17: Motor Vehicle Safety Data," December, 2002, http://www.bts.gov/publications/national_transportation_statistics/2002/html/table_02_17.html.

[85] Paul L. Wachtel, *The Poverty of Affluence: A Psychological Portrait of the American Way of Life* (Gabriola Island, B.C.: New Society, 1983), 33.

[86] Bernie Fischlowitz-Roberts, Earth Policy Institute, "Air Pollution Fatalities Now Exceed Traffic Fatalities by 3 to 1" 17 September 2002, http://www.earth-policy.org/Updates/Update17.htm.

[87] International Council for Local Environmental Initiatives (ICLEI), "US Communities Acting to Protect the Climate" (Toronto: ICLEI,1998), 21.

[88] Bill McKibben, *The End of Nature* (New York: Doubleday, 1989), 143.

[89] Matthew L. Wald, "EPA Says Catalytic Converter Is Growing Cause of Global Warming," *New York Times* 29 May 1998, A1, A16.

[90] Jeffrey Lughole, Ph.D., and Kelly Turner, *You Can Prevent Global Warming (and Save Money!): 51 Easy Ways* (Kansas City, MO: Andrews McMeel Publishing, 2003), 301.

[91] John De Graaf, et al., *Affluenza: The All-Consuming Epidemic* (San Francisco: Berrett-Koehler Publishers, 2001), 90.

[92] De Graaf, 89.

[93] Better World Club, "Carbon Offsets - Guilt Free Travel," 28 August, 2002, http://www.betterworldclub.com/links/offsets.htm.

[94] Hybridcenter.org, "Hybrids Under the Hood (Part 1)" 28 May, 2005, http://www.ucsusa.org/hybridcenter/page.cfm?pageID=1698.

[95] Bay Area Action, "The SUV Ticket," 30 January, 2004, http://www.baaction.org/SUVticket/.

[96] http://www.baaction.org/SUVticket/.

[97] John A. Larson, M.D., *Road Rage to Road-Wise* (New York: Forge Books, 1999), 20.

[98] Alan Reder, *75 Best Business Practices for Socially Responsible Companies* (New York: Jeremy P. Tarcher, 1995), xiii.

[99] Reder, 126.

[100] U.S. Department of Energy, "Cutting Paper," 13 July 2002, http://eetd.lbl.gov/paper/ideas/html/copyfactsA.htm.

[101] U.S. Environmental Protection Agency, "Indoor Air Facts No. 4 (revised): Sick Building Syndrome (SBS)" August 2006, http://www.epa.gov/iaq/pubs/sbs.html.

[102] Martin J. Walker, "Home Sickness," *The Ecologist,* 22 April 2001, 40-43.

[103] CDC, "Chronic Disease Overview," 15 October 2004, http://www.cdc.gov/nccdphp/overview.htm.

[104] AskDr.Sears.com, "Phytonutrients," 15 April 2003, http://askdrsears.com/html/4/t044200.asp#T044205.

[105] Salli Rasberry & Padi Selwyn, *Living Your Life Out Loud* (New York: Pocket Books, 1995), 129.

[106] CDC, "Aging Boomers Drive Up Doctor Visits," 11 August 2003, http://www.cdc.gov/nchs/pressroom/03news/agingvisits.htm.

[107] Organic Consumers Organization, Organic Bytes #66, 29 September 2005, http://www.organicconsumers.org/bytes/092905.cfm.

[108] ArthritisSupport.com, "Study Shows Long-Term Use of NSAIDs Causes Severe Intestinal Damage," 4 January 2005, http://www.arthritissupport.com/library/showarticle.cfm/ID/936.

[109] Target Marketing, "A Beauty of a Market-Multichannel Approach to Cosmetics," 10 August 2004, http://www.backchannelmedia.com/newsletter/story/3087795286/A_Beauty_of_a_MarketMulitchann.html.

[110] Martin J. Walker, "Home Sickness," *The Ecologist* 22 April 2001, 40-43.

[111] "Statement of Senator Edward M. Kennedy: FDA Reform and Cosmetic Preemption," 5 September 1997, http://www.healthy-communications.com/statement_of_senator_edward_m.htm.

[112] Kim Erickson, *Drop-Dead Gorgeous* (New York: Contemporary Books, 2002), 217.

[113] David Steinman and Samuel S. Epstein, M.D., *The Safe Shopper's Bible* (New York: Macmillan, 1995), 119, 199.

[114] Diane di Costanzo, "The Dirty Dozen Ingredients in Personal Care Products" *The Green Guide* January/February 2004, http://www.thegreenguide.com/doc.mhtml?i=100&s=10uglies.

[115] Technology Transfer Network Air Toxics Web site, 22 February 2005, http://www.epa.gov/ttn/atw/hlthef/formalde.html.

[116] Jeffrey Hollender, "Vanity, Thy Name Is Poison" *Non-Toxic Times,* Vol. 3, No. 8, June 2002, http://www.seventhgeneration.com/page.asp?id=1334.

[117] S.M. Duty, et al. "Phthalate Exposure and Human Semen Parameters," *Epidemiology* 14:269–277, 2003, http://www.protectingourhealth.org/newscience/infertility/2003/2003-0519dutyetal.htm.

[118] I. Colón, D. Caro, C.J. Bourdony and O. Rosario, "Identification of Phthalate Esters in the Serum of Young Puerto Rican Girls with Premature Breast Development" *Environmental Health Perspectives* 108:895-900, 2000, http://www.ourstolenfuture.org/NewScience/reproduction/Puberty/colonetal2000.htm.

[119] Erickson, 188.

[120] Lynn Marie Bower, *The Healthy Household* (Bloomington, IN: Healthy House Institute, 1995), 65.

[121] Epsom Salt Industry Council, 10 May 2005, http://www.epsomsaltcouncil.org/beauty_usage_tips.htm.

[122] Walker, 40-43.

[123] Georgia Podiatric Medical Association, "Foot Facts" 1 May 2005, http://www.gapma.com/FootFacts.htm.

[124] Gary Polakovic, "Chemicals in Home a Big Smog Source," *The Los Angeles Times* 9 March 2003, B1+.

[125] B. Sanders, "News and Updates," *Greenkeeping: The Environmental Consumer's Guide*, Vol. 2, No 2, Lebanon, NH, May/June 1992, 3.

[126] Jeffrey Hollender, *The Non-Toxic Times*, Vol. 2, Number 10, August, 2001, http://www.seventhgeneration.com/site/pp.asp?c=coIHKTMHF&b=84963.

[127] Annie Berthold-Bond, "Vinegar Kills Bacteria, Mold and Germs," *Care2 Ask Annie*, 1 May 2005, http://ww.care2.com/channels/solutions/healthy/164.

[128] Health & Environment Resource Center, "Make the Connection: Health & Environment Volume 1, Hazards of Household Products and Recipes for Less Toxic Alternatives," 1997-2002, http://www.herc.org/maketheconnection/docs/Volume1.pdf.

[129] Juliet B. Schor, *The Overworked American* (New York: Basic Books, 1992), 109.

[130] David Pearson, *The New Natural House Book* (New York: Simon & Schuster, 1998), 57.

[131] IARC Monographs, *Occupational Exposures in Paint Manufacture and Painting* (Vol. 47, 1989, p. 329), 21 January 1998, http://www-cie.iarc.fr/htdocs/monographs/vol47/47-13.htm.

[132] Diane di Costanzo, "The Dirty Dozen Ingredients in Personal Care Products," *The Green Guide* 9 February 2004, www.thegreenguide.com/gg/pdf/dirtydozenpalm.pdf.

[133] Sarah Ban Breathnach, *Simple Abundance* (New York: Warner Books, 1995), May 11.

[134] National Center for Chronic Disease Prevention and Health Promotion, "Physical Activity and Health At-A-Glance" 17 November 1999, http://www.cdc.gov/nccdphp/sgr/ataglan.htm.

[135] EPA.gov, "Municipal Solid Waste Generation, Recycling, and Disposal in the United States: Facts and Figures for 2007," http://www.epa.gov/osw/nonhaz/municipal/pubs/msw07-fs.pdf.

[136] Robert Lilienfeld & William Rathje, *Use Less Stuff* (New York: Ballantine Publishing Group, 1998), 162.

[137] Lilenfeld & Rathje, 108.

[138] "Matters of Scale: Visible vs. Invisible Waste," *World Watch*, November/December 1999, 37.

[139] The Non-Toxic Times, "Protecting Those Least Able to Protect Themselves, A Few Thoughts from Jeffrey Hollender, President," February 2003, http://www.seventhgeneration.com/site/pp.asp?c=coIHKTMHF&b=84882#6.

[140] "Residential Trash & Recycling Service, City of Hermosa Beach, CA," 15 May 2005, http://www.hermosabch.org/departments/publicworks/recycle1.html.

[141] Nikki Goldbeck & David Goldbeck, *Choose to Reuse* (Woodstock, NY: Ceres Press, 1995), 109.

[142] Goldbeck & Goldbeck, 109.

[143] *Utne*, Jan-Feb, 2003, No. 115, 18.

[144] Goldbeck & Goldbeck, 153.

[145] Jeffrey Lughole, Ph.D., and Kelly Turner, *You Can Prevent Global Warming (and Save Money!): 51 Easy Ways* (Kansas City, MO: Andrews McMeel Publishing, 2003), 280.

[146] Kathy Stein, *Beyond Recycling* (Santa Fe: Clear Light Publishers, 1997), 62.

[147] John C. Ryan, *Seven Wonders* (San Francisco: Sierra Club Books, 1999), 59.

[148] PlasticsResource.com, "US EPA Recycling Goal Exceeded," 1 May 2005, http://www.plasticsresource.com/s_plasticsresource/doc.asp?TRACKID=&CID=99&DID=196.

[149] "Designing the Future" *Newsweek*, 16 May 2005, 40-45.

[150] Heather Rodgers and Christian Parenti, "The Hidden Life of Garbage" from *The Brooklyn Rail*, in *Utne*, Nov/Dec 2002, 46.

[151] Tasaday, Laurence, *Shopping For a Better Environment* (New York: Meadowbrook Press, 1991), 27.

[152] "Eco-Friendly Printing and Writing Papers More Reduce, Reuse, Recycle Solutions: A Green Seal Choose Green Report," 19 January 2004, http://www.care2.com/channels/solutions/home/67.

[153] *Mother Earth News.com*, Issue 196, February/March 2003, http://www.motherearthnews.com/library/2003_February_March/Green_Gazette.